Thoughts
on my
Thoughts
II

Thoughts

on my
Thoughts

II

*The **TALES** That Wagged This Veterinarian*

Walter R. Hoge, DVM

Printed in the United States of America
ISBN 978-1-958434-86-4 (sc)
ISBN 978-1-958434-87-1 (hc)
ISBN 978-1-958434-88-8 (e)

Library of Congress Control Number: 2022922117

2023.03.08

MainSpring Books
5901 W. Century Blvd
Suite 750
Los Angeles, CA, US, 90045

www.mainspringbooks.com

Table of Contents

**Part II   Thoughts Shared with
              Family and Friends**

It is a common theme in many books and films: when people get lost in a desert or a jungle and try to walk in a "straight line", they end up walking in circles. No matter how hard they try, at some point they will cross their own tracks and despair, because they realize that they will never make it back to civilization. Surprisingly enough, the belief that people walk in circles when lost is mainly based on anecdotal evidence and has never been studied systematically in a real desert or forest.

Scientists have now presented the first empirical evidence that people can't walk in a straight line and really do walk in circles when they do not have reliable cues to their walking direction.

It turned out that these circles were rarely in a systematic direction. Instead, the same person sometimes veered to the left, sometimes to the right. Walking in circles is therefore not caused by differences in leg length or strength, but more likely the result of increasing uncertainty about where straight ahead is.

Thinking about walking in circles and trying to walk a straight line—even with all the volumes of information we have accumulated about how life began we still find ourselves getting lost and turning in circles trying to solve one of science's greatest outstanding mysteries. Even the individual pathways in metabolism are intricate. It is hard to imagine how such an intricate process could have started by itself.

Complicating things further, each step is controlled by a molecule called an enzyme, which speeds up the chemical reactions in question. Enzymes are complicated molecules that can only be made through metabolism, under the control of genes.

So, scientists face a biochemical chicken-or-the-egg dilemma: *Which came first, the chemical engine to build the cell, or the cellular mechanisms needed to build the engine?*

In the quest for finding certainty in our pursuit for truth and understanding, it seems to me good council to consider what is written in 1Kings 19:11-12. The Lord is not found in the strong winds, disasters, earthquakes or fire. After all is done, His answer will be found in "a still small voice."

CHAPTER

PREFACE

WHAT IS LIFE?

It is a common theme in many books and films: when people get lost in a desert or a jungle and try to walk in a "straight line", they end up walking in circles. No matter how hard they try, at some point they will cross their own tracks and despair, because they realize that they will never make it back to civilization. Surprisingly enough, the belief that people walk in circles when lost is mainly based on anecdotal evidence and has never been studied systematically in a real desert or forest. (Current Biology, 2009)

Scientists in the Multisensory Perception and Action Group at the Max Planck Institute for Biological Cybernetics have now presented the first empirical evidence that people can't walk in a straight line and really do walk in circles when they do not have reliable cues to their walking direction.

Their study examined the walking trajectories of people who walked for several hours in the Sahara desert and in the forest area of Germany. The scientists used the global positioning system (GPS) to record these trajectories. The results showed that participants were only able to keep a straight path when the sun or moon was visible. However, as soon as the sun disappeared behind some clouds, people started to walk in circles without even noticing it.

One explanation offered in the past for walking in circles is that most people have one leg longer or stronger than the other, which would produce a systematic bias in one direction. To test this explanation, we instructed people to walk straight while blindfolded, thus removing the effects of vision. Most of the participants in the study walked in circles, sometimes in extremely small ones (diameter less than 20 m)."

However, it turned out that these circles were rarely in a systematic direction. Instead, the same person sometimes veered to the left, sometimes to the right. Walking in circles is therefore not caused by differences in leg length or strength, but more likely the result of increasing uncertainty about where straight ahead is.1

Thinking about walking in circles and trying to walk a straight line—even with all the volumes of information we have accumulated about how life began we still find ourselves getting lost and turning in circles trying to solve one of science's greatest outstanding mysteries. We know it happened early in our planet's history because there are fossil microorganisms in rocks laid down 3.5 billion years ago, a mere billion years after Earth formed. But how and where it happened remain uncertain.

A key problem is that living organisms are extraordinarily complicated. Even the simplest bacterial cell has hundreds of genes and thousands of different molecules. All of these building blocks work together in an intricate dance, shuttling food into the cell and passing waste out, repairing damage, copying genes, and much more.

The scale of this complexity is illustrated by research published in 2021 that compares the DNA of 1,089 bacteria, which are the simplest living organisms. The researchers, led by bioengineer Joana C. Xavier, who was at Heinrich Heine University Düsseldorf in Germany at the time, looked for protein families that were common across the species of bacteria, as these were likely to be truly ancient—dating back over three billion years to the last common ancestor of all bacteria. They found 146 such protein families, revealing that even the earliest bacteria were extraordinarily intricate and the product of a long period of evolution.

All hypotheses about the origin of life attempt to strip away this complexity and imagine something far simpler that could have arisen spontaneously. The difficulty is deciding what this proto-life would have been like. What parts of the living cells we see today were the first to form?

Many ideas have been put forward, including a molecule that can copy itself such as a strand of RNA, or a fatty "bubble" or "blob" that could have acted as the foundational structure of a cell. But a growing group of scientists believe that before genes or cell walls, the first thing life needed was an engine.

Life is fundamentally active. Even in seemingly stationary organisms like trees, there is furious activity at the microscopic scale. Xavier, who is now based at University College London, compares a living cell to a cup of water with a hole in the bottom and a faucet pouring in. If the two flows are equal, the volume of water in the cup stays the same, "but there is transformation going on."

Similarly, every living thing takes in nutrients and uses them to build and repair its body. For humans, that means eating foods and then using our digestive systems to break them down into simple chemicals that our bodies can use. Other organisms get their energy from sunlight, or from chemicals like methane, but the same principle applies. Thousands of reactions are constantly transforming one substance into another and shuttling things to where they are needed. All of these processes make up an organism's metabolism. If metabolism stops, the organism dies.

It is hard to imagine how such an intricate process could have started by itself. Complicating things further, each step is controlled by a molecule called an enzyme, which speeds up the chemical reactions. But enzymes are complicated molecules that can only be made through metabolism, under the control of genes.

The chemistry of metabolism is so central to life that many researchers believe it must have been at the core of the first living cells. Once a metabolic engine was up and running, the thinking goes, it could create the other chemicals that life needs, and gradually cells would self-assemble. However, all metabolism-first hypotheses for the origin of life face the same problem: Metabolism, like life itself, is remarkably complex. In Xavier's study of the last bacterial common ancestor, she estimated that this ancient organism's genes could produce 243 chemicals through metabolic processes, as well as transforming chemicals into one another.

Even the individual pathways in metabolism are intricate. It is hard to imagine how such an intricate process could have started by itself. Complicating things further, each step is controlled by a molecule called an enzyme, which speeds up the chemical reactions in question. Enzymes are complicated molecules that can only be made through metabolism, under the control of genes.

So, scientists face a biochemical chicken-or-the-egg dilemma: Which came first, the chemical engine to build the cell, or the cellular mechanisms needed to build the engine?2

There are nine theories often mentioned on the origin of life:

- Lightning may have provided the spark needed for life to begin. Experiments in 1952 showed that electric sparks can generate the building blocks of amino acids and sugars from an atmosphere loaded with water, methane, ammonia and hydrogen.
- The first molecules of life might have met from clay crystals that preserved their structure as they grew and stuck together to form areas exposed to different environments. They trapped other molecules along the way and organized them into patterns much like our genes do now.
- The deep-sea vent theory suggests that life may have begun at submarine hydrothermal vents spewing elements key to life, such as carbon and hydrogen.
- Ice might have covered the oceans 3 billion years ago and facilitated the birth of life. Key organic compounds thought to be important in the origin of life are more stable at lower temperatures. At normal temperatures these compounds, such as

simple sets of amino acids, are sparsely populated in water, but when frozen become concentrated and facilitate the emergence of life.

- DNA needs proteins in order to form, and proteins require DNA to form, so how could these have formed without each other? The answer may be RNA, which can store information like DNA, serve as an enzyme like proteins, and help create both DNA and proteins. Later DNA and proteins succeeded this "RNA world," because they are more efficient.

- Instead of developing from complex molecules such as RNA, life might have begun with smaller molecules interacting with each other in cycles of reactions. These might have been contained in simple capsules akin to cell membranes, and over time more complex molecules that performed these reactions better than the smaller ones could have evolved.

- Perhaps life did not begin on Earth at all, but was brought here from elsewhere in space, a notion known as panspermia. For instance, rocks regularly get blasted off Mars by cosmic impacts, and a number of Martian meteorites have been found on Earth that some researchers have controversially suggested brought microbes over here. Other scientists have even suggested that life might have hitchhiked on comets from other star systems.3

- The theory of intelligent design is not creationism. It simply is an effort to empirically detect whether the "apparent design" in nature acknowledged by virtually all biologists is genuine design (the product of an intelligent cause) or is simply the product of an undirected process such as natural selection acting on random variations.

- Creationism typically starts with a religious text and tries to see how the findings of science can be reconciled to it. Intelligent design starts with the empirical evidence of nature and seeks to ascertain what inferences can be drawn from that evidence. Unlike creationism, the scientific theory of intelligent design does not claim that modern biology can identify whether the intelligent cause detected through science is supernatural.

In Roman times, sculptors sometimes sought to conceal breaks and cracks and chips in statues with melted beeswax mixed with marble dust. The purchaser, thus deceived and believing that he was buying a flawless piece of marble, would place such a statue proudly in his atrium.

Over time the beeswax would dry out, crumble away, and expose the ugly defects. This practice of beeswax trickery became so widespread that reputable sculptors guaranteed their works sine cera, which literally translated means "without wax." Our word sincere comes from this rebellion against the use of wax to deceive and to cheat. The saying "Mind your own beeswax," may originate from the beeswax seals used on important documents to preserve their confidentiality.4

It is written in 1 Kings 19:11-12, "he said, Go forth, and stand upon the mount before the LORD. And, behold, the LORD passed by, and a great and strong wind rent the mountains, and brake in pieces the rocks before the LORD; but the LORD was not in the wind: and after the wind an earthquake; but the LORD was not in the earthquake: and after the earthquake a fire; but the LORD was not in the fire: and after the fire a still small voice."

All theories on the origin of life have cracks in the shaping of their sculptors of truth. The pathways to truth are not straight and the beeswax—theories, translation errors, misinterpretations etc. with or without marble dust will be refined or replaced over time by our ever increasing understanding of the forces of nature. Progress will most likely be obtained from the small voices of truth coming from study, observation, inspiration, revelation or other powers that be. Watching us get there is very exciting to me.

There are treasures laid up in the heart,—treasures of charity, piety, temperance and soberness. These treasures a man takes with him beyond death when he leaves this world. *Buddhist Scriptures*

1. *People Really Walk in Circles When Lost, Max Planck Institute for Biological Cybernetics, Tubingen, Germany, 08/20/2009.*
2. *Science, 'Impossible' Chemistry May Reveal Origins of Life on Earth, 04/04/2022.*
3. *Life Science, "7 theories on the origin of life", Charles Q. Choi, Scott Dutfield, 02/14/2022.*
4. *pureazcandles.co.nz/sacred-history.*

PART I

ANIMALS AND US FOLKS

1

IN PURSUIT OF INEBRIATION

An opium den was an establishment in which opium was sold and smoked. Opium dens were prevalent in many parts of the world in the 19th century, most notably China, Southeast Asia, North America, and France. Throughout the West, opium dens were frequented by and associated with the Chinese because the establishments were usually run by Chinese, who supplied the opium and prepared it for visiting non-Chinese smokers.

Opium smoking arrived in North America with the large influx of Chinese, who came to participate in the California Gold Rush. The jumping-off point for the gold fields was San Francisco, and the city's Chinatown became the site of numerous opium dens soon after the first Chinese arrived, around 1850. However, from 1863 to the end of the century, anti-vice laws imposed by the new municipal code book banned visiting opium rooms in addition to prostitution. Despite this, the 1870s attracted many non-Chinese residents to San Francisco's dens, prompting the city fathers to enact the nation's first anti-drug law, an 1875 ordinance banning opium dens. In the early 20th century, huge bonfires, fueled by confiscated opium and opium paraphernalia, were used to destroy opium and create a public venue to discuss opium use.1

The poppy plant, Papaver somniferum, is the source of opium. It was grown in the Mediterranean region as early as 5000 B.C., and has since been cultivated in a number of countries throughout the world. The milky fluid that seeps from its incisions in the unripe seedpod of this poppy has been scraped by hand and air-dried to produce what is known as opium.

A more modern method of harvesting for pharmaceutical use is by the industrial poppy straw process of extracting alkaloids from the mature dried plant (concentrate of poppy straw). All opium and poppy straw used for pharmaceutical products are imported into the United States from legitimate sources in regulated countries. Common names are morphine, codeine, hydrocodone, heroin, methadone, hydroquinone, fentanyl and oxycodone.

Opium can be a liquid, solid, or powder, but most poppy straw concentrate is available commercially as a fine brownish powder. Opium can be smoked, intravenously injected, or taken in pill form. Opium is also abused in combination with other drugs.

The intensity of opium's euphoric effects on the brain depends on the dose and route of administration. It works quickly when smoked because the opiate chemicals pass into the lungs, where they are quickly absorbed and then sent to the brain. An opium "high" is very similar to a heroin "high"; users experience a euphoric rush, followed by relaxation and the relief of physical pain.

Side effects of opium is caused by inhibiting muscle movement in the bowels leading to constipation. It also can dry out the mouth and mucous membranes in the nose. Opium use leads to physical and psychological dependence, and can lead to overdose effects which include: Slow breathing, seizures, dizziness, weakness, loss of consciousness, coma, and possible death.2

Heroin is a very addictive opium drug made from morphine and overdose deaths have dramatically increased over the last decade. This increase is related to the growing number of people misusing prescription opioid pain relievers like OxyContin and Vicodin. Some people who become addicted to those drugs switch to heroin because it produces similar effects but is cheaper and easier to get.

In fact, most people who use heroin report they first misused prescription opioids, but it is a small percentage of people who switch to heroin. The numbers of people misusing prescription drugs is so high, that even a small percentage translates to hundreds of thousands of heroin users. Even so, some research suggests about one-third of heroin users in treatment simply started with heroin. Maybe they were mistakenly told that only one use cannot lead to addiction. Both heroin and opioid pill use can lead to addiction and overdose.3

In the opium dens of the Orient domestic cats become addicted to the opium smoke permeating the rooms, and it is common to see these cats approach the smokers, waiting for them to expel mouthfuls of smoke, which the animals then inhale repeatedly. That these creatures are addicted to opium is proved by the fact that normal cats turn away in disgust to avoid the exhaled smoke, as well as the fact that when the opium-den cats are deprived of their daily fumes they are seized by obvious symptoms of withdrawal, which in some cases result in their death. Even the mice that live in and around the dens approach the smokers—who are generally undisturbed by the intrusion—and stand up on their hind legs in an attempt to inhale the opium.4

Not many of us realize that entirely on their own and without the influence of captivity or conditioning wild animals, birds and even insects do indeed drug themselves? This deliberate seeking of inebriation among all the classes of animals is perfectly natural, normative behavior. Indeed, the pursuit of inebriation is so ubiquitous that it has been proposed as a kind of fourth drive akin to hunger, thirst and sex.

* In the Canadian Rockies, lichen grows in some of the most inhospitable, hard-to-reach terrain in the region, which is the perfect place for bighorn sheep to climb and get high. The sheep have been known to traverse paths far too risky for humans and find lichen growing on the rocks. Some of the lichens have psychoactive substances in then. Some will chip their teeth all the way down trying to scrape lichen off the rock.

* When dolphins are catching their prey they often toss them around for a while before eating them. This might not seem such a wise idea when trying to eat a pufferfish, which emits one of the deadliest poisons in the world when it feels it's being threatened. It is thought that small doses its tetrodotoxin numbs the mouth and is mildly hallucinogenic. They don't injure the pufferfish;

they just bite it enough to get it to release its neurotoxins.

* Though they're not necessarily using them to get high Madagascar's red-fronted lemurs have been observed picking up highly toxic millipedes, rubbing them all over their nether regions, and eventually swallowing them.

While primates routinely use insects as a sort of topical ointment to relieve irritations, chewing them is far less common, and little is known about why lemurs do this. The millipede's toxin is not scientifically known to be a hallucinogenic, But some will ingest the millipede to help with parasites. It's pretty much a medicinal use.

* Jaguars are fond of ayahuasca vines. In the same way that people flock to the Amazon for ayahuasca ceremonies with mystical shamans, the native jaguars in the region eat yage. No one is exactly certain why jaguars do this, but the yage vines contain harmala alkaloids—a key component of the ayahuasca drink recipe which activates DMT (dimethyltryptamine) in other ingredients. And it turns these fierce predators into rolling goofballs.

* In the great plains of America's Midwest, one of the first plants to bloom in the spring is locoweed (which means 'crazy' in Spanish), a low-growing, high-protein plant with colorful flowers and a deadly phytotoxin. This plant that livestock actively seek out produces swainsonine, which can cause grazing animals to go into a calm trance where

they are lethargic and stand around, starve from malnutrition, or become agitated have seizures and die.

* Humans are mostly to blame for Australian wallabies' relatively new found penchant for poppies. In its rush to become one of the world's leading producers of legal poppy plants, Australia cleared much of the wallaby's natural habitat. The displaced wallabies still often wander into poppy fields and many of them eat the opiates and get high. It's thought to be the reason the wallabies return again and again, though the phenomenon has not been conclusively studied.5

Catnip is a plant that has been used extensively for human illness and, more recently, in toys for pets. It is a plant with which some veterinarians have little familiarity. Catnip (Nepeta cataria) is a perennial herb belonging to the mint family, Labiatae. The term "catnep" is thought to originate from the fondness that cats show for the plant. The plant is indigenous to Europe, and was supposedly introduced to North America with European settlement. It is cultivated easily and is now a common garden plant on this continent. It is found in hedges, fencerows, roadsides, stream banks, and waste places.

The entire plant is harvested when in flower, which occurs from June to September. It has a mintlike taste and odor and is strongly scented. Compounds in catnip alter the behavior of wild and domestic cats, other mammals, and insects.

Cats can respond behaviorally to air concentrations of 1:109 to 1:1011. The response to catnip is characterized by sniffing, then licking and chewing with head shaking, followed by chin and cheek rubbing and then a head over roll and body rubbing. Spontaneous vocalization occurs occasionally and has been interpreted as a response to hallucinations. This reaction is similar to estrous rolling patterns and this probably made people think that catnip is an aphrodisiac. Hatch suggests that the response is not the same as estrous behavior but some sexual stimulation is apparent. The reaction is independent of sex and gonadal state, and neutering has no effect on the response to catnip.

The plant appears to be pleasurable as cats seek the source of the scent and return daily to eat and roll in the foliage. Catnip can be used either as the leaf or in a liquid aerosol extract. An older reference notes that the plant will make cats "frolicsome, amorous and full of battle." Another said that cats eat the leaves for their medicinal properties.

The heredity of the response has been shown to be an autosomal dominant trait. There is no correlation with breed or color. Most non domesticated felids also react, but there is a suggestion that tigers may not respond. If a kitten is less than six to eight weeks old, it will not react and the full behavioral pattern may not be evident until they are three months old. Not all cats will respond to catnip.

Catnip has been prepared and used by people for many years. It was originally used as a tea, juice, tincture, infusion, and poultice and has been smoked and chewed. It fell out of favor with the development of more effective drugs.

In the 1960's, catnip was used in place of marijuana or as a filler in marijuana. Even toys for pets were bought to get the catnip for use. Because catnip burned too fast by itself, it was usually mixed with tobacco. A more intense effect could be obtained by spraying the alcohol extract on tobacco and then smoking it. More recently, it has been used by people for its hallucinogenic effects.

Catnip produces visual and auditory hallucinations. It makes people feel happy, contented, and intoxicated, like marijuana. It has not been used recently because marijuana seems to be more readily available and is more dependable in its effects.

In conclusion, catnip is presently used in cats to bring about a euphoric state. It does not appear to be harmful and is very appealing to some cats, though some fail to respond at all. Catnip has had brief, recent popularity as a hallucinogenic drug in people, and was popular formerly as a home remedy.6

All living species are characterized by a few primary functions, such as nutrition and reproduction, which are indispensable to their preservation. But these alone are not enough; for the species to be able to preserve itself over time it must include the capacity to evolve, adapting and modifying itself in response to continual environmental changes. The principle of conservation tends to rigidly preserve established schemes and patterns, but modification requires a depatterning instrument, or function, capable of opposing the principle of conservation.

Since it is almost always only a certain percentage of members of any given species that engages in such behavior, this percentage may perform a depatterning function not only for itself but for the species as a whole.4

I understand how animals must evolve to meet the changes of an everchanging world. It is calculated by experts that between 0.01 and 0.1% of all species will become extinct each year. If the low estimate of the number of species out there is true—i.e. that there are around 2 million different species on our planet- then that means between 200 and 2,000 extinctions occur every year.

After 250 years of professionals documenting thousands of new plants and animals every year, the rate at which new species are discovered remains relatively stable. Somewhere between 15,000 and 18,000 new species are identified each year, with about half of those being insects.

However, I have a hard time understanding how animals or man for that matter increases their chances of survival of themselves or their species by losing their mental faculties in a competitive world. I think in most cases the participants risk receiving an undesirable "Darwin Award."

The Darwin Awards are a tongue-in-cheek honor originating in Usenet newsgroup discussions around 1985. They recognized individuals who have supposedly contributed to human evolution by selecting themselves out of the gene pool by dying or becoming sterilized via their own actions.

Fentanyl is a synthetic opioid that is 80-100 times stronger than morphine. Pharmaceutical fentanyl was developed for pain management treatment of cancer patients, applied in a patch on the skin. Because of its powerful opioid properties, Fentanyl is also diverted for abuse. Fentanyl is added to heroin to increase its potency, or be disguised as highly potent heroin. Many users believe that they are purchasing heroin and actually don't know that they are purchasing fentanyl—which often results in overdose deaths. Clandestinely-produced fentanyl is primarily manufactured in Mexico.

Rates of overdose deaths involving synthetic opioids were nearly twelve times higher in 2019 than in 2013. The latest provisional drug overdose death counts through May 2020 suggest an acceleration of overdose deaths during the COVID-19 pandemic.7

I remember a "principals of anesthesia" class conducted while I was attending veterinary school. The class introduced us to the anesthetic effects of fentanyl on laboratory rats.

Why I remember this class was that a short time after fentanyl was given to the rats their muscles became ridged. The systemic rigidity was severe enough that we could place the rats into different positions and they would stay in place like a statue.

Recent research describes the fate of rats on Fentanyl. Photos showing the "Muscular rigidity in the 2,000 µg/mL test group: Before injection, (photo) showed rat tails on the floor (normal condition). Fifteen minutes after injection of 2,000 µg/mL fentanyl. The tail tone was increased, and systemic rigidity occurred within 5 minutes later. Thirty minutes after injection of 2,000 µg/mL fentanyl. The rats regained consciousness."8

During the 70s and 80s I used fentanyl (called Sublimaze) under the trade name of Innovar Vet. It was a great drug to use when performing c-sections on dogs. During delivery the puppies had good color, were actively moving and it didn't take long for them to start nursing.

We were also able to reverse the mother's anesthesia; thus, quickly awakening her, allowing good milk letdown, and she and her puppies were able to go home in a short time.

It just so happens that I still have some fentanyl in my safe that shows a lot number of 9056 with an expiration date of March 1994. Its use was discontinued at Camden Pet Hospital thanks to abuse, addiction by the human animal, and strict monitory requirements by the FDA as a control drug.

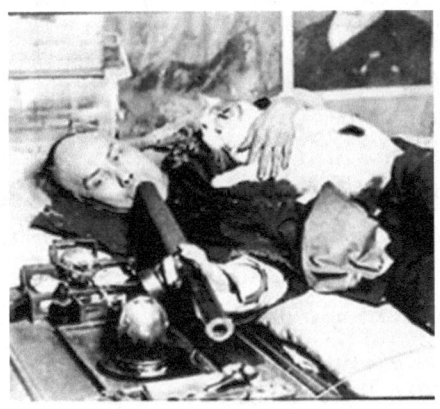

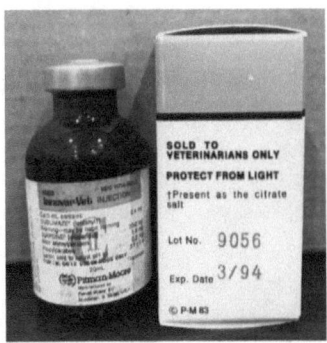

1. *Wikipedia.*

2. *DEA (Department of Drug Enforcement) WHAT IS OPIUM?*

3. *Compton WM, Jones CM, Baldwin GT. Relationship between nonmedical prescription-opioid use and heroin use. The New England Journal of Medicine 2016; 374:154-163.*

4. *Animals and Psychedelics, The Natural and the Instinct to Alter Consciousness, Giorgio Samorini, 2000.*

5. *Ronald K. Siegel, Intoxication: Life in Pursuit of Artificial Paradise, 01/01/1989.*

6. *Jeff Grognet, Canadian Veterinary Journal Vol 31: 455-456 June 1990.*

7. *CDC Health Alert Network Advisory: Increase in Fatal Drug Overdoses Across the United States Driven by Synthetic Opioids Before and During the COVID-19 Pandemic. CDCHAN-00438, 2020 Dec 14.*

8. *Neurotoxicity of Intrathecally Administered Fentanyl in a Rat Spinal Model Pain Medicine, Volume 12, Issue 5, May 2011, Pages 717–725.*

2

ALCOHOL, HAMSTERS
AND US

Alaska Natives abuse alcohol at a higher rate than all ethnic groups in the US, mirroring those of all the Native American tribes in the lower 48 states. Even for non-native Alaskans, drinking runs deep in the state's way of life, so for a population as vulnerable as tribal residents, the problem becomes magnified.

In 2015, the Daily News-Miner wrote that Alaska is among the national leaders in per capita alcohol consumption, and with high rates of drinking come some serious consequences, such as high rates of violent crime, domestic violence, sexual abuse, and suicide, all of which have been linked to the dangerously high rate of drinking in the state. Alaska's remote geographic location has contributed to the "Last Frontier mythology," where fur-trading, gold mining, logging, oil, and fishing contributed to the modern Alaska economy, but, in many cases, are no longer viable. Drinking—and drinking heavily—has been a part of that image, especially among men who keep isolation and boredom at bay by engaging in risky behavior, like substance abuse.

Figures from the Centers for Disease Control point out that the state had the national highest rate of fatal incidents involving firearms and as many as 80% of the firearm fatalities "were from intentional self-inflicted injuries." On the whole, Alaska averages 136 suicide deaths every year, meaning that in this state there are 10 people taking their own lives every month. Native Alaskans have the highest rate of suicide across all demographics in our country. These are "crisis level" numbers, says the Huffington Post, where tribes become so overwhelmed with the grief of losing their members that the traditional process of grieving is replaced by more self-destructive behavior, like substance abuse.

Why Alaska? Some have blamed it on the long, dark winters of the Arctic Circle, where "darkness and depression descend," in the words of The New York Times. In 1992, the American Journal of Psychiatry noted that almost one in 10 Alaskans suffers from seasonal affective disorder, a form of clinical depression that is triggered by the changing of particular seasons. Some Alaskans, notes the Times, cope with the use of bright-light therapy (artificial lights that dim and brighten to simulate natural sunlight patterns); others move away; and yet others turn to drugs and alcohol.

Some blame Alaska's struggles on the state's remoteness. The state's most rural communities, where many native tribes have their reservations do not have highways; the only access in or out is by aircraft or snowmobile, and only during good weather. This makes medical care hard to come by in the best of times; specialized care, like mental health counseling and substance abuse treatment, is all but impossible for many.

The isolation and barren landscape make for a perfect storm of what the Seward Times calls "a recurring theme of tragedy in the Last Frontier." At 571,951 square miles, Alaska is the largest state in the US, but with less than 750,000 residents, it is also one of the least populated states in the country. When problems develop, they develop in isolation and silence, especially among rural communities.

A 2006 report published in the American Indian and Alaska Native Mental Health Research journal noted that indigenous Alaskans have experienced an increase in alcohol availability from bars and liquor stores outside of tribal areas, but a lack of easily accessible and culturally responsive treatment programs. Survey respondents report regular binging, followed by loss of consciousness, domestic violence, suicide, legal problems, and "feelings of intergenerational grief." The researchers wrote that the Native Alaskans they talked to called for rehabilitation approaches that combine family with tribal customs and values.1

Alaska also has the heaviest alcohol drinkers in the animal kingdom living in their state. They are much punier than you might expect. Elephants, for example, are massive, but they are relative lightweights—they lack a gene for alcohol metabolism. Humans actually rank pretty highly, thanks to our ancestors' propensity for picking fermented fruit off the ground. But to find the real champs, you have to think smaller. Think the mighty hamster. In the wild hamsters hoard ryegrass seeds and fruit in their burrows, then eat this stockpile as it ferments and becomes alcoholic over the winter.

In the laboratory, rodents prefer 190 proof Everclear spirits to sweetened or regular water—they seem to drink not for pleasure but for calories. Everclear is a brand name of rectified spirit (also known as grain alcohol and neutral spirit) produced by the American company Luxco (formerly known as the David Sherman Corporation). It is made from grain and is bottled at 60%, 75.5%, 94.5% and 95% alcohol by volume (120, 151, 189, and 190 U.S. proof respectively). There is 190 calories per ounce in 95% proof. With seven calories per gram, alcohol is an extremely concentrated source of calories. In fact, it's second only to pure fat, which has nine calories per gram. Protein and carbs, meanwhile, come in at four calories per gram.

Research suggests a low to moderate amount of alcohol may have certain protective factors for the cardiovascular system. However, a robust 2018 study published in The Lancet suggests the only truly "safe" level of drinking alcohol is zero. As phrased in the U.S. Dietary Guidelines for Americans, "If adults age 21 years and older choose to drink alcoholic beverages, drinking less is better for health than drinking more."

The guidelines suggest that men who choose to drink should limit drinking to no more than two drinks per occasion, and women should have no more than one. The reason being that a woman's body absorbs more alcohol and reaches higher blood alcohol concentrations than men who drink the same amount. This is because their bodies take longer to metabolize, break down and remove, alcohol. One reason is that women pound for pound have less body water than men and alcohol resided mainly in water. Drinking less is better for your health, and among those who do drink, higher average alcohol consumption is associated with an increased risk of death from all causes compared with lower average alcohol consumption.2

"You just put a bottle of unsweetened Everclear in the cage and they love it," says Gwen Lupfer, a psychologist at the University of Alaska Anchorage who has studied alcohol consumption in hamsters. They regularly down 18 grams per kilogram of body weight a day, the alcoholic equivalent of a human drinking a liter and a half of 190-proof Everclear. In the wild, hamsters hoard ryegrass seeds and fruit in their burrows, and they eat this fermenting store as it becomes more and more alcoholic over the winter. In the lab, well, they're pretty happy with Everclear. Given the choice between water and alcohol, they go for the booze.

Humans have known about hamsters' affinity for alcohol since at least the 1950s, when scientists in Texas found that hamsters could outdrink the common lab rat. Rats can be made to drink alcohol—either by selectively breeding genetic lines or by feeding them a mix of sugar and ethanol until they develop a taste for the latter. (Ethanol is the specific type of alcohol found in alcoholic drinks.) But with hamsters, "you could take a hamster right from the pet store and give it grain alcohol," says Danielle Gulick, an addiction researcher at the University of Florida. "It would happily drink."

And they can drink a lot before getting drunk. When Lupfer was studying dwarf hamsters, she and her students rated the animals' drunkenness on a literal wobbling scale. They scored the hamsters from zero, for "no visible wobbling," to four, for "falls onto side and does not right itself." (They had previously, unsuccessfully, tried to track the hamsters' walking by dipping their paws in watercolor—they couldn't tell the drunk and sober hamsters' paw prints apart.) The hamsters never averaged above 0.5 on the wobbling scale—even at the highest oral doses. But when Lupfer and her team instead injected the ethanol directly into the hamsters' abdomens, the animals didn't do so well. They started wobbling and falling over at much, much lower doses.

Consumed orally, Lupfer explains, alcohol goes straight from the gut to the liver, which starts breaking down the mind-altering toxin that is ethanol. Hamster livers are "so efficient" at processing ethanol that very little ends up in their blood, says Tom Lawton, a critical-care doctor in Bradford, England. But when the hamsters got injected with ethanol, the substance could bypass the liver and go into their bloodstream and then their brain—hence much wobbling and falling over.

Hamsters' alcohol tolerance is likely an adaptation to their hoarding lifestyle. (Other animal hoarders might have evolved a similar tolerance, but they haven't been as easy to study in a lab.) They would have a tough time getting through the winter if they didn't like their own food that they'd hoarded or if they got sick from the alcohol in it.

Hamsters don't just tolerate alcohol, though; they prefer it to water—and that might be because they're drinking for the calories. (Alcohol has seven calories per gram, almost as many as does fat, which clocks in at nine.) Gulick has found that giving hamsters sucrose water can suppress their boozing, but calorie-free saccharin water cannot.

And in the '90s, scientists investigating whether hamsters could be a good model for alcoholism studies decided to test ethanol against carefully calorie-matched offerings of tomato juice, peach juice, mango juice, sugar water, and a chocolate Ensure Plus nutrition shake. The hamsters indeed started drinking less alcohol when given sweet, calorie-rich alternatives. Chocolate Ensure Plus worked the best, which the researchers chalked up to a preference for its taste.3

Human ancestors may have begun evolving the knack for consuming alcohol about 10 million years ago, long before modern humans began brewing booze, researchers say. The ability to break down alcohol likely helped human ancestors make the most out of rotting, fermented fruit that fell onto the forest floor. Therefore, knowing when this ability developed could help researchers figure out when these human ancestors began moving to life on the ground, as opposed to mostly in trees, as earlier human ancestors had lived.

"A lot of aspects about the modern human condition—everything from back pain to ingesting too much salt, sugar and fat—goes back to our evolutionary history," said lead study author Matthew Carrigan, a paleogeneticist at Santa Fe College in Gainesville, Florida. "We wanted to understand more about the modern human condition with regards to ethanol," he said, referring to the kind of alcohol found in rotting fruit and that's also used in liquor and fuel.

To learn more about how human ancestors evolved the ability to break down alcohol, scientists focused on the genes that code for a group of digestive enzymes called the ADH4 family. ADH4 enzymes are found in the stomach, throat and tongue of primates, and are the first alcohol-metabolizing enzymes to encounter ethanol after it is imbibed.

The researchers investigated the ADH4 genes from 28 different mammals, including 17 primates. They collected the sequences of these genes from either genetic databanks or well-preserved tissue samples.

The scientists looked at the family trees of these 28 species, to investigate how closely related they were and find out when their ancestors diverged. In total, they explored nearly 70 million years of primate evolution. The scientists then used this knowledge to investigate how the ADH4 genes evolved over time and what the ADH4 genes of their ancestors might have been like.

Then, Carrigan and his colleagues took the genes for ADH4 from these 28 species, as well as the ancestral genes they modeled, and plugged them into bacteria, which read the genes and manufactured the ADH4 enzymes. Next, they tested how well those enzymes broke down ethanol and other alcohols.

This method of using bacteria to read ancestral genes is "a new way to observe changes that happened a long time ago that didn't fossilize into bones," Carrigan said.

The results suggested there was a single genetic mutation 10 million years ago that endowed human ancestors with an enhanced ability to break down ethanol. The scientists noted that the timing of this mutation coincided with a shift to a terrestrial lifestyle. The ability to consume ethanol may have helped human ancestors dine on rotting, fermenting fruit that fell on the forest floor when other food was scarce.

Just because they were adapted to be able to ingest it doesn't mean ethanol was their first choice, nor that they were perfectly adapted to metabolize it.4

Like other addictions, alcoholism appeals to the pleasure centers of the brain. When you drink alcohol regularly, your brain begins to associate the drinks with sensations like euphoria, relaxation, and loss of inhibitions. This results in cravings and, in some cases, dependency.

Alcohol triggers your brain to release the reward-system chemical dopamine. This leads your brain to link positive feelings with drinking and motivates you to crave more. It also affects serotonin, which plays a role in things like mood and sleep.

As you drink more and addiction takes hold, you will develop tolerance and experience less pleasure, and you may have withdrawal symptoms when you try to stop drinking. Heavy drinkers will begin to drink even more in an attempt to keep withdrawal at bay.

Early signs of problem drinking or alcohol misuse can be subtle. It often starts by starting to prioritize activities that involve alcohol that leads to a shift in daily routines and relationships. Latter changes such as sleep patterns, mood, energy, and interests occur because alcohol intake increases in an attempt to alleviate the very challenges it is creating.5

An interesting story about overcoming addictions to coffee and alcohol is recorded about Heber Jeddy Grant (November 22, 1856—May 14, 1945). He was an American religious leader who served as the seventh president of The Church of Jesus Christ of Latter-day Saints (LDS Church). Grant worked as a bookkeeper and a cashier, then was called to be an LDS apostle on October 16, 1882, at age 25. After the death of Joseph F. Smith in late 1918, Grant served as LDS church president until his death.

He was born twelve years after the Section 89 of the Doctrine of Covenants revelation on The Word of Wisdom that was given through Joseph Smith the Prophet, at Kirtland, Ohio, February 27, 1833.

According to Paul H. Peterson, "Interpretations and attitudes have changed toward the Word of Wisdom over the years. Before 1840 many Mormons considered abstinence important though Joseph Smith stressed moderation. Observance became lax as Mormons treked westward to settle Utah territory. Brigham Young stressed obedience to the revelation in the 1860's but never made observance obligatory. Under John Taylor in 1883, a Word of Wisdom reformation began. Taylor stressed that Church officers should obey the revelation as did successors, Wilford Woodruff and Joseph F. Smith. None of them required rigid compliance for procurement of a Temple recommend. Heber J. Grant preached the Word of Wisdom with zeal and during his administration, strict observance became a criterion of orthodoxy. Attitudes have changed little since Grant's time and today Word of Wisdom adherence is a distinguishing characteristic of Mormon society."6

Young Heber J. Grant had greater difficulty overcoming the habit of drinking beer over coffee. Fearing an early death like his father's and convinced of the virtues of insurance, Salt Lake City's youngest agent repeatedly sought coverage to protect his mother. Nineteenth century actuarial tables however discriminated against slender girths and no company would issue Heber a policy. Determined to gain weight Heber sought out Dr Benedict who had an immediate solution. If Heber would drink four glasses of beer daily, Dr Benedict prescribed, within two years he would have the additional twenty pounds necessary for coverage.

At first Heber found beer "bitter and distasteful" like his mother's herbal "kinnikinnick" tea. But he quickly acquired both a business and a personal taste for it. Within a year he secured the fire insurance business of most Salt Lake City saloons and Utah breweries, an additional ten pounds and a growing relish for the savor of hops his daily four glass limit became five and occasionally grew to six.

He warred with his acute sense of conscience rereading the word of wisdom he resolved to abandon his drinking and place his health and his mother's future with the lord, "insurance or no insurance." But resolutions were easier made than kept. "I wanted some beer so bad that I drank it again," he confessed. Finally, he found strength in the same formula that he had used with coffee by telling himself he was free to take a drink whenever he wished. He overcame his obsession and ceased drinking. As quickly, he lost his insurance trade with the saloons and breweries of the territory.7

Experiencing the addictive effects of alcohol and coffee on the pleasure centers of the human brain during President Grant's youth must have left a deep impression on the value of the teachings in the 89th section of the Doctrine and Covenants. "Heber J. Grant preached the Word of Wisdom with zeal and during his administration, strict observance became a criterion of orthodoxy."6

I remember my father the MD confronting his mother about how she needed to gain some body weight. He brought her a six pack of beer and told her the calories would help put weight on her. She told him that she was not going to disobey the scripture's teachings on abstinence from drinking alcohol as stated in the Word of Wisdom and refused his offer.

I also remember my dad overcoming dependance on alcohol and how our family life and his general disposition improved.

I also remember being an underage college student getting into Mort's Club in downtown Moscow Idaho. I ordered a beer and sat down at a table. Sheryl's, the future mother of my children, cousin came over and sat down beside me. Good thing he promised not to tell or I may have had children that don't look so much like her. Also, I still remember the taste I got in my mouth after drinking Jack Daniel's Whiskey with a couple of friends. Both events helped me stay away from developing alcohol dependance.

I also remember a mouse that a roommate caught in our dorm. We fed it only beer and leftover snacks. It became friendly, fat and had a beautiful hair coat. As I recall, it went home with the roommate for summer break.

Looking back—maybe a mouse alcohol tolerance study in my 1967 animal science experimental lab studies class would have placed some light on rodent alcohol metabolism years before the hamster studies. After all, an MD named Lawton's comments were mentioned in the hamster study, "who recently tweeted about hamsters and alcohol in a delightful thread, told me that he bred hamsters in his youth in Yorkshire. He did not learn until medical school that very serious scientists had studied hamsters' alcoholic preferences. But as a teenager, he made a related discovery of his own. When his house got so cold that the hamsters would start hibernating, a spot of brandy would perk them right back up. Cheers."3

1. *Native Alaskans Alcohol Use, Statistics, Editorial Staff, July 5, 2019.*

2. *The Lancet, Vol 132, Issue 10152, P987-988, 09/22/2018.*

3. *You Have No Idea How Hard It Is to Get a Hamster Drunk, "You just put a bottle of unsweetened Everclear on the cage and they love it.", by Sarah Zhang—staff writer at The Atlantic & Tom Bingham, December 26, 2021, SHARE.*

4. *Origins of Human Alcohol Consumption Revealed, Charles Q. Choi published December 01, 2014, journal Proceedings of the National Academy of Sciences.*

5. *What Causes Alcohol Addiction?, WebMD, By Marta Manning.*

6. *An Historical Analysis of the Word of Wisdom, Paul H. Peterson MA, Brigham Young University—Provo.*

7. *BYU Studies Quarterly, Young Heber J. Grant's Years of Passage, pages 144-145, Ronald W. Walker, 04-01-1984.*

3

TOBACCO

When German pathologist Robert Koch discovered the bacterium behind tuberculosis in 1882, he included a short guide for linking microorganisms to the diseases they cause. It was a windfall for germ theory, the modern understanding that pathogens can make us sick. But it didn't only shake up the field of medicine: Botanists took note, too.

When a blight of mosaic disease threatened European tobacco crops in the mid-1800s, plant pathologists set out to identify its root cause. For decades, only one forward-thinking botanist, Martinus Beijerinck, realized the source was neither a bacterial nor a fungal infection, but something completely different: a virus (Latin for liquid poison).

Today, we know that viruses can be found nearly anywhere in the air, oceans and soil and that a tiny percentage of these are dangerous pathogens that cause disease. Yet the study of viruses started not in medical science, but in botany, the study of plants. Viruses are so small—and so strange—that it would take decades for scientific consensus to agree that they exist at all.

The idea that microorganisms could cause plant disease wasn't entirely new even in the late 19th century. In the 1840s, Reverend Miles Berkeley, also a botanist, identified the fungus behind Ireland's potato blight, despite the clergy's notion that the devil was to blame.

In 1857, farmers in the Netherlands reported a disease threatening another economically vital crop: tobacco. The leaves began turning a mottled dark green, yellow, and grey, causing farmers to lose up to 80 percent of crops in affected fields. Massive fields of tobacco that had been planted with the same crop repeatedly were especially susceptible. Once the disease reached a farmer's field, it spread rapidly.

In the Netherlands, plant pathologist Adolf Mayer began researching the disease in 1879 and named it the "mosaic disease of tobacco." He tried to use Koch's guidelines, which call for a series of germ isolations and re-infections, to find its cause. But Mayer ran into trouble. Although he showed that the sap from a sick tobacco leaf could pass the disease to a healthy leaf, he couldn't produce a pure culture of the pathogen and the virus is too small to be seen under a microscope. Other studies found that the pathogen was smaller than bacteria and was growing in the leaves, but strangely, it couldn't reproduce without them. Questions about whether these tiny germs were small bacteria, molecules secreted by bacteria, or something else remained unanswered into the 1920s. Some people would probably say the questions went on until they could be seen with an electron microscope.

In 1935, chemist Wendell M. Stanley created a crystallized sample of the virus that could be visualized with X-rays. The first clear, direct photographs of tobacco mosaic virus would not come until 1941 with the invention of powerful electron transmission microscopes, which revealed the pathogen's skinny, sticklike shape.

Tobacco use has been documented for over 8,000 years. Tobacco cultivation likely began in 5000 BC with the development of maize-based agriculture in Central Mexico. Radiocarbon methods have established the remains of cultivated and wild tobacco in the High Rolls Cave in New Mexico from 1400-1000 BC. It was originally used by Native Americans in religious ceremonies and for medical purposes. Early in tobacco's history, it was used as a cure-all remedy, for dressing wounds, reducing pain, and even for tooth aches. (My wife, Shauna, informed me that her grandfather blew pipe smoke in her ears for ear aches).

In the late 15th century, Christopher Columbus was given tobacco as a gift from the Native Americans. It gained instant popularity in Europe, for they believed that tobacco had magical healing powers. Soon, the smoking of tobacco was promoted as a viable way to get your "daily dose of tobacco."

By the early 17th century, scientists and philosophers were discovering the consequences that smoking tobacco had on their lives, including difficulty with breathing and trouble with quitting. In 1632, Massachusetts passed a state law making smoking in public illegal. This was the earliest legislation recorded regarding smoking.

In 1760 Pierre Lorillard established the first company that processed tobacco to make cigars and snuff. Today, over 200 years later, P. Lorillard is the oldest tobacco company in U.S. history. As tobacco usage continued to grow, scientists began to study and further understand the chemicals in tobacco and the harmful health effects of smoking.

It wasn't until the 1900's that cigarettes were made and sold as a major tobacco product in the U.S. In 1901, 3.5 billion cigarettes were sold in the U.S. and more and more tobacco companies were established, creating an entire industry that gained a lot of power.

In 1964, the Surgeon General's report on smoking tobacco was released, shining light on the serious health effects cigarettes were causing. This report also allowed the government to initiate the regulation of the production and sales of cigarettes. In 1985, less than a century after cigarettes became popular, lung cancer became the number one cause of death in women. Rates for lung cancer were even higher than breast cancer at this time.1

Stuffing cigarette butts into the lining of nests may seem unwholesome. But a team of ecologists says that far from being unnatural, the use of smoked cigarettes by city birds may be an urban variation of an ancient adaptation. Birds have long been known to line their nests with vegetation rich in compounds that can drive away parasites. Chemicals in tobacco leaves are known to repel arthropods such as parasitic mites, so Monserrat Suárez-Rodríguez and her colleagues wondered whether city birds were using cigarette butts in the same way. In a study published in Biology Letters, the researchers examined the nests of two bird species common on the North American continent. They measured the amount of cellulose acetate (a component of cigarette butts) in the nests, and found that the more there was, the fewer parasitic mites the nest contained.

The team also used heat traps to test whether the repellent effect of the cigarette butts was related to their nicotine content, rather than to their structure or other features. They placed traps in the nests of 27 house sparrows (Passer domesticus) and 28 house finches (Carpodacus mexicanus) on their university campus. The traps, which use warmth to lure parasites close, were fitted with cellulose fibers and filters from either smoked or unsmoked cigarettes, as well as adhesive tape to catch the arthropods.

After 20 minutes, the team found that devices with unsmoked butts had many more parasites attached to them than devices with smoked butts—which contain more nicotine from the cigarette smoke passing through them. Indeed, in nests that contained bird eggs, traps with unsmoked butts caught on average more than twice as many parasites.

The results raised the question: might these birds show a preference for cigarette brands high in nicotine? If they do, that might suggest this behavior has truly evolved as an adaptive response to challenges from parasites.

As well as having anti-parasite effects, there may be as-yet unknown negative effects for the birds, because many compounds in cigarette butts are known carcinogens, and some are pesticides.[2]

Although there were already clear links between tobacco and human cancer, researchers spent decades forcing beagles to smoke cigarettes and painting tar on the backs of mice. Physicians were encouraged to keep quiet while researchers spent years performing animal tests.

In tobacco inhalation experiments, dogs, primates, guinea pigs, hamsters, rabbits, lambs, chickens, rodents and other animals were given nicotine and forced to inhale smoke. Dogs were forced to inhale cigarette smoke on mechanical ventilators. In one experiment, researchers cut openings in the throats of beagles' (tracheotomy) and forced them to breathe concentrated cigarette smoke for an entire year.

Other tests have involved inserting electrodes into dogs' penises to measure the effect of cigarette smoke on sexual performance. Masks were strapped on to the faces of rats and mice while cigarette smoke was pumped directly into noses. Rhesus monkeys were confined to chairs with head devices, while being exposed to nicotine and caffeine to study effects on breathing. In 1996, the National Institutes of Health (NIH) funded 123 grants for tobacco research, with 40% slated for animal testing. According to a 1957 medical journal, except for a few cases—there was failure by many investigators in inducing experimental cancers during fifty years of trying. This casted serious doubt on the validity of the cigarette-lung cancer theory.

At the time, 27 human studies had already established a clear link between smoking and cancer. In spite of reams of data establishing the tobacco/cancer link, the tobacco industry still conducts tobacco testing on animals, spending millions of dollars and killing hundreds of animals in an attempt to manipulate data. Tobacco testing on animals has been illegal in Britain since 1997.3

An abstract from an article published in 2005 stated, "this study demonstrates that lifetime whole-body exposure of B6C3F 1 mice to high doses of cigarette smoke robustly increases lung cancer incidence compared with sham exposed animals. *This is the first study to demonstrate a strong effect of inhaled cigarette smoke on lung cancer in an animal model* (italics added). This commentary attempts to put the new results in perspective with the existing literature on cigarette smoke inhalation studies in animals and discusses strengths, limitations and possible applications of available models.4

We all probably pretty much know that cigarette smoking kills you. We also have a good idea that cigarettes contain chemicals—a mix of over 7,000 chemicals, in fact—that can cause diseases including cancer, cardiovascular disease, and COPD. We may not know that other tobacco products, like e-cigarettes, hookah, and smokeless tobacco, contain some of the same chemicals as cigarettes or what these chemicals are, and how might they affect your health?

Nicotine is a highly addictive chemical found in the tobacco plant itself and is therefore present in all tobacco products. While nicotine is what addicts and keeps people using tobacco products, it is not what makes tobacco use so deadly. It's the chemicals in tobacco and tobacco smoke, not nicotine, that causes serious disease and death in tobacco use.5

While attending the University of Idaho in 1964-1968 several of my class mates would play cards and showing our macho manhood smoked cigarettes. Because we did not bet, I didn't lose any money but did gamble on my future health and happiness by risking addiction to nicotine. I haven't smoked since I was in college but it wasn't because I wasn't affected by our card games. It was for several reasons:

I don't smoke partly because I tried to light up in front of my future kid's mom while driving from Moscow Idaho to Spokane Washington. I don't remember much about her rage, but I do vividly remember almost driving off the road, realizing she had principles I needed to follow if she was going to be my eternal mate and her throwing the cigarettes out the window.

Fortunately, I had constant breathing problems from allergies. I also had two anaphylactic reactions before I reached high school age. One of them occurred when my father was not at home and my mother had to find epinephrin in his medical emergency bag for injecting into me. My sister Pat recalls how I looked, my anxiety, and how she tried to keep me calm and under control while waiting for mom to get instructions from my dad. I'll never forget the racing of my heart rate and fear of dying induced by the drug.

Allergies worsened when I moved to Purduc University mostly caused by Indiana's late summer and fall ragweed population plus inhalant plant particles present in the large animal university barns. I was treated with cortisone, antihistamines and desensitization injections. The only lasting benefit I had from the injections was that whenever I had an allergy attack there would be an itchy swelling on my arm where I had received them.

Doctors warned me that I was an asthma attack waiting to happen and that it would be wise choosing research over exposing my health to animal allergens. However, my interests in practicing veterinary medicine overrode wisdom, I did develop asthma that was controlled by medication and my almost always plugged nose at night began to open up when I reached my mid fifty's. I'm now able to get by without the use of decongestants or nose drops.

I believe my good fortune is mostly due to desensitization to allergens from a lifelong exposure mostly from work. Much like the injections I received from an allergist in Indiana hoped they would do. Comments made by an allergist in 2019 leads me to believe I'm at least partially right: "Allergies aren't just for kids. Some adults may actually experience a change in allergies as they age. From developing springtime allergies for the first time, to realizing that your family cat doesn't cause you the misery it once did—allergies can shift and change at different phases of your life."6

Smoking followed me from the University of Idaho, into a marriage and to graduate school at Purdue University. Fortunately, I didn't make it easy to smoke by letting my wife know what was going on or smoking in front of others. This helped me use cigarettes sparingly, increased guilt of what I was doing and reinforced the knowledge that I must quit for my own welfare. However, the feeling of taking in a deep breath filled with nicotine was hard to get out of my mind.

A single 15-minute exposure to nicotine causes a long-term increase in the excitability of neurons involved in reward, according to a study published in The Journal of Neuroscience. The results suggest that nicotine and cocaine hijack similar mechanisms of memory on first contact to create long-lasting changes in a person's brain. Smoking is a very long-term behavioral change, but everything starts with the first exposure. That's what the study was trying to understand—when a person first is exposed to a cigarette, what happens in the brain that might lead to a second cigarette?7

Nicotine has been proven to be as addictive as cocaine and heroin and may even be more addictive. Many people who smoke develop nicotine dependence, which makes quitting all the harder, especially when they try to stop smoking on their own. In fact, 70 percent of smokers report wanting to quit, but many wait until they develop a significant tobacco-related disease such as heart disease, cancer or stroke.

I don't remember the last cigarette I smoked. I do remember being involved at school and socially with people that did not smoke and the inhaled smoke lift became more and more not worth it. Also, having allergies and potential asthma risks really helped me discontinue the use of tobacco.

However, I must confess that I do prescribe a nicotine-based product for the dogs and cats I care for. It is placed just behind the base of the neck and it kills fleas that get on them for at least one month.

The chains of habit generally too small to be felt
until they are too strong to be broken—
Samuel Johnson (1709-84)

1. *Science, How a Few Sick Tobacco Plants Led Scientists to Unravel the Truth About Viruses, March 24, 2022.*
2. *Might these birds show a preference for cigarette brands high in nicotine? Monserrat Suárez-Rodríguez, an ecologist at the National Autonomous University of Mexico in Mexico City & Timothy Mousseau, an ecologist at the University of South Carolina in Columbia.*

3. *The Faces of Devocalization, Coalition to Protect and Rescue Pets (PETA), September 2009.*

4. *Carcinogenicity studies of inhaled cigarette smoke in laboratory animals: old and new, Stephen S. Hecht Carcinogenesis, Volume 26, Issue 9, September 2005, Pages 1488 - 1492.*

5. *Matt Kaplan, Nature, 2012.*

6. *October 31, 2019 / Allergies, Can Allergies Go Away or Develop as You Age?*

7. *UChicago Medicine, Nicotine and cocaine leave similar mark on brain after first contact, 2011.*

4

IF IT SOUNDS TOO GOOD TO BE TRUE . . . IT PROBABLY IS—STILBESTEROL

DES (Diethylstilbestrol) was first synthesized in early 1938 by Leon Golberg, then a graduate student of Sir Robert Robinson at the Dyson Perrins Laboratory at the University of Oxford. Golberg's research was based on work by Wilfrid Lawson at the Courtauld Institute of Biochemistry, (led by Sir Edward Charles Dodds at Middlesex Hospital Medical School now part of University College London). A report of its synthesis was published in Nature on 5 February 1938. DES acts three times more powerfully than natural estrogen and is effective when given orally.

DES is a derivative of stilbene, Stilbenes are a class of phenolic metabolites found in various edible plants, such as grapevine, berries and peanuts. Their bioactivity and their potential benefits for human health have been the subject of several studies.

Among all identified stilbenes, resveratrol has been particularly studied and results from literature showed that it presents several biological activities, including antioxidant, anti-inflammatory and antiproliferative effects. It is produced by serval plants in response to injury or when the plant is under attack by pathogens, such as bacteria or fungi. It is made from red grape products that I take as a supplement to hopefully help my body age more slowly. The usage instructions states that it is a highly concentrated standardized extract used to support immune system health and provide overall antioxidant support.

In humans DES has been used to treat quite a list of conditions in the past: Recurrent miscarriage in pregnancy, menopausal hormone therapy for the treatment such as hot flashes and vaginal atrophy, hormone therapy for hypoestrogenism, postpartum lactation suppression and breast engorgement, prostate cancer and breast cancer, prevention of tall stature in tall adolescent girls, acne in women, an emergency post coital contraceptive, a means of chemical castration for hypersexuality and sex offenders, and feminizing hormone therapy.

Use of DES as a feminizing hormone made history in the 1950s. Alan Turing was noted as being an outstanding mathematician whose work had an impact on computer science, the use of artificial intelligence and a war hero. He is best known for work devising code-breaking machines during the Second World War and was also openly gay. In the 1950s he was convicted of gross indecency for his relationship with a man and homosexual acts. He avoided prison by agreeing to take DES chemical castration, was removed from his government work and felt himself to have been placed under observation.1

Soy beans and other plants that contain isoflavones and lignans are consider to be phytoestrogens that have been suggested to be anticarcinogenic and have anti DES qualities. The mechanisms by which they exert cancer-preventive effects may involve modulation of estrogen synthesis and metabolism. To evaluate this hypothesis, a randomized, cross-over soy isoflavone feeding study was performed in 12 healthy premenopausal women. These data suggested that soy isoflavone consumption may exert cancer-preventive effects by decreasing estrogen synthesis and altering metabolism away from genotoxic metabolites toward inactive metabolites.

Where DES increases the amount of estrogen like activity isoflavones and lignans have been proposed to help prevent cancers by decreasing the natural levels of estrogen in the human body.

DES has been very successful in treating spayed female canine incontinence stemming from poor urinary bladder sphincter control. It has been replaced for use by Estriol (Incurin) that was discovered about the time (1930) DES came into use. It has the same effect of strengthening the sphincter muscles with less side effects. A big plus for both of these compounds is they can both be given by mouth.

Before Estriol we used DES for many years to aid in urinary bladder control and as an emergency contraceptive for birth prevention in dogs with an unplanned mating.

We also use a product called phenylpropanolamine to help directly tighten the bladder sphincter muscles. It is also used in decongestants for allergies and colds. If you have a prostate problem be careful using this medication. Just like in the dog it will also tighten the muscles around your sphincter near the prostate and may prevent you from voiding. I've had prostate cancer therapy and it took me serval hours before I could void after taking this decongestant. I mentioned this to my urologist who told me not to use the decongestant. He has cared for patients that needed to be catharized until the affects wore off.

James Herriot describes a case regarding treating a small dog's testicular Sertoli cell tumor in his 1974 book *All Things Bright and Beautiful*. Herriot decided to prescribe a high dose of the new drug Stilboestrol (DES) for the recurring tumor, with the amusing side effect that the male dog became "attractive to other male dogs", who followed the terrier around the village for a few weeks. Herriot comments in the story that he knew "The new drug was said to have a feminizing effect, but surely not to that extent."

The greatest usage of DES was in the livestock industry. During the 1960s, it was used as a growth hormone in the beef and poultry industries. It was later found to cause cancer by 1971, but was not phased out until 1979. Although DES was discovered to be harmful to humans, its veterinary use was not immediately halted.

By 2007, DES was only used in the treatment of prostate cancer and breast cancer. In 2011, Hoover and colleagues reported on adverse health outcomes linked to DES including infertility, miscarriage, ectopic pregnancy, preeclampsia, preterm birth, stillbirth, infant death, menopause prior to age 45, breast cancer, cervical cancer, and vaginal cancer.[2]

While visiting Idaho a high school class mate of mine shared a book titled, *"DOCTORS WITH BUGGIES, SNOWSHOES, AND PLANES" (One Hundred Years and more—Of Idaho Medicine)*, published in 1993 by Louise

Shadduck. The book contained a summary of my father's professional career including his studies at four universities, the degrees of BA, MS and MD, captain in the US Army serving in Germany, Chief of staff for two terms at the Idaho Falls Hospital in Idaho, Chairman of Record Committee and staff member of Sacred Heart Hospital in Idaho Falls, Necrologist, and secretary of the Idaho Academy of General Practice for two years. The final note was that he and his wife had four children.

It looks like my dad had a wonderful professional career. Funny thing, I was aware of only a few of these accomplishments and to me he was the one that seemed to be always doing rounds at the hospital, seeing patients in his office or too busy to go on vacations or take me duck hunting or fishing. It wasn't until later when I was pursuing my professional career that we talked some about his experiences.

He passed in 2001 and I have finally reached the point in my life where his life story is important to me. Too bad I have to learn about his life in a book and he can't "fill in the blanks" with a personal touch explaining the "how's" and "why's" that helped him become who he was. I'm sure if I asked my father what was one of his most important accomplishments he achieved during his professional career, near the top of the list would probably be the early diagnosis of a malignant growth in my sister Patricia that resulted in saving her life.

During dad's seventy-fifth year he decided it was time to retire. As a final act he informed all his four children and their spouses that he would give all of them a physical exam. I don't need to tell you how much all of us looked forward to such an activity. I remember how my kid's mom wanted to "get out of Dodge and pay for the physical back in California."

All of us showed up for the ordeal, went on our way and all seemed fine. At the time nothing was mentioned about the discovery a few years earlier of cancer in my younger sister or the challenges that confronted her during treatment. Fortunately, she successfully went through the treatments, is living a full life, has raised 6 children, and currently is with her husband serving his calling as mission president of the Mongolia Mission.

Becoming established in my business and starting a family I hadn't thought much about what my sister was going through during treatment. The information coming from home at the time didn't concern me. I knew that she was able to care for her children and helped some in her husband's office.

Many years later my children's mom was being treated for cancer. When she became terminally ill my sister called and told me that one mistake she made during her illness was that she felt her family could take care of their needs and she didn't want others to feel obligated to help care for her.

She emphasized to me the importance of our family opening our hearts to those who wanted to serve. For "when we are in the service of our fellow man we are in the service of our God" *Mosiah 2:17* and we shouldn't deny them from receiving those blessings of service ". . . come into the fold of God, …be called his people, and…willing to bear one another's burdens, that they may be light; Yea, . . . willing to mourn with those that mourn; yea, and comfort those that stand in need of comfort, and to stand as witnesses of God at all times and in all things, and in all places that ye may be in. . . . *Mosiah 18:8-9.*

My older sister, Bobbie, and I knew that dad's diagnosis of Pat's cancer was a surprise to the oncologist that cared for our sister but we weren't sure about the particulars. Therefore, I sent an email to my sister in Mongolia and some of her response is included below. To me these comments give confirmation to the statement—I didn't say it would easy. I said it will be worth it. Thank you for letting me share some of her comments with you:

Tuesday, April 30, 2013 8:59 AM

Dear Rich,

We finally got through the big 20th Anniversary of the dedication of the church in Mongolia. We are still recovering . . . and trying to catch up on everything (including sleep). I'm sorry I couldn't get this to you sooner. Hopefully it will be of some use to you. We miss being closer to all of you—even a closer time zone would help! We'll be home the first part of July . . .

Bobbi gave a fairly good account, but discredited Dad by saying it was an "old" technique that found my cancer. It was actually a "new" cervical brush technique that was being criticized by some of the doctors as "being more painful for the patient so they didn't use it even though it was more accurate." It went farther in and was able to find problems that couldn't be detected by the older "scrape the outer area" technique.

We had just moved to Orem (Feb. 1985) Shawn was barely 3 (6th child). We were in the middle of starting a new practice along with a new office building, etc. That summer we started furnishing the operating suite. We were under a lot of stress—financial, worried about Medicare approval of the facility, etc. The state of Utah was either going to give us a cease and desist order or allow us to do surgery in the facility.

Dad called me and said he was worried about Jay. He knew he had gained weight and was terribly stressed over all the problems going on. He wanted Jay to go to Blackfoot for a physical—especially to check his blood pressure. I let him know that Linnea needed a pre-school kindergarten physical and I was due for a pap smear (before starting on a new baby.) (Of course, I didn't mention the "starting of a new baby" to him. I had always put off exams until after conception, but I really felt strongly I should get it done.) He said he'd take care of all of us. At the last minute Jay decided he couldn't go so

I went anyway (the first time ever driving that far alone with the "fearsome six" in the car). I almost cancelled out, but felt impressed that I needed to go.

Linnea was in great shape to start school (other than her second broken arm that was still in a cast.) But my tests came back "conclusive for malignancy—late stages." Dad called Jay and told him so he "got" to tell me. We were at the office and I drove the car home alone in a state of shock . . . not a very good idea.

After having biopsies by a GYN in Orem, the news got worse because it was adenocarcinoma of the cervix which spreads very quickly via the lymphatic system to other organs and it was definitely in the invasive late stages. He sent me to a gynecological oncologist in SLC. The gynecologist asked, "How did you ever catch this with a PAP smear? You just don't find this with a PAP smear." I told him of Dad's new technique and he said, "That explains it. You are so fortunate."

They suggested radiation, or surgery. Radiation was their first option because they thought it would be less invasive and "might" work to keep me comfortable—for a while. However, if I lived longer my abdominal organs would all be in terrible shape as time went along.

We opted for the radical hysterectomy because I wanted to know where we really stood because of the young children. They would remove the uterus, cervix, and the surrounding tissues, etc. They would also remove all the lymph nodes they could find from my diaphragm all the way into the groin area. They warned me of complications from destroyed nerves that were wrapped around the lymph nodes which would interfere with bowel and bladder functions, etc. I would need to have a catheter and wear a bag for a few months after surgery.

Jay gave me a blessing before going to SLC for surgery. In it he said that I would be "healed according to MY faith." That was not what I wanted to hear. I did not doubt that Heavenly Father could heal me. That was not an issue. I had complete faith in Him. But I thought, "I'm nobody special. He's got a lot of children to take care of. Why didn't Jay say something like, I would be healed according to the faith of my family or friends or somebody else—not just MY faith?"

It seemed to be all on my shoulders at that point, but I knew that any and all prayers would certainly help a lot. I appreciated everyone's prayers so much. I also realized that this certainly was a test of my faith and I needed to better understand how it worked.

After surgery I was so weak and so sick and couldn't even drive the kids to lessons or to shop in a store. I had a hard time remembering anything. I forced myself to get up and tried to keep going, but I really couldn't keep going. I got down to 80 pounds before I quit weighing myself. I caught every cold or sore throat that anybody had. I was dizzy and lightheaded.

I forced myself to eat. I still can't remember most of what happened for the next 6 months. I do remember the entire neighborhood's kids running through the house slamming doors and not being able to do anything about it. Luckily, we had a lot of food storage so I didn't need to go to the store very often.

My daughter Linnea still remembers my reading to her at nap time or bed time and falling asleep in the middle of sentences. I would just speak slower and slower until I stopped. Sometimes she would fill in the words for me.

I love having a well-managed home. Fortunately, some of my children were old enough to help cook, vacuum, dust, do the dishes, wash the clothing, put it away etcetera. Dust still piled up, the floors hadn't been mopped or shampooed for a long time and the windows were dirty.

My poodle Tiffy was concerned about me and followed me everywhere. She slept by me and wanted to be on my lap whenever I sat down. She, also, was neglected. Her hair was getting longer and more matted by the day. She could hardly see out of her eyes for all the hair around them. She would bark at the children when they were being rowdy and tried to look after me.

Six or seven months after my surgery the bishop called me into his office for an interview. I parked in the back of the building and stopped, out of breath, at the drinking fountain. Dizziness overcame me as I leaned down for a drink. I didn't pass out, but I knew it was close. He asked me to be the new YW (Young Woman's) President. I was surprised and in my mind I thought, "How can I do this? I can't even take care of my family." Of course, I told him, "Yes."

It was at that point that my health began to improve. I slowly got stronger and started to gain a little bit of weight. I could do short shopping trips to the grocery store. I was able to vacuum and dust again.

Things just kept going uphill little by little. By July I was actually able to go to Girls' Camp and even be useful. I knew a miracle had happened in my life. Sometimes I wondered if I would have continued to improve if I hadn't accepted that call.

I learned many things from this experience a few of which I will attempt to share:

- We need to follow our promptings.
- We need the prayers of the righteous in our behalf, but they can't always pray for us unless we share our problems with them. However, sometimes they are prompted to pray in our behalf even if they don't know what is going on.
- We need to understand how faith works and do everything in our power to truly believe and not doubt the power of our Heavenly Father in our lives. Each of us is loved by our Heavenly Father.
- We don't need to be "somebody special" to receive His blessings because everybody is special to Him. We truly are his precious sons and daughters.
- Innate objects are just not that important. It doesn't matter how dirty the floors get or how many inches of dust are on the furniture. It doesn't hurt the house at all. As soon as it is clean again, all is back to normal.
- Living things are extremely important and must never be neglected. Relationships cannot be put on hold. Love must be ongoing. Care must be ongoing. Understanding must never stop.

I realized this acutely when I finally had the energy and strength to trim my small poodle's hair. It was tangled and matted. She could hardly see through the matted hair and gunk around her eyes. I couldn't comb through it without really hurting her. So, I talked quietly and lovingly to her as I hacked at it with my hair scissors until I got rid of most of the mats.

It was painful for both of us. Occasionally she would yelp and I felt terrible. We both did some whimpering. Then I carefully combed through it, still causing her some pain. Eventually I used the clippers to even it up. She looked more like an ugly white rat than a cute poodle.

It was not a good experience for either one of us. It took months before all was back to normal—just because I had been neglectful.

-We must constantly nurture and spend meaningful time with those we love, including our Heavenly Father. If we don't, our relationships will become like Tiffy's coat— all matted and messed up. And it may take some long, painful experiences to get things back to normal again.

-This experience brought me closer to my Heavenly Father because so much of my time was spent on my knees praying for my family and for my health.

I would wake up in a panic in the middle of the night due to nightmares of my children not having a mother to raise them. The only way I could receive comfort was to slide out of bed onto my knees and pray until I could feel the comfort of the spirit again.

I knew I couldn't give in to negative thoughts that would decrease my faith. My life depended on it then.

Now I realize that my soul also depended on it then and continually depends on it now.3

Elder Jeffrey R. Holland stated, "Let us always remember that we do not have to walk down the long, lonely path that Jesus did during his sacrifice for our sins. He has opened the door for, 'the merciful care of our Father in Heaven, the unfailing companionship of His Beloved Son, the consummate gift of the Holy Ghost, angels in heaven, family members on both sides of the veil, prophets and apostles, teachers, leaders, friends.' All of these and more have been given as companions for our mortal journey because of the Atonement of Jesus Christ and the Restoration of His gospel."5

Diethylstilbestrol (DES) was prescribed for pregnant women between 1940 and 1971 to prevent miscarriage, premature labor, and related complications of pregnancy. The use of DES declined after studies in the 1950s showed that it was not effective in preventing these problems.

In 1971, researchers linked prenatal (before birth) DES exposure to a type of cancer of the cervix and vagina called clear cell adenocarcinoma in a small group of women. Soon after, the Food and Drug Administration (FDA) notified physicians throughout the country that DES should not be prescribed to pregnant women.

The daughters of women who used DES while pregnant—commonly called DES daughters—have about 40 times the risk of developing clear cell adenocarcinoma of the lower genital tract than unexposed women. However, this type of cancer is still rare; approximately 1 in 1,000 DES daughters develops it.

The first DES daughters who were diagnosed with clear cell adenocarcinoma were very young at the time of their diagnoses and later research has shown that the risk of developing this disease remains elevated as women age into their 40s.

DES daughters have a 2 times more likely chance of an increased risk of developing abnormal cells in the cervix and the vagina that are precursors of cancer (dysplasia, cervical intraepithelial neoplasia, and squamous intraepithelial lesions). They also show an increased risk of breast cancer after age 40 and problems with fertility and pregnancy.

Commonly referred as "DES daughters" and "DES sons" these women are recommended by the United States National Cancer Institute to be aware of these health risks, share their medical history with their doctors, and get regular special medical examinations to screen for complications as a result of this medication. DES, it has largely been discontinued and is now mostly no longer marketed.4

Dad wrote in his journal, "The day the Japanese attacked Pearl Harbor, 7 December 1941, I heard the news by radio while dissecting a cadaver with some students in the anatomy laboratory. This was on a Sunday morning (in Honolulu), and I could picture such a morning...Pressure was applied to all medical students to enlist in the Army or Navy. I applied to the Navy, but the examiner thought I was too much underweight. For all I know this may have been for the best. I joined the Army as Pvt (lowest rank they have) and they took us to camp for a couple of weeks and returned all of us with rank of Pfc, private first class."

He graduated from Northwestern Medical School on September 14, 1945 with a Doctor of Medicine and headed by ship off to Germany just before my birth on February 23, 1946. My younger sister Pat was born in the late 1940s. I don't know if dad or another doctor prescribed DES for my mother during her pregnancies. I have found evidence that at the time it was a new big deal, dad was a brand new up to date MD and I know how I felt about great and wonderful new treatments when I graduated as a DVM.

Regarding our earthly journey, the Lord has promised:

"I will go before your face. I will be on your right hand and on your left, and my Spirit shall be in your hearts, and mine angels round about you, to bear you up".

(D&C 84:88)

1. *Stilboestrol—Gone but not forgotten. Prescriber Update 27(1): 9-11. May 2006. Professor Charlotte Paul, . Department of Preventive and Social Medicine, Otago University Medical School, Dunedin; and Dr Mira Harrison-Woolrych, New Zealand Pharmacovigilance Centre, Dunedin*
2. *1101-8Clinical Trial, Cancer Epidemiol Biomarkers Prev, 1998 Dec;7(12):1101-8. Effects of soy isoflavones on estrogen and phytoestrogen metabolism in premenopausal women X Xu 1, A M Duncan, B E Merz, M S Kurzer.*
3. *Patricia Clark, personal communication, April 30, 2013.*
4. *Wikipedia.*
5. *Elder Jeffrey R. Holland, "None Were with Him", Ensign, May 2009.*

5

COMPANIONS—YOUR MICROBIOME

Our bodies are crawling with bacteria, yeast, fungi and virus cells. Their total population is grouped together and called microbiome. In any human body there are around 30 trillion human cells, but our microbiome population living on and in us is an estimated 39 trillion. Due to their small size, these microbes make up only about 1-3 per cent of our body weight, but this belies the microbiome's tremendous power and potential.

Placing things into a little more perspective let's assume that I had all my 39 trillion microbes removed from my body and shared them equally with all the living people on the earth. In 2022 the official population count was just under 7.95 billion and I could give 4,905 microbes to each of them and still have 4,905 living on my body.

The New York Times reported that during the Covid-19 pandemic the United States Government stimulus money given out between 2021 until March 2022 was 1.8 trillion to individuals, 1.7 trillion to businesses, 745 billion to state and local governments, 482 billion to health care and 288 billion to other expenses for a grand total of 5 trillion dollars.

If I were given a dollar for each of the microbes living on and in me—that would be 39 trillion dollars. If I paid off the 5 trillion dollars the government spent for the pandemic, I would still have enough left over to give $4,276.73 to every man, woman and child living on this earth in 2022 + have the same amount left for me.

We have around 20-25,000 genes in each of our cells, but the human microbiome potentially holds 500 times more. The large numbers of genes in microbiome life allows the microbes to evolve quickly, swap genes, multiply and adapt to changing circumstances given them. All living hosts that harbor these microbiomes receive benefits that scientists are just beginning to fathom. The human microbiome contains beneficial and pathogenic microbes competing for dominance. Disease occurs when the bad microbes over populate the beneficial ones.

Each part of the body is a different type of ecosystem, like a planet with different continents and climates, the inhabitants of which have adapted to the characteristics of each location. Three-quarters of your microbiome can be traced back to your mother. The womb is a sterile place, free of microbes (at least we think so at the moment). But when we exit via the birth canal, we're bathed in vaginal microbes.

This literal baptism of bacteria may be vital to a healthy start in life—babies who are born through caesarean section are more likely to develop allergies, asthma, coeliac disease and obesity later in life Scientists suspect that a lot of common modern allergies, such as hay fever, are triggered by an immune system that didn't learn to live with such microorganisms at an early age.

We also ingest around a million microbes in every gram of food, and our diet has a direct impact on which species thrive in our gut microbiome. If we change diets, from meat-eater to vegetarian, for example, the gut bacteria changes accordingly.1

The most commonly found pathogenic microbe found in my practice is yeast. They primarily are found on damaged skin from allergies, contact irritants or parasites that cause scratching and licking. We usually find the heaviest infection in the ear canals of dogs. The yeast grows rapidly in the ear because it is moist, warm and dark inside. I often take a Q-tip with dark yeast smelling material from an ear canal and ask the owner if they would like to take it home to make wild yeast sourdough starter. It only requires a mixture of flour, water and time. In a short time, the microbial action of the yeast and beneficial lactic acid found in air (or from an ear canal) will ferment the flour and water to make a sourdough starter that will nurture your family for generations. It takes about two weeks for a sourdough starter to be ready for bread baking. Natural yeasts take time to populate and ferment the starter and make it active.

So far—I've had no takers. If yeast floating around a kitchen can be used to make starter; why not ear canal yeast? I don't seriously suggest anyone try it. The ear canal has many other micro-organisms that may affect the yeast fermentation and even though cooking kills all the microbes, toxic materials may be left behind that may affect taste or one's personal health.

The ingredients found in food that help sustain the microbes in the digestive tract are called prebiotics, and adding additional beneficial microbes are called probiotics. It is called a symbiotic relationship when prebiotics work in tandem with probiotics for the overall good of an animal. For this reason, you'll often see prebiotics paired with probiotics in many products.

Around the mid-1900s, scientists began to explore the benefits of rumen removing ingesta (probiotics) from a normal cow's rumen and transplanting the fluid into another cow's rumen to treat indigestion on dairy and livestock (other ruminants) operations.

The most important roles that we think of microbes having that live in the digestive tract is helping extract energy from our food or producing vitamins; but they also have a large role in aiding our immune system and recently there has been a lot of evidence building on how they help us with glucose regulation and overall metabolism. To top it off they also have the ability to protect us from invading pathogens.

Think as the microbiome as having a little army of microbes in your gut. When you ingest a pathogen, they actually help to fight off that infection. And so, they're pretty powerful and they're essential for our well-being. When the microbiome in the digestive tract is taken over by disease causing microbes that antibiotics, change of diet or other methods fail, doctors are reaching out more and more to inoculating the intestinal tract with new microbes— much like farmers share rumen fluid in cows. How do they do that—they basically feed you with human poop that hopefully does not contain parasites or microbes that can act as pathogens.

In human medicine, using poop to restore normal microbiomes in the GI tract has been around since the fourth century. Chinese medicine appears to be the first documentation of using fermented fecal material and giving it to patients who have diarrhea and showing it helps improve symptoms. There has been little human scientific literature written until about 2010,2012.

Inoculating the GI tract with poop is called Fecal Microbial Transplantation (FMT) and you take fecal material from a healthy donor and put that fecal material into a diseased recipient. The poop can be administered in a lot of different ways. Most commonly it's given via an enema, as a slurry during an endoscopic exam and more products for oral FMT are becoming available. There are frozen products where a capsule is filled with feces and given orally, but there's also lyophilized products where feces is freeze-dry and encapsulated. It can be stored at room temperature and taken orally.

But it's really taking that fecal material and in that fecal material are all those great microbes, and it's not just bacteria, that's what we tend to talk about, but it's that whole microbial community and that microbial community then has the opportunity to engraft or take up a niche or a home within the new recipient. And there is a lot of encouragement that FMT can be used in human and animal medicine to help cure or help prevent disease.

The epidemic of obesity is huge when it comes to quality of life, risk of disease and life expectancy. There have been lots of rodent studies that have shown that you can actually transmit phenotypes with fecal material. Probably the most well-known example is a study in mice taking microbes from obese animals and putting them into germ-free mice that don't have any microbiota associated with them, and they go on to develop that obese phenotype.

If you take microbes from a lean individual, you can actually augment the microbiome to actually change their overall physiology. Currently there are research projects planned to use FMT to reduce obesity in dogs and cats. I'm going to watch the progress carefully and if all goes well maybe I can be one of the first volunteers when they launch human studies.2

There are several ingredients placed in dog foods that increase bulk and reduce calories. One of the ingredients manufacturers used to add fiber and bulk with low calories to the diet was peanut hulls. During the late 70's or early 80's there was a shortage of peanut hulls and the dog food was on back order for as I remember several months. This occurred at the time peanut farmer Jimmy Carter was president of the United States (1977-1981) and he had a brother Billy who was a bit of a character. Billy also was a peanut farmer and had received a Libyan Government loan for $220,000 during Jimmy's term as president. It became a scandal that was given the name Billy gate by the press. He also helped launch a product called Billy Beer in July 1977 by a brewery company that closed in 1978.

When there was the peanut hull shortage, Billy Beer being promoted and Billy gate rummers in the air I couldn't help but think that the lack of weight reducing diet available, because of a peanut hull shortage, had something to do with Billy. I pictured him like Scrooge Mc Duck in his room with piles of money throwing it into the air. However, in Billy's case it was grain bins filled with peanut hulls waiting for a rise in the market value.

This story was a good one that I have enjoyed sharing over the years with my clients while discussing obesity and weight reducing diets. The company no longer uses peanuts hulls and switched to a product known as a prebiotic called beet pulp. Sugar comes from two main crops in the United States, sugar cane and sugar beets. Beet pulp is left over from the sugar beet once the sugar has been removed, and is commonly used as an ingredient in animal feeds. This fiber is a high energy, low protein and high fiber source that is added to horse, cattle, sheep and goat diets. It is also used in pig diets at relatively high amounts, but only in relatively limited concentrations in diets for poultry.

Sugar beets are not used as a supplement or prebiotic for humans. However, there was a dairy farm across the street from my youth home and I used to take beet pulp, meant to be mixed with the cow's feed, and ate it. It had at first a sugary flavor and after chewing it for a short time it had more of a bitter taste. It didn't seem to hurt me and I suspect it might have been used as a prebiotic for humans if it didn't have the high energy level.

I also liked to take wheat out of a grain bin and chew it. The wheat gluten mixed with saliva turns into chewy gum and there was some sweetness present—like when you chew bread a short time and the enzyme amylase in saliva breaks down the wheat carbohydrates into sugar.

Red beets are used as a supplement for humans to "support blood pressure, respiratory system through nitric oxide production, promote heart health, antioxidant and a source of vitamin C."

In 1976 I started practice at Camden Pet Hospital. The owner Dr. Jack Hylton had practiced most of his career in large animal medicine. After his passing his colleague Dr. Patrick H. Baymiller sent me his life sketch which included, "Hylton developed and purchased and maintained the bulls and ran one of the early dairy artificial insemination herds in America. Most current people in this valley do not realize this was an important San Francisco Milk Shed. As late as 1958 Jack averaged two rumenotomies (surgery than enters into a portion of the stomach) on dairy cows daily. Jack sold his herd to the American Dairy Breeders Assn. who moved their operation to the University of Wisconsin."

I am certain Dr. Hylton was very familiar with the procedure and most likely transplanted probiotics (culture of microbes) from a healthy cow's rumen to one with digestive problems.

He taught me how to apply the principle of fecal microbial transplantation (FMT) by taking feces from a healthy cat, placing it into a pill capsule and giving it by mouth to a cat with untreatable diarrhea. And, I saw cats actually return to have normal bowel movements.

Within the next 10 to 15 years there will continue to be more interest in the makeup of the organisms in the gut (microbiome) and its relationship to our and our and animal's health. Current research is focusing on treating inflammatory bowel syndrome, controlling obesity, preventing and improved recovery from strokes, and better quality of sleep patterns by just changing which microbes live in the digestive system.

The day may well come when you are asked by your doctor to bring in a poop sample, (like veterinarians currently ask their clients to do), for your physical exam. During your visit you will be asked to fill out a questionnaire concerning eating habits, possible developing disease processes or conditions that may be attributed to microbes living in your microbiome.

If a disease process is discovered you may receive a notification letter in a package of freeze-dried fecal material with a code attached identifying the contributor, manufacturer and the condition(s) to be treated. It will also give directions on how to take the fecal medication and any possible side effects.

Fable of the Microbiomes

Adapted from the lyrics to the tune of *Button Up Your Overcoat* . . . Brown Lew et al.

Listen, big boy, you have great friends—us microbiomes.
Goodness but are you ever afraid,
Something's going to happen to us?
Because you could not live if you should lose us - ooh, ooh, no.
    Never forget your microbiome friends.
When eating out stay away from food that is sweet or fat.
Take good care of yourself.
You belong to us - ooh, ooh.
    Eat your prebiotics containing fiber foods at least each day.
Get lots of sleep and don't drink or smoke.

Oh, take good care of yourself.
You belong to us—ooh, ooh.

Daily be sure and take a supplement of some of our probiotic relatives.
Remember to eat prebiotic fiber foods and make eating a late meal against your religion.
If you break the rules, you may get an upset stomach, GERD or something worse.
Resulting in vomiting, a juicy stool and need to use POO-POURRI to hide your remorse—ooh, ooh, no.

We microbiomes can boost your immunity, maintain beautiful skin, maintain your normal daily constitutional, make vitamins and cure diseases too.
If you take care of yourself, we'll take care of you.
You belong to us and we belong to you.
We'll take care of you—ooh, ooh.

Hope you have a long, long life taking care of us microbiomes.
We have dedicated our lives to take care of you with not a fuss.
Because when you're called home to your father on high.
And your family buries you deep after being sure your life is truly over.
All us 39 trillion microbiomes will still be with you buried deep under the grass and sweet clover—ooh, ooh, no.

If you removed your face from your microbiome it would still look like you...

1. *Everything you need to know about the 39 trillion microbes that call our bodies home, Mun-Keat Looi, BBC Science Focus Magazine, 2020.*

2. *Morris Animal Foundation, Episode 40: The Amazing Science of Fecal Microbial Transplantation, Dr. Kelly Diehl & Dr. Jenessa Winston, Ohio State University, 2022.*

6

THE DEAF ANIMALS

While I was serving as Cub Scout Master we had a pack meeting on appreciating what it is like to get older. I brought safety glasses that they smeared with Vaseline, thick gloves, ear plugs and I wanted to bring unlaced adult boots (didn't for safety reasons). They were asked to read for us with the smeared glasses on, do skill tests wearing gloves and hear with ear plugs in place while being spoken to in a noisy room. The young men had a great time while doing these activities. I'm sure they did not comprehend what an affect losing just one sense can have on quality of life.

Born in 1770 the German Ludwig Van Beethoven regarded as the Greatest Classical Composer ever began to lose his hearing gradually, from about the age of 28, telling the English pianist Charles Neate that his hearing loss came from a fit (suspected from a disease called typhus—lead poisoning) he suffered in 1798 induced by a quarrel with a singer.

In the early years of his hearing loss at the age of 31 Beethoven wrote to his brothers in 1802 telling them he had even considered suicide because of it:

"Oh you men who think or say that I am malevolent, stubborn, or misanthropic, how greatly do you wrong me? You do not know the secret cause which makes me seem that way to you. From childhood on, my heart and soul have been full of the tender feeling of goodwill, and I was ever inclined to accomplish great things. But think that for six years now I have been hopelessly afflicted, made worse by senseless physicians, from year to year deceived with hopes of improvement, finally compelled to face the prospect of a lasting malady (whose cure will take years or, perhaps, be impossible).

Though born with a fiery active temperament, even susceptible to the diversions of society, I was soon compelled to withdraw myself, to live life alone. If at times I tried to forget all this, oh how harshly I was flung back by the doubly sad experience of my bad hearing. Yet it was impossible for me to say to people, 'Speak louder, shout, for I am deaf.' Ah, how could I possibly admit an infirmity in the one sense which ought to be more perfect in me than others, a sense which I once possessed in the highest perfection, a perfection such as few in my profession enjoy or ever have enjoyed.—Oh I cannot do it; therefore forgive me when you see me draw back when I would have gladly mingled with you.

My misfortune is doubly painful to me because I am bound to be misunderstood; for me there can be no relaxation with my fellow men, no refined conversations, no mutual exchange of ideas. I must live almost alone, like one who has been banished; I can mix with society only as much as true necessity demands.

If I approach near to people a hot terror seizes upon me and I fear being exposed to the danger that my condition might be noticed. Thus, it has been during the last six months which I have spent in the country. By ordering me to spare my hearing as much as possible, my intelligent doctor almost fell in with my own present frame of mind, though sometimes I ran counter to it by yielding to my desire for companionship. But what a humiliation for me when someone standing next to me heard a flute in the distance and I heard nothing or someone heard a shepherd singing and again I heard nothing.

Such incidents drove me almost to despair; a little more of that and I would have ended my life—it was only my art that held me back. Ah, it seemed to me impossible to leave the world until I had brought forth all that I felt was within me...I hope my determination will remain firm to endure...Perhaps I shall get better, perhaps not; I am ready...'Divine one, thou seest my inner most soul thou knowest that therein dwells the love of mankind and the desire to do good'."1

According to the World Health Organization (WHO) deafness is the number one birth defect in the U.S., about half is due to heredity, half avoidable through primary prevention, 20% of us have some form of hearing loss, deaf children have a high risk of abuse and few have contact with a church.

I remember playing with cap guns with my cousin while staying with our grandmother Hoge in Paris Idaho. We were taking a roll of caps and hitting them with a brick against the sidewalk. For days my ears rang. I also remember my grandpa Rich watching a black and white

TV with a speaker held to his ear in order to hear a baseball game.

No wonder since my early years I haven't been able to recognize words being said when I'm whispered to, the words in a song, people speaking in a crowded room, movies with soft speaking or background music. An audiologist showed me a chart from my hearing test and at certain frequencies my hearing dropped off that chart. He mentioned that with the sound frequencies I didn't detect (which are typical of a female's voice) and the background of barking dogs it was obvious why I had trouble hearing at work.

I remember hearing birds chirping as I was leaving a doctor's office and trying out hearing aids for the first time. I'm sure the WHO organization would attribute my hearing loss both to heredity and preventable causes. However, I never felt abused as a child from hearing issues.

My father the M.D. complained a lot about my mother's hearing (she was from the Rich side of the family) and as they aged he wanted her to get her hearing tested—which she declined. I approached dad and mentioned that if he wanted mom's hearing checked he might suggest to her that they both go in and have a hearing test. His reply, "I don't have a hearing problem and don't need my ears checked!"

One of the more significant things that is associated with coat color in dogs is the fact that the color of a dog's fur can predict the likelihood that a dog's hearing will be normal or not. Perhaps the most prominent researcher associated with this issue is George Strain of Louisiana State University in Baton Rouge, who has reported data on over 11,000 dogs using the Brainstem Auditory Evoked

Response (BAER) test that looks at brain activity caused when sounds are registered by the ears.

He has been looking at the factors that predict congenital hearing loss or deafness. A congenital hearing loss is one that is present at birth, although it may take many weeks for it to be recognized by a pup's breeder or veterinarian. Congenital hearing loss is mostly due to genetic factors, and these are found to be associated with certain coat colors. The coat colors associated with the highest risk are white, some spotting (dalmatian like), roan (white or gray hairs mixed through the coat) and merle (desaturated colors, especially where blacks become grays or blues).

According to Dr. Strain's research the classic example of a spotted dog is the Dalmatian. In this breed 22 percent are deaf in one ear, and 8 percent are deaf in both ears, amounting to an amazing 30 percent born with some form of hearing deficit. In the Bull Terrier individuals can be either white or can have prominent color patches. Among those Bull Terriers who are white, the rate of congenital deafness is 20 percent, while for those with color patches it is only around 1 percent.

The gene that causes whiteness in a dog's coat also tends to make it more likely that it will be blue eyed. Thus, it seems sensible to expect that blue-eyed Dalmatians would be even more likely to be deaf. This prediction is true and the effect is quite dramatic. Among blue-eyed Dalmatians, about one out of every two are deaf in at least one ear. What is the worse is the fact that even if the Dalmatian has brown eyes, if one of his parents had blue eyes the chance of being deaf increases.

In certain breeds of dogs, the association between dogs' coat colors and the likelihood of deafness was noted by early breeders. For example, some Boxer breed clubs report that white Boxers are almost as likely to be congenitally deaf as Dalmatians. For this reason several national Boxer clubs have written into their regulations the requirement that white Boxers are to be culled (the polite word for being killed at birth). The argument is that in puppies it is difficult to sort out the deaf ones from those with normal hearing. Bruce M Cattanach of the MRC Mammalian Genetics Unit Harwell England claims that the rate of deafness in white Boxers is 18%. It is true that detecting deafness in young pups at home is difficult, since the deaf pups cue off the behavior of their littermates. A puppy that does not awaken in response to a loud noise is almost certainly deaf in both ears, but a pup that is deaf in only one ear cannot be detected with any reliability. Boxer breeders argue that the most efficient means of dealing with the problem is to destroy all of their white pups. This is unfortunate since although 1 in 7 white Boxers may be deaf that still means that 6 out of 7 such dogs will still have normal hearing.[2]

Not only does the color of the hair coat and eyes have a genetic relationship with deafness in dogs it also affects cats. Researchers have found that 17 to 22 percent of white cats with non-blue eyes are born deaf. The percentage rises to 40 percent if the cat has one blue eye, while upwards of 65 to 85 percent of all-white cats with both eyes blue are deaf. Some of these cats are deaf in only one ear. Interestingly, if a white cat with one blue eye is deaf in only one ear, that ear will invariably be on the same side of the head as the blue eye.

Cats with just one deaf ear may appear perfectly normal, and their problem may never become known to their human companions. Even cats that are totally deaf from birth can make perfectly satisfactory companions as long as a few precautions are heeded. Try to keep them out of situations where their safety depends upon their ability to pick up auditory cues. Don't let them go outside where they can be killed or injured by threats they cannot hear, like from roaming dogs and speeding cars. There is no treatment for hereditary deafness.3

In my experience it is common to observe older dogs becoming deaf. Usually upon examination of the ear canals and drums they will appear normal and a diagnosis of deafness over a cognitive attention disorder is best done at home. I recommend that the owner test hearing when their pet is looking away and not using sounds that will cause vibrations from the floor—like stomping. Increasing noises from two pots or pans coming together usually does the trick. Not only can one determine if the dog does or does not hear but if louder noises can be detected.

Treatment with anti-inflammatory or other medications rarely improves hearing loss. I suspect most of senile deafness occurs from a genetic factor.

Besides keeping white cats away from roaming dogs or speeding cars, their skin is subject to sun burn and I have surgically removed many an outdoor white cat's ear tips and/or the skin over the nose due to skin cancer. Cats also tend to not appreciate sun screen placed on their ears and on the nose will be licked off and is a no-no. Thankfully I have never had a Boxer breeder request euthanasia of white pups.

In a summary, "Deafness is observed in various dog breeds with different clinical characteristics (e.g., congenital, environmental, age-related) and different genetic architecture. There are more than 100 genes known to be involved in non-syndromic hearing loss in humans, and, therefore, studying breed-specific hearing loss in dogs suggests a promising translational value toward the better understanding of the genetics of hearing loss in humans."5

Interesting experiences of a few who helped change history and were deaf:

- Ludwig Van Beethoven was a German pianist born in 1770, and is regarded as the Greatest Classical Composer ever. By the age of 52 he was presumed to be completely deaf. However, this is when he produced some of his most important works. As his hearing got worse Beethoven struggled to communicate with people.

The biggest challenge for him was conducting and performing in concerts as he couldn't hear when the music stopped and the audience applauded.

- Alexander Graham Bell the famous inventor that most people don't know was deaf. There's a layer of irony to Alexander Graham Bell's hearing loss because he invented the telephone. Bell's mother and wife were both deaf, his father pioneered deaf education, and he himself was also a deaf educator, but his methods continue to cause controversy even to this day. Even though he married a deaf woman, he strongly opposed intermarriage among deaf people.

A eugenicist, Bell even tried to pass legislation to stop deaf people from marrying each other, fearing that it would somehow "contaminate" the human race, even though most deaf people are born from hearing parents.

-   Vint Cerf is known as one of the 'fathers of the internet'. He is a mathematician and inventor who co-invented TCP/IP protocol with Robert E. Kahn in 1974, which paved the way for the invention of the internet we use today.

When he was born six weeks premature in 1943, Cerf was placed in an oxygen tent to help him breathe. Doctors now believe that this might have caused his progressive nerve loss and increasing hearing loss.

-   Clayton Valli a deaf linguist and American Sign Language (ASL) poet was the first person to identify ASL poetry as a literary genre. He also created unique and beautiful poetry with sign language.

Valli's poetry used handshape, hand movement, facial expression, space and repetition to convey the meaning of his works. Many of his poems use the theme of nature to communicate about the deaf experience.

-   Thomas Edison known by many as America's greatest inventor spent much of his life with little to no hearing. Edison is famous for engineering world-changing devices including the light bulb, the phonograph (the first device to record and play back sound), and the microphone used in telephones.

There's much mystery surrounding the cause of Edison's hearing loss, which he claims began as young as 12 years old. Some suggest that a case of Scarlet Fever during childhood and recurring untreated middle-ear infections were the cause. Others believe it was passed down within his family. Edison claimed that he was picked up by the ears after falling out of a train, hearing a 'pop' inside his ears. Edison was thought to be completely deaf by the time he turned 18.

Edison said that he was better able to concentrate on his work due to his hearing loss, suggesting that deaf people (like himself) should 'take to reading' because "it beats the babble of ordinary conversation."

My wife mentioned that she felt my hearing loss also helped me, like Edson, reach for goals that may have been sidestepped. It definitely helped increase my reading time, reduced time spent on entertainment, and I find it comforting when lost in the "soul of my mind" to not be interrupted by environmental sounds.4

Thomas Paine wrote, "I love the man who can smile in trouble, who can gather strength in distress and grow brave by reaction. Tis the business of little minds to shrink, but he whose heart is firm, and whose conscience approves his conduct, will pursue his principles to the death."

Just when all seems to be going right, challenges often come in multiple doses applied simultaneously. When those trials are not consequences of your disobedience, they are evidence that the Lord feels you are prepared to grow more...He therefore gives you experiences that stimulate growth, understanding, and compassion which polish you for your everlasting benefit. To get you from where you are to where He wants you to be requires a lot of stretching, and that generally entails discomfort and pain.6

Beethoven decided not to be defeated, even by what was for him the worst catastrophe imaginable. And we know that his decision to live beyond his deafness, to refuse to accept it as the ultimate and terminal tragedy, allowed the creation of his greatest works. One of the greatest myths about this man regarded by generations of musicologists and music lovers alike as the greatest composer who ever lived, is that he was universally misunderstood, unrecognized, and unrewarded during his own lifetime, that only after his death was his greatness appreciated.1

If Ludwig van Beethoven had nothing ever go wrong with his hearing, could he have written the late piano sonatas, the late string quartets, or the Ninth Symphony? Would you be where you are in your life if you hadn't had challenges that helped you smile in trouble, gain strength in distress and grow brave by reaction?

Do you want to be a Hereford cow or just a cow? An old cowboy said he had learned life's most important lessons from Hereford cows. All his life he had worked cattle ranches where winter storms took a heavy toll among the herds. Freezing rains whipped across the prairies. Howling, bitter winds piled snow into enormous drifts. Temperatures might drop quickly to below zero degrees. Flying ice cut into the flesh. In this maelstrom of nature's violence most cattle would turn their backs to the ice blasts and slowly drift downwind, mile upon mile. Finally, intercepted by a boundary fence, they would pile up against the barrier and die by the scores.

But the Herefords acted differently. Cattle of this breed would instinctively head into the windward end of the range. There they would stand shoulder-to-shoulder facing the storm's blast, heads down against its onslaught.

"You always found the Herefords alive and well,"
said the cowboy. "I guess it's the greatest lesson I ever learned on the prairies—just face life's storms."

It is a matter of the lemon and the lemonade, after all. In adversity we can complain bitterly, "Why me? Why now?" and wallow in self-pity, thus denouncing God. Or we can find our way by asking that all-important question: "Which of my Heavenly Father's principles will help me now?" And when we find that appropriate principle, the next step is to live that law, "irrevocably decreed" upon which the particular blessing that we need is predicated. (See D&C 130:21).7

1. *Heiligenstadt Testament & Profiles in Audacity, Alan Axelrod, 2006, p30-34.*
2. *Stanley Coren, Your Dog's Coat Color Predicts His Hearing Ability, White, piebald, roan and merle colored dogs may have hearing deficits, Posted July 10, 2012.*
3. *Cornell Feline Health Center, Health Information, Ask Elizabeth: White Cats and Blindness/Deafness.*

4. *Google Searches.*
5. *Early onset adult deafness in the Rhodesian ridgeback dog is associated with an in-frame deletion in the EPS8L2 gene, published 04/06/2022.*
6. *Richard G. Scott, "Trust in the Lord," Ensign, November 1995.*
7. *Elaine Cannon, Adversity (Salt Lake City: Bookcraft, 1987), pp. 133- 34.*

7

BUTTERFLY GIFT
AND EPILEPSY

Doctors in Belgium have discovered that a Chinese herb already linked to kidney failure, may cause cancer as well. Patients at a Belgian weight loss clinic were given this herb in error. Staff at the clinic had prescribed an herb from a group of plants from the genus species Aristolochia commonly called birthwort.

Birthwort plants are eaten by swallow tailed caterpillars that makes them toxic when eaten. The toxin is called Aristolochic acid (which means "excellent birth") and in California the musty unpleasant odor of its pipevine flower contains the toxin which attracts the pipevine swallowtail butterfly to lay eggs on the plant. It's the only food source for the red-spotted black caterpillars that consume the leaves of the plants, and then use the flowers as a secure, enclosed place to undergo metamorphosis. The plant toxins ingested by the caterpillars makes them and the mature butterfly unpalatable to predators.

Since there is virtually no control over the quality of these herb products, it is not unusual not to know what is actually in herbal preparations used as dietary supplements. The findings reinforced the idea that the use of natural herbal medicine may not be without risk. Cases of kidney failure from aristolochic acid have been reported in France, Britain, Spain, Japan, Taiwan, and the United States.1

Birthwort plants, and the aristolochic acids they contain, were quite common in ancient Greek and Roman medical texts, and well-established as an herb there by the fifth century BC. Birthworts appeared in Ayurvedic texts by 400 AD, and in Chinese texts later in the fifth century. In these ancient times, it was used to treat kidney and urinary problems, as well as gout, snakebites, and a variety of other ailments. It was also considered to be an effective contraceptive.

In many of these cases, birthworts were just some of the many ingredients used to create ointments or salves. By the early first century, in Roman texts, aristolochic acids are first mentioned as a component of frequently ingested medicines to treat things such as asthma, hiccups, spasms, pains, and expulsion of afterbirth.

The word *aristo* from Greek means "best." One of the best in human history was *Aristo*tle. It makes me wonder if the Romans and Greek *aristo*crats thought the birthwort containing *aristo*lochic was one of the best medicines that could be used for host of diseases.

A client of mine had a cat with epilepsy that was controlled by phenobarbital. This drug has been used for many years and works by slowing down brain activity. I had never seen the cat during a seizure, which is not unusual in cats, but the owner clearly described a seizure in a cat and convinced me that it was epileptic.

The owner usually asked for a written prescription for phenobarbital and seldom did the owner have it filled at Camden Pet Hospital. The cat was brought in for scheduled health visits, blood tests, and during visits I found the owner pleasant and concerned about his cat's health.

He was a collector of butterflies and gave me one as a gift. I keep it in my "world of weirdness" trophy case at home. It contains everything from ostrich eggs, to shark's jaws, my wisdom teeth, supposed petrified dinosaur dung and a portion of rail track and cable from the San Francisco Cable Car Company.

The butterfly is a swallowtail from Papua New Guinea and was collected on June 6th 1995. It is a species that eats birthwort plants that contain aristolochic acid as a caterpillar and is considered to by poisonous throughout its life cycle.

Barbiturates are a family of drugs that come from barbituric acid, a substance that was first synthesized in 1864 by the German chemist Adolf von Baeyer. The synthesis of barbituric acid was carried out through the combination of urea (a product obtained from animal waste) and malonic acid (an acid derived from apples). Phenobarbital is one of the pharmaceutical products made from barbiturates.

Phenobarbital functions by depressing the central nervous system. The medication slows down brain activity, which suppresses seizures and panic attacks. By slowing brain activity, phenobarbital also relieves the symptoms of drug and alcohol withdrawal. Drinking alcohol with phenobarbital or taking it in combination with other drugs will increase adverse effects, including your risk of fatality.

Nowadays phenobarbital is in some disuse due to the high addiction produced by its consumption and the limited range of beneficial effects of barbiturates.

When a butterfly goes into its chrysalis stage the enzymes present breaks down its body into a material that looks like oozy Jell-O. The cells within the ooze migrate to the proper locations and create a whole new body. Scientists wondered until recently if the adult insect remembered any experiences it had during its life as a caterpillar. The brain is composed of many different parts, making it difficult to confidently pinpoint which parts undergo modifications in the chrysalis.

Debate has been whether this completely different looking adult butterfly is a new organism. It does still have aristolochic acid poison in its body from eating birthwort plants as a caterpillar, it uses the cells of a caterpillar to develop into a butterfly, but does it have any memory of the experiences it had as a caterpillar?

A recent study provided evidence of memory retention by literally shocking some hookworm butterfly caterpillars. The caterpillars were trained to dislike and avoid the scent of ethyl alcohol by subjecting them to mild electrical shocks whenever they smelt it. 78% of the conditioned larvae crawled away from a scented arm with ethyl alcohol into fresh air. 77% of conditioned caterpillars that had developed into butterflies continued to go down the arm with fresh air when re-introduced to ethyl alcohol. This study proved that the neural tissue responsible for taste, smell, memory and learning remain intact during metamorphosis.[2]

One day working at Camden Pet Hospital I returned a phone call from a pharmacist. He requested information about a phenobarbital prescription refill request written for the cat with epilepsy that was owned by the client that gave me the poisonous swallowtail butterfly. The pharmacist verified the prescription and then in a stern voice said as I remember, "Do you realize that this client has prescriptions for phenobarbital written by several veterinarians and they are being filled by pharmacies in our area? It's obvious to us all this medication is not just for the cat!"

Evidently the good client with the epileptic cat that gave me a beautiful swallowtail butterfly containing poisonous aristolochic acid was illegally purchasing for his individual use a potentially poisonous substance that effects mood and behavior. Even under a doctor's care phenobarbital can lead to addictive behavior and death. Killing one's self with a drug made out of pee and apples doesn't make a lot of sense.

It's very interesting—you can train a butterfly in its youth to stay away from alcohol but the supposed "most intelligent species on earth" in its youth hasn't obtained enough understanding to stay away from dangerous substances. An addicted man or women will obtain a narcotic any way they can even if it has the potential of killing them.

Maybe the principle of God giving man his free agency wasn't such a good idea. "We are free to take drugs or not. But once we choose to use a habit-forming drug, we are bound to the consequences of that choice. Addiction surrenders later freedom to choose. Through chemical means, one can literally become disconnected from his or her own will!"3

If the client who was illegally purchasing phenobarbital for his addiction had been purchasing the narcotic directly from each prescribing veterinarian's pharmacy, he would probably have never been caught. Veterinarians at the time were not required to keep track of drugs purchased between veterinary hospitals the way pharmacies monitored purchases.

Unless his family or friends were aware of the problem, he was found over dosed, admitted himself for rehab or was autopsied no one would have known about his little secret. Forest Gump would probably have said about such a man, "Stupid is as stupid does."

I'm left with memories of hope for my client that he was able to enjoy life with his cat and without the crutch of narcotics, the good pharmacist that alerted me about the prescription problem without getting the FDA involved with my drug license, and a beautiful swallowtail butterfly from Papua New Guinea that reminds me to look deeper than what you see for true beauty. Below is a photo of the butterfly that I keep in my home museum.

"For 'tis the mind that makes the body rich, And
as the sun breaks through the darkest clouds,
So honor peereth in the meanest habit."4

1. *BMJ Publishing Group Last Updated: 28th February, 2020.*
2. *Do Butterflies Remember Being Caterpillars? Updated On: 4 Jan 2022 By Saloni Hombalkar.*
3. *Russell M. Nelson, MD, Addiction or Freedom, October 1988.*
4. *Shakespeare, William (1564-1616).*

8

EMPATHY AND SELF MEDICATION

Two of my children used their pediatrician to care for their children. My youngest gave me the opportunity to attend his first son's circumcision. Before the doctor injected a nerve block that serves the groin area, he filled a baby bottle nipple with sugar water and introduced Ivan to his first foreign object and sugar into his mouth. He sucked away during the surgery enjoying the taste of sweets and the feeling of a pacifier oblivious to the procedure.

Raising babies, or for that matter puppies, requires constant awareness as to what goes into their mouths? I don't know all the whys or what's for this behavior but BeBe will never forget the time she bit through an electric cord. The alternating electric current rapidly stimulates and then lets the muscles of the jaw relax preventing the victim from releasing the cord from its mouth. Fortunately, my wife was present, did not get shocked and when she couldn't release BeBe's mouth unplugged the cord. BeBe was fortunate to survive with only some marks left on her teeth. She now ignores electric cords as if they do not exist.

However, I do know that she does remember. Recently, a new cat addition to our family named Boo, was playing with a Velcro strap attached to an electric cord. BeBe went over and jumped on the 4 month old kitten until he ran away from the cord.

Especially during the spring it is not uncommon for dogs to graze on grass. Common thought for this behavior is that the dog is trying to make themselves vomit or is in need of nutritional supplements missing in their food. Dr. Wailani Sung discussed that there have been many speculations and theories, but there is limited research on why dogs eat grass. The truth is that no one knows for sure. However, scientists have formed a few theories and disproved some myths based on the research we do have.

Some scientists speculate that eating grass is an instinctive behavior for dogs that evolved from their wolf ancestors. We know from research on wolves that 2-10% of their stomach contents may contain plant material. Wild canids (from the Canidae family, which includes wolves, jackals, foxes, and coyotes) also have been observed to eat grass. It may provide adequate fiber, vitamins, minerals or some energy in the diet.

Dogs are primarily carnivores, meaning they eat meat. Recent studies have shown that dogs have evolved the ability to digest some carbohydrates in response to coevolving with humans. Carbohydrates are sugar, starches, and fibers mainly found in fruit, grain, vegetables, and milk products. If dogs can digest some carbohydrates, then does this mean our dogs can really digest grass? The answer is no, not really. Grass mainly passes through the dog's intestinal tract undigested.

Researchers have found this behavior is influenced by how hungry your dog is and the time of day. There was less grass eating when the dog had eaten a meal, and increased grass eating beforehand. Grass eating also occurred less frequently later in the day. The researchers believed that grass eating was normal dog behavior and was not indicative of an underlying illness.

In a study one group of dogs were fed a diet containing fructo-oligosaccharide (FOS). The other group of dogs were fed a standard diet. FOS is extracted from sugar beets and passes undigested through the small intestines and into the large intestine where it ferments. Large quantities of FOS can cause watery, loose stool. The dogs fed the standard diets had more episodes of grass eating compared to the FOS dogs that had diarrhea. This meant that dogs with gastrointestinal upset were less likely to eat grass. However, in this particular study, the diarrhea originated in the large intestines, so it doesn't give us insight on grass-eating behavior in dogs that have gastrointestinal upsets in their stomach or small intestines.

Dogs, especially younger dogs, often explore with their mouths. Eating grass may be something that they try, just like some children eat dirt. Some dogs may learn to like the taste of grass.

Other dogs may have learned that when they eat grass, their pet parents pay them more attention. You may talk to your dog more or offer your dog treats to get them to stop eating grass. Sometimes, pet parents pull their dogs away from a patch of grass. This restriction may spur a dog to eat any grass as soon as they find it because it's forbidden.

In other studies it was found that there were 5 episodes of vomiting out of 709 grass eating incidents. They concluded that dogs do not eat grass to cause themselves to vomit. Out of 1,571 survey responders, 9% of dogs were reported ill by the owners prior to eating grass. Only 22% of the owners reported that their dogs frequently vomited after eating grass. They found that younger dogs ate more grass than older dogs. It was reported that there were only two vomiting episodes out of 374 grass-eating events.

These studies provide some evidence that dogs do not eat grass to induce vomiting.1

Even though vomiting studies of dogs concluded that there is only some evidence that dogs eat grass to induce vomiting for medicinal purposes—many animal species have created their own pharmacies from ingredients that commonly occur in nature.

Birds, bees, lizards, elephants, and chimpanzees all share a survival trait: They self-medicate. These animals eat things that make them feel better, or prevent disease, or kill parasites like flatworms, bacteria, and viruses, or just to aid in digestion. Even creatures with brains the size of pinheads somehow know to ingest certain plants or use them in unusual ways when they need them.

A dog eating grass and vomiting may have had an upset stomach or intestinal parasites that stimulates eating enough grass to induce vomiting or help eliminate infected feces.

It's not clear how much knowing or learning is involved, but many animals seem to have evolved an innate ability to detect the therapeutic constituents in plants. Although the evidence is entirely circumstantial, the examples are plentiful. The practice is spreading across the animal kingdom in sometimes surprising ways: 1-Bears, deer, elk, and various carnivores, as well as great apes, are known to consume medicinal plants apparently to self-medicate. 2-Some lizards are believed to respond to a bite by a venomous snake by eating a certain root to counter the venom. 3-Baboons in Ethiopia eat the leaves of a plant to combat the flatworms that cause schistosomiasis. 4-Fruit flies lay eggs in plants containing high ethanol (alcohol) levels when they detect parasitoid wasps, a way of protecting their offspring. 5-Red and green macaws, along with many animals, eat clay to aid digestion and kill bacteria. 6-Female woolly spider monkeys in Brazil add plants to their diet to increase or decrease their fertility. 7-Pregnant lemurs in Madagascar nibble on tamarind and fig leaves and bark to aid in milk production, kill parasites, and increase the chances of a successful birth. 8-Pregnant elephants in Kenya eat the leaves of some trees to induce delivery.

Most studies of animal self-medication, however, are in the great apes. In the 1960s, chimpanzees were not chewing but swallowing whole aspella leaves, which have no nutritional value. So why do they do it?

In 1996, it was suggested the chimps were self-medicating. They observed that parasite-ridden, constipated chimpanzee in Tanzania and across Africa chewed on the leaves of a noxious plant it would normally avoid. By the next day, the chimpanzee was completely recovered. The plants had bristly leaves, rough to the touch. They theorized the chimps were swallowing the plants to take advantage of that roughness, using the leaves and stems to scour their intestines and rid themselves of parasites.

Michael Huffman has defined medicinal use of a substance requires that—First, the plant eaten cannot be a regular part of the animal's diet; it is used as medicine not food. Second, the plant must provide little or no nutritional value to the animal. Third, the plant must be consumed during those times of year (for example, the rainy season) when parasites are most likely to cause infections. Fourth, other animals in the group don't participate. If the activity meets these standards, it is safe to assume the animal is self-medicating. Researchers have observed the practice in 25 regions involving 40 different plants.[2]

Recently it has been observed that animals not only self-medicate but use medications to care for others. Chimpanzees were spotted capturing insects and applying them to their own wounds, as well as the wounds of others, possibly as a form of medication. This behavior of one animal applying medication to the wounds of another has never been observed before, and it may be a sign of helpful tendencies in chimpanzees similar to empathy in humans.[3]

Sympathy involves understanding from your own perspective. Empathy involves putting yourself in the other person's shoes and understanding why they may have these particular feelings. In becoming aware of the root cause of why a person feels the way they do, we can better understand and provide healthier options.

People usually become more empathic after going through hardship and pain. It's easier to understand what someone else is going through when you've already experienced something similar. However, we are truly empathic when we are simply sensitive to how other people are feeling. For example, we don't necessarily have to lose someone to realize how painful it can be.

Empathy is something that can be taught. Adults can help children develop higher levels of empathy by exposing them to different worldviews and by teaching them to be kind, generous, patient and forgiving.

Learning how to care for others is crucial for our personal development and for creating healthy and meaningful relationships. Being empathic is a key ingredient to make the world around you a better place and to become the best person you can be.

To the extent that our experience of suffering reminds us of what everyone else also endures, it serves as a powerful inspiration to practice compassion and avoid causing others pain.4

Chimpanzees tending to others needs is prosocial, or positive behavior that is in the interest of helping others— something that isn't often observed in animals. This is especially breathtaking because so many people doubt prosocial abilities in other animals. Suddenly we have a species where we really see individuals caring for others.

Prosocial behaviors have long posed a problem for evolutionary theory, because it was not immediately clear why organisms might help others in the face of selection operating in the interest of self. It's difficult to say if what the chimps are doing is motivated by empathy, but the researchers were surprised to see that the chimps recognized that how they treat their own wounds can be applied to others and helped one another even if they weren't related.

We do not know whether the observed behavior involves empathy. We know that it may qualify as prosocial behavior, meaning it may increase the welfare of another animal—feeling better via the social attention and caring, or via substances in the saliva-insect mix that may be soothing or anti-inflammatory. There are examples of chimpanzees adopting and rescuing other chimpanzees, which may involve empathy.3

"Is there no balm in Gilead?," asked the prophet Jeremiah. Anciently, an ointment known for its power to heal and soothe came from Gilead, near the Jordan River. Made from the gum of a tree, the balm was in high demand as a trade commodity at the time. Today we talk of the symbolic power of the balm of Gilead to "make the wounded whole."

Recently, a wise physician told his patient, "There is no cure for what you have, but there is healing." The physician understood that sometimes the healing we need does not come from medical treatment. Healing of the soul comes from unselfish concern for others, from integrity and goodness, from repentance and forgiveness. Every time we reach past personal concerns to encourage and lift others, we can experience a healing of the heart. When we feel anguish or animosity, we can find healing by letting go of anger and blame. When we feel troubled and afraid, we can find peace in the words of scriptures and hymns. When we feel like we can't face another day, we can find courage in sweet assurances and the quiet confidence of family and friends.

Humility and meekness are the balm of Gilead. Kindness and empathy are healing ointments. Sincere prayer and meditation soothe the worried soul. Even the beauties of nature can lift our spirits and help us look to a higher source for healing.

> The Lord's promise is sure: "I have heard thy prayer,
> I have seen thy tears: behold, I will heal thee."5

1. *PETMED, Vet written—Vet reviewed, Why Do Dogs Eat Grass, Wailani Sung, MS, PhD, DVM, DACVB, 08/31/2021.*
2. *Proceedings: National Academy of Science, 111(49): 2014/12/09: 17339-17341.*
3. *CNN, Ashley Strickland, Chimpanzees apply 'medicine' to each other's wounds in a possible show of empathy, Updated 2022/02/07.*
4. *Dalai Lama.*
5. *Empathy and the Pure Love of Christ, Music & the Spoken Word, Program #3967.*

9

STARVING KITTY—ATE THE WHOLE THING

On July 23, 2008 early in the morning client Donna Howe brought in a small tortoiseshell kitten that she found on the side of the road in a gutter. The kitten was unconscious but responded to noxious stimulus. Her temperature was less than 94 degrees and she weighed 1 pound 2 oz.

We administered fluids and attempted to warm up the kitten. Upon examination she had a firm large distended abdomen. Doctor Hoffman notes that the stomach was full of something. The client offered to pay $300 if we could help the kitten but she did not want the kitten. We agreed to try although we weren't sure she would make it. By 2:15pm the temp was now 103 and the kitten was eating and grooming herself.

We took x-rays and there appeared to be a granular material and wiry metallic material in her abdomen. On 7/24 we found out that she had a gastrointestinal parasite called coccidia. Palpation of the abdomen "still firm contents with wiry brush/Brillo pad feel." Recheck abdomen still shows metallic material.

Dr Hoffman took the kitten to VSA (now Sage), an emergency/specialty practice, and consulted with Dr's Julie Smith, Bill Scherrer, Andrea Struble, Bridgette Nicholson and Andrea Fineman. They all agreed that kitten had possible obstruction but that surgery would be very risky with a guarded prognosis due to friability of young kitten tissue. They advised against surgery as long as the kitten was still eating and drinking. For the next 5 days we would watch kitten.

On 7/29 we rechecked x-rays. On 7/30 Dr Jim Hoskinson reviewed x-rays. He felt it was a cord or rubber band in the belly. Something elastic.

For 6 more days we monitored the kitten. On 8/6 her temperature was now 104.5 at 3:35pm. We treated with 35cc SQ Fluids and started an antibiotic called Clavamox. (Notes from kitten's file).

Watching this kitten's condition deteriorating for two weeks reminds me of a story told by Elder David B. Haight: James Peter Fugal was an honest man! He herded sheep much of his life in the rolling hills of Idaho—both his own sheep and sheep for others.

On one bitterly cold winter night, he was herding sheep for another man when a blizzard set in. The sheep bunched together, as sheep do, in the corner of a fenced area, and many died. Many other sheep on surrounding ranches also died that same night because of the weather.

Though the death of the sheep was no fault of his and it appears that he had no contract to compel his actions, James Fugal felt responsible and spent the next several years working and saving to repay the owner for his lost sheep.1

The longer time went by, Nancy was becoming more attached to this kitten and it was getting more difficult for her or the staff at Camden Pet Hospital to "let her go." The specialists in the area felt the kitten had a guarded prognosis surviving surgery and her condition had deteriorated more since their evaluation. If the kitten were placed in my trust and I performed surgery that failed, I would feel some responsibility and I could not replace this particular cat. The easiest thing would be to stay out of the case, continue hospital care and see if the kitten's condition would turn around.

On 8/7 the kitten now weights 1 pound 8 oz. Dr Hoge approached me and said I can go in and do surgery. You may lose her if I do, you may lose her if I don't.

It seemed like it was only about 20 minutes before the surgery was started and done. He removed "a large amount of firm latex material".

Recovery was uneventful and I took her home to monitor that night. By 8/22 she weighed in at 2 pounds 7 ounces and by 9/15 3 pounds 10 ounces. (Notes from kitten's file entered by Nancy Itri, office manager).

Phoebe is now 14 years old and weighs in at 7 pounds 1 ounce. (October 17, 2022).

It seems that failure tends to be more public than success. Or at least that's what we perceive it to be. We fret it, we try to avoid it, and we question ourselves every time we have unconventional ideas. But the simple truth is—no great success was ever achieved without failure. It may be one epic failure. Or a series of failures—such as Edison's 10,000 attempts to create a light bulb or Dyson's 5,126 attempts to invent a bagless vacuum cleaner. But whether we like it or not, failure is a necessary stepping stone to achieving our dreams.2

Examination of the foreign body I removed from Phoebe's stomach fourteen years ago revealed a used condom. Evidently the hungry kitten found a meal from the protein remaining in the rubber contraceptive.

"It's impossible." Said pride. "It's risky."
Said experience. "It's pointless." Said reason.
"Give it a try." Whispered the heart.

1. *1-David B. Haight, "Ethics and Honesty," Ensign, November 1987, 13.*
2. *2-Ekaterina Walter, writes about leadership, business culture, and marketing innovation, 2013.*

10

VULTURES

Diclofenac is a nonsteroidal anti-inflammatory drug (NSAID) used to treat pain and inflammatory diseases such as gout. It is taken by mouth or rectally in a suppository, used by injection, or applied to the skin. Improvements in pain last for as much as eight hours.

It is believed to work by decreasing the production of prostaglandin. It blocks both COX-1 (like aspirin) and COX-2 (like celecoxib), hence is a COX-2 inhibitor. Diclofenac was patented in 1965 and came into medical use in the United States in 1988. In 2019, it was the 74th most commonly prescribed medication in the United States, with more than 10 million prescriptions.

In 2007 diclofenac sodium was approved as a rub on topical gel medication for temporary relief of joint pain due to osteoarthritis. In 2020 the FDA changed its status from prescription to non-prescription through a process called Rx-to-OTC switch and is available as under genetic labels.

Common side effects and precautions include abdominal pain or history of heart burn, gastrointestinal bleeding, nausea, dizziness, headache, high blood pressure, asthma, and swelling. Serious side effects may include heart disease, stroke, kidney problems, and stomach ulceration.

Recently a friend of mine saw me walking down the hall limping, in church of all places, and mentioned this newly OTC rub on medication that really was helping her and her husband with arthritis of her knee and his two knee replacements.

Rub on is easy, generic usually means pretty safe (even though the precaution list includes several of my health concerns), and since it was dosed topically instead of systemic—what could it hurt to give it a try?

In veterinary medicine the product is recommended for treatment of certain kinds of inflammation within the eye of dogs and cats and on horses. My physician's desk reference states, "While, theoretically, diclofenac could be used systemically (orally) in other veterinary species, there are other FDA-approved and safer alternatives."

For religious and cultural reasons, most people in India don't eat beef. Cows are precious and even revered assets, pulling plows and carts, giving milk, and producing dung used for fertilizer and fuel.

Slaughtering cattle is taboo to Hindus, so aged animals are allowed to die naturally, with the carcasses left in open fields or taken to dump sites and are left on the ground (sky burial) for vultures and other scavengers to consume.

Sky burial (Tibetan: "bird-scattered") is a funeral practice in which a human corpse is placed on a mountaintop to decompose while exposed to the elements or to be eaten by scavenging animals, especially carrion birds. It is a specific type of the general practice of excarnation. It is practiced in areas of China and India. The locations of preparation and sky burial are understood in the Vajrayana Buddhist traditions as charnel grounds.

In Tibetan Buddhism, sky burial is believed to represent their wishes to go to heaven. It is the most widespread way for commoners to deal with the dead in Tibet.

If a Tibetan dies, the corpse is wrapped in white Tibetan cloth and placed in a corner of the house for three or five days, during which monks or lamas are asked to read the scripture aloud so that the souls can be released from purgatory. The Family members stop other activities in order to create a peaceful environment to allow convenient passage for ascension of souls into heaven.

Later, the Family members will choose a lucky day and ask the body carrier to take the body away to the celestial burial platform. On the day before the burial, the family members take off the clothes of the dead and fix the corpse in a fetal position. Specifically, the body is bent into a sitting position, with the head against the knees. At dawn on the lucky day, the corpse is sent to the burial site among mountains which are always far from residential areas. Then "Su" smoke is burned to attract condors, Lamas chant sutras to redeem the sins of the soul, and a professional celestial burial master deals with the body.

Practice of sky burial is closely related to philosophy of Tibetan Buddhism. Tibetans believe that if the vultures come and eat the body, it means that the dead has no sin and that his or her soul has gone peacefully to the Paradise. And the condors on the mountains around the celestial burial platform are "holy birds" and only eat the human body without attacking any small animals nearby. Any remains left by the holy birds must be collected up and burnt while the Lamas chant sutras to redeem the sins of the dead, because the remains would tie the spirits to this life.

There are a lot of taboos in the process of the celestial funeral in Tibet. Strangers are not allowed to attend the ceremony, for Tibetans believe it will bring negative efforts to the ascending of the souls. So, visitors should respect this custom and keep away from such occasions. The family members are also not allowed to be present at the burial site.

As India's population soared during the 20th century, its farmers' herds of cows, goats, water buffalo, and other livestock also expanded—and so did the number of vultures, reaching as many as 40 million by the 1980s. They were a nuisance at the time. Thirty-five percent of all planes that were hit by birds at New Delhi airport were vultures. The civil aviation department there hired people to shoot vultures around airports. Vultures pooped everywhere and owners of parked cars left for a few days would often find vultures nests built on top of their cars.

Vultures do face some challenges in India and elsewhere around the world. They die of electrocution on power lines or are hunted. They swallow poisonous lead bullets in carrion and their forest habitats where vultures nested and bred are dwindling.

In 1985 and 1986, in Keoladeo National Park, there were so many vultures it was difficult to conduct an actual count. There had been seen at least 1,800 white-backed vultures then, but in 1998 and 1999 only 86 were seen, representing a decline of about 96%.

The reasons why the birds had been nearly wiped out were a complete mystery. There was no shortage of food in Keoladeo Park; old, abandoned cows wandered the grounds and died, and healthy cows sometimes perished after getting stuck in the park's marshes, providing easy food sources for scavengers.

During one study of 100 carcasses found only 8 had vultures on them.

Theoretically disease or poisoning could be the culprit, but evidence was lacking. Vultures produce highly corrosive stomach acids, allowing them to consume highly toxic bacteria, such as anthrax and cattle dying from rodenticides.

For centuries a Zoroastrian community in India called the Parsis, as well as Vajrayana Buddhists in Tibet, disposed of their dead through "sky burials," setting them out in high places where vultures and other birds quickly turned the bodies into bare skeletons.

Other animals, such as dogs and rats, can fill the same ecological niche, but vultures are vastly preferable. From 1987 to 1997, as the vulture population cratered in India, the number of feral dogs increased from 18 million to 25.5 million, according to one estimate. As a result, an estimated 20,000 Indians die from rabies annually, mostly poor people and children; many others are injured in dog attacks.

Most investigators had thought the culprit was likely an infectious disease, but it soon became clear to the research team that vultures were dying in clusters, which suggested sudden exposure to a highly lethal toxin. Consistently they found the internal organs of the dead birds were covered with a chalky white paste indicating visceral gout, a result of kidney failure. People and animals develop gout when they don't properly metabolize purines, which are nitrogen-containing compounds common in meat products, especially organs and wild game. The body turns purines into uric acid, which birds normally excrete in their characteristically white poop, the avian form of urine. After two years of grueling and expensive studies they could not identify a cause for the die-offs.

They had a strong suspicion the birds were getting something from their food, which is mainly cattle and livestock, so they began looking closely at the livestock industry. Researchers surveyed local farmers and veterinarians, asking about new medicines they had recently started using. What they were looking for was something that was readily available over the counter, that was inexpensive, and had the ability to cause kidney failure. And diclofenac stood out, just like that."1

Wow! The same drug I've started rubbing on my knee killed 96% of the vulture population, resulted in an increased rat population where dead animals are laid to rest on the top of the ground and there is an increase in feral dog attacks and rabies from breeding and feeding in the area.

And, according to the drug insert's potential side effects, it also has the possibility of affecting areas of my body that are already under the care of the medical profession.

After I rub diclofenac topical gel on my right knee twice a day, I keep the area bare for several minutes and use a hair dryer to help it dry a little before putting on my pants. During this ritual, my mind wrestles about India with all these dead animals being piled up, releasing toxic gases into the atmosphere and supporting rodents, feral dogs and deadly diseases.

I also think about the hundreds of corpses that for centuries have been found disposed of in the Ganges. The

Ganges is the largest river in India, providing water to more than 500 million people. It also has extremely important religious significance in Hindu culture—personified as the goddess Ganga. Hindu faith holds that bathing in the river can absolve one's sins, and that anyone who is cremated on the river's banks, or whose ashes are submerged within it, will achieve salvation.

Traditionally, Hindus cremate their dead. But many communities follow what is known as "Jal Pravah"—the practice of floating in the river the bodies of children, unwed girls, or those who die from infectious diseases or snake bites. Many poor people also cannot afford cremation, and so they wrap the body in white muslin and push it into the water. Sometimes, the bodies are tied to stones to ensure they remain submerged. In normal times, corpses floating in the Ganges are not an uncommon sight.

At times during the Covid-19 pandemic all electric crematoriums were running 24/7 and only bodies that were coming from hospitals with Covid-19 certificates were accepted. A large number of people were dying at home, without getting any tests. Their families took the bodies to the outskirts of the city and when they couldn't find wood or a cremation spot, they just buried them on the river bed.

Back in the early 1990s, the government hit upon a strange and novel solution for the problem of the corpses: flesh-eating turtles. This unusual plan was made easier by the fact that the soft-shelled species found in and around the Ganges, had already demonstrated a taste for deceased flesh by raiding extinguished funeral pyres. In addition, turtles also have religious significance, so it was culturally acceptable for people to imagine the final fate of their physical selves as food for the aquatic creatures.

About 25,000 turtles were released into the Ganges over a decade. The animals were bred on a governmental farm in nearby Banares, raised on a diet of exclusively dead fish so that they wouldn't develop a taste for the living as well. They eat everything except the bones and ten adult turtles could consume an entire human body in two days.2

I also ponder the items that could be produced from rendering the deceased animals left to be recycled by nature. They might help lift the economy of segments of India's society that are trapped in poverty.

According to the North American Renderers' Association (NARA), rendering is the cooking and drying of meat and/or other animal by-products not used for human consumption in order to recover fats and proteins. The process reuses materials that would otherwise be discarded and repurposes them for various applications, such as fuel and livestock feed. It's a highly sustainable solution to food waste, recycling meat processing leftovers for other essential uses, and saving landfill space.

People use rendered products every day in soaps, paints, varnishes, lubricants, caulking compounds, candles, cleaners, paints, polishes, rubber products, plastics, fertilizers, and even explosives.

For hundreds of years, renderers have been recycling unwanted meat into animal food and fertilizer. Rendering produces valuable fats and proteins that improve nutrition in foods used by consumers and farmers to feed their pets as well as livestock, poultry, and fish. Also, leftovers, like organ meats, are used to produce rendered end products contain valuable fats and proteins containing vitamins and minerals.

I cringe thinking about leaving a loved one naked on the ground waiting to be devoured by vultures, birds and other living things, or being torn apart by flesh-eating turtles in the Ganges. Would rendering, cremation, liquification with sodium hydroxide, composting, cryogenics or seeing a casket being buried with dirt make it any easier when we've lost a loved one?

Best not to spend much time contemplating these things. If I'm to worry—maybe thinking about whether or not I'm poisoning my body as I rub diclofenac topical gel on my knee twice daily might be more productive for my brain to dwell on.

1. *Science History Institute, Poison Pill: The Mysterious Die-Off of India's Vultures, Meir Rinde, 2019. Atlas*
2. *Obscura What Became of India's Corpse-Eating Turtles?, Atlas Obscura, Oriana Leckert, 2014.*

11

WALKING BACKWARDS TO GO FORWARD

Every day, tiny, red insects called Spanish desert ants make several trips from their nest in search of food. When they find a small snack like a seed or crumb, they can hold it aloft in their tiny jaws and carry it home. But when they encounter a larger meal, say, a dead cricket or a piece of popcorn, they often have to drag it, walking backward, to get it to the nest.

Scientists used to think the insects needed to see something from the front to recognize a familiar location. Now, a research team has shown that the ants use a number of methods to find their way, and that they can recognize familiar scenery even when they're walking backward—a high level of visual sophistication for such a tiny animal.

When walking forward, Spanish desert ants (Cataglyphis velox) use a strategy called "path integration": They remember the feeling of the twists and turns they took and how many steps they are from the nest, which they use to compute the fastest route back home. They also rely on the angle of the Sun to get their bearings, and they look around at the passing scenery and remember certain landmarks that can help them on their return journey.

But how they know where they're going while walking backward is less clear. Sometimes the ants drop their food and turn around to see the path ahead—a behavior called peeking—before picking up the crumb again and trudging along on their backward way.

Wanting to know if desert ants could recognize anything visually while walking backwards, researchers selected ants that had already establishing a path by walking to a feeder from their nest in the desert so they knew where they were. The scientists also ant-napped some insects from right outside the nest who thought they were home. They deposited the ants some distance away from the nest with a giant crumb of ant-approved cookie.

As the ants began to drag the cookie back to the nest, the researchers would sometimes change the scenery around them, mimicking strange mountains by adding black plastic bags and tarps alongside the path. When confronted with such new landmarks, the ants peeked after walking only 3.2 meters along the 8-meter path, whereas ants on familiar paths could go nearly 6 meters without turning around. The observations reveal that the insects were taking in their surroundings as they walked backward and using them to navigate and decide when to peek.[1]

Deciding to look back and take a peek on his past, Darryl Strawberry said, "Eleven years ago I stuck a needle in my arm for the first time and that's when I realized I was really sick," said Strawberry. "I used drugs and alcohol for a long time and it started when I was 21 years old...

It was about 11 years ago I realized that I could reach for something greater than myself and got well."

Strawberry was suspended by Major League Baseball on three occasions for substance abuse. He was given a 140-game suspension in 1999 for possession of cocaine and soliciting sex from a prostitute. He then violated his probation from that charge in September 2000 after blacking out from taking painkillers while driving and causing an accident, which led to two years of house arrest.

Strawberry was also arrested and put in prison on several occasions for leaving court-ordered treatment centers to score drugs. After violating several non-drug rules at the Florida treatment center he was on probation in, he was sentenced to 18 months in jail in March 2002. Strawberry was released after 11 months and has reportedly been sober since then.2

Many years ago, a family experienced a little annoyance (like the kind we all face)—they had a leaky pipe in the bathroom ceiling. Drip, drip, drip, until a plumber was called, and the leak repaired. To access the broken pipe, the plumber had to cut a hole in the ceiling. As he finished his work, he instructed the family to wait several days for everything to dry before patching the hole.

But several days turned into several weeks, then months, then more than a year. Over time, the family didn't really see the hole in the ceiling anymore. One day, a young daughter's friend came to play, and when she went into the bathroom, she exclaimed, "Why do you have a hole in your ceiling?" As the family gathered and recounted the story, it was as if they saw the hole again for the first time.

It's easy to grow accustomed to the way things are, and in time, problems that were once so obvious, even urgent, become invisible to us. It often takes someone else to lovingly point out the gaping holes in our lives. A trusted friend or family member, a person who truly wants the best for us, can offer a fresh perspective, can see things we can't, and can even help us make those needed repairs. But that takes sincerity and humility from both those who give and those who receive the feedback.

The truth is we can all benefit from some repairs in our lives. Perhaps our hearts have been damaged by harsh feelings or the slow drip of unnoticed patterns of anger, impatience, or cynicism. Maybe we need to patch some holes in our relationships with forgiveness and compassion. Whatever the needed repairs, we don't have to make them alone. We have each other, and above all, we have the Lord Jesus Christ, who said, "My grace is sufficient for thee: for my strength is made perfect in weakness" (2 Corinthians 12:9). Ultimately, the Lord gives us power to heal, to turn our weaknesses into strengths, and to repair what is broken.3

After battling cocaine and alcohol addiction throughout much of his famed baseball career, Darryl Strawberry has now been clean and sober for the last 11 years. Not only is he now committed to helping others beat their own addictions, he's even started a treatment center to help facilitate the movement.

He has continued to work on the Darryl Strawberry Foundation, which supports children with autism and he recently opened The Darryl Strawberry Recovery Center in St. Cloud, Florida and is looking to eventually open up two more rehab facilities. "It's not about me," he said. "Sometimes people too often think celebrities and athletes are all about themselves and I was at one point...I was a great baseball player and had a chance to do that. I just want to be able to help some of those that are less fortunate than me."

The biggest lesson that Strawberry appears to have learned is that recovery is a journey. While he stumbled several times in his attempts to get well, his determination to succeed has led to his sobriety today. It should be noted that a relapse, even a significant one, does not mean that sobriety is an impossible feat.2

Unfortunately, some make errors in judgement great enough that they may not have the opportunity for a second chance. In a scriptural theme for this discussion, Jeffery Holland chose to discuss Luke 17:32, where the Savior cautions, "Remember Lot's wife." What did He mean by such an enigmatic little phrase? To find out, we need to do as He suggested. Let's recall who Lot's wife was.

The story, of course, comes to us out of the days of Sodom and Gomorrah, when the Lord, having had as much as He could stand of the worst that men and women could do, told Lot and his family to flee because those cities were about to be destroyed. "Escape for thy life," the Lord said. "Look not behind thee . . . ; escape to the mountain, lest thou be consumed" (Genesis 19:17; emphasis added).

With less than immediate obedience and more than a little negotiation, Lot and his family ultimately did leave town but just in the nick of time. The scriptures tell us what happened at daybreak the morning following their escape:

"The Lord rained upon Sodom and upon Gomorrah brimstone and fire from the Lord out of heaven;

"And he overthrew those cities" (Genesis 19:24-25)... Surely, with the Lord's counsel—"look not behind thee"— ringing clearly in her ears, Lot's wife, the record says, "looked back," and she was turned into a pillar of salt (see verse 26).

Just what did Lot's wife do that was so wrong? As a student of history, I have thought about that and offer a partial answer. Apparently, what was wrong with Lot's wife was that she wasn't just looking back; in her heart she wanted to go back. It would appear that even before she was past the city limits, she was already missing what Sodom and Gomorrah had offered her. As Elder Neal A. Maxwell (1926-2004) of the Quorum of the Twelve Apostles once said, such people know they should have their primary residence in Zion, but they still hope to keep a summer cottage in Babylon.

It is possible that Lot's wife looked back with resentment toward the Lord for what He was asking her to leave behind. We certainly know that Laman and Lemuel were resentful when Lehi and his family were commanded to leave Jerusalem. So, it isn't just that she looked back; she looked back longingly. In short, her attachment to the past outweighed her confidence in the future. That, apparently, was at least part of her sin.

I was told once of a young man who for many years was more or less the brunt of every joke in his school. He had some disadvantages, and it was easy for his peers to tease him. Later in his life he moved away. He eventually joined the army and had some successful experiences there in getting an education and generally stepping away from his past. Above all, as many in the military do, he discovered the beauty and majesty of the Church and became active and happy in it.

Then, after several years, he returned to the town of his youth. Most of his generation had moved on but not all. Apparently, when he returned quite successful and quite reborn, the same old mind-set that had existed before was still there, waiting for his return. To the people in his hometown, he was still just old "so-and-so"—you remember the guy who had the problem, the idiosyncrasy, the quirky nature, and did such and such. And wasn't it all just hilarious?

Little by little this man's Pauline effort to leave that which was behind and grasp the prize that God had laid before him was gradually diminished until he died about the way he had lived in his youth. He came full circle: Again, inactive and unhappy and the brunt of a new generation of jokes. Yet he had had that one bright, beautiful midlife moment when he had been able to rise above his past and truly see who he was and what he could become. Too bad, too sad that he was again to be surrounded by a whole batch of Lot's wives, those who thought his past was more interesting than his future. They managed to rip out of his grasp that for which Christ had grasped him. And he died sad, though through little fault of his own.4

Strawberry hasn't returned to the mistakes of his youth. He is engaged in a work that constantly reminds him of a place that he doesn't want to return. "The biggest lesson that Strawberry appears to have learned is that recovery is a journey. While he stumbled several times in his attempts to get well, his determination to succeed has led to his sobriety today. It should be noted that a relapse, even a significant one, does not mean that sobriety is an impossible feat." Unless one looks back and stumbles longingly like Lot's wife, there is always hope and changing is not an "impossible feat."

As the ants began to drag the cookie back to the nest, the researchers would sometimes change the scenery around them, mimicking strange mountains by adding black plastic bags and tarps alongside the path. When confronted with such new landmarks, the ants peeked after walking only 3.2 meters along the 8-meter path, whereas ants on familiar paths could go nearly 6 meters without turning around. The observations reveal that the insects were taking in their surroundings as they walked backward and using them to navigate and decide when to peek.

The ants' eyes have a wide angle of view—they have nearly 360° vision, whereas humans can only see about one-third of their surroundings without turning their heads. The insects are likely taking in information from beside and behind them as they walk away from the nest, then using it to guide them back as they are dragging food. After analyzing the behavior of the ants, researchers were able to create a model showing the circumstances in which the insects rely on their visual surroundings versus other sources of information like the angle of the Sun or their internal step-counter to find their way home backward.[1]

May we not "return to thoughts of the towns of our life" where peers have pulled us down and constantly reminded us of a place we don't want to return. Always remember that it's not unusual that we may stumble many times, recovery is a journey and not an impossible feat. Understand that some stumble from looking back "longingly", like Lot's wife, to our old ways and may turn into an unmovable pillar of salt with little chance of recovery. Helping others in need will help us stay on the right path.

May we think of the desert ants: As the ants began to drag the cookie back to the nest, the ants that already knew where they were did much better regardless of the scenery. They could walk for longer distances before they peeked behind them, and more of them made it home with their cookie. A few "clueless" ants got lost, but surprisingly, others were able to find their way back to the nest even when they hadn't previously tracked where they walked using path integration, which means they must have only been using their visual memories of their surroundings and possibly the angle of the Sun.1

1. *How ants walking backward find their way home. Insects can recognize scenery forward and backward, by Eva Frederick, Dec 2019.*

2. *Darryl Strawberry Talks Addiction and Recovery update, McCarton Ackerman, December 2021.*

3. *Repairing What is Broken, Music & The Spoken Word, #4858, 10-23-2022.*

4. *The Best Is Yet to Be, By Elder Jeffrey R. Holland, Of the Quorum of the Twelve Apostles, BYU devotional address, January 2009.*

12

MY EXPERIENCE
WITH RACCOONS

While visiting home our daughter noticed rather quiet chattering sounds coming from the attic in her bedroom during the night. We did not notice anything during the day and I did not find anything visually in the attic. However, night noises continued and the ceiling in the bedroom she was sleeping had a light brown spot that looked like we had a leaking roof.

I began posting myself quietly every evening by my car parked in the street where I could see the roof. I noticed a raccoon emerging nightly from an attic vent hole onto the roof. It went to the back of the house and I later found the raccoon would go to the top of the gazebo, onto the fence and disappear into the neighbor's yard. I then placed spotlights on the roof at night so she could not see me. She became less cautious and I observed her nightly activities on a regular basis.

I was contemplating the stupid fantasy of trying to catch her with an open garbage can as she jumped to the gazebo. One evening I was standing under the roof next to the gazebo, she came to the edge of the roof over where I was standing on the deck and started to jump. Fear struck me and the only think I could think to do was bark like a dog—it worked. Thoughts of a garbage can capture ceased.

Even when raccoons are quiet vocally, they still make noise. The sound of an animal rustling or scurrying about the attic or in the chimney is a common sign that a raccoon has moved in. Typical raccoon sounds also occur when the pests walk across rooftops, construct their dens, or attempt to gain entry through holes or other small openings that lead to attractive denning sites. People tend to hear raccoon sounds most frequently at night due to the nocturnal behavior of the pests.

We later found the noises in our house were from a mother raccoon and her two babies living in the attic above Tiffani's bedroom. The water spot on the ceiling wasn't water but leakage from the raccoon's latrine. Evidently, raccoons keep their home nice and clean by eating and sleeping in places other than where they use the bathroom.

A raccoon's face has several markings that help it stand out. The most noticeable marking is the black "mask"—large black markings around each eye. They extend from the edge of the nose to the lower part of the cheek. In addition, raccoons have whitish patches on top of the eyes and around the nose. Raccoons have grayish-brown fur over most of their body, and their tails have four to six black rings.

Raccoons live throughout the continental United States in woods, wetlands, suburbs, parks, cities, and anywhere there is cover, food, and water. Predators of raccoons include the coyote, fisher, bobcat, red fox, and great horned owl.

Raccoons are omnivores, meaning they will eat both meat and vegetables. They like grasshoppers, nuts, berries, mice, squirrels, and bird eggs. They are nocturnal and search for food at night. Raccoons are opportunistic feeders and are well known by people for their skillful attempts at stealing food from garbage cans in parks and neighborhoods. They love corn and cause damage in the fields by not only eating the corn but knocking down the stalks. In a study of corn crop plundering by wild animals, Purdue University researchers found that raccoons were responsible for 87 percent of the 73,000 damaged plants they evaluated.

What makes raccoons so good at snatching food? Check out their forepaws. Raccoons' forepaws, each with five fingers, are surprisingly dextrous. They can easily grasp, hold and manipulate objects in their forepaws, similar to primates. While raccoons' flexible forepaws help them with food procurement and tree climbing, the animals don't display any sort of traits related to tool use like primates. Raccoons actually have the same nerve grouping on the hairless parts of the forepaws as primates have, including humans, making them very sensitive to touch.

When raccoons perform their dunking ritual, the water on their paws could excite the nerves in their forepaws. That, in turn, gives them a more vivid tactile experience and provides precise information about what they're about to eat. This is a beneficial trait since the raccoon's hunt in the dark and their vision isn't its keenest sense.1

Raccoons are known to defecate and urinate in swimming pools, and even destroy pool lining, filters, and more. If these critters live in your neighborhood, it is important to invest in a quality pool cover, and have it on whenever your pool is not in use. If you cannot get a pool cover that protects the entire pool, at least get one that covers the shallow-end where the steps are located. They commonly hide their feces and urinate in the water on the first step.2

Raccoons are solitary, except during the breeding season, which occurs from January to June. Females usually have one litter a year, with three to seven offspring per litter. The gestation period is roughly two months. Young stay with their mother for their first winter, then venture off on their own in spring. A raccoon can live for 16 years in the wild, but often only live for an average of five years.

Raccoons can be dangerously aggressive if cornered or provoked. During my veterinary career I've seen severe wounds inflicted on a dog from tangling with a raccoon. I've seen dogs kill opossums but never a raccoon.

Raccoons can carry rabies which is a fatal virus to both animals and people if left untreated. Being nocturnal, humans rarely encounter or are bitten by raccoons. Skunks, bats, and foxes also commonly contract rabies; but, contact with infected bats is the leading cause of human rabies deaths in this country. At least 7 out of 10 Americans who die from rabies in the US were infected by bats.

These masked creatures can also carry and transmit other diseases including distemper, salmonella, and leptospirosis. But that's not all! These animals can be carriers of fleas, lice, roundworms, and other parasites that can make humans very sick.3

While pet raccoons are uncommon, over the years, some Americans have kept these animals as pets including past US President Calvin Coolidge who kept a pair as pets while he resided in the White House. Even though they are cute animals, most animal experts do not recommend keeping raccoons as pets because these animals are known to be unpredictable and full of trouble. Unlike easily domesticated dogs, raccoons are not social and are animals that exhibit hostile and instinctual behaviors toward humans and other animals. While dogs easily bond with humans, raccoons are unable to form close emotional connections to humans even after several breeding attempts. Many people have tried to breed raccoons over the years to try to make them good pets. However, these attempts have failed time and time again. Regardless of how many generations of raccoons that have been bred, these animals always fail to form deep connections to humans like dogs or even cats. By nature, raccoons are independent, curious, aggressive, and unpredictable.

It's illegal in most states to keep raccoons as pets. As of this writing, there are only 15 states that allow raccoons to be kept as pets. Many of the states that allow pet ownership of raccoons require wild animal permits.4

I have a photo of a raccoon that I spayed. The uterus and internal abdomen looked very similar to a dog. I don't remember the owner or what became of the raccoon. I do know that treating or spaying a raccoon today would be a no-no and a possible reprimand or more from the California Fish and Game Department or the Veterinary Medical Board.4

Pulling into my driveway after work I noticed a police car parked on the street in front of my house and our son Dustin visiting with him at the front door. Dustin being a teenager, I suspected the worst was coming his way. Instead, the officer was there to visit with the owner of the home—me.

Apparently, my family had been throwing our dog's poop over the fence into our neighbor's swimming pool. I had no idea what he was talking about. Finding out that I was a veterinarian and worked as a leader with a San Jose Police Department employee in the Boy Scouts of America, the officer felt it ridiculous that my family would be doing such a thing. He left and I heard no more about the accusations.

My first reaction to raccoons in our attic was excitement. What a cool thing to have such a beautiful and reclusive animal living almost like a pet in my home. I had a mini zoo in my youth and was able to befriend several wild animals. Googling my new find quickly changed my attitude about having these pests on my property. I found videos where closing access to an attic from a mother raccoon with offspring inside resulted in the critter tearing off shingles and tar paper from the roof of a home to get to her young. It was obvious that just closing the vents to the attic and letting the young get hungry enough to go into a trap was out of the question.

Having a family of raccoons take up residence on my property put me in a tough spot. I didn't want to harm the animals, but they weren't welcome to dig up my yard, chew my home's wiring and cables, and use my attic for a latrine. I had a dog in the yard, pest resistant garbage cans and kept pet food and debris from around the home. The only thing left would be to evict the raccoon family from my attic and seal off the vent holes. I didn't even know if trapping and having the game warden or pest control relocate or dispose of them was legal. But I decided to give it a try.

The literature I found suggested baiting traps with sweet and chewy marshmallows, wet stinky cat food, bacon, the sweet aroma of fresh fruit, the strong scent of canned tuna or salmon, whole uncooked eggs, sweet corn on the cob, a fatty meal, sugar-coated veggies and a wad of tin foil may stimulate their curiosity enough to enter a trap.5

I placed a Havahart live animal two-door trap in my attic that we used regularly for clients to trap cats for medical care or neutering. Different varieties of suggested baits were used and I didn't even find a hint that the raccoons had even investigated the trap.

I finally contacted a pest control company that I had taken care of the owner's dog. He mentioned that he hated raccoons because they were intelligent enough to be very hard to trap. Still giving it a try, he set up several traps over the roof areas to try his luck. Several days went by before he gave up.

He then took the traps down and arranged a day to investigate the attic. He told me that he didn't want me to be at home and it would be best for me to be at work. Just leave the door unlocked and he would let me know how things worked.

In the afternoon he called and let me know that everything was under control. He and his Jack Russel Terrier entered the attic, beamed a flashlight at the raccoons and with his dog in pursuit let off several shots with his 410-shotgun as the critters were trying to exit the attic. One raccoon was dead (he would take care of the remains), one injured enough to leave blood on the parking cement on the side of the house and the mother got away. The attic vent holes were now raccoon proof and it was all good. He used the 410-shotgun because the BB shot would have little chance of penetrating the attic and hitting a neighbor's home.

The exterminator wanted me to know nothing about what he planned on doing because I being a veterinarian may have declined his plan or my license may have been at risk for an inhumane act and using a gun in the city limits of San Jose. Also, the local humane society or California Veterinary Medical Board might get involved and not be pleased with my presence. I was relieved that I hadn't known what was going to transpire at my home and knew nothing about the course of action. The raccoons needed to leave their home to help keep mine functioning without pest damage.

Getting home from school Dustin recalls, "All I remember about that day was coming home and going up the stairs to see how the exterminators were doing. About halfway up the stairs he fired his shotgun and it startled me so bad that I thought I'd been shot. I tumbled down the stairs to the ground floor clutching my chest."6

The incident bothered me enough that I found a source where I could buy in bulk up to 200 raccoon tails. I had a plan to buy some raccoon tails, place a note on them about my experience and place one on the doorstep of every house in the immediate neighborhood.

Time passed and I wasn't sure the neighbors would appreciate my scheme. Instead, I found a Daniel Boone hat in Alaska with a genuine raccoon tail attached to the back of it that I placed in my museum.

Oh, and by the way—the neighbor who accused me of throwing poop in his swimming pool. One day I had a chance to chat with him about the incident. He told me that he set up a motion camera to catch me in the act. Instead, he found a raccoon walk over to the shallow end of his swimming pool, wash and eat some food, take a poop (not sure of a pee) in the pool and proceed to climb over the fence into my yard.

1. *How Stuff Works, Why Do Raccoons Wash Their Food?, Cristen Conger.*
2. *raccoonatticguide.com.*
3. *Animal Diversity Web, University of Michigan Museum of Zoology, Adirondack Ecological Center, College of Environmental Science and Forest, State University of New York + other.*
4. *Petkeen.com.*
5. *Best Raccoon Bait for Traps: What to Use to Trap Raccoons, Sep 16, 2020 by Victoria Moore.*
6. *Dustin Isaacson, personal communication, 04/22/2022.*

13

BRAIN FOG

Thinking hard for several hours can leave us feeling mentally tired. If this leads to a general feeling of fatigue and cognitive inefficiencies, such as reduced concentration and difficulty with memory, a common term for this is brain fog.1

Most people have experienced mental fog or brain fog. It is often described as a cloudy-headed feeling. Forgetfulness is a common complaint among older adults. As we grow older, we experience physiological changes that can cause glitches in brain functions we have always taken for granted. It takes longer to learn and recall information. We are not as quick as we used to be.

Also, lack of sleep, overworking, and stress can cause brain fog. Depression has a range of symptoms, including cognitive changes that people commonly refer to as brain fog. These symptoms often occur during depressive episodes, but they can develop before these episodes begin and continue during remission.

Recent research has found what causes mental tiredness. Prolonged concentration leads to the build-up of a compound called glutamate, which is potentially harmful, in regions at the front of the brain. This may provide an explanation as to why we avoid difficult tasks when mentally fatigued: the glutamate overload makes the brain try to avoid further mental work difficult.

Many of us have experienced mental weariness after a hard day of thinking, but until now, we didn't know why. The brain doesn't seem to run out of energy after working hard and even when we aren't deliberately thinking about anything specific, some brain regions, called the "default mode network", are as active as ever.

To learn more, researchers used a technique called magnetic resonance spectroscopy (MRS), which measures levels of various chemicals in living tissue harmlessly. They focused on a region towards the front and sides of the brain called the lateral prefrontal cortex, which much previous work has shown is involved in difficult mental tasks.

The team asked 40 people to do memory tasks while lying in an MRS scanner. These included watching sequences of numbers appear on a screen and stating if the current number was the same as a previous one. Twenty-six of the participants did a harder version of this task, while the other 14 were given an easier one.

Levels of eight different brain chemicals were measured, including glutamate, which is the main signaling chemical between neurons. At the junctions between neurons, called synapses, electrical signals can't leap the gap. Instead, tiny particles of compounds such as glutamate are released, which transmit the signal.

After completing the memory tasks for 6 hours, those doing the harder version had raised levels of glutamate in their lateral prefrontal cortex and those doing the easier task, levels stayed about the same. Across all participants, there was no rise in the other seven brain chemicals that were measured.

Among the participants doing the harder tasks, their glutamate level rise tallied with dilation of the pupils in their eyes, another broad measure of fatigue. Those doing the simpler task reported feeling tired, but had no glutamate rise or pupil dilation.

The researchers also investigated if mental fatigue affected decision-making. They did this by interspersing the memory task with different exercises, such as one where people had a choice between getting a sum of money right away or a different one later.

As the participants doing the harder task felt more tired and had an accumulation of glutamate, they shifted to options that gave a small reward immediately. This could be an example of us avoiding difficult mental tasks, such as calculating which choice to make, to prevent the accumulation of potentially harmful glutamate levels.2

If you've ever felt like you can't think straight or concentrate on a task when it's hot and humid, you're not alone. Many individuals experience this brain fog when temperatures rise to uncomfortable levels especially during the summer.

There is a growing body of research that demonstrates how environmental conditions, heat in particular, can affect mental performance. A 2006 study showed that an increase in indoor temperature can reduce work productivity in the office. Researchers evaluated how well participants carried out common office tasks and saw that there is a consistent decrease in performance when the temperature rises above 75.2°F.

This decline in mental function isn't limited to office workers or adults, and it has been observed in high school students as well. A 2018 study illustrated how a hot 90°F day can reduce educational performance on exams up to 14 percent and result in a 10.9 percent lower likelihood of passing a subject.3

Consistent with previous work, new results indicate that some aspects of cognitive function are reduced during acute cold exposure. The current study extends these findings and demonstrates that cognitive dysfunction persists into the recovery period after removal from the cold. This pattern emerged despite multiple measures of cold stress (e.g. core/skin temperatures, thermal sensation) being at baseline levels.

This is the first report of this phenomenon in healthy human subjects and they speculate that the causes are due to both physiological and psychological factors.4

All living plants and animals adjust on a daily to ambient temperature change. The artic ground squirrel adjusts enough to cold that it is considered to be both a warm and a cold-blooded animal.

As an adaptation for coping with the harsh, inclement weather of the winter months, they hibernate for about eight months out of the year. Their chosen hibernacula have coverage provided by vegetation, rather than open, windswept burrows. This vegetation coverage allows for a higher accumulation of snow and warmer soil temperatures.

The artic ground squirrels usually start winter hibernation in August or September, enter into a state of torpor in which their metabolic rate and body temperatures are drastically lowered for up to three weeks at a time. Their body temperature drops from about 99 degrees F to as cold as 27 degrees F, below freezing. Between these states of torpor, they arouse and will either shiver or use their stored fat to bring their body temperatures back to a euthermic, or comfortable state of about 93-97 degrees F. This rewarming period usually lasts one to two days and then they return to their state of torpor in order to conserve energy.

There is a large variation between species of animals as to what would happen if they were awakened during hibernation or in a torpor state. For some animals, it would be a major disruption or even fatal. For others it would be more of a minor, but significant annoyance. For others, it may just be a bit earlier than they would have awakened. For many species survival depends on their body condition.

Different species vary in the time it takes to become functionally alert. Black bears usually take 2 to 10 minutes to be aroused. I could not find data on other animals; but I'll bet if aroused during hibernation or torpor there is reduced cognitive function and cloudy headed groggy brain fog for a long enough period in all animals hibernating or in a torpor state to be vulnerable to predation.5

People strolling through New York City's parks witness how the tree squirrels adjust to overheating. The squirrels sprawl out on the ground, face down, limbs outstretched and lying still. The parks agency advise that if a squirrel was seen lying face down on the ground, don't worry. On hot days, squirrels keep cool by splooting (stretching out) on cool surfaces to reduce body heat. It is sometimes referred to as heat dumping. Looking at the posturing, they look like they are suffering some mental fatigue and brain fog.

I see this behavior from our Manchester Terrier that weighs just over ten pounds and has a thin coat of fur. She sploots (see photo below) like a squirrel on the cement to get warm in the morning and on the grass or in the shade to cool in the warm afternoon. This is a common behavior in dogs and at my work has been in the past called splayed out or spread out.

Etymologically, spooting may be a variant of splat, but there are suggestions that it is a blend of splay and scoot. It has been quite closely associated with dogs and I suspect I'll need to start entering the new word spooting in my medical records. Maybe in a couple of years we'll also need to buy a new dictionary and veterinary students will see the word on their veterinarian board of exams.6

King Ahab married Jezebel, who worshiped the idols of Baal, and provoked the Lord to anger. In response Elijah seals the heavens with a drought that results in more than two years of famine. Elijah meets with Ahab and challenges the priests of Baal to call down fire from heaven to consume their sacrifice. The prophets of Baal called and called from morning to evening, but to no avail, even after hours of ritual bloodletting and prophesying.

Elijah called the people to himself. He repaired the altar of I AM who I AM which had been torn down. Then he dug a trench around the altar and called for enough water to be poured on the altar until it filled the trench. Elijah prayed to the Lord that the people would know that he was God and the fire of the Lord fell and consumed the burnt offering and the wood and the stones and the dust, and licked up the water that was in the trench.

Elijah prayed to end the feminine, and the Lord sent rain. Queen Jezebel is angry at what Elijah has done to the prophets of Baal and tries to kill Elijah. He flees into the wilderness, after a day's journey sat down under a juniper tree and is so discouraged that he requested that he might die.

As he lay and slept under the juniper tree an angel of the Lord touched him and said for him to arise and eat the food and water that had been prepared for him and then he laid himself down again to rest. The angel came again a second time and touched him and said arise and eat because you have a long journey. He ate again and the rest and nourishment he had received gave him enough strength to travel forty days and forty nights in the wilderness. *1 Kings 17-19.*

Here we have Elijah the prophet in a heap of trouble. He has maddened King Ahab by calling upon the Lord for a famine that has lasted for over two years, the wicked prophets of Baal could not call down fire to burn their sacrifice, Elijah puts water on his sacrifice, God responds to his request and sends down fire that consumes the sacrifice as well as the alter, the Lord kills the prophets of Baal, and the wicked Queen Jezebel (who worships Baal) has orders to kill him.

Elijah flees into the wilderness for a day, is temporally and spiritually exhausted, and is sitting alone under a tree with no one or place to turn for help. I suspect he was totally worn out, dehydrated, had been over heated, was without shelter to warm him for the night, not able to slept, and fearful and anxious about what method Jezebel would like to use when she kills him.

He feels there is no hope, is in deep depression, his brain's glutamate levels are at a high enough level to place him in a deep state of brain fog, and he is not capable of making good cognitive decisions resulting in the depressing thoughts that all is lost and that death is imminent. Even though the Lord had allowed Elijah to perform many miracles, his exhausted state resulted in the performance of such mental tasks as prayer, exercising faith and having hope the Lord would come to his rescue were too difficult to perform in his glutamate saturated brain.

No matter how difficult our trials may be, it is hard to imagine what Elijah or for that matter Job must have gone through during their earthly trials: Maynard Dixon, a prolific artist from the previous century, is best known for his vibrant paintings of the American West. He spent much of his life roaming the western United States, which he loved so much, capturing on canvas images of the peoples and places he saw. But during the Great Depression in the 1930s, Dixon's artistic focus changed: he painted a series of images depicting striking and displaced workers. One of those paintings, *Forgotten Man*, captured the poignant feelings of so many people during that time.

A man sits on the curb with his head down and his back against a wall of anonymous legs. The people behind him seem to pass by quickly—they are engaged in life, purposeful, going somewhere. But this person, this forgotten man, sits unseen, cast aside and ignored by those around him. He seems dejected, worn out, exhausted with life.

Maynard Dixon's painting has a certain timelessness about it. Who has not felt lonely or forgotten at times? At times it seems like everyone else is moving forward, productive and successful. Meanwhile, we may feel that the world is passing us by—that we are forgotten.

At such times, it's helpful to remember that no matter how we are treated by others, we are never forgotten by God. He has placed good things in our lives that can brighten our outlook if we will only seek them. He has sent us here with a purpose to bring goodness to our little part of the world. We can start by realizing that we aren't the only ones who may feel forgotten. We can notice the unnoticed. We can strive to do something each day, perhaps just some little thing, that helps lift someone who is down. We can do our part to help ensure that there are no forgotten men or forgotten women.

If we can do this, the seed of hope will begin to take root and grow in our heart. Most often, it won't be a quick or dramatic change, but in small and simple ways, the light of hope and the promise of better days will come.7

The seed of hope began for Elijah as he splayed out (splooted) on the ground, rested from his worries and began sleeping in an attempt to remove his physical exhaustion, brain fog and depression while under the juniper tree. Then an angel of the Lord touched him and said for him to arise and eat the food, and water that had been prepared to restore his physical health.

Once filled with nourishment he then splooted himself down and rested again to help restore him mentally and spiritually.

With his restored confidence, the angel came again a second time and touched him and said arise and eat to prepare your body to carry you on a long journey.

He ate again and the rest and nourishment he had received gave him enough mental and physical strength to travel forty days and forty nights in the wilderness.

Through the experiences of Elijah, it appears that the Lord is instructing us to recognize that there are times we've overdone, are cold, over heated or stressed, and anxiety or depression has taken over our wellbeing—and we crash. Glutamate levels in our brain have risen to dangerous levels, and brain fog takes over.

It's okay to back off, rest from our labors, get the help we need and take care of our physical, mental and spiritual concerns before jumping back into the jungle of life.

"And see that all these things are done in wisdom and order; for it is not requisite that a man should run faster than he has strength. And again, it is expedient that he should be diligent, that thereby he might win the prize; therefore, all things must be done in order." Mosiah 4:27

1. *Cynthia Funes, PhD, University Medicine Neurosurgery Clinic, Phoenix, AZ, 2021.*
2. *Why thinking hard for several hours can leave you mentally exhausted, Clare Wilson, Mind, 2022.*
3. *How Does Extreme Heat Affect Our Brains?, Carla Delgado, Discover, 2021.*
4. *Acute Cold Exposure and Cognitive Function: Evidence for Sustained Impairment, Ergonomics, 2012.*
5. *Alaska State Department of Fish and Game.*

6. *What does 'splooting' mean? And why are squirrels doing it?, Washington Post, Adela Suliman, 2022.*
7. *The Promise of Better Days, Music & the Spoken word, Lloyd D. Newell, October 30, 2016.*

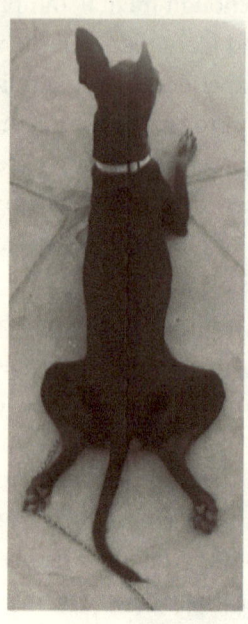

14

BOBBIE THE TRAVELING WONDER DOG'S TRAVELS HOME

In August, 1923, while on a family road trip in Indiana, Frank and Elizabeth Brazier, with their daughters Leona and Nova, were visiting relatives in Wolcott, Indiana. Their two-year-old Scotch Collie/English Shepherd mix dog Bobbie (1921-1927) was attacked by three other dogs and ran away. After an exhaustive search the broken-hearted Brazier family was unable to find Bobbie and continued their trip before returning home to Silverton Oregon, never expecting to see their dog again.

In February, 1924, six months later, Bobbie returned to Silverton mangy, dirty, and scrawny, with his toenails worn down to nothing. He showed all the signs of having walked the entire distance, including swimming rivers and crossing the Continental Divide during the coldest part of winter. Robbie became known as the "Wonder Dog" when the news media got the word out that during his ordeal he had crossed at least 2,551 miles (4,105 km) of plains, desert, and mountains in the winter to return home, an average of approximately 14 miles (23 km) per day.

His story drew national attention and was featured in numerous newspapers. People who had fed and sheltered Bobbie on his journey wrote the family to tell about their time with Bobbie. The Humane Society of Portland concluded that after returning to Wolcott Bobbie eventually headed west. During their original trip, the Braziers had parked their car in a service station each night. Their dog visited each of these stops on his journey, along with a number of homes, and a hobo camp. In Portland, an Irish woman took care of him for a period of time when she found he had been injured, leaving his legs and paws gashed.

Upon his death in 1927, he was buried with honors at the Oregon Humane Society's pet cemetery in Portland. A week later, German Shepherd film star Rin Tin Tin laid a wreath at his grave. His grave is sheltered by a "fancy white and red dog house." Bobbie's demonstration of loyalty is celebrated during Silverton's annual children's pet parade that serves as a reminder of the special place animals and pets have in people's lives.1

Even compared to Bobbie the Wonder Dog, migrating hummingbirds are amazing. Most are only about 3 to 3.5 inches long and weigh 3 grams to 6 grams (or from the weight of a penny to the weight of a nickel), they have a brain the size of a rice grain, live for 3 to 5 years, feed on flower nectar, insects and spiders, and have many migrating flight patterns.

Hummingbirds are beautiful jewels of color and marvels of aerodynamics. Their wings beat up to 80 beats per second, and they are the only birds that can fly backwards. They have amazing endurance, and certain species migrate up to 4,000 miles from Mexico to Canada and Alaska. Some fly non-stop 500 miles across the Gulf of Mexico during their migration.

At night humming birds go into a very deep sleep called Torpor. This allows them to slow down their metabolism and lower their body temperature. Torpor saves over half of their energy at night. When hummingbirds sleep and are in the Torpor state, they have been known to hang upside-down.

When in torpor they may appear to be dead and will probably not even respond if you touched them. It takes anywhere from 20 minutes to an hour for a hummingbird to warm up and fully recover from torpor. Once they are up and about, the first order of business is food. The hummingbirds will eat 25% of their daily intake as soon as they recover from torpor.

Most of these birds DO return to the same feeders or gardens to breed year after year. What's more, they often stop at the same spots along the way and arrive on the same date! Not bad for birds with brains no bigger than a grain of rice. The real puzzle is how these creatures of habit remember where they had a meal 8 months earlier, and then, navigate right to that spot.

Scientists aren't exactly sure how hummers home in on home. The birds are too small to track with transmitters, so they have used research on other birds with transmitters to establish theories how hummingbirds migrate by instinct and the environment help them steer course:

- Spurred on in search of food and warmth.

- Respond to photoperiod (the number of hours of sunlight) at a certain time of year. This releases hormones that "tell" hummers it's time to go.
- Cue into the Earth's magnetic field. Like some other birds, they may have substances in their bodies that can sense the magnetic field. By knowing which way is north, they are better able to steer.
- Use the sun as a "compass." They use the sun's position in the sky, where it is at different times of day, to stay on course. Scientists think the pineal gland on the top of the bird's brain is sensitive to light.
- They notice and recall landmarks such as rivers, coastlines, mountain ranges, and even highways.
- Some scientists wonder whether birds even use their senses of smell and hearing to locate familiar places.2

Elder Dieter F. Uchtdorf stated, "When scientists study this fascinating behavior, they ask questions such as 'How do they know where to go?' and "How does each successive generation learn this behavior?'

When I read of this powerful instinct in animals, I can't help but wonder, "Is it possible that human beings have a similar yearning—an inner guidance system, if you will—that draws them to their heavenly home?"

I believe that every man, woman, and child has felt the call of heaven at some point in his or her life. Deep within us is a longing to somehow reach past the veil and embrace Heavenly Parents we once knew and cherished. Some might suppress this yearning and deaden their souls to its call. But those who do not quench this light within themselves can embark on an incredible journey—a wondrous migration toward heavenly climes . . .

God knows your every thought, your sorrows, and your greatest hopes. God knows the many times you have sought Him. The many times you have felt limitless joy. The many times you have wept in loneliness. The many times you have felt helpless, confused, or angry. Yet, no matter your history, if you have faltered, failed, feel broken, bitter, betrayed, or beaten, know that you are not alone. God still calls to you.

The Savior extends His hand to you. And, as He did to those fishermen who stood long ago on the banks of the Sea of Galilee, with infinite love He speaks to you: "Come, follow me." If you will hear Him, He will speak to you this very day.

When you walk the path of discipleship—when you move toward Heavenly Father—there is something within you that will confirm that you have heard the call of the Savior and set your heart toward the light. It will tell you that you are on the right path and that you are returning home.

Since the beginning of time, God's prophets have urged the people of their day to "hearken unto the voice of the Lord thy God, . . . keep his commandments and his statutes . . ., (and) turn unto (Him) with all thine heart, and with all thy soul." . . .

On your journey back to Heavenly Father you will soon realize that this journey isn't just about focusing on your own life. No, this path inevitably leads you to become a blessing in the lives of God's other children - your brothers and sisters. And the interesting thing about the journey is that as you serve God, and as you care for and help your fellowmen, you will see great progress in your own life, in ways you could never imagine.

Perhaps you don't consider yourself all that useful; perhaps you don't consider yourself a blessing in somebody's life. Often, when we look at ourselves, we see only our limitations and deficiencies. We might think we have to be "more" of something for God to use us - more intelligent, more wealthy, more charismatic, more talented, more spiritual. Blessings will come not so much because of your abilities but because of your choices. And the God of the universe will work within and through you, magnifying your humble efforts for His purposes.

His work has always advanced on this important principle: Out of small things proceedeth that which is great."3

Unfortunately, during my life I have never been able to find my way using the photoperiod changes during different seasons of the year, the Earth's magnetic forces or using the sun as a guide. And, without a satellite global positioning system (GPS) network available on my cell phone, I'd often be lost just trying to find my way to a meeting, doctor's office or the restaurant with the great meal I had two weeks before.

The animal kingdom appears to have genetically imprinted guidance systems helping them make the correct choices for survival. Man must seek to find the correct course for survival through the Master of us all.

1. *Wikipedia*
2. *Various sources*
3. *A Yearning for Home, Dieter F. Uchtdorf, 09/30/2017.*

15

GREAT PYRENEES GUUARDING THE FLOCK

According to my family, in 2008 Shauna and I were driving on U.S. 55 east from her mother's home in Caldwell Idaho and her daughter Tiffani happened to be driving west from Nampa towards Caldwell. Abruptly our cars were stopped and a flock of sheep tended by sheep herders and large white dogs engulfed our cars like a flooding river across the highway. Soon, Tiffani frantically called on the phone informing us that sheep were surrounding her, they blocked her view and she was afraid they were going to overturn her car. Her fears were heightened due to a not long before incident when she feared rolling down a highway embankment when her leak free GEO tracker floated nearly off the road during a short burst of heavy rain. She was amazed how a man was able to easily push the small SUV with her inside it back onto the road.1

There are many sheep ranches in Idaho. Most are owned and operated by Basques that are indigenous to and primarily inhabit a region that is located around the western end of the Pyrenees on the coast that straddles parts of North-central Spain and south-western France. Some herders, most noteworthy the Basque, took part of their pay in sheep. This eventually gave the herders enough capital to buy land and become prosperous sheep producers. They are a very proud people—while visiting a Basque's home I noticed a sign on the wall that read, "Eat, Drink and be Basque."

On January 10, 2004 the Herold Journal-Logan Utah wrote about one Great Pyrenees guard dog in Logan Canyon that was proving that he's a sheep's best friend. Despite hunger and severe cold, the dog stayed with a small flock that was left behind after grazing season and were now snowbound about 100 yards north of U.S. 89 near Beaver Mountain. Great Pyrenees are used by ranchers to protect their herds against attacks by coyotes and other wild animals.

Some felt that the dog was going to die protecting the sheep if somebody did not help. Jim Stone an outfitter, who travels the canyon once or twice a day, began feeding the dog shortly after he first noticed it in October. However, it was getting difficult to get food to the animal because it was too far from the road and the snow was becoming too deep. He feared it would freeze to death or starve, and he was trying to get someone to do something about it.

One local sheep rancher said the situation was not uncommon, and both dog and sheep would be fine. However, the Division of Wildlife Resources and the Cache County Sheriff's Office said they planned on taking action if nothing more than filing animal-neglect charges against the dog's owner. They felt that the dogs posed risks to wildlife and humans, and could end up getting shot or run over by a car. It's a problem they see every year. "You start leaving dogs up there and that causes problems. Let's do something, contact the Humane Society, determine who owns the animals—whatever it takes."

It was suggested that the Search and Rescue Team could use snowmobiles to get to the animals and shoot the dog with a tranquilizer gun. But, the president of the Utah Woolgrowers Association, "said that's unnecessary. There's still forage on the trees for the sheep, and food is being left for the dog. The best thing for people to do is just leave the dog alone and let the owner come get him. People don't understand what's going on." He admitted that he knew the owner but declined to give his name. He said the owner has tried to retrieve the animals, and planned to try again.

One individual was quoted as saying that he couldn't understand how someone would allow the animals to suffer and possibly die. He thinks some "old-school" ranchers had the attitude that a dog and a few sheep aren't worth the effort. "It just really gets me in the heart that somebody would leave that dog there like that," he said. "It's just kind of a sad deal."

According to the Herold Journal, the problem is that Pyrenees guard dogs are very skittish and often difficult to coax. They're very wild dogs and when they're little pups, you never touch them and you never do anything with them. Because of that, they're a little hard to handle. The dog will not leave because its instincts are to protect the sheep. That's what they are bred to do and are wonderful dogs. It's unlikely the dog would harm a human being, but concern was expressed that no one wanted to go up there and fight with the dog in deep snow where the dog could get them. Stone said he had been leaving food by the side of the road once or twice a day, and the dog comes down to retrieve it after he leaves, but he couldn't get within 60 or 70 yards of him. He even left hay for the sheep next to the dog's food and noted that the dog was so smart that it came down to the road and hauled the hay back up to the sheep.2

The Great Pyrenees is an old breed of dog and their fossils have been found around 3000 B.C. where sheep were raised. The American Kennel Club describes the breed as a large, thickly coated, and immensely powerful working dog bred to deter sheep-stealing wolves and other predators on snowy mountaintops. Pyrs today are mellow companions and vigilant guardians of home and family. Frequently described as 'majestic,' Pyrs are big, immensely strong mountain dogs standing as high as 32 inches at the shoulder and often tipping the scales at more than 100 pounds. These steadfast guardians usually exhibit a Zen-like calm, but they can quickly spring into action and move with grace and speed to meet a threat. The lush weatherproof coat is all white, or white with markings of beautiful shades of gray, tan, reddish-brown, or badger.

I noticed when I looked up dog rescues there are numerous adoption groups dedicated to finding homes for the Great Pyrenees. It appears that the main reason for putting them up for adoption is that the beautiful puppy just got too big for the family. I have cared for numerous Great Pyrenees dogs in my practice over the years. I can't remember a behavior incident but most weigh over 100 pounds.

I found this follow up to the story about the Great Pyrenees wintering with the sheep in Logan Canyon Utah.

Elder Gary E. Stevenson wrote this story. "My friend of many years spent his life as a rancher, doing the hard work of raising cattle and sheep in the rugged Rocky Mountains. He once shared with me the challenges and hazards associated with raising sheep. He described that in early spring, when snow on the expansive mountain range had mostly melted, he placed the family herd of approximately 2,000 sheep in the mountains for the summer. There, he watched over the sheep until late fall, when they were moved from the summer range to a winter range in the desert. He described how tending a large flock of sheep was difficult, requiring early days and late nights—waking well before sunrise and finishing long after dark. He could not possibly do it alone. Others helped tend the flock, including a mix of experienced ranch hands assisted by younger hands who were benefiting from the wisdom of their companions. He also relied on two old horses, two colts in training, two old sheepdogs, and two or three sheepdog pups. Over the course of the summer, my friend and his sheep faced wind and rainstorms, sickness, injuries, drought, and just about every other hardship one can imagine. Some years they had to haul water all summer just to keep the sheep alive. Then, every year in late fall, when winter weather threatened and the sheep were taken off the mountain and counted, there were usually more than 200 that were lost.

The flock of 2,000 sheep placed in the mountains in early spring was reduced to less than 1,800. Most of the missing sheep were not lost to sickness or natural death but to predators such as mountain lions or coyotes. These predators usually found the lambs that had strayed from the safety of the flock, withdrawing themselves from the protection of their shepherd.

My shepherd friend shared another important element in the watch care of sheep on the range. He described that lost sheep were particularly vulnerable to the dangers of predators. In fact, up to 15 percent of his and his team's total time was devoted to finding lost sheep. The sooner they found lost sheep, before the sheep drifted too far from the flock, the less likely the sheep were to be harmed. Recovering lost sheep required much patience and discipline.

Some years ago, I found an article in a local newspaper so intriguing that I saved it. The front-page headline read, "Determined Dog Won't Abandon Lost Sheep." This article describes a small number of sheep belonging to an operation not far from my friend's property that were somehow left behind in their summer range. Two or three months later, they became stranded and snowbound in the mountains. When the sheep were left behind, the sheepdog (Great Pyrenees) stayed with them, for it was his duty to look after and protect the sheep. He would not go off watch! There he remained—circling about the lost sheep for months in the cold and snowy weather, serving as a protection against coyotes, mountain lions, or any other predator that would harm the sheep. He stayed there until he was able to lead or herd the sheep back to the safety of the shepherd and the flock.

Who is a shepherd? Every man, woman, and child in the kingdom of God is a shepherd. No calling is required. From the moment we emerge from the waters of baptism, we are commissioned to this work. We reach out in love to others because it is what our Savior commanded us to do. Alma emphasized: "For what shepherd … having many sheep doth not watch over them, that the wolves enter not and devour his flock? … Doth he not drive him out?" Whenever our neighbors are in distress temporally or spiritually, we run to their aid. We bear one another's burdens that they may be light. We mourn with those who mourn. We comfort those who stand in need of comfort. The Lord lovingly expects this of us. And the day will come when we will be held accountable for the care we take in ministering to His flock."3

The prophet Mormon described the Spirit of Christ as one of the most fundamental means God uses to sustain and guide us: "For behold, the *Spirit of Christ* is given to every man, that he may know good from evil; wherefore, I show unto you the way to judge; for everything which inviteth to do good, and to persuade to believe in Christ, is sent forth by the power and gift of Christ; wherefore ye may know with a perfect knowledge it is of God. But whatsoever thing persuadeth men to do evil, and believe not in Christ, and deny him, and serve not God, then ye may know with a perfect knowledge it is of the devil; for after this manner doth the devil work, for he persuadeth no man to do good, no, not one; neither do his angels; neither do they who subject themselves unto him.4

There were many proposals and opinions on how best to save the lost sheep in Logan Canyon during the winter of 2004. It was common knowledge that the longer the sheep remained in the canyon the more vulnerable they were to the dangers of predators and starvation. However, an experienced sheep herder knew the situation well and advised that this was not an uncommon occurrence and if left alone the Great Pyrenees would lead the flock home to safety.

God the Father knows some of His flock gets lost, finding themselves in danger and that the condition is worsening the longer they are unaccounted for—He also knows that each one can be found and led home to safety if they will but follow His son.

1. Her car was a first-generation Chevrolet (though built in partnership with Suzuki Motor) 2,365 pound (our 2011 Ford Explorer weighs 4,732 pounds) small SUV built from 1989 until 1997 under the now extinct GEO brand.

2. Herald Journal-Logan, January 10, 2004, Safe or stranded? John Wright Record Number: 10926085039D86D8.

3. Elder Gary E. Stevenson, Oct 8, 2018, General Conference.

4. Moro. 7:16-17.

16

JONAH SWALLOWED IN THE BELLY OF A WHALE

In February, 1891, the "Star of the East", a whaling ship from Liverpool, England was hunting whales in the South Atlantic near the Falkland Islands. A whale was sighted and two boats sent to kill it. The first boat successfully harpooned the whale, but the whale swam away, dragging the boat for about five miles. Later, the harpooner in the accompanying boat also succeeded in harpooning the whale. Both boats were towed about three miles by the whale, then it "sounded" or went below the surface, then later came back to the surface but in its death throes, capsized one of the whaling boats. All but two crew members were rescued by the other boat and presumed lost at sea.

A few hours later, the now dead whale was lashed to the side of the ship and the crew began the task of cutting it up. When they came to the stomach, they hoisted onto the deck and were shocked to see something moving around inside. They quickly cut the stomach open and found one of the missing sailors, thirty-five year old James Bartley, inside alive, but unconscious. He was soon revived, but for two weeks was delirious. By the end of the third week he had recovered sufficiently to go about his duties again.

The sailor remembered the beginning of his ordeal and being lifted into the air then dropping into the water. After that he said he heard a horrible rushing sound, which he thought might have been the beating of the water by the whale's tail, and then he was enveloped in a terrible darkness and found himself slipping along a smooth passage that seemed to carry him forward. He finally realized he had been swallowed by the whale, and although he tried to be brave, he passed out and didn't remember anything beyond that.

Back in England, Bartley was taken to a London hospital. His skin had been bleached and wrinkled to the appearance of old parchment by the gastric juices of the whale's stomach, and never looked normal again although he enjoyed good health.1

"Bartley did not equal the prophet Jonah in the duration of his ordeal, for Jonah was in the whale's belly 'three days and three nights.' It is rarely mentioned also, that Our Lord Himself corroborated the Jonah story in a passing reference (Matthew, 12:40). Those who, in spite of this, condemn the Biblical tale of Jonah and his whale as 'just another fish story' cannot have heard of James Bartley and his."2

The City of Nineveh: Jonah lived when Nineveh was at the height of her violence and glory. She was proud, powerful, and licentiously wicked. The prophet Nahum (3:1-4) later described the crimes of these people, particularly the way the Assyrians treated those whom they captured: "Woe to the bloody city! It is all full of lies and robbery; the prey departeth not; the noise of a whip, and the noise of the rattling of the wheels, and of the prancing horses, land of the jumping chariots. The horseman lifteth up both the bright sword and the glittering spear: and there is a multitude of slain, and a great number of carcases; and there is none end of the corpses; they stumble upon their corpses: Because of the multitude of the whoredoms of the well-favored harlot, the mistress of witchcrafts, that selleth nations through the whoredoms, and families through her witchcrafts."

Who would dare call such a violent city to repentance? When the Lord told Jonah to go up to Nineveh and "cry against it," the scripture leaves no question as to Jonah's personal reaction. He was absolutely terrified. The map will show that Jonah's mission to Nineveh was toward the east, but to our amazement we discover that Jonah girt up his skirts and begat himself forthwith toward the west. Jonah was running away! Jonah was the first and only prophet on record to actually flee from an assignment. He raced down toward Joppa, the main Mediterranean seaport lying west and a little north of Jerusalem. There he took passage on a freighter destined for the most distant land he could reach—Tarshish! Even at the risk of offending the Lord, he was determined to get himself removed so far from the scene of this awful assignment that the Lord might get someone else to do it. His idea was to get himself out of sight and out of mind—the Lord's mind (Jonah 1:3).

How far Jonah's freighter progressed before a violent storm struck we are not told, but the experienced seamen in charge of the craft knew they were in desperate straits. The force of the smashing hurricane threatened to swamp the ship and rip the timbers apart. The sailors at first thought they could save her by heaving their "wares" overboard so as to "lighten it," but they soon found it was not enough. The fury of the gale became so ferocious that the sailors became afraid that "the ship was like to be broken."

The shipmaster had ordered all his mariners to pray "every man to his own god," but the prophet Jonah did not. For whatever reason he was found by the captain sleeping and the captain cried out, "What meanest thou, O sleeper? Arise, call upon God, if so be that God will think upon us, that we perish not!"

By the time Jonah struggled up on deck the sailors were in the process of drawing lots and Jonah drew lots with them. They felt this storm must be the result of some offense by one of them which had aroused the wrath of that man's god. Ironically, the lot accidentally fell to Jonah and he confessed about the Lord's revelation to him and his missionary call to go to Nineveh. After some discussion they first tried to row to shore and when that failed they cast Jonah into the sea. He wrote, "The waters compassed me about, even to the soul; the depth closed me round about, the weeds were wrapped about my head. I went down to the bottoms of the mountains; the earth with her bars was about me forever."

Then it happened. There was a sudden rushing of water, a monstrous mouth gaped wide, and almost before Jonah could discover what was happening he had been plucked from the water and was slithering down into the gastric cavity of some large sea animal which the Bible says the Lord had "prepared." The book of Jonah says it was a "fish" but Jesus called it a "whale." Jonah said, "Out of the belly of hell cried I," and "when my soul fainted within me I remembered the Lord: and my prayer came in unto thee, into thine holy temple." And, when the timing was right the Bible says, "And the Lord spake unto the fish, and it vomited out Jonah upon the dry land."

Jonah returned to Nineveh, walked "a day's journey" into the labyrinth of this vast human beehive, and cried he: "Yet forty days, and Nineveh shall be overthrown" throughout the city. And, as he did, he must have expected to have some barbarous act preformed on him from such a wicked city. But, "the people of Nineveh believed God, and proclaimed a fast, and put on sackcloth, from the greatest of them even to the least of them."

Even the haughty king listened intently when the message was brought to him. His officers quoted the Hebrew prophet as saying, "Yet forty days, and Nineveh shall be over thrown!" he threw off his vestments and went into mourning with sackcloth and ashes. Then he sent out a decree to all the people. It was an absolute command issued jointly by the king and his nobles.

It declared, "Let man and beast be covered with sackcloth, and cry mightily unto God; yea, let them turn everyone from his evil way, and from the violence that is in their hands. Who can tell if God will turn and repent, and turn away from his fierce anger, that we perish not?"

Jonah removed himself a safe distance from Nineveh and waited the forty days to watch his delivered proclamation to come true. But it didn't happen and Jonah was very disappointed: For "God saw their works, that they turned from their evil way." The Lord therefore resolved to suspend the terrible destruction which He had prepared for them.

And later said to Jonah, "And should I not spare Nineveh the great city, wherein are more than six score thousand persons that cannot discern between their right and their left hand…?" Jonah was only thinking of himself and the wicked men and women in Nineveh—God was thinking about the 120,000 innocent children and their parents that had repented.3

People all over the world, in every culture and clime, pursue greatness. The desire to succeed and excel is as universal as it is natural. But what is true greatness? How do we know when we have achieved it? Some might say that greatness happens in rare, extraordinary moments when someone of unusual ability rises above his or her peers.

Howard W. Hunter, himself a great man and beloved spiritual leader, offered a different definition of greatness when he said, "To do one's best in the face of the commonplace struggles of life—and possibly in the face of failure—and to continue to endure and to persevere in the ongoing difficulties of life when those struggles and tasks contribute to others' progress and happiness, . . . this is true greatness."

In my opinion, Jonah, at least for the moment, looked for other kinds of success, based on worldly praise, reward, and recognition, that are really just an illusion. "Not loud or pretentious, true greatness does not shout from the rooftops or seek attention among the crowds. Most often, true greatness doesn't grab headlines. It's usually quiet, often unseen, and frequently unspoken. And the rewards of true greatness are without price or parallel. They include meaningful relationships, the enduring gratitude of loved ones, and the satisfaction of a life well lived. Long after public applause has died away, true greatness lives forever in every heart it has ever touched."4

Questions have been raised over the years about whether the James Bartley story is true. The diameter of a whale's esophagus is small and felt to be incapable of passing an adult human down into its stomach, the environment of the stomach contains toxic digestive enzymes and there is not a good oxygen supply in a whale's digestive tract. Still, stories have surfaced from time to time confirming that the Bartley encounter did occur.

Julie McSorley relates a true whale of a tale: I live with my husband, Tyrone McSorley, in San Luis Obispo, California, about three miles from the beach. Every few years, the humpback whales come into the bay for a few days while they're migrating. November 2020 was one of those times, so we took out our yellow double kayak to watch the wildlife. We paddled out the length of the pier and saw seals, dolphins, and about 20 whales feeding on silverfish. We were in awe watching these graceful behemoths—each one about 50 feet long—breach and spray though their blowholes. We laughed when they turned their side fins so that it looked as if they were waving at us.

At the time my friend Liz Cottriel was staying with us. The next day, I asked her if she wanted to go out on the water to see them. "No way," said Liz, now 65. She was not an experienced kayaker and was terrified that the kayak would overturn while we were surrounded by hungry whales. "There's nothing to worry about," I assured her. "The craft is stable, and we can turn back anytime." After some cajoling, she finally agreed to join me. I didn't want her to miss this magnificent experience and regret it later.

Liz and I got out on the water at 8:30 the following morning. There were already about 15 other kayakers and paddleboarders in the bay. It was warm for November—about 65 degrees—so we wore T-shirts and leggings. After a half-hour, we had our first whale sighting just past the pier: two humpbacks swimming toward us. How amazing to be that close to a creature that size, I thought as the whales dipped under the waterline.

When whales go down after breaching, they leave what looks like an oil slick on the water. I figured if we paddled toward that spot, we'd be safe from the whales, since they'd just left. We followed them at a distance—or what I thought was a distance. I later found out that it's recommended to keep 300 feet away. We were more like 60 feet away.

Suddenly, we were being pelted. A tightly packed swarm of fish, known as a bait ball, started jumping out of the water into our kayak. Their movement sounded like crackling glass all around us.

What should have been a comical moment was actually terrifying. Their actions meant they were escaping the whales, which meant that we needed to get out of there too. But before we could paddle to safety, our kayak was lifted out of the water about six feet, bracketed by massive jaws. Liz and I slipped out of the kayak into the whale's mouth. My body was ingulfed except for my right arm and paddle. Liz, meanwhile, was looking up directly at the whale's upper jaw, which she later described as a big white wall.

As the whale's mouth closed, Liz thrust her arm up to block it from crushing her. I felt the creature begin to dive and had no idea how deep we'd be dragged. Still, I didn't panic. I just kept thinking, I've got to fight this. I've got to breathe.

Whales have enormous mouths but tiny throats. Anything they can't swallow they spit right out. That included us. As soon as the whale dipped underwater, it ejected us. And we popped back up onto the surface about a foot apart. The entire ordeal lasted only about 10 seconds.

A few kayakers paddled over. One was a retired firefighter, who asked us if we had all of our limbs. "We thought you were dead!" he said.

We were not, of course. But I am much more aware of the power of nature and the ocean than I was before. Liz was shaken up, likening the ordeal to a near-death experience, and she says her whale-watching days are over. But even she had to laugh when she got home that afternoon and realized she'd brought back a souvenir. When she pulled off her shirt, six silverfish flopped out.5

In 1907, new information came out in The Expository Times. A gentleman named A. Lukyn Williams had made some basic inquiries with the hope of getting a statement from the captain of the Star of the East concerning the incident. He found that the Star of the East was a British ship that had sailed from Auckland, N.Z., on December 27, 1890, and had docked in New York on April 17th, 1891, and was commanded by a Captain Killam. On November 27, 1906, the captain's wife wrote to Williams from Yarmouth (Nova Scotia): *"My husband asked me to write. There is not one word of truth in the whole whale story. I was with my husband all the years he was in the Star of the East. There was never a man lost overboard while my husband was in her. The sailor has told a great sea-yarn. I wish, if it is not too much trouble, to send us one of the papers with the yarn in."*

Ironically, the final coffin nail was driven into the Bartley story in 1991... ironic because no one seems to have noticed. Edward B. Davis, associate professor of science and history at Messiah College in Grantham, Pennsylvania, did his own research into the story of James Bartley's survival. He queried the Maritime History Archive at Memorial University in St. John's, Newfoundland, for documents relating to the Star of the East, and received both the captain's full name—John Killam—and a complete listing of the crew members that served on board the ship during the fateful year of 1891... and James Bartley's name wasn't on the roster. Yet still the story is repeated, and people ask if it's true.

In the end, some stories will survive, not because they are true, but because many people think they should be.6

1. *Newspaper, James Bartlett swallowed by whale 1892*
2. *Sir Francis Fox*
3. *The Fourth Thousand Years, W Cleon Skousen, Jonah.*
4. *Howard W. Hunter, Music & the Spoken Word, #4,522, 05-15-2016.*
5. *Reader's Digest, told by Emily Landau, March/April, 2022.*
6. *Anomalyinfo.com, Garth Haslam, James Bartley: The Modern Jonah.*

17

CAN DOGS SHOW LOVE?

Humans don't question their ability to love their dogs. We feed and exercise them, set our schedules based on their needs, get up with them in the middle of the night, buy them silly toys, and tell them our deepest secrets. They are there to greet us at the door whenever we come home and never seem to have a bad day. Even if they have soiled or ripped up your house they may great you with complete submissiveness and the look of shame on their face but still are in hopes that you will forgive their behavior quickly so they can get on with how glad they are that you have opened the door.1

Dogs often get treats as rewards. A new experiment shows that dogs who get fed, when given the chance to reciprocate, usually won't pay their owners back with food. The rapport started with our ancestor's sharing food with wolves, and today, we show our love to our canine pets with treats and train them with goodies as motivation. However, close the bond is between humans and dogs, though, food sharing may just be a one-way street: Dogs don't seem to pay back the hand that feeds them.

That lack of reciprocated food sharing in dogs is the key finding of a study published in 2021 by dog researcher Jim McGetrick and his team who found that in lab experiments, dogs who received treats by humans pushing a button didn't then return the favor by pushing the same button so humans gained a treat in kind.

"In terms of dog domestication and the evolution of dogs as a species, their cooperativeness with humans might not be related to this form of cooperation where I help you and then you help me at some point in the future. Previous studies have observed that dogs repay other generous dogs with food tit-for-tat, and take the initiative to rescue distressed humans from entrapment. The current study is the first to look at whether fed dogs would reward food to beneficent humans.

To probe this question, the researchers trained 37 pet dogs to press a button for food from a dispenser. These dogs came from over ten different breeds and mixes, with diverse idiosyncrasies to match. Some dogs were gentle, laying their paws delicately on the button and nibbling their reward. Other dogs mauled the button and chewed on the box that enclosed it. One dog only pressed the button with its hind leg.

Once each dog associated the button with food, the button was placed in an adjacent room with a human stranger inside. The dog would remain in a different room with the food dispenser. A wire mesh fence separated the two rooms and the dog could observe the human controlling the coveted button. A helpful human would press the button and the dog would receive food and if the unhelpful human pushed button would not release food.

When the dogs didn't get food in a situation where they expected to get food they whined, made a fuss and looked effectively like they were throwing a tantrum.

The researchers then reversed the situations. The working button was transferred to the room with the dog, and the food dispenser filled with chocolate candy replacing the kibble was relocated to the human's room. This time, the dogs weren't nearly so eager to press the button in their room when the food ended up with the human next door. Moreover, when it came to reciprocating the helpful human who had previously fed the dog via the button or the unhelpful one who had refused, the dogs didn't seem to distinguish between the two. The dogs pushed the button equally for both groups.

Moreover, after each button-pressing experiment, the dogs and humans had the chance to interact with each other. The dogs didn't seem to hold the volunteers' unhelpfulness against them. They approached the volunteers equally, whether the humans had been helpful or not. The dogs did not seem to hold a grudge or show any signs of gratitude or reciprocity towards the humans that pushed the button for food.

Jeffrey Stevens, a psychology researcher at the University of Nebraska-Lincoln who wasn't involved in the study, said there are still studies that need to address the key thing of whether they were asking the question in the right way. Dogs have a completely different world than we do. For example, dogs perceive their environment mainly with their sense of smell rather than their sight.2

For years scientists and animal behaviorists have researched whether our dogs have the ability to return our love. Are we being anthropomorphic (having human characteristics) when we interpret our dogs' behavior in human terms of love? The reason I got started researching whether a dog can show love or not was because my wife mentioned that our dog BeBe loves me more than her. I told her that BeBe has no idea what love is. I suddenly was focused on whether a dog really can show love and why or why not it has that ability.

In a genetic study conducted at Duke University, scientists compared how wolf pups and dog pups responded to humans. They took young wolf pups away from their mothers and litters and raised them in human homes. The dog pups had very little human contact while they stayed with their mother and littermates. When they observed all the pups' responses to people, the dog puppies were much more likely to be attracted and make eye contact. The researchers concluded that "dog puppies are more attracted to humans, read human gestures more skillfully, and make more eye contact with humans than wolf puppies do."

Another study focused on the tendency of our dogs to stare right into our eyes, communicating love and devotion. Wolves will not look humans in the eye. Researchers found that during domestication, dogs developed a facial muscle that enables them to raise the inner eyebrow intensely. The theory is that this muscle developed from dogs' motivation to establish eye contact with humans - something they do especially when they need help solving a problem or need to know when communication from humans is directed at them.

Since dog's brains are highly dependent on their remarkable sense of smell to evaluate the world around them, animal cognition scientists at Emory University decided to measure the canine brain's response to the smell of familiar and unfamiliar people and dogs. They taught their subjects to lie still in magnetic resonance imaging (MRI) machines, so they could observe the dogs' reactions to five different scents.

When these dogs smelled the odor of their owners, as compared to other odors, the caudate nucleus (known as the reward center of the brain) showed activation. "This provides important clues about the importance of humans in dogs' lives," the researchers concluded.

Another study of canine and human brain responses, conducted at Eotvos Lorand University in Budapest, focused on sounds made by humans and dogs. The scientists observed that human and dog brains react similarly to emotion-laden sounds. For example, happy sounds light up the same area of the brain—the auditory cortex—in both. These similar reactions seem to indicate a strong ability to communicate types of emotions across species.

Oxytocin, known as the love hormone, is present when humans and animals interact. University of Tokyo scientists studied the role of oxytocin in a dog's brain as an influence on social interactions with humans and with other dogs. They found evidence that oxytocin enhances social motivation in dogs to approach and interact with their dog partners (picture Lady and the Tramp) and their human partners.

Researchers in Sweden also studied oxytocin levels in dogs and their owners. They observed that dogs and their owners responded in similar ways to their interactions, such as petting, regarding oxytocin levels. Calm, anti-stress behaviors in the human caused a similar response in the dog.

They concluded that "the owners and the dogs could mutually sense the other's emotional state based on an increased ability to read the other's behavioral cues . . . oxytocin can facilitate and stimulate friendly social interactions, induce anti-stress effects, and increase trust."[1]

Mary Temple Grandin (born August 29, 1947) is an American scientist, academic and animal behaviorist. She is a prominent proponent for the humane treatment of livestock for slaughter and the author of more than 60 scientific papers on animal behavior. Grandin is a consultant to the livestock industry, where she offers advice on animal behavior, and is also an autism spokesperson.

Grandin is one of the first autistic people to document the insights she gained from her personal experience of autism. She is currently a faculty member with Animal Sciences in the College of Agricultural Sciences at Colorado State University.

Being autistic Dr. Grandin has given great insight into the emotions of animals compared to humans. In her book *Animals in Translation* she comments, "the main difference between animal emotions and human's emotions is that animals don't have mixed emotions the way normal people do. Animals aren't ambivalent (having mixed feelings or contradictory ideas about something or someone); they don't have love-hate relationships with each other or with people. That's one of the reasons humans love animals so much; animals are loyal. If an animal loves you he loves you no matter what. He doesn't care what you look like or how much money you make.

This is another connection between autism and animals; autistic people have mostly simple emotions, too. That's why normal people describe us as innocent. An autistic person's feelings are direct and open, just like animal feelings. We don't hide our feelings, and we aren't ambivalent. I can't imagine what it would be like to have feelings of love and hate for the same person.

Some people will probably think this is an insulting thing to say about autistic people, but one thing I appreciate about being autistic is that I don't have to deal with all the emotional craziness my students do. I had one fantastic student who flunked out of school because she broke up with her boyfriend. There's so much psychodrama in normal people's lives. Animals never have psychodrama.

Children don't, either. Emotionally, children are more like animals and autistic people, because children's frontal lobes are still growing and don't mature until sometime in early adulthood. I mentioned earlier that the frontal lobes are one big association cortex, trying everything together, including emotions like love and hate that would probably be better off staying separate. That's another reason why a dog can be like a person's child: children's emotions are straightforward and loyal like a dog's. A seven-year-old boy or girl will race through the house to greet Dad when he comes from work the same way a dog will. I think animal, children, and autistic people have simpler emotions because their brains have less ability to make connections, so their emotions stay more separate and compartmentalized."3

I remember my youngest daughter Kara always running like my dog to the front door when I came home from work. She would jump into my arms and welcome me home. The reason I remember this is because these special moments became less special as she gained weight and it was difficult for me to hold her. Running to daddy stopped about the age Dr. Grandin mentioned and even though physically I was relieved, I to this day miss those special moments coming home from work and her response as I walked through door.

My son Brad and his new wife lived in our home for a short time. Jill would be waiting for Brad every night near the front door when he came home from work for what seemed like a couple of weeks. Then the greetings came from her sitting in the living room couch and shortly thereafter Brad would come in the door and call out, "Jill I'm home" to locate her presence.

Clive Wynne, a psychologist and founder of the Canine Science Collaboratory at Arizona State University, is the author of a book called *Dog Is Love: Why and How Your Dog Loves You*. Wynne writes about research conducted in his laboratory, as well as other studies that focus on the affectionate nature of dogs. In an interview in The Washington Post, when asked whether his dog Xephos loves him, he said: "I know that sometimes Xephos just wants dinner. But I'm pretty convinced that that's not the whole picture. She really does feel a bond, a connection toward me that's as real as any other connection that any other individual in my life might feel toward me. I'm not saying human and dog love are identical. I'm just saying there's enough similarity between how dogs form strong emotional bonds and how people form strong emotional bonds that it's fair enough to use the love word."

What have we learned:

*Dogs do not seem to hold a grudge or show any signs of gratitude or reciprocity towards the humans that feed them.

*Dog puppies are much more attracted to humans and adjust better than wolf puppies.

*Human and dog brains react similarly to the love hormone oxytocin levels, emotion-laden sounds, and dogs and their owners respond in similar ways to their interactions such as petting. Calm, anti-stress behaviors in the human causes a similar response in the dog.

*Animals aren't ambivalent (having mixed feelings or contradictory ideas about something or someone); they don't have love-hate relationships with each other or with people. That's one of the reasons humans love animals so much; animals are loyal. If an animal loves you, he loves you no matter what. He doesn't care what you look like or how much money you make.

*Emotionally, children are more like animals and autistic people.

Research findings may or may not tell you whether dogs are capable of feeling the strong emotion of love, but the answer for every dog owner lies in your own personal definition of love. Is love defined as a strong bond, a show of affection, the desire to be with you always?

Does my dog offer real love? Does yours? The answer lies in the happiness your dog brings you. Author Carolyn Knapp summed up my answer to the question in her book "Pack of Two": "Before you get a dog, you can't quite imagine what living with one might be like; afterward, you can't imagine living any other way."1

In conclusion I'm happy that the research and discussions have points that make my wife and me right in our own ways. We can continue pursing our Love relationship and not mess up our lives with any Hateful thoughts about who is right. And BeBe can continue confusing us as to which one she likes the most as if she ever thinks about it.

1. *American Kennel Club, Do Our Dogs Really Love Us?, By Harriet Meyers, Feb 10, 2022.*
2. *Dogs fail to reciprocate the receipt of food from a human in a food-giving task, Jim McGetrick et al, PLOS, Published: July 14, 2021.*
3. *Animals in Translation, Temple Grandin, Pg 88-89, 2005.*

18

PLACEBO EFFECT

Elisha Perkins (January 16, 1741—September 6, 1799) was a United States physician who created a fraudulent medical device, the "Perkins Patent Tractors". Although they were made of steel and brass, Perkins claimed that they were made of unusual metal alloys. Perkins claimed his rods cured inflammation, rheumatism and pain in the head and the face; he applied the points on the aching body part and passed them over the part for about 20 minutes. Perkins claimed they could "draw off the noxious electrical fluid that lay at the root of suffering"

Perkins was born in Norwich, Connecticut. He was educated by his father Joseph Perkins in Plainfield, Connecticut, where he later practiced medicine with success. When the American Revolutionary War broke out, Elisha Perkins served as a surgeon for the Continental Army during the Battle of Bunker Hill in the Siege of Boston. During the late 18th century, the progression of medicine due to the

Enlightenment increased the consumer demand for new therapies, such as therapeutic devices and inventions. Consequently, around 1795–96, Perkins invented his

"Tractors", for which he took out a 14-year patent on February 19, 1796. The tractors consisted of two 3-inch metal rods with a pointed end; the term is from the old meaning of tractor, "that which pulls", as in the term "tractor beams". Perkins claimed they could "draw off the noxious electrical fluid that lay at the root of suffering". The device was later the subject of the first placebo research.1

Elisha Perkins healing process with "Tractors" reminds me of a deep tissue penetrating laser light procedure that is described by the manufacturer as, "the problem-solver for your veterinarian team that is fast-acting and versatile. This doctor-prescribed, technician-driven modality effectively treats a wide variety of conditions including pre-surgical, post-surgical, acute, and chronic disease states. Photobiomodulation (PBM) therapy results are achieved when a sufficient dose of light energy reaches target tissue and results in decreased inflammation, decreased pain, and accelerated healing."

Specific conditions recommended for its use are infections, sprains and strains, dental procedures, post-surgical, inflammation, osteoarthritis, degenerative joint disease, inflammatory bowel disease, fractures, wounds and lick granulomas.

My son and I attended a presentation on the mode of action PBM has on the tissues of the body and tried it out on an experimental basis. We had the technicians use the light energy on surgical incisions and report back if they felt the wounds healed quicker and if there were less post op complications.

They reported positive results, we purchased a machine and now after each surgical procedure (except cancer or eye), protective dark glasses are placed on the tech and the light beam with the correct energy setting and prescribed length of time is directed on the area.

Trusting the manufacturer, the observations of our hospital staff and feedback from clients of pets receiving the therapy -we also use it for other recommended procedures.

Perkin's invention also makes me think about my childhood where my friends and I would place the forked end of a stick in our hands, pass the end of the stick (Tractor) along the ground (dowsing) and quivering and shaking the stick pretending to find water under the ground. Were we imagination playing or copying a scientific principle?

Wherever the line blurs, you're bound to find contentious debates. One of the longest-running of these disagreements center on dowsing, a supposed sixth sense that enables people to find underground water using a forked branch, pendulum or pair of bent wires (Tractors). There is no scientific reason why dowsing should work. Yet, many believe that it apparently works well enough and reliably enough to keep the practice alive.

Dowsing originated in ancient times, when it was treated as a form of divination (the practice of seeking knowledge of the future or the unknown by supernatural means). The Catholic Church, however, banned the practice completely. Reformer Martin Luther perpetuated the Catholic ban, in 1518 listing divining for metals as an act that broke the first commandment (i.e., as occultism).

Old texts about searching for water do not mention using the divining twig, and the first account of this practice was in 1568. Sir William F. Barrett wrote in his 1911 book Psychical Research that: ...in a recent admirable Life of St.

Teresa of Spain, the following incident is narrated: Teresa in 1568 was offered the site for a convent to which there was only one objection, there was no water supply; happily, a Friar Antonio came up with a twig in his hand, stopped at a certain spot and appeared to be making the sign of the cross; but Teresa says, "Really I cannot be sure if it were the sign he made, at any rate he made some movement with the twig and then he said, 'Dig just here'; they dug, and lo! a plentiful fount of water gushed forth, excellent for 'drinking, copious for washing, and it never ran dry." " As the writer of this Life remarks: "Teresa, not having heard of dowsing, has no explanation for this event", and regarded it as a miracle. This, I believe, is the first historical reference to dowsing for water.2

The professed modern-day prophet, Joseph Smith and his contemporaries, believed in supernatural entities with real power? And so does every Christian, Jew, or Muslim who believes in God, angels, and divine power to reveal, heal, etc. However, to label these beliefs as "magic" is to beg the question—to argue that Joseph believed in and sought help from powers besides God. Nobody disputes that Joseph and his family believed in the Bible, which condemns divination and witchcraft:

"There shall not be found among you any one that maketh his son or his daughter to pass through the fire, or that useth divination, or an observer of times, or an enchanter, or a witch." *Deuteronomy 18:10*

Therefore, Joseph and his family viewed folk magic and the use of seer stones as not falling under this Biblical condemnation. It is clear that Joseph and his contemporaries believed that one could gain knowledge from such activities as dowsing [using a rod (Tractor) to find water, ore, or buried treasure] and the use of the seer stones. This does not mean, however, that Joseph understood such activities to be a form of magic.

In Joseph's time, the power of (for example) dowsing was seen as a manifestation of "how the world worked." An article published in 1825 described how the downward bob of a divining rode "closely resembles the dip of the magnetic needle, when traversing a bed or ore." A journal of science reported the idea that "the rod is influenced by ores."

An early British dowser denounced the idea that dowsing for ore was based on magic. "It [the rod] guided me to the orifice of a lead mine. [The rod is] of kin to the Load-stone [magnet], drawing Iron to it by a secret virtue, inbred by nature, and not by any conjuration as some have fondly imagined."

Using a divining rod (Tractor) was seen in these examples as a manifestation of natural law, and requiring the grace of God to operate. Thus, divining was seen in these examples as a manifestation of natural law. Just as one might use a compass or lode-stone to find true north, without understanding the principles or mathematics of magnetism which underlay it, so one could use dowsing as a tool, without understanding the principles by which it operated.

It is further clear that those who used divinization by rods, for example, believed that the rod's natural ability also required the grace of God to operate. Hence, practitioners would consecrate their rods, and pray to God to bless their efforts. Of such matters, Oliver Cowdery was told in an early revelation, "without faith you can do nothing." Like any natural ability, Joseph believed that the gift and tools of seership (in the broader sense) could be misused. As he told Brigham Young, "most...who do find [a seer stone] make an evil use of it." And, Emma Smith's hostile brother Alvah would later remember that Joseph told him, "His gift in seeing with a [seer] stone and hat, was a gift from God."3

Was Joseph Smith's dowsing activities with "tractors" science, science fiction, a sixth sense or was he visited by aliens (influenced by spirits or God)?

The success of dowsers doesn't surprise the people who know the most about finding underground water, hydrogeologists for the United States Geological Survey (USGS). They point out that the United States is so water-rich you can get wet drilling just about anywhere, if you drill deep enough. Far harsher criticism of dowsing and dowsers using (Tractors) comes from outside the mainstream scientific community. Two organizations, the Committee for the Scientific Investigation of Claims of the Paranormal (CSICOP), and the James Randi Educational Foundation (JREF), are actually working to discourage the practice, which they both dismiss as paranormal nonsense. To make their point that dowsing is a sham each has staged demonstrations in which dowsers were asked to find buried pipes. Dowsers did no better than the laws of chance predict. JREF is so confident of its position it promises to pay $1.1 million to anyone who can "prove" dowsing works.

Dowsers don't let the skeptics get them down. In fact, the ranks of dowsers have been steadily growing, the American Society of Dowsers (ASD) has about 4200 members, and there is a 16th century drawing of men wearing traditional miners' clothing holding the same type of forked stick in use by many dowsers today.

There is a massive set of data that suggests there may be some validity to dowsers' claims. The encouraging words are contained in a study financed by the German government and published in the Journal Of Scientific Exploration, which is a peer-reviewed scientific journal published at Stanford University.

The project was conducted in the hope of finding cheaper and more reliable ways of locating drinking water supplies in Third World countries. Researchers analyzed the successes and failures of dowsers in attempting to locate water at more than 2000 sites in arid regions of Sri Lanka, Zaire, Kenya, Namibia and Yemen over a 10-year period.

To do this, researchers teamed geological experts with experienced dowsers and then set up a scientific study group to evaluate the results. Drill crews guided by dowsers didn't hit water every time, but their success rate was impressive. In Sri Lanka, for example, they drilled 691 holes and had an overall success rate of 96 percent. In hundreds of cases the dowsers were able to predict the depth of the water source and the yield of the well to within 10 percent or 20 percent. Carefully considered statistics of these correlations far exceeded lucky guesses.

What's more, virtually all of the sites in Sri Lanka were in regions where the odds of finding water by random drilling were extremely low. As for a USGS notion that dowsers get subtle clues from the landscape and geology, it was pointed out that the underground sources were often more than 100 ft. deep and so narrow that misplacing the drill only a few feet would mean digging a dry hole.

As impressive as this success rate may seem, it doesn't do much to change the minds of skeptics. Their anticipating this criticism, the German researchers matched their field work with laboratory experiments in which they had dowsers attempt to locate water-filled pipes inside a building. The tests were similar to those conducted by CSICOP and JREF, and similarly discouraging.

Skeptics see the poor showing as evidence of failure. Researchers see the discrepancy as an important clue. They suspect that subtle electromagnetic gradients may result when natural fissures and water flows create changes in the electrical properties of rock and soil. Dowsers, it's theorized, somehow sense these gradients and unconsciously respond by wagging their forked sticks, pendulums or bent wires.

There is ample evidence that humans can detect small amounts of energy. All creatures with eyes can detect extremely small amounts of electromagnetic energy at visible light wavelengths. Some researchers believe the dark-adapted human eye can detect a single photon, the smallest measurable quantity of energy. Biologists also have found nonvisual electric and magnetic sensing organs in creatures from bacteria to sharks, fish and birds. Physiologists, however, have yet to find comparable structures in humans.

Results confirm from the study two things that they believe are certain: After 10 years of field research, a combination of dowsing and modern techniques can be both more successful, and far less expensive, than had been thought."4

In science fiction, "tractor beams" and pressor beams can be used together as a weapon: by attracting one side of an enemy spaceship while repelling the other, one can create severely damaging shear effects in its hull. Another mode of destructive use of such beams is rapid alternating between pressing and pulling force in order to cause structural damage to the ship as well as inflicting lethal forces on its crew.

Two objects being brought together by a "tractor beam" are usually attracted toward their common center of gravity. This means that if a small spaceship applies a "tractor beam" to a large object such as a planet, the ship will be drawn toward the planet, rather than vice versa.

In Star Trek, "tractor beams" are imagined to work by placing a target in the focus of a subspace/graviton interference pattern created by two beams from an emitter. When the beams are manipulated correctly the target is drawn along with the interference pattern. The target may be moved toward or away from the emitter by changing the polarity of the beams. Range of the beam affects the maximum mass that can be moved by the emitter, and the emitter subjects its anchoring structure to significant force.2

The Connecticut Medical Society (CMS) condemned the "tractors" as "delusive quackery", and expelled Perkins from membership on the grounds that he was "a patentee and user of nostrums". Perkins nevertheless managed to convince three US medical faculties that his method worked.

In Copenhagen, Denmark, twelve surgeons at the royal Frederik's Hospital also began to support the method. Even George Washington is said to have bought a set. Other physicians' criticisms were met with charges of elitism and professional arrogance. Perkins boasted of 5,000 cured cases. The cures were certified to by eight professors, forty physicians, and thirty clergymen. Of the purchase made by Washington, Perkins' son, Benjamin Perkins, said that the "President of the United States, convinced of the importance of the discovery from experiments in his own family, availed himself of its advantages by purchasing a set of the 'Tractors' for their use."1,2

What the CMS did was probably taking proper action against Elisha Perkins and expelling him from their membership—but missed recognizing his important contribution to medicine known as the placebo effect. The placebo effect is when a person's physical or mental health appears to improve after taking a placebo or 'dummy' treatment. Placebo is Latin for 'I will please' and refers to a treatment or an event that appears real, but is not designed to have any therapeutic benefit.

During World War II, Henry Beecher, MD, a Harvard-trained anesthesiologist, ran out of morphine to use for anesthesia. He turned to a placebo and began injecting patients with saline instead. That simple salt water worked well enough for him to perform surgery on many of his patients. The reason? They believed it would.

The placebo effect is a phenomenon in which patients can take a nonmedical substance, whether it's a saline injection or a sugar pill, and experience a positive response. In 1955, Dr. Beecher estimated that 35 percent of any treatment success was due to the placebo effect. Today, we know that the response rate ranges from 26 to 50 percent, and depends on several factors.

In a review published in 2017 in the journal Annual Review of Clinical Psychology, it was shown that the more bells and whistles attached to a placebo, the higher the effect. For example, placebo acupuncture was more powerful for relieving pain than a placebo pill, and as powerful as actual acupuncture. In the review, placebo pills and injections had about a 26 percent placebo response, placebo acupuncture had a 38 percent response, and placebo surgery had a 50 percent response.

Placebos work best in diseases with symptoms like pain, itching, or fatigue and less well on symptoms like high blood pressure, fever, or abnormal heart rate. A placebo may not stop a tumor from growing, but it can help reduce pain and the side effects of cancer treatment. Mental health disorders respond very well to placebos, especially anxiety, panic attacks, and depression. A possible explanation is that the anticipation of an effect boosts dopamine, which can decrease depression and anxiety.

A review of 215 studies that was published in the journal Pain found that up to 75 percent of any pain treatment is due to the placebo effect. Getting a placebo from a trusted health-care provider also makes any placebo more powerful.

The gold standard to determine the safety and effectiveness of a new treatment or medication is to use a randomized, placebo-controlled trial in which one group of volunteers is randomly assigned to a placebo group and the other is assigned to a real treatment group. Neither group knows if they are getting the treatment or the placebo. The placebo response is generated solely by the patient. Anything beyond that response is attributed to the new medication or treatment.

New research, however, is complicated by the growing power of the placebo response. More patients in placebo groups are experiencing symptom relief than ever before, which makes the active treatments in the study appear to be less effective by comparison.

A study published in the journal Pain reported that, in 1996, clinical trial participants reported a 27 percent difference between the effectiveness of placebo and active drugs. In 2013, the difference was just 9 percent.

Interestingly, this association is seen only in the United States. There are two possible explanations: First, American drug trials tend to be larger, longer, and have more clinical staff interacting with study participants. Both factors—complexity and relationships with health-care providers—have been shown to increase the placebo effect. In addition, the United States is the only country that allows pharmaceutical companies to market their products directly to patients, so patients may be primed by advertising to expect greater benefits.5

According to David Ramey, DVM, one of the occasional arguments used in support of "alternative" approaches to human medicine is the observation that since "alternative" medicine is used (with true or reliable success) in animals, and animals don't know anything about the treatment that they're getting, then one must assume that the treatment works." Of course, the fallacy of such an observation is pretty obvious to anyone with a logical/skeptical frame of mind, because it assumes that the therapies do work (even though there's little evidence of that).

Clearly, however, some people perceive that the therapies work, including veterinarians—there are veterinary acupuncturists, chiropractors, homeopaths, etc., etc. Since there's very little scientific support for the idea that the therapies actually have any clinically significant effect on biological processes, including the processes that result in disease, questions arise as to whether there are other effects of "alternative" treatments on animals. Specifically, people may wonder whether or not animals can benefit from placebo effects.

Regardless, whether or not placebo effects exist in human medicine, there is little evidence that they exist in animals. In general, for a placebo response to occur, it would require that the patient being treated recognizes that there is an intentional effort to treat. Animals would appear to lack the ability to comprehend such intentions (other than they may not like a particular intervention). As such, animals would not be able to participate in placebo-generating experiences. So, for example, one couldn't rationally suggest to a dog that a particular therapy might help it get better, or that it was beneficial because it was "natural;" one presumably wouldn't be able to let a horse know that a particular therapy might give it a window of hope for recovery. They just wouldn't understand.

Still, there are many explanations for how a placebo-like effect might be explained in animals. Take conditioning. Conditioning theory proposes that bodily changes result following exposure to a stimulus that previously produced that change. This is perhaps the most intuitively acceptable explanation for any placebo effects in animals. Indeed, animal studies support such a model for placebo effects, starting with the first descriptions on salivating dogs by Pavlov. Both human and animal studies support the idea that conditioning forms some basis for placebo responses. Since conditioning requires learning, it would be expected that repeated visits to a practitioner might increase the strength of the association between a learned stimuli and response in animals, good or bad. There are numerous examples of dogs shaking in fear when being taken into a veterinary clinic; on the other hand, a dog that enjoyed being handled in a soothing environment might appear to receive some relief from a chronic condition; as it learned to associate its visits with the comforting handling, conditioning effects could occur. This could certainly serve as reasonable explanations for purported placebo effects in animals. Nevertheless, the hypothesis that a healing or therapeutic effect can be dependably provoked as a result of conditioning cannot be supported at this time by any evidence.

Expectancy theory proposes that bodily changes may occur to the extent that the person receiving the therapy expects them to. There is considerable overlap between expectancy and conditioning, because learning is one of the major ways that expectancies are formed. To the extent that therapies are expected to provide relief from disease, or at least provide the client and/or veterinarian with a feeling of control over the disease process, they may alleviate adverse mental states (in the humans). Certainly, in humans, therapies that help restore patient control may evoke therapeutic effects, at least short term, but studies that investigate the expectancy model in animals have so far not been performed. Still, if animals were able to form an association between treatment-related signals (the attention and handling received, the way that the owner behaves towards the animal when it is receiving treatment) and the relief of its distress, expectancies of treatment effects might develop (on the part of both animal and owner).

There is a good body of research that demonstrates that human contact has measurable effects on animals. For example, petting by humans reduces heart rates in dogs and horses and causes major vascular changes in dogs. Gentle handling increases productivity in dairy heifers and increases reproductive efficiency in sows. Thus, it is plausible that human-animal contact might play an important role in the observed responses to therapeutic interventions.

To take an "alternative" example, it has been shown that a single acupuncture treatment is as effective as petting a horse, when it comes to relief of signs of chronic airway disease; that is, there's no demonstrable effect of acupuncture beyond simple handling. On the other hand, handling may also be stressful to animals, so responses to handling may not necessarily be beneficial. Still, there's no question that human contact can invoke responses from animals and animals may behave quite differently when they are not being observed; those shouldn't be confused with placebo-effects, however.

The reported intensity of subjective symptoms such as pain, fatigue, and depressed mood in an animal may vary over time for all sorts of reasons, not all of which have to do with actual changes in symptom severity. Further complicating such analyses are treatment effects that might exist on the part of both the animal owner, as well as the veterinarian with a personal investment in an "alternative" approach.

Client expectations can be very powerful motivators. Having participated in a therapeutic transaction, clients generally expect to see some results. Optimistic owners may be more likely to diligently pursue treatments. Even failing obvious results, normal reciprocal responses often result in clients reporting improvement, at least initially, even when no improvement has occurred. At the very least, veterinarians can help clients understand what problems are occurring in the animal—such comfort and reassurance may make a problem easier for the client to deal with. That's a good thing, mostly, unless the veterinarian steers the client into areas that are unsupported by evidence.

Good veterinary care should include a healthy dose of understanding and compassion, and veterinarians should be interested in proven effective care. However, there's no evidence whatsoever that animals can benefit from, or even experience, placebo effects. Indeed, when doctors claim effectiveness for a treatment beyond the evidence in the belief that they are doing the patient a favor by inducing a "placebo effect" to the animal's supposed benefit, they are abusing three trusted roles: expert, authority figure, and comforter.6

I might add to Dr. Ramey's comments on the placebo ('I will please') effect in animals. In my experience one placebo effect that often pleases my clients and results in a patient's improvement or cure: "Is there a glimmer of hope that the passage of time will bring relief? Hold on to that. Deal with what you must in the present, but rest in the peace that the tincture of time has an amazingly good track record of salving wounds." *Beyourself-blog, 2016*.

Client loyalty is often used to expand a business by taking advantage of the placebo effect. Through endorsements or testimonials clients are projecting to others the Latin meaning of placebo, 'I will please'.

Have you ever given someone a testimonial? Did they use it on their website? Don't you feel honored and appreciated? Giving a testimonial increases your emotional bond with that business and with the person who asked. Imagine the results of making every one of your clients feel appreciated.

This is why you want to ask for a testimonial every time someone thanks you. It's not about getting enough testimonials, it's about making those who appreciate you feel appreciated by you. Turn thankful clients into loyal, raving fans.

Recommending someone can be awkward—we may not know the right things to say. It's a mental roadblock. It's just easier to keep our mouth shut than to feel uncomfortable. However, when someone raves about you, they're mouthing the words. Those kind words about you will spill out more easily at the next opportunity to do so. What's the Golden Rule of referrals? The more you rave about others, the more others will rave about you.

You should ask for permission before showcasing a customer's testimonial. And you should also be sure to give them credit? When clients give you a testimonial, they won't use your carefully crafted corporate words. They'll talk like normal people. They'll express your unique selling proposition and distinctive value prop in everyday language.

Sometimes feedback isn't 100% positive. Or maybe the testimonial mentions something that you'd prefer not to highlight. Either way, collecting feedback is a great learning experience.

If you're the business owner, ask your clients to give a testimonial about your staff. You will look honorable to your client, and it's a great way of appreciating others. Showcasing staff compliments on your website is a win-win-win. Testimonials about your workplace also help with HR recruitment.

Testimonials are more productive when shared by raving fans. Social media seems tailor-made for this. It's fantastic to see testimonials about you on someone else's social media. Moreover, their friends, family and colleagues will see them raving about you. That's proactive word-of-mouth marketing! Blogs are engineered to boost your search engine optimization (SEO).7

Seeking client loyalty testimonials about how good you are can be tricky. Deep inside you know how good your business is. Are you asking others to promote the placebo effect "I will please" when things are not as they seem to that client? There are also legal ramifications if you or a client get caught projecting something being too good and not true.

The Federal Trade Commission (FTC) has the power to stop and penalize parties "using unfair or deceptive acts or practices in or affecting commerce." This makes it a crime to break official rules imposed by the FTC. And the FTC forbids the use of fake testimonials.

Dozens of FTC documents explain the details of "misleading advertisements," but it boils down to a simple Truth in Advertising statement; "When consumers see or hear an advertisement, whether it's on the Internet, radio or television, or anywhere else, federal law says that ad must be truthful, not misleading." The FTC had made a number of guides explaining how truth in advertising works in different situations, but fake testimonials are actually illegal under Section 5 of the FTC Act (15 USC 45).

Fake testimonials are considered false or deceptive advertising—and therefore against the law—for several reasons. First, they are not based on a real customer's experience, which a testimonial must be. Second, it misleads the customer. Claiming a happy customer exists when they don't is misleading in itself, but whatever the fake testimonial claims is also misleading. Third, it encourages customers to spend money on a product or service they otherwise might not, thereby financially defrauding the customer, which is an especially notable offense for the FTC.

Fake Testimonials are illegal on Third-Party Websites. Reviews and testimonials on sites like Google, Yelp, and Amazon can go a long way towards increasing a businesses' popularity. Some business owners have been tempted to create false reviews on these sites. Not only is this practice forbidden by the FTC, but these websites also take a hard stance against it. Fake reviews decrease the overall reputation of the site itself and make users less likely to trust it. For this reason, among others, every major review site, including Google, Amazon, Yelp, TripAdvisor, and others, have all clearly stated that reviews must be true statements by real customers.

Social media has become a prominent tool for marketing. This includes sharing reviews and testimonials. With the ease of sharing information to be seen by millions, social media may seem like the go-to place to create fake testimonials or reviews. However, the FTC's rules still apply here and expressly forbid fake testimonials, reviews, and endorsements on social media.

Recently, the FTC sent a notice of penalty to more than 700 companies, including Amazon.com Inc. and Facebook Inc, for fake reviews and misleading endorsements online. There is a fine line between authentic content and advertising when it comes to social media. This has led to an increase in deceptive endorsements across various social platforms.8

It's not a new idea in marketing; celebrity endorsements sell products. And while not all brands subscribe to the celebrity endorsement theory, it's based in pretty simple logic. People idolize celebrities, so when famous people are seen in advertisements promoting a new product, audiences are prompted to buy that product, either subliminally or directly.

According to Ad Age, a brand that inks an endorsement contract with a celebrity or an athlete can see their stock rise up to .25 as soon as the news is made public. This represents an increase in perceived legitimacy from the celebrity's endorsement, even though the product has not changed at all.

The same article claims that on average, audiences are exposed to some 3,000 advertisements today across all media, leading to an element of marketing overexposure. Studies have shown that advertisements that use a celebrity, about whom many people already have positive feelings and impulses, grab an audience's attention more easily than a standard ad.

It seems obvious, but in order for their impact to be shown, endorsements have to have a similar target audience that the "influencer" has to begin with. As Convince and

Convert notes, using celebrities or athletes to promote something that their audience has little interest in will not produce a big marketing splash.9

We are being bombarded 24/7 by placebo promises intended to please ("I will please") our inner selves and help make us happy, healthy, wealthy &/or wise if we will but partake of suggested treatments, products or events -even though they are often of questionable value and may be potentially harmful.

I'm thinking about all the "just trust me, just partake, your health will improve, you will sleep better, your retirement account will grow, you will be relieved of debt, your family life will improve... and especially, "you can feel, be and look like the successful person promoting the product." These folks are attracted to us because of their accomplishments and they promote a product or service that is associated with their success. Their testimonials or endorsements are carried on social media, radio, TV, printed media or direct contact from friends or salespersons.

I think about companies using the placebo effect to increase sales and the huge sums of money given to "the important people", idolized by thousands of people, who encourage us to buy products they promote through testimonials or endorsements of products or services.

Imagine getting paid an estimated $6 million for your involvement in this three-word jingle: "I'm Lovin' It." Yep, Justin Timberlake inked a lucrative deal with McDonald's. (Guess you could say he wants you to "buy buy buy.") Or how about earning an estimated $50 million to promote Pepsi products? That's the endorsement deal that megastar Beyonce signed up for back in 2012.

A study published in the journal Pediatrics describes the lucrative endorsement deals of 65 music celebrities—including Britney Spears, Maroon 5, Timberlake and other stars popular with teens and young adults. These celebrities promoted 57 different food and beverage brands, ranging from soda to energy drinks to pizza, Pop-Tarts and candy. The vast majority of food and beverage products were unhealthy according to researcher Marie Bragg of New York University.

Musicians can influence the thinking—and perhaps the habits—of their young fans. A published study found that teens and young adults who reported enjoying hit songs that referenced brands of alcohol (think Kesha and her bottle of Jack) were more likely to drink compared with those who didn't like these songs.

When it comes to food and non-alcoholic beverage choices, the influence of TV advertising has been well-documented. As the Institute of Medicine concluded, "television advertising influences children to prefer and request high-calorie and low-nutrient foods and beverages."

The food industry has pledged to cut back on marketing unhealthful foods to children ages 12 and under. More than a dozen of the largest food companies—including Coca-Cola, McDonald's and Kellogg—have joined this self-policing effort, called the Children's Food and Beverage Advertising Initiative.

Now, there's pressure on the industry from some public health advocates to cut back on advertising directed at teenagers. Experts point to rising obesity rates among teenagers, as reported by the Centers for Disease Control and Prevention this week. "Given that we have a childhood and teen obesity problem in the country, [these endorsements of unhealthy foods] are sending the wrong message to young people, and likely contributing to poor dietary habits," according to author Marie Bragg.10

Richard Schiffman published a post on the physiological and psychological effects of prayer and meditation. The piece summarized some of the latest scientific research on how spiritual practices help to lessen stress levels and improve our health. He mentioned that he was surprised when many of the comments on the article focused less on the substance of these findings than on the reputed sins of religion.

Some mocked the act of prayer as "childish behavior," "a primitive superstition" and "sending telepathic thought messages to an invisible being in the sky." Several people suggested that the effects of prayer were imaginary, or the results of what they called "the placebo effect." Others pointed out that any relaxation technique where one sits quietly and let's go of the stress of the day can lead to the improvements cited in the studies.

I didn't disagree. The research which correlates spiritual practices with health benefits does not ascribe these benefits to the intervention of a supernatural being. It does not prove that the God who people are praying to actually exists. It merely establishes that those who pray and meditate tend to be statistically healthier than those who don't—end of story. And as for the placebo effect, you will get no argument from me there either. It is when people say "just a placebo effect" that my hackles rise.

The placebo effect is arguably the most underrated discovery of modern medicine. Replace "just the placebo effect" with "the amazing placebo effect," "the mindboggling placebo effect." To my way of thinking, the very existence of this mysterious effect proves that God exists. That's right, you can find evidence for the foundational truths taught by religion in virtually every double-blind medical research study!

Remember the part of the Ten Commandments where the Lord commands the Israelites to "make no images"? That is precisely the place where most people—including religious believers—go wrong. We make an image in our minds of what God is, and then we proceed to either argue for it or against it.

But this is idolatry. Anyone who clings to a fixed position on the nature of the sacred is an idolator, because Spirit, according to mystics in all traditions, has no form. Or to put it more precisely, spirit is the ground of all forms, it is the source and foundation for all that exists.

This may sound hopelessly abstract and philosophical. But it is actually very concrete. We are talking about the most immediate and intimate reality of all. Allah in the Holy Koran proclaims, "I am closer to you than your own jugular vein."

Granted, this is hard to grasp until we actually experience it (touched by the spirit?). Yet all of us get glimpses at moments of the existence of a higher, more loving and expansive potential within ourselves. When mystics speak about being "one with God," they are not making an egotistical statement. It flows from their experience that the ego is but a thin veneer painted over their real selves. And the real self cannot be defined in any way. What we are (to quote Winston Churchill out of context) is "a riddle, wrapped in a mystery, inside an enigma."

Which brings us back to the placebo effect. It is mysterious, right? We don't know how it happens. A person was sick and they take a sugar pill and next thing you know—voila—they are healthy. To call this "the placebo effect" is to dress up our ignorance in words. What has actually happened is nothing short of a miracle. Science has got no explanation for it—something immaterial (a thought?) has impacted something material (our body) in a way which utterly defies logic.

And that is what prayer is all about. Prayer is based upon the conviction that the immaterial is more powerful than matter itself. Whether we call this immaterial force "God," "the ground of our being," "Spirit," or "higher consciousness" doesn't matter. The point is—there is an uncanny power (which all of us without exception have got access to) which performs miracles. The sick can be cured, the broken can feel whole again.

And the greatest miracle of all is that this power can connect us to a place within ourselves of boundless love, peace and wellbeing. Do we need any other proof for the existence of God?11

The availability of brain imaging studies like MRIs and PET scans has given brain researchers a window into understanding how the placebo effect works. The current theory is that there are three important components: classic conditioning, expectations, and neurobiology.

Classic conditioning is the most basic component. It is a learned, automatic reaction gained from prior experience. If a lab animal is fed every time a bell rings, it will start to salivate at the ring of the bell, whether it receives food or not.

Brain imaging shows that brain neurons that recognize an injection of morphine will become wired to brain neurons that release pain-relieving brain messengers called neurotransmitters. Over time, triggering the injection neurons will automatically trigger the pain-relieving neurotransmitters, even if the injection is just salt water, because neurons that fire together wire together.

Expectation is a higher brain function that involves memories, emotions, and evaluations. Brain imaging shows that areas of the brain that are responsible for hope and belief are activated during a placebo response.

The placebo response can generate the same neurotransmitters that are generated by real medications or treatments. They include the neurotransmitters serotonin, dopamine, and endorphins.[5]

Besides inventing the "Tractors" of quackery and bringing attention to the "placebo effect" in modern medicine during the late 1700s; Elisha Perkins also invented purported antiseptic medicine and used it for dysentery and sore throat.

Perkins also claimed to have discovered a cure for yellow fever. This consisted of vinegar with muriate of soda which he tested in New York City during an outbreak in 1799. The cure had no effect and Perkins contracted the fever and died.[1,2]

"When pain is to be born, a little courage helps more than much knowledge, a little human sympathy more than much courage, the least tincture of (time), the love

of God ("I will please") more than all."
C.S. Lewis

1&2. Wikipedia.

3. *Fair, Faithful Answers, Informed Response, Question: Did Joseph Smith and his contemporaries believe in supernatural entities with real power?*

4. *Finding Water With A Forked Stick May Not Be A Hoax, Popular Mechanics, 2004.*

5. *The Power of the Placebo Effect, Bottom Line Health, Yoni K. Ashar, PhD, 10/08/2022.*

6. *Is There a Placebo Effect for Animals? David Ramey, DVM, on October 25, 2008.*

7. *Top Seven Overlooked Benefits Of Testimonials, Vidram Rajan, Forbes, 2017.*

8. *Are Paid or Fake Testimonials Illegal?, By Sam Stemler, October 25, 2021.*

9. *How Brands Should Use Celebrities For Endorsements, Steve Olenski, Forbes contributor, 2016.*

10. *This Is How Much Celebrities Get Paid To Endorse Soda And Unhealthy Food, All Things Considered, Allison Aubrey, 2016.*

11. *How the Placebo Effect Proves That God Exists, Richard Schiffman, HuffPost, 2012.*

19

JUMPING TO CONCLUSIONS

Some species of moth with long, specialized proboscises are uniquely adapted to suck the nectar from the flower of the datura, a plant that is notoriously hallucinogenic for human beings. In Arizona a moth lives on a diet of Datura nectar and in doing so contributes to the pollination of flowers.

Only after countless observations did researchers realize that these moths appeared to be drunk after they had sucked the nectar. Some researchers reported that after the moths suck the nectar of several flowers, "they seem clumsy when they land on the flowers and often miss the target and fall onto the leaves or the soil. They right themselves slowly and awkwardly. When they take flight again their movements are erratic, as if they were confused. But the moths seem to like this effect and return to suck more nectar from those flowers."

The psychoactive alkaloids which are harvested by human beings for its hallucinogenic properties appear to be the same material that intoxicates the moths. Their resulting behavior can prove extremely dangerous to the moths: to lie, even briefly, in a daze on the ground or to fly slowly and awkwardly is also to fall easy prey to avid predators, insects, reptiles or amphibians, that have learned to wait under the datura mushrooms for their complacent victims. Some believe that the word toadstool came from the toads that congregate under the mushrooms to feed on the intoxicated insects.1

The mushroom Amanita muscaria plant hallucinogen must be considered potentially poisonous. These attractive fungi often appear in groups and are a common sight in all kinds of woodlands. Usually recurring in the same place for several years. When they first emerge from the leaf litter of the forest floor, the young fruitbodies are covered entirely in pointed white warts. As the caps expand the red pellicle shows through until eventually the cap comprises mainly red skin with white warts distributed more or less evenly across its surface.

It's interesting to me how it took researchers countless observations to find that moths were being affected by a plant that humans harvest for its hallucinogenic properties. Four-year-old children were tested by watching as a monkey hand puppet approaches a vase containing a red and a blue plastic flower. The monkey sneezes. The monkey backs away, returns to sniff again, and again sneezes. An adult then removes the red flower and replaces it with a yellow one. The monkey comes up to smell the yellow and blue flowers twice and each time sneezes. The adult next replaces the blue flower with the red one. The monkey comes up to smell the red and yellow flowers and this time does not sneeze.

The child is then asked, "Can you give me the flower that makes Monkey sneeze?" When psychologists Laura E. Schulz and Alison Gopnik, both then at the University of

California, Berkeley, did this experiment, 79% of four-year-old's correctly chose the blue flower. Their research makes clear, even very young children have begun to understand cause and effect. This process is critical to their ability to make sense of their world and to make their way in it. With such powers of discernment already in place by age four, people should be highly skilled at identifying cause and effect by the time they are adults, shouldn't they?

Schulz presented some evidence that gives the impression that everyday causal reasoning of the average adult regarding familiar topics appears highly fallible. People connect two events as cause and effect based on little or no evidence, and when they act on these judgments—they jump to conclusions.

There are studies that show college students don't jump to conclusions as often and display good ability in performing skill tasks. The question is - do they represent the cognitive performance of average people in their thinking about everyday affairs?

To address this question 40 people waiting for a train were asked if they would spend 10 minutes answering a survey in exchange for five dollars. It was explained that a group was trying different combinations of entertainment features at fund-raisers, to see which would sell the most tickets, and showed each person a diagram with some of the results. The sign for the first party listed door prizes, comedian, costumes; its sales were "medium." The second party listed door prizes, auction, costumes; its sales were "high." The third party listed door prizes, auction, comedian, costumes; its sales were "high."

A diagram was left in view as the interviewees were asked, "Based on their results, does the auction help ticket sales?" It was also asked how certain they were about their answers. They could choose "very certain," "certain," "think so but not certain" or "just guessing." The same questions were asked for each of the three remaining features: comedian, door prizes, costumes.

If you examine the first and third parties, adding the auction boosts sales. By comparing the second and third parties, you can see that adding a comedian has no effect on sales. Yet the information available is insufficient for assessing the causal status of door prizes or costumes (because they are always present).

Did the forty people waiting for the train stack up to the four-year-old's who had a 79% success rate and the highly cognitive college students? In a word, no.

83% judged that two or more of the features caused sales to increase, and 45% claimed that three or all four of the features did so (only the one feature auction boosted sales). Even more striking, most respondents were quite confident that they were correct. For two of the four features, the average certitude reported was greater than "certain" (tending toward "very certain"), whereas for the three or all four features they were slightly below "certain." Gender was not a factor: men and women did not differ significantly in either their judgments or levels of certainty.

Respondents judged door prizes to affect outcome (83%) much more commonly than they judged costumes to affect outcome (33%), although the affect on sales for each feature was identical.

As the research at the train station suggests, consistency and avoiding undue certainty in one's judgments is important. Undue certainty and jumping to conclusions reflects a failure in "knowing what you know" and underlies the rigidity in thinking that is a major contributor to human strife.

Inconsistency can be similarly self-serving, allowing us to protect our favorite theories without subjecting them to the same standards of evidence to which we subject those of others.2

The curious relationship of certain moths to the flowers of the datura plant led people to reevaluate the singular behavior of the common housefly (Musca domestica) when presented with fly agaric, or the toadstool Amanita muscaria (Samorini 1999). So long has this relationship been remarked on, that the very name of the mushroom derives from the Latin word for fly, musca. Another common name for the fungus is fly-killer, since the insects that are so enticed by its cap fall "stone dead" after tasting it. For centuries, in fact, people have scattered fly agaric caps on their windowsills as an insecticide. To enhance their effect, they were often crushed and missed in with a little milk or sugar; this not only attracted a larger number of flies but induced them to consume a greater quantity of the intoxicating substance. It appears that many flies perished from a simple case of overdose.

In fact, people were jumping to the conclusion that the victims of fly agaric intoxication all had died. There they were lying perfectly stiff on their backs with their legs folded up in the air. In reality, however, they had not died at all; if left alone, you can come back in an hour or a day to find, surprisingly, that they have flown away. Of course, usually the "dead" flies are swept up and thrown out or those that had woken up and flown off were replaced by others who had become intoxicated.

It looks like adding a little milk or sugar to the crushed mushroom had the only beneficial effects of attracting more flies, keeping them intoxicated for a longer time and having a mess on the windowsill to clean up.1

While getting acquainted with my current wife she asked me to send her a picture of myself. I sent her one of my family at the gravesite of my children's mom. Her mother looked at the photo and said, "he's a lonely man." She was partially right but jumped to the conclusion that I was so lonely that I wouldn't make a good companion for her daughter. She was also informed by her aunt that she had better look out if she was going to marry a person with so many children and grandchildren.

It seems like whenever there is a personal, family, community or world event of interest someone jumps to conclusions and tells the story with the ending long before the truth can be known. And guess what -to them it is the Gospel truth.

Just a few minutes ago we heard two loud bangs near a neighbor's house across a creek from us and two more that sounded near another neighbor's home. I commented that if there were shots fired, we would shortly hear sirens. No sirens but a short while later our cat tripped off the night light in our back yard and it startled my wife—the jump to a conclusion we made about the event was still on her mind. It turned out to be a car engine back firing as it came around the hill and down an incline on the road.

The story of the "Gerbil-Caused Accident", described by Jan Harold Brunvand in his Encyclopedia of Urban Legends, is a perfect illustration of jumping to conclusions:

In the story, a woman is driving to her son's show-and-tell session at school, with a pet gerbil in a box on the passenger seat. The gerbil escapes and starts crawling up her leg inside her pants. The woman pulls over, gets out of the car, and begins to jump up and down, shaking her leg to get rid of the gerbil. A passerby thinks the woman is having a seizure, so he approaches her and wraps his arms around her to help. Another passerby sees the struggle, and assumes the first passerby is an attacker, so he punches him in the face. The gerbil finally gets out of the woman's pant leg, and she embarrassingly tries to explain what really happened.

Temple Grandin in *Animals in Translation* page 266 states, "One thing we do know about humans is that the left brain, which is the conscious language part of the brain, always makes up a story to explain what's going on. Normal people have an interpreter in their left brain that takes all the random, contradictory details of whatever they're doing or remembering at the moment, and smooths everything out into one coherent story. If there are details that don't fit, a lot of times they get edited out or revised. Some left brain stories can be so far off from reality that they sound like confabulations."

Oh, about the popular belief that fly agaric is a fatal poison to flies. Centuries past there were mycologists and entomologists who realized that flies that had tasted the mushroom were only in a state of lethargy and who counseled people who used it as an insecticide to gather up the stupefied insects and throw them into the fire.

But during as recent as the last half of the 1960's some collaborators of the great mycologist Roger Heim—one of the founding fathers of modern ethnomycology and a pioneer in the study of hallucinogenic mushrooms—undertook to determine the mushroom's level of toxicity for the fly. They placed a certain number of flies in a petri dish in direct and prolonged contact with the fly agaric or a liquid extract of it. As a result, they observed a high mortality rate in the intoxicated insects. They jumped to the conclusion that the toadstool intoxication had caused the death.

In reality, the death may have been due to the phenomenon of overdose induced by the conditions of the experiment, or even—as was suggested by the researchers themselves—to the production of carbon dioxide produced within the petri dish, which kills flies by asphyxiation.[1]

A story where one did not jump to conclusions was clueless Alice in Wonderland. She eats part of one side of a mushroom and grows shorter; a piece from the other side would make her taller. A sleepy caterpillar sitting on the mushroom spoke to Alice:

'Who are you?' said the Caterpillar. This was not an encouraging opening for a conversation. Alice replied, rather shyly, 'I—I hardly know, sir, just at present—at least I know who I WAS when I got up this morning, but I think I must have been changed several times since then.'

'What do you mean by that?' said the Caterpillar sternly. 'Explain yourself!'

'I can't explain myself, I'm afraid, sir' said Alice, 'because I'm not myself, you see.'

I don't see,' said the Caterpillar.

'I'm afraid I can't put it more clearly,' Alice replied very politely, 'for I can't understand it myself to begin with; and being so many different sizes in a day is very confusing.'

Oh, if we could be like Alice: In the absence of information not jumping to conclusions . . .

1. *Animals and psychedelics, The Natural World and the Instinct to Alter Consciousness, Giorgio, Samorini, 2000.*
2. *Can people be counted on to make sound judgments? Deanna Kuhn on February 1, 2007 This article was originally published with the title "Jumping to Conclusions" in SA Mind 18, 1, 44-51.*

20

ANIMALS WHO
COMMIT SUICIDE

Iselin Aspen relates the first time she heard about them from her mother. I turned on the tap water to plunge my head in and get a drink, like all Norwegian children would do. We have one of the world's most excellent tap water, and what is exported as first class bottled water around the world, is by many Norwegians regularly used to mop the floor.

My mother rushed forward to turn it off. "Stop! Don't drink it. We have to boil it first." What? Boil the water? Why on earth would someone boil water before drinking it? My mother turned me around and smiled slightly. "It's the lemmings. They're flooding the mountain and we have to boil the water for now. The municipality just announced it."

From then on I learned that there's a small rodent infesting Norwegian mountain tops. They're always there, as tasty staples for owls, foxes and eagles. But every three to four years or so, they tend to explode in numbers, and just take over everything in areas with some altitude. This is what's called a "lemming year." To this day, no one has really been able to prove scientifically why this explosion of the lemming population occurs. And by explosion I literally mean it. Norwegian children are taught that lemmings explode when they get angry. So whatever you do, don't agitate one! It will explode in your face.

The other major exceptionality we are told about lemmings, is that during lemming years, they will horde migrate to the nearest high cliff, and commit mass suicide by throwing themselves over the edge and into the waters below. No one knows exactly why they do this, but it's probably for the best, since otherwise every year would be a lemming year.

Some lemming years are more extreme than others, while during the 1990's and early 2000's they hardly occurred at all, except very locally in a few areas. But the lemming years were observed by our ancestors as well.

Bishop Olaus Magnus of Upsala described the phenomenon in his Latin work "History of the Nordic peoples" from 1555 A.D. There, he explained that every three years or so, lemmings would grow extraordinarily in size and their fur would also grow much longer, to the great benefit of traders of fur…

His theory was that the growth was due to a sudden excessive appetite. The bishop could also report that during storms and heavy rainfall, lemmings would fall from the sky in large numbers, littering the ground, though no one knew from where they came.

Bishop Magnus speculated if the lemmings might have been brought by the winds from some remote island, or if they were actually formed in the skies and tossed down to earth? Some of them would burst open upon arrival, and in their intestine could be found undigested herbs.

Like a swarm of locust, these rodents would consume everything green on their way, before either bursting asunder and dying in masses all over the place, or by being consumed by predators. They could also bite, and anything that came in close contact with them died.

After a rainfall of lemmings, widespread disease often occurred, and the air was filled with rottenness and stenches from the dead rodents and their many victims. It's a dire account from the past, and I am sure the kids were scared of the lemmings even back then.

Apparently, there were also good consequences of lemming committing suicide years in the past. The bishop related that after the worst wave was over, nature seemed to flourish. Carcasses fertilized the ground and other species would have lots of new offspring. The animals who feasted on lemmings, grew large and strong, and their fur became increasingly long and beautiful. The traders of fur were also happy, and they would export the lemming furs abroad in bunches of 40! But the bishop was quick to condemn this behavior, and believed it safer to never touch a piece of lemming fur without wearing gloves.1

In his early adulthood, before he and his family were taken away to the Nazi internment camps, Viktor Frankl (1905-1997) had established himself as one of the leading psychiatrists in Vienna and the world. As a 16-year-old boy, for example, he struck up a correspondence with Sigmund Freud and one day sent Freud a two-page paper he had written. Freud, impressed by Frankl's talent, sent the paper to the International Journal of Psychoanalysis for publication. "I hope you don't object," Freud wrote the teenager.

While he was in medical school, Frankl distinguished himself even further. Not only did he establish suicide-prevention centers for teenagers—a precursor to his work in the camps—but he was also developing his signature contribution to the field of clinical psychology: logotherapy, which is meant to help people overcome depression and achieve well-being by finding their unique meaning in life. By 1941, his theories had received international attention and he was working as the chief of neurology at Vienna's Rothschild Hospital, where he risked his life and career by making false diagnoses of mentally ill patients so that they would not, per Nazi orders, be euthanized.

That was the same year when he had a decision to make, a decision that would change his life. With his career on the rise and the threat of the Nazis looming over him, Frankl had applied for a visa to America, which he was granted in 1941. By then, the Nazis had already started rounding up the Jews and taking them away to concentration camps, focusing on the elderly first. Frankl knew that it would only be time before the Nazis came to take his parents away. He also knew that once they did, he had a responsibility to be there with his parents to help them through the trauma of adjusting to camp life. On the other hand, as a newly married man with his visa in hand, he was tempted to leave for America and flee to safety, where he could distinguish himself even further in his field.

As Anna S. Redsand recounts in her biography of Frankl, he was at a loss for what to do, so he set out for St. Stephan's Cathedral in Vienna to clear his head. Listening to the organ music, he repeatedly asked himself, "Should I leave my parents behind?... Should I say goodbye and leave them to their fate?" Where did his responsibility lie? He was looking for a "hint from heaven."

When he returned home, he found it. A piece of marble was lying on the table. His father explained that it was from the rubble of one of the nearby synagogues that the Nazis had destroyed. The marble contained the fragment of one of the Ten Commandments—the one about honoring your father and your mother. With that, Frankl decided to stay in Vienna and forgo whatever opportunities for safety and career advancement awaited him in the United States. He decided to put aside his individual pursuits to serve his family and, later, other inmates in the camps.2

In September 1942, Viktor Frankl (prisoner number 119104) was arrested and transported to a Nazi concentration camp with his wife and parents. The selection procedure upon arrival at the camp was carried out on the ramps as follows: families were divided after leaving the train cars and all the people were lined up in two columns. The men and older boys were in one column, and the women and children of both sexes in the other. Next, the people were led to the camp doctors and other camp functionaries conducting selection. They judged the people standing before them on sight and, sometimes eliciting a brief declaration as to their age and occupation, decided whether they would live or die.

Age was one of the principal criteria for selection. As a rule, all children below 16 years of age (from 1944, below 14) and the elderly were sent to die. As a statistical average, about 20% of the people in transports were chosen for labor. They were led into the camp, registered as prisoners, and assigned the next numbers in the various series. Of the approximately 1.1 million Jews deported to Auschwitz, about 200 thousand were chosen in this way. The remainder, about 900 thousand people, were killed in the gas chambers.

Historians estimate that around 1.1 million people perished in Auschwitz during the less than 5 years of its existence. The majority, around 1 million people, were Jews. The second most numerous group, from 70 to 75 thousand, was the Poles, and the third most numerous, about 20 thousand, the Gypsies. About 15 thousand Soviet POWs and 10 to 15 thousand prisoners of other ethnic backgrounds (including Czechs, Byelorussians, Yugoslavians, French, Germans, and Austrians) also died there.[3]

It was not without reason that the Nazi concentration camps were referred to as death factories, for their chief objective was the mass extermination of people, mainly those of Jewish origin. Death and dying were such mass and everyday phenomena in concentration camps that prisoners quickly became largely indifferent towards the death of fellow prisoners, and even their own death (Ryn & Kłodziński, 1982). In this context, death through suicide receded into the background, and was often treated as an escape from everyday sufferings. Perhaps this is why, among the multitude of papers dealing with life in concentration camps, so few articles have been devoted to this particular problem.

It is the direct contact between doctors and former prisoners of these camps, and above all former prisoners of the Auschwitz-Birkenau camp, which has uncovered a high incidence of suicide in concentration camps. Thus, interviews with former prisoners constitute our main source of information concerning this problem (Ryn & Kłodziński, 1976).

The statements made by the former prisoners suggested that motives for suicide committed in the concentration camp could be classified as "direct" and "indirect". The first group would include all traumatic factors connected with the incarceration period, such as imprisonment, changes in the camp hierarchy, drastically difficult financial situation and living conditions, starvation, diseases, extremely hard work, and the constant danger of repressive measures and death. The second group would consist of any psychological and somatic traumata (when a person has a significant focus on physical symptoms, such as pain, weakness or shortness of breath, to a level that results in major distress and/or problems functioning. The individual has excessive thoughts, feelings and behaviors relating to the physical symptoms) or any circumstances directly connected with a prisoner that might constitute a cause of attempted suicide. The motives in this group would also include intra-psychological factors, such as mental illness.

The most frequently encountered motives for suicide in the concentration camp were as follows: psychological disturbances (mainly states of depression of varying intensity and etiology), somatic illnesses, fear of torture, fear of being denounced, loss of a relative or friend, disappointment in love, physical assault, and feelings of patriotism and altruism.4

Before Viktor Frankl became a renowned psychologist; before he survived a Nazi concentration camp; and before he wrote Man's Search for Meaning, a bestselling book about his experiences; he was a high school student who thought deeply about life - more deeply than perhaps most teenagers do. One day his science teacher declared to the class, "Life is nothing more than a combustion process, a process of oxidation." Young Viktor leaped from his chair and countered, "Sir, if this is so, then what can be the meaning of life?"

Science class is not typically the best place to find answers to that kind of question. Viktor instead learned about life and its meaning in the cruel classroom of the concentration camps. There he was taught by experience what he already felt in his heart: those who are most resilient, who are most likely to survive horrific conditions, are those who have a sense of meaning in their lives. In his words: "A man who becomes conscious of the responsibility he bears toward a human being who affectionately waits for him, or to an unfinished work, will never be able to throw away his life. He knows the 'why' for his existence, and will be able to bear almost any 'how.'"

For some, the "why" of existence may be that our children or grandchildren need us. Perhaps we have an unfinished project that keeps us going. Or we may find meaning in giving back to a group or an individual who depends on us. It could be said that this ability to look outward, to feel a sense of purpose beyond just satisfying our own desires, is what makes us human, what distinguishes us from all other life on earth. It's also what brings true happiness - have you noticed that you never find a truly selfless, service-minded person to be disgruntled?

In 1945 Three years after interment, when his camp was liberated, most of his family, including his pregnant wife, had perished - but he, prisoner number 119104, had lived. In his bestselling 1946 book, Man's Search for Meaning, which he wrote in nine days about his experiences in the camps, Frankl concluded that the difference between those who had lived and those who had died came down to one thing—the meaning of life which he came to understand as a high school student when one of his science teachers declared to the class, "Life is nothing more than a combustion process, a process of oxidation." Frankl jumped out of his chair and responded, "Sir, if this is so, then what can be the meaning of life?"

The meaning of life is found in the face of another. It is found as we sacrifice and get outside ourselves in some way, large or small. It is found as we strive to make life better for those who follow us. It is found as we commit ourselves to something larger—more meaningful—than ourselves.5

According to Gallup in 2013, the happiness levels of Americans are at a four-year high and that nearly 60 percent all Americans today feel happy, without a lot of stress or worry. On the other hand, according to the Center for Disease Control, about 4 out of 10 Americans have not discovered a satisfying life purpose. Research has shown that having purpose and meaning in life increases overall well-being and life satisfaction, improves mental and physical health, enhances resiliency, enhances self-esteem, and decreases the chances of depression. On top of that, the single-minded pursuit of happiness is ironically leaving people less happy, according to recent research. "It is the very pursuit of happiness," Frankl knew, "that thwarts happiness."

This is why some researchers are cautioning against the pursuit of mere happiness. In a new study, which will be published this year (2013) in a forthcoming issue of the Journal of Positive Psychology, psychological scientists asked nearly 400 Americans aged 18 to 78 whether they thought their lives were meaningful and/or happy. Examining their self-reported attitudes toward meaning, happiness, and many other variables - like stress levels, spending patterns, and having children - over a month-long period, the researchers found that a meaningful life and happy life overlap in certain ways, but are ultimately very different. Leading a happy life, the psychologists found, is associated with being a "taker" while leading a meaningful life corresponds with being a "giver."

"Happiness without meaning characterizes a relatively shallow, self-absorbed or even selfish life, in which things go well, needs and desire are easily satisfied, and difficult or taxing entanglements are avoided," the authors write.

Roy Baumeister, social psychologist at Florida State University wrote, "What sets human beings apart from animals is not the pursuit of happiness, which occurs all across the natural world, but the pursuit of meaning, which is unique to humans." He states in his book, *Willpower*: Rediscovering the Greatest Human Strength, "Partly what we do as human beings is to take care of others and contribute to others. This makes life meaningful but it does not necessarily make us happy. Meaning is not only about transcending the self, but also about transcending the present moment - which is perhaps the most important finding of the study, according to the researchers. While happiness is an emotion felt in the here and now, it ultimately fades away, just as all emotions do; positive affect and feelings of pleasure are fleeting. The amount of time people report feeling good or bad correlates with happiness but not at all with meaning.

Meaning, on the other hand, is enduring. It connects the past to the present to the future. 'Thinking beyond the present moment, into the past or future, was a sign of the relatively meaningful but unhappy life,' the researchers write. Happiness is not generally found in contemplating the past or future. That is, people who thought more about the present were happier, but people who spent more time thinking about the future or about past struggles and sufferings felt more meaning in their lives, though they were less happy."

The wisdom that Frankl derived from his experiences there, in the middle of unimaginable human suffering, is just as relevant now as it was then: "Being human always points, and is directed, to something or someone, other than oneself - be it a meaning to fulfill or another human being to encounter. The more one forgets himself - by giving himself to a cause to serve or another person to love—the more human he is."

Baumeister and his colleagues would agree that the pursuit of meaning is what makes human beings uniquely human. By putting aside our selfish interests to serve someone or something larger than ourselves - by devoting our lives to "giving" rather than "taking" - we are not only expressing our fundamental humanity, but are also acknowledging that there is more to the good life than the pursuit of simple happiness.2,6

It turns out lemmings do not explode because of anger and they do not willingly commit mass suicide.

What is true though, is their sudden excessive population growth. When this happens, they will eat everything like locusts, and the vegetation is so drastically changed that it can be seen on satellite images.

The explosion myth has a relatable explanation. Lemmings become very agitated when their numbers increase. The animals have been observed falling into cramping and convulsions, probably due to stress, and this often results in death and skin rupture.

When a large number of lemmings die, their predators also live in abundance, and become more picky. Animals will then consume only the more nutritious intestine, while leaving the rest of the carcasses behind to rot.1

The suicidal migratory behavior of lemmings more than likely influenced the Medieval fable of a mysterious Pied Piper dressed in colored clothes from Hamlin, Lower Saxony, Germany. To save the people from the plague the Piper led the vast host of rodents out of town and into the sea where they drowned.

Lemming, any of 20 species of small rodents, some of which undertake large, swarming migrations. They are found only in the Northern Hemisphere. They have short, stocky bodies with short legs and stumpy tails, a bluntly rounded muzzle, small eyes, and small ears that are nearly hidden in their long, dense, soft fur. They measure 3 to 10 inches in body length and weighing 1 to 4 ounces. The color of some species varies seasonally. During the summer its coat is gray tinged with buff or reddish brown and with dark stripes on the face and back. In the winter they molt into a white coat and develop forked digging claws. Other species are gray, sandy yellow, various tints and tones of brown, or slate gray and black.

Lemmings live throughout temperate and polar regions on North America and Eurasia inhabiting steppes and semideserts, treeless alpine or arctic tundra, sphagnum bogs, coniferous forests, and sagebrush-covered slopes.

They are solitary and generally intolerant of one another. Active year-round, they feed on almost any sort of vegetation, including roots, buds, leaves, twigs, bark, seeds, grasses, sedges, and mosses.

Lemmings scamper along extensive runway systems and construct nests in burrows or beneath rocks. Some make nests on the tundra surface or beneath the snow.

Breeding from spring to fall, females can produce up to 13 young after a gestation period of about 20 to 30 days.

Are lemmings suicidal? NO! Jordon Jarrell, a retired biologist at the University of Alaska Museum of the North in Fairbanks, says the myth may have its roots in the animals' cyclical population booms, which are driven by factors such as food availability.

In Sweden and Finland, these springtime spikes push lemmings to disperse from the mountains in search of better accommodations, a journey described by *National Geographic magazine in 1918.*

When lemmings encounter water bodies, some are jostled into swimming and being unable to swim far, huge numbers wash up on the beaches. As for the migrating lemmings that avoid a watery death, they often survive and produce colonies for where you wouldn't ordinarily find them—"quite the opposite of self-destructive."

A 1958 Disney nature documentary, *White Wilderness*, also reinforced the suicidal myth by fabricating scenes of lemmings leaping to their deaths, according to the Alaska Department of Fish and Game.7

Suicide is a crime the most revolting of the feelings; nor does any reason suggest itself to our understanding by which it can be justified. It certainly originates in that species of fear which we denominate poltroonery. For what claim can that man have to courage who trembles at the frowns of fortunes? True heroism consists in being superior to the ills of life in whatever shape they may challenge him to combat. Napoleon Bonaparte, Emp of the French (1769-1821).

1. *History | Nature, Iselin Aspen, Lemmings From the Sky, 04/20/2021.*

2. *Viktor Frankl: A Life Worth Living—December 18, 2006, by Anna S. Redsand (Author).*

3. *http://www.auschwitz.org.*

4. *Medical Review Auschwitz, Suicide in Nazi concentration camps, 08/10/2017.*

5. *From: Emily Esfahani Smith, 01-09-2013, Anna S. Redsand, Viktor Frankl: A Life Worth Living July 2016, Music & The Spoken Word 02-28-2016.*

6. *Roy Baumeister & John Tierney, Willpower, 2018.*

7. *National Geographic, Are Lemmings Really Suicidal? The Truth Behind Animal Myths, Liz Langley, 05/23/2015 & others.*

21

DO ANIMALS GO TO HEAVEN

Kelsey Berteaux wrote, "I remember the first time I went to put a dog down. Her name was Maggie. She was a beautiful, black Great Dane with a love for life and eating socks. But she was only 4 when Wobbler syndrome necessitated we take her to the vet. And not come home. I remember how the vet explained it wouldn't be painful, that she'd just drift off and "go to sleep," like so many people say. I remember petting her softly, whispering her name, and wondering, after she was "gone," how she was still warm and then, how long it would take for her to turn cold.

Maggie didn't get to come back to our home that day; I had never before hoped so desperately that she had gone to another, more glorious home."1

I have assisted many companion animals reach the moment when they pass on to their next estate. In fact, my choice to become a veterinarian was strongly influenced by the stress and anxiety I noticed when my father was caring for the terminally ill. Dad was a surgeon and general practitioner medical doctor that returned to the small town he grew up in to practice medicine. He cared for teachers, relatives and friends that he had known from his youth and their passing took a part of him with them.

As a veterinarian the choice to not continue life if an animal is suffering is not necessarily easy for an owner but an acceptable option. The pet has an IV catheter placed into a vein in a leg in the same manner as when being prepared for an anesthetic surgical or medical procedure. A preanesthetic is placed in the catheter, the patient becomes semi conscience and an overdose of an anesthetic given. The procedure usually takes less than five minutes and the owner often chooses to be with their companion and friend.

These are often soul-searching moments for those present during euthanasia. Often the owners will bring up the subject of the importance of pets in their life and question if I felt they would ever see their friend again? My answer is that there are recorded personal experiences and scriptures that animals have a spirit that upon death leaves them and goes to Heaven. However, this is a GOK (God only knows) question. I relate to them that I have had experiences during the passing of an animal where I have felt there was something (spirit?) more than life that was leaving the pet.

I had similar feelings when I was with my wife during her mother's passing and as a young father when a friend of mine's newly born son suffered anemia from an Rh Factor incompatibility with his mother. The baby was on life support and dying. Their physician advised them that their baby was in organ failure and their decision was that it was best to take him off life support and allow him to return to his Heavenly Father. The father asked me if I would assist him in naming and giving a father's blessing to the child before death. Being both ordained Elders in our faith, we exercised our priesthood authority and placed our hands on the baby and the father gave the infant a name and a blessing. I left the room with the parents holding their child for the last few minutes of life.

The most revealing information I've found to share with my clients about what happens to animals after death was written by Gerald E. Jones, director, Institute of Religion, Berkeley, California. "Nature helps us to see and understand God. To all His creations we owe an allegiance of service and a profound admiration." Thus, the General Superintendency of the Deseret Sunday School Union, President Joseph F. Smith, President of the Church, and Elders David O. McKay and Stephen L Richards, members of the Council of the Twelve, editorialized in the April 1918 Juvenile Instructor.

Recognizing that the "love of nature is akin to the love of God" they reminded the members of the Church that "men learn more easily in sympathetic relationships of all life than they do in the seclusion of human interest." (P. 183.) Many families recognize the importance of pets and the resultant loving and sharing among their children. Caring for pets can also develop a sense of responsibility.

Devotion of animals to families can be inspiring as well as practical. A recent news item related the bravery of a dog in saving the life of a small girl by breaking the window of a burning automobile and pulling her to safety.

A number of questions have been asked concerning the place of animals in the gospel plan: Do animals have spirits and are they resurrected? Yes. The Prophet Joseph Smith received information concerning the eternal status of animals. Answers to questions he posed are in the Doctrine and Covenants, section 77. He also spoke about the resurrection of animals in a sermon but did not expand on the subject. (History of the Church, 5:343.)

To what degree of glory do animals go? The scriptures speak only of animals being in the celestial kingdom. Whether they go to other kingdoms is a matter of conjecture. Elder Joseph Fielding Smith on one occasion said the distribution of animals into all three degrees of glory is "very probable," (Improvement Era, Jan. 1958, pp. 16–17.) To my knowledge, no other prophet has published an opinion on the subject.

Are animals judged and resurrected according to their obedience to laws? According to Elder Joseph Fielding Smith, animals do not have a conscience. They cannot sin and they cannot repent, for they have not the knowledge of right and wrong. (Man: His Origin and Destiny, Deseret Book Co., 1954, pp. 204–5.)

Can animals be with their owners in the hereafter? There is no revealed word on this subject. Reason would tell us that a rancher or farmer may not want all of the cattle he has owned during his life. On the other hand, emotional ties may be honored and family pets may well be restored to their owners in the resurrection. Elder Orson F. Whitney wrote that Joseph Smith expected to have his favorite horse in eternity. (Improvement Era, Aug. 1927, p. 855.)

Just what is the relationship between men and animals? Men are children of God. Animals are for the benefit of man. This does not mean, however, that man is not to have a concern for this part of his stewardship. The prophets in all ages have indicated that man will be accountable for his treatment of animals and that justice and mercy should be exercised concerning them. Alma encourages us to pray over our flocks. (Alma 34:20, 25.) There are numerous examples in Church history of animals being administered to by the anointing of oil and their resultant healing. In the best-known incident, Mary Fielding Smith's oxen were spared to bring her pioneer family, including a future President of the Church, Joseph F. Smith, to Utah. (Preston Nibley, Presidents of the Church, Deseret Book Co., 1959, pp. 234–35.)

Though the prophets have spoken frequently about man's responsibility to show proper treatment to animals in this world, very little detail is known about the states of animals in the eternities. Greater emphasis is rightly placed upon man's need to live the gospel and be worthy to return to his Heavenly Father where he will then learn the answers to such questions. Quoting again from the editorial cited at the beginning of this article: "Men cannot worship the Creator and look with careless indifference upon his creations. The love of all life helps man to the enjoyment of a better life. It exalts the spiritual nature of those in need of divine favor." (Juvenile Instructor, Apr. 1918, p. 182.2

Will Rogers said, "If there are no dogs in Heaven, then when I die I want to go where they went." And,

an unknown author stated, "Heaven is the place where all the dogs you've ever loved come to greet you."

These thoughts express my feelings that Heaven can't be Heaven without the presence of animals.

*"If having a soul means being able to feel love and
loyalty and gratitude, then animals are better
off than a lot of humans. James Harriot*

*"One day, we will see our animals again in
the eternity of Christ. Paradise is open to
all of God's creatures." Pope Frances*

1. *Animals and the Afterlife: Do All Dogs Go to Heaven?,
   Kelsey Berteaux August 12, 2017.*
2. *Gerald E. Jones, director, Institute of Religion, Berkeley,
   California "Nature helps us to see and understand God,
   March 1977.*

22

A STROKE OF LUCK

You know that you are in trouble when you wake up with an IV in each arm dripping fluids into you, you're lying near venetian blinds that at specified times open so nurses can eves drop and you see your wife (that should be in Idaho) watching you with a long face sitting in a chair near you. You are told by a neurologist that you have had a stroke, holds up a pen and asks you to tell him what the parts are. You can't remember the name plunger that exposes or retracts the ink cartridge. After each visit and his same questions, you remember trying to remember the word stroke and plunger because you know the next day you are going to get another try. It was several days and a bout of gout in my big toes (ouch) before he said good boy and let me go home.

I remember visiting my great grandmother Grimmett as a young boy. She would get out pictures of her family, point and try to tell me who they were. My mother told me that she had a stroke and got around fairly well but her ability to communicate had been reduced to pointing and making what noise she could from her vocal cords. At the time I don't believe I was able to read and I don't remember her attempting to write me messages.

Currently, my family is close friends with a stroke victim that we see most weeks at church and go out for social events on a regular basis. He was a successful business man at IBM and now doesn't recognize letters of the alphabet and can't read.

The two main causes of stroke are a blocked artery (ischemic stroke) or leaking or bursting of a blood vessel (hemorrhagic stroke). Some people may have only a temporary disruption of blood flow to the brain, known as a transient ischemic attack (TIA), that doesn't cause lasting symptoms. They all damage or cause death to the portion of the brain that is void of a good blood supply.

If I'm paying attention, every time I walk into my bedroom closet, I'm reminded what the symptoms of a stroke are and what to do by a magnetic sticker in my face on the safe:

- Sudden numbness or weakness in the face, arm, or leg, especially on one side of the body.
- Sudden confusion, trouble speaking, or difficulty understanding speech.
- Sudden trouble seeing in one or both eyes.
- Sudden trouble walking, dizziness, loss of balance, or lack of coordination.
- Sudden severe headache with no known cause.

Dogs can also have strokes with the most common symptoms being blindness and/or loss of balance. As in human medicine, the word 'stroke' is used in veterinary medicine to mean a sudden loss of blood supply to a region of the nervous system. They can be either be caused by a blockage or bleeding of a blood vessel. Most often they occur in the spinal cord and do not affect the brain.

The cause may be from accidental trauma, infectious diseases, genetic disorders, cancer or no cause may be found. In the brain, strokes may cause sudden loss of balance, blindness, or seizures. In the spinal cord, strokes can cause sudden weakness or paralysis of one or more limbs.

The most common strokes we see at Camden Pet Hospital are from trauma to the spinal cord. It may be stretched enough and/or there may be bleeding and tissue swelling around the cord that results in partial or total paralysis of the rear legs. Fortunately, most dogs recover from care, rest, time and occasionally surgery.1

Strokes are most often diagnosed in cats that are about nine years old. They can occur due to an underlying illness such as cancer that metastasizes (spreads) to or within the brain, kidney disease, heart disease, hyperthyroidism or parasites. However, in many cases it may be impossible to pinpoint.

Cats are at risk of a stroke from loss of blood supply to an area from a narrowed artery that has been clogged or from an artery bleeding resulting in pressure or loss of blood supply to the brain or spinal cord.

The most common stroke seen at our hospital in cats is from a blood clot that has lodged in the aortic artery (called a saddle thrombus) where it separates and supplies blood to each back leg. The cat usually shows pain in the rear legs and often can't walk. Activation of the blood clot is usually caused by heart disease or to a lesser extent cancer of the thyroid gland (hyperthyroidism).

Following is a statement written by my son Jeremy Hoge, at my request in 2022, three years after my stroke. I include it because it may help alert those who read it how important it is to recognize a stroke and getting care ASAP. Here we have a father and son who are veterinarians that work together examining companion pets that from time to time have strokes. Even with our intimate relationship with animals and education, neither one of us thought stroke until prompted to do so.

"Hey Pop's, I will try to remember the best I can about out visit with Dr. Yeh the back surgeon:

During our lunch break we were set to eat and to get to your appointment with Dr. Yeh... I do not remember if we ate lunch or not prior. That day seemed like a "bad" Walter day where during the AM you seemed to be asking more questions about treatments you knew and actually taught me after graduation . . . what's this medication or when do I recheck something or other . . . I just wrote it off as you had a lot going on and just off that morning. On our way to your appointment you did seem to be in some distress, talking faster but mumbling more and not seeming comfortable in the car, but I figured well the back pain was bothering you.

At the appointment you started off your "normal" self-trying to make small talk and your white coat hypertension and your anxiety with doctor's appointments. I do not remember the exact BP but I swear it was like 220 or 230. During that process of the nurse check in, you started to speak faster, became flushed, and were kind of off. We went into the exam room where you met with his PA Jessica and him. She did the initial evaluation but you were not able to remember or answer some of her questions. We could see in your face the frustration but you kept asking me to respond to her. More of the same when Dr. Yeh came in.

You also said you had a migraine that day and it was making things difficult for you to remember. We headed out, I cannot remember what was finally discussed besides surgery is recommended but you needed to get some diagnostics done first before scheduling. I do remember Dr. Yeh asking me if this was "normal" for you which I stated no, this is worse than usual :)

On our way to the car I started pushing you to answer various questions. You were having a terrible time coming up with some simple answers and were getting mad at me for being mean to you with your migraine. Once in the car and driving back to CPH (Camden Pet Hospital) I literally took my pen and some scratch paper and wrote a "B" on it and asked you what that was... I can't remember what you said but it was not even close to "B". I pulled off Highway 85 and Camden Avenue but turned to go back to the hospital. You made me pull down the street just N of 85 onto Camden to then again tell me "No, I have a migraine, I need to just go home and sleep!" I told you that I will take you back to work but I wanted you to stay there.

Once at CPH in the parking lot Dr. Yeh called me. He asked me how you were doing. I told him that I was concerned based on your behavior but you were not allowing me to take you back to the hospital. Dr. Yeh told me I needed to just make the decision for you since he was concerned that you might be having a stroke... which my reply was I AGREE!

When we parked at CPH I hopped out of the car and told Nancy and Dana to NOT let you leave. I told them I needed to take you to the hospital but wanted to get the two clients in the building out of there since we were late and they had been waiting. Dana was the one that took the brunt of your . . . frustration? . . . but she did the job of distracting you for 10 minutes or so for me to get those clients taken care of and my phone and keys.

I drove you back to the ER at Good Samaritan Hospital. You kept asking me why we were going back and any time I said stroke you were mad but if I just said tests for Dr. Yeh you were fine with it. We walked in, just to the left was the acute triage area that when we started to fill out the touch screen the nurse asked me what was going on and I said I think he is having a stroke, they sat you down, wheeled you right over to the acute care doctor and within about 3 minutes you were getting a CT and hooked up to IVs and blood testing. When they took you into the CT area, they took me to the ICU treatment area where they were going to bring you once they were done.

I reached out to Brad (son) and Shauna (wife) to give them an update on what I knew and what was going on. The ICU nurses started asking me what treatments were allowed.... I kept thinking to myself my dad will kill me if he is on coumadin the rest of his life! Here they are asking me if it is ok to give blood thinners!!!! I told them to move forward with the clot buster shot and I hoped I could beg for forgiveness later."2

The National Institute of Health report states, "Each year, about 795,000 people in the United States have strokes, and of these incidents, 137,000 of the people die. About 610,000 of these cases are first strokes, and 185,000 people who survive a stroke will have another stroke within 5 years.

Ischemic strokes make up about 87% of all strokes. Hemorrhagic strokes make up the remaining 13%.

Stroke is a leading cause of death and disability in the United States. People of all ages and backgrounds can have a stroke."

John Hopkins Medicine listed the effects of a stroke: Included was changes in movement and sensation; speech and understanding language, eating and swallowing; vision, cognitive (thinking, reasoning, judgment, and memory) ability, perception and orientation to surroundings; self-care ability, bowel and bladder control, emotional control, sexual ability; right or left-sided weakness or paralysis and sensory impairment; inability to localize or recognize body parts, understand maps and find objects, such as clothing or toiletry items; memory problems, behavioral changes, such as lack of concern about situations, impulsivity, inappropriateness, and depression; impaired ability to do math or to organize, reason, and analyze items; impaired ability to read, write, and learn new information; inability to walk and problems with coordination and balance (ataxia), dizziness, headache, nausea and vomiting; problems with breathing and heart functions, body temperature control, coma, death and acquired savant syndrome.

Looking over the list of all the things I'm thankful did not happen to me, I noticed the words savant syndrome.

It is a rare condition in which persons with various developmental disorders, including autistic disorder, have an amazing ability and talent. The condition can be congenital (genetic or inborn), or can be acquired later in childhood, or even in adults.

Autistic are people who can do things like tell you what day of the week you were born based on your birth date, or calculate in their heads whether your street address is a prime number or not. They usually have IQs in the mentally retarded range, though not always, yet they can naturally do things no normal human being can even be thought to do, no matter how hard he tries to learn or how much time he spends practicing.

Take, for example, a child who is mute and non-communicative but has the bizarre ability to do any jigsaw puzzle placed in front of him picture side down, with machine-like rapidity. Just by looking at the shapes of, say, 200 pieces, he can quickly put the puzzle together. Or consider another savant, blind from birth, who, at 14 years old, played Tchaikovsky's Piano Concerto #1 from beginning to end flawlessly, having heard it just once. Or the late Kim Peek (who inspired Dustin Hoffman's portrayal in the film Rain Man), who would read books extremely rapidly—one page with the right eye and the other with the left. He also memorized literally thousands of books, each from reading just once.

Acquired savant syndrome occurs when the brain responds to trauma. The syndrome refers to the new skills or abilities that emerge in a previously "normal" person. These new abilities follow brain injury, stroke, or other central nervous system incidents, and even dementia. In acquired savant syndrome astonishing new abilities, typically in music, art or mathematics, appear unexpectedly in ordinary persons after a head injury, stroke or other central nervous system (CNS) incident where no such abilities or interests were present pre-incident.

Take the 56-year-old builder who, after surviving a stroke, "began filling several notebooks with poems and verse; he hadn't written poetry prior to that time. Following that, he began to paint expansively and expressively, spending almost all of his time painting and sculpting." Or consider the 42-year-old orthopedic surgeon who, in the aftermath of being struck by lightning, developed an insatiable desire to listen to classical piano music. He sought out Chopin recordings, and had such a strong desire to play them that he taught himself. Or Jason Padgett's who after an attack outside of a karaoke bar in 2002, the furniture salesman had a concussion and became a mathematical genius. Padgett developed the ability to visualize complex math and physics topics even though he didn't go beyond pre-algebra in his studies.

Dr. Temple Grandin DVM, PhD, who has autism and specializes in animal behavior, mentioned that she would go so far as to say that animals might actually be autistic savants. Animals have special talents normal people don't; and at least some animals have special forms of genius normal people don't, the same way some autistic savants have special forms of genius.

She sees genius when birds and animals learn complicated navigational skills and can travel hundreds of miles to escape winter and return to the same area in the spring.3

My mentor, Dr. Hylton, at Camden Pet Hospital raised and raced homing pigeons that when released many miles away could find their home nest. Homing pigeons have been recorded returning home after being released over 1000 miles away.

Discussing why animals migrate, Science Focus wrote: you may have heard about some of the animal kingdom's epic migration, such as humpback whales traveling from the poles to the equator, or hundreds of thousands of monarch butterflies arriving in Mexico every winter. Many animals make long, treacherous journeys year after year, so why do they go to all that effort?

Many birds, mammals, fish, reptiles, amphibians, crustaceans and insects migrate, and they usually do it to find food, a safe place to breed, or a suitable climate. For example, European swallows migrate south every winter to Africa or Asia where the climate is warmer, and food is more plentiful. Flying 200 miles a day, they use fat reserves to avoid starvation on their long journey. Another famous migration is that of wildebeests in Serengeti, which follow the seasonal rains that nourish the grasses on which they graze.

But not all migrations are seasonal; Atlantic salmon spend most of their lives in the sea, and when it is time to reproduce, they travel thousands of miles to return to the exact river where they were born. A study published in 2021 found they can travel up to 2,000 miles to return to their birth river, all to ensure their offspring get the best start in life.

Although their feats of endurance are incredible, animals that migrate tend to be more vulnerable to climate change, deforestation and habitat fragmentation because they rely on multiple habitats, across countries or even continents, to survive or complete their life cycle.4

For me I consider my stroke as being a "stroke of luck." If it hadn't occurred where and when it did, Dr. Yeh had not called Jeremy and I was allowed to go home to sleep off my "migraine" headache; I can only imagine where I would be or not even be today.

On the other hand, I also can only imagine what it would be like if I had awakened to the elevated stature of an acquired savant syndrome victim and had genius capabilities. My family would have difficulty adjusting to that!

I might also hear with less difficulty, be able to instantly remember names, not struggle with recognizing things, places, and orientation when looking at a map, find objects I've misplaced and be free of migraine headaches.

Since my stroke I find myself in a more structured life style. I practice my counting skills twice a day as I prepare my supplements and medications, I at least once daily take my blood pressure and an electric cardiogram, I wear my CPAP every night and clean it every morning, at night I wear a ring that continuously records my oxygen level and vibrates if it gets below 90%, I have eleven doctors on my team and couldn't feel better.

The photo on the left is of an MRI that was taken a few days before my fateful visit with Dr. Yeh. If you look carefully at the upper white spot it looks like a rabbit looking down. If you look next to the vertical white line that ends at the bottom of the photo, to the right you will see a dark area that looks to me like my wife's hair. It lightens some at the bottom and there are two dark dots that to me look like eyes. In the white area below, you can see a nose and a mouth.

If you look in the center of the next photo you will see two eyes and a beak with two large feet below. Ears are found on each side of the eyes and the dome of the head above. Just above the ears you will see two of her children showing their faces.

When I went into see Dr. Yeh I intended showing him these objects on the MRI. The only thing I remember about my visit that day, besides walking out of his office, of the stroke was trying to show him these objects in a fun way and him telling me that he could not see them. He stated that these were bone structures and not my wife, an Easter Bunny head and creatures living in my body. From Jeremy's description my verbal skills were not as good as I remembered.

The last photo on the right shows the hardware Dr. Yeh put in my back.

When I had a pre surgical interview, following recovery from my stroke, Dr. Yeh told me that I was going to have such pain that I would hate him. I told him that I would not hate him if I had a lot of pain and I couldn't imagine hurting any more than I was from arthritis in the disks I had ruptured 35 years previously. Other than a spinal leak that gave me a head ache and kept me lying flat on my back for several days, from day one I had less pain than before surgery.

On my first post op visit Dr. Yeh asked me how I was feeling. I asked him how he pronounced his name? He had a questioning look on his face (probably thought I was having another stroke) and replied that his name was pronounced Yeh. I told him, "I feel Yeah!" After that visit we had a relaxed wonderful relationship.

The dressed-up selfie of me was for my one-year post stroke neurological exam. We were in the mist of the Covid-19 pandemic and the exam was via Zoom. The receptionists seemed to get quite a kick out of my gig. Dr. Sachdev with a stern look asked me serious thoughtful questions, had me add and subtract numbers, hold my arms out, stand on the left and right foot, verify that I had peripheral vision and other stuff I can't remember. At the end of the visit without any recognition of how I was dressed or even a smile, as I recall he said, "I knew that you were nuts during my first visit with you in the hospital and it's obvious to me that you are still nuts. I think you need another MRI." The MRI was never ordered and I haven't seen the doctor for another visit.

I guess I'll always be nuts and I'll always wonder if he thought the way I was dressed was a joke. I'm sure being a neurologist he's seen some pretty strange folks.

The dressed-up image is a selfie of me during my Zoom one year post stroke exam with the neurologist.

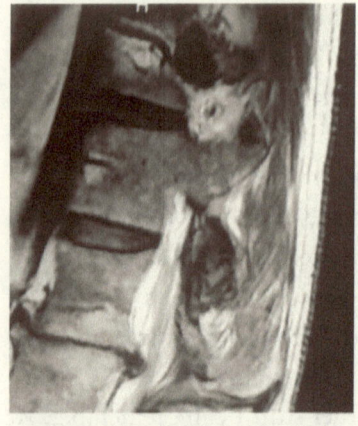

Two views of the MRI of my back taken just before Easter. The one on the left shows a rabbit's head / looking down below the image it looked to me like my wife's head.

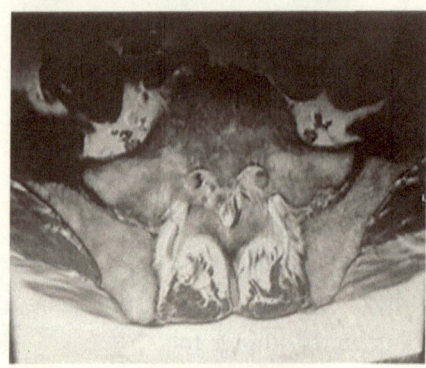

The next photo shows the beaked face of a mother whatever & 2 babies above her ears.

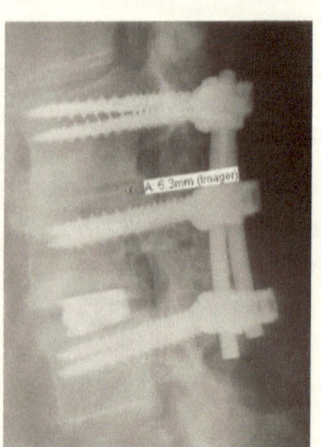

The x-ray is the surgery Dr. Yeh performed on my back.

1. *Texas A&M University, Veterinary Medicine & Biological Science, Strokes in Dogs, CVMBS NEWS, 2016.*
2. *Hey Pops I will try to remember the best I can about our visit with Dr. Yeh, summer 2022.*
3. *Temple Grandin, Animals In Translation, 2005.*
4. *July 2022 Science Focus, CrowdScience, Why do Animals Migrate, page 82, July 2022.*

23

MY FRIEND ROGER

My client Roger has been very successful in business and as a family man. His family-owned business services and repairs large 18 wheeler or semi-trailer trucks that carry freight. His sons are caring for most of the business, but Roger is still very important since they serve clients that have established long term relationships with him. The truckers often "want to see or speak with Roger" when they need services performed or have concerns about their expensive trucks. They are their source of income and often used as a home away from home.

I started seeing his wife's special friend, Scooter, in December of 2005. He came in for well puppy care and over the years I saw him as a frequent visitor. Roger's wife took Scooter everywhere she went. I got to know Roger and the family through her stories. They not only worked together, they played together and she was the matriarch of the family.

Over the last five years Roger started coming in more often with his wife for Scooter's visits. The last time I spoke with Roger was 2 ½ years ago when he mentioned that his wife had just received her first chemo treatment for lung cancer and handled it like "a trooper."

When Roger brought Scooter in, during the early spring of 2022, we were still seeing our patients using curb side service because of the Covid-19 pandemic. I saw Scooter's file and went directly to the parking lot. Roger told me that he had recently lost his wife to cancer. He described his last day with her at their cabin in Lake Tahoe. She was in good spirits but had been losing strength and got out of breath easily. He assisted her to the upstairs bathroom, bathed her and was drying her off when she passed.

He was distraught, depressed and at a loss as to how he was going to get along without his wife. He told me how she was his best friend, treated him like a king, the house was always kept immaculate, she did all the errands caring for his every need and just in case she missed something Roger needed he found a stash of money hidden away to take care of it. He told me the only store he remembers going into for years was Home Depot. He didn't want to continue on without her.

We discussed how his grandchildren, those at his work, and Scooter needed him. I sent him home with a week's supply of pain medication (I usually sent home with him a month's supply) Scooter had used in the past for his arthritis, discussed a cancer he's had for many years and a newly developing cough. On the bottle I had the receptionist write for him to call me before the medication ran out. I shortened Scooter's usual medication in hopes of checking up on Roger.

Not knowing anything else I could do for Roger—I sent him a book called *The Birth We Call Death* along with a note about the experiences I had losing my kid's mom to cancer.

A few weeks later Scooter's cough was getting worse, x-rays and lab work was done and I referred him to see a specialist. They placed Scooter on medication for the cough and felt he would do okay. Things continued to worsen and Roger had Scooter euthanized (put to sleep) because of the struggling he was having getting his breath.

Searching my soul about this "circle of life" we are going through and the quickening and warm spirit I've experienced from time to time—logic tells me there must be more than the time we spend on this earth.

It is often asked, If God really lives, how could he allow his children to suffer so much? If He lives, then where did I come from, why am I here and where do I go after death? Will I ever have the chance to see again those I love that have died before me? Are we just weak, having difficulties in our life and using a god for a crutch? Is there anything beyond what you see and experience on this earth?

Addressing his people Korihor said, "O ye that are bound down under a foolish and a vain hope, why do ye yoke yourselves with such foolish things…they are foolish traditions of your fathers." *Alma 30:13-14*

The concept that all of us living on this earth are part of a three act play of life has helped give me a better understanding that I'm not here just because of the creation of this earth over millions of years by chance and that when I'm dead there is nothing. There just must be a plan that gives everything the spark of energy and purpose for all living things on this planet.

We're in the middle of a three-act play that we don't fully understand, but focusing on Christ's teachings can help us find an eternally happy ending.

The lights dim. The plush red curtain rises. The costumed figures around you spring into action. Who is the hero? Who is the villain? It's hard to say. You stand center stage, unable to make sense of it all. Everyone seems to understand what's going on but you. "This is act 2," one actor whispers. "Look over this script."

We may not all be actors, but the notion of such a play is not that far from reality. Imagine the plan of salvation, also called "the great plan of happiness" (Alma 42:8), as a three-act play. Act 1 is where we came from, act 2 is our life on earth, and act 3 is where we are going. During act 2, we have no memory of our past and little knowledge of our future, but fortunately the gospel of Jesus Christ—the play's script—puts our mortal life in context.

Act 1 - Understanding Our Beginnings: From the scriptures and the words of living prophets, we learn of our premortal existence (see Abraham 3:22–24). Before we came to earth, we participated in a council with our Heavenly Father. We learned that we would come to earth to gain a body, have posterity, face opposition, and increase in light and truth. If we were obedient and became more Christlike, we could one day live with our Father again.

Because we would make mistakes along the way, Jesus Christ was chosen as our Savior to pay the price of sin. He suffered for each of us, and because of His sacrifice, we can be cleansed through repentance.

But Satan (or Lucifer, as he was called in the premortal existence) rebelled and sought to remove our ability to choose right or wrong. A War in Heaven began. Upon his defeat, Satan was cast out of heaven, along with the spirits who chose to follow him (see Moses 4:1–4).

Though we can't remember this premortal existence, we know that we promised to do all we could to return to God's presence once we were on earth. And He promised us agency, allowing us to choose to follow Him.

Act 2 - Using Our Agency: Now we are here in act 2, and God has provided the script to guide us back to Him—the gospel of Jesus Christ. Our challenge is to use our agency to follow the script so we can prepare to return to our Heavenly Father (see Abraham 3:25). Like a complex play full of subplots, our mortal life can be complicated. It is riddled with temptations, trials, and tragedies of every kind. But the truth is that act 2 is all about choosing whether we will follow the teachings of Christ so we can become more like Him.

The scriptures provide the perfect pattern for happiness, encouraging us to "press forward, feasting upon the word of Christ, and endure to the end" (2 Nephi 31:20). We grow as we make and keep covenants, obey the commandments, and repent when we sin. As we immerse ourselves in the scriptures and teachings of our prophets, we will stay focused on the plan we joyfully agreed to follow in act 1.

Act 3 - Embracing Eternity: Our physical bodies may die at the end of act 2, but the story doesn't end there. In fact, act 3 has no closing curtain—it is eternal (see Abraham 3:26).

Because of the Atonement of Jesus Christ, all of God's children who come to earth will be resurrected. What could be more joyful than resurrection? (see D&C 93:33).

Nearly all will also receive a degree of glory depending on their works: the telestial kingdom, with a glory like that of the stars; the terrestrial kingdom, with a glory like that of the moon; or the celestial kingdom, with the ultimate glory like that of the sun (see D&C 76:50–113). In the celestial kingdom we will dwell with the Father and the Son. A relative few will remain "filthy still" (2 Nephi 9:16) and be cast into outer darkness, where they can never progress.

What Will Your Story Be? If we follow the gospel of Jesus Christ in act 2, act 3 of our play will be glorious beyond belief. The curtains are up. The action is underway. What will you do on stage?1

When I lost my parents and the mother of my children, I felt pain that I still can't put into words. However, going through the pains of loss and loneliness and other personal challenges during my life, I better understand and am beginning to appreciate why we must go through trials to truly enjoy the goodness life has to offer.

Elder Orson F. Whitney wrote, "No pain that we suffer, no trial that we experience is wasted. It ministers to our education, to the development of such qualities as patience, faith, fortitude and humility. All that we suffer and all that we endure, especially when we endure it patiently, builds up our characters, purifies our hearts, expands our souls, and makes us more tender and charitable, more worthy to be called the children of God . . . and it is through sorrow and suffering, toil and tribulation, that we gain the education that we come here to acquire and which will make us more like our Father and Mother in heaven." *Orson F. Whitney (1855-1931).*

Pain stayed so long, I said to him today,
"I will not have you with me anymore,"
I stamped my foot and said, "Be on your way,"
And paused there, startled at the look he wore.
"I, who have been your friend," he said to me;
"I, who have been your teacher—all you know
Of understanding love, of sympathy
And patience I have taught you. Shall I go?" *Unknown*

Roger now has a new four-legged friend, the breeder personally flew the puppy from Indiana and delivered him at Roger's front door. He takes him to work each day and is getting back into a normal routine. The crisis is gone for the time being.

I hope Roger has been able to replace the terrible loss of his wife with faith and hope that he will one day have the opportunity of being with her again. My prayer is that both he and I can keep in perspective the why we need to go through the refiner's painful fire of sorrow and suffering, toil and tribulations throughout our lives. That we can prepare ourselves and look with joy and anticipation forward as we struggle to endure all that comes our way until we cross the veil into our loved one's arms.

1. *Life's a Play: The Plan of Salvation in Three Acts, author Margaret Willden, 2017. Based on a talk, "The Play and the Plan," given by President Elder Boyd K. Packer (1924–2015) in a Church Educational System fireside for young adults on May 7, 1995.*

24

I FEEL YOUR PAIN

In 1992, presidential candidate Bill Clinton famously told an activist who was heckling him at a rally, "I feel your pain," and that statement quickly entered the popular vernacular as a clichéd expression of sympathy.

Most of us have at one time or another found ourselves telling someone who is complaining to us about something that we, like Bill Clinton, "feel" his or her pain. Whether our offer of sympathy is intended to be taken sincerely or ironically, however, we almost certainly do not intend for it to be taken literally. No matter how empathetic we may like to imagine ourselves, we cannot actually feel someone else's physical pain. Or can we?

At the Oregon Health and Science University suggests that physical pain may, indeed, be transferrable from one individual to another. In the Oregon study, one group of mice was subjected to a variety of pain-inducing stimuli (inflammation from a local injection of a noxious substance, and withdrawal from opiates and alcohol). Other "bystander" mice, not subject to the pain-inducing stimuli, were housed in different degrees of proximity to the primary mice in order to test whether or not their pain would be transferred to the bystander mice. All the mice were housed in open cages, but while one group of bystander mice was housed in the same room as the mice suffering inflammation and withdrawal, another group was housed in a separate room.

As expected, the mice that had been subjected to noxious stimuli soon developed hyperalgesia, or a measurable increase in sensitivity to pain. Interestingly, the bystander mice housed in the same room with the hyperalgesic mice exhibited a similar heightened sensitivity to pain. Even without any direct exposure to noxious stimuli, the bystander mice "felt" the pain of the primary mice who were suffering the effects of inflammation and withdrawal.

Catherine Matthews Pavia related this family story, It had been four years since I had come home for Easter, so I had looked forward to the break from school and the Easter activities with my family. We were in the kitchen fixing supper Friday night when I asked Mom about the family reunion she was organizing.

"Everyone wants to go back to the lake," she told me as she chopped vegetables. "But during the six-hour car trip last year ..." I looked up as the chopping ceased and her voice broke. Tears crept from the corners of her eyes, and her face crumpled. "I thought I was going to die. I really thought I was going to die."

I didn't know how to respond to my gentle, patient mother when she talked about the possibility of her death. I wanted to hug her until her shoulders stopped shaking. I wanted to tell her everything would be all right—the doctors would find out what this disease was and give her medicine and fix everything. But I couldn't.

I had refused to think of death throughout the year of her sickness, even as I fasted and prayed and hoped. Still, I watched her weaken and suffer. She wasn't vocal in her suffering. She just worked harder because she was unable to sleep at night or even sit down. The pain clutched at her heart and made her shake whenever she tried to relax. But soon her suffering became visible in the dark circles around her eyes and the fatigue deep in her eyes themselves.

Discouragement soon accompanied the pain. After a full year of visiting doctors and undergoing tests, she was distressed when the specialists were unable to discover what was causing the intense pain around her heart. The test results all came back normal. Nothing was wrong, the doctors said. But we knew the situation wasn't normal. My mother did not normally pace the floor at night or stop in the middle of vacuuming to sob. And my mother, who had faced many types of pain in her life without ever complaining, did not normally talk about dying.

During the two days before Easter, I tried again to think of something I could do to help her. But her disease had left us all feeling powerless. Even my father, a doctor, could not fix the situation, in spite of his years of training, experience, and knowledge. I could not alleviate her burdens—she even wanted to do most housework herself, because resting made the pain worse. So, she was always working, working to the point of exhaustion. And because there was so little we could do to relieve her suffering, she seemed to suffer alone.

Not surprisingly, the mice housed in a separate room—cut off from visual and auditory cues related to the pain sensitivity of the other mice—showed no initial signs of hyperalgesia. When a small amount of bedding from the cages of the hyperalgesic mice was placed in the cages of the mice housed in the separate room, however, those mice too began to exhibit hyperalgesia.

In the absence of visual and auditory information from the other two groups of mice, olfactory cues from their bedding induced hyperalgesia in the physically separated group of mice. While only one group of mice was actually subjected to a noxious stimulus, all three groups ended up displaying pronounced hyperalgesia. In other words, the pain of the mice in the first group was effectively transferred to the mice in the other two groups.

This study reinforces the conclusions of other studies on the transferability of pain. It covers new ground, however, in its demonstration of olfaction as a major mechanism in the social transfer of pain. There is still a great deal to be learned about the manner in which these cues trigger the experience of hyperalgesia, but a mounting body of evidence suggests that we may, indeed, be able to feel each other's pain.[1]

Plants or animals maybe "can't feel the pain" President Clinton expressed in 1992 or stress in the same way we do, but scientists have found that plant cells can communicate stress in a way that's not so different from animals. The findings show that plants use a compound, called gamma-aminobutyric acid or GABA, to create signals that regulate growth when facing drought, viruses or extreme temperatures. This is the same compound used as an essential neurotransmitter found in animal brains.

In other words, this is how plants manage stress without having a central nervous system. Animals have long lines of nerve cells to send messages throughout its body. This discovery suggests that there is a cell-to-cell communication in plants that is intrinsically a part of all plant tissues. The cells are not very isolated and the neurotransmitter is able to shuttle from one cell to another fairly rapidly. While the compound is exactly the same among plants and animals, the proteins that bind to it are very different within the two kingdoms of life.2

We went to church on Easter morning. As I glanced at my mother sitting beside me, my thoughts wandered back to her high, cracked voice and the chilling sentence that had consumed me since Friday night - "I thought I was going to die."

Suddenly my mother rose from the bench and made her way to the pulpit. "On this Easter Sunday," she began, "I want to bear my testimony of Jesus Christ's Atonement. King Benjamin said that Christ 'shall suffer temptations, and pain of body, hunger, thirst, and fatigue, even more than man can suffer.'3 Many of you may not know that I have been sick lately. The nights have been long" - her voice softened as she continued - "but not lonely. During the worst of it, the Savior has been my friend, my support. I testify that Jesus Christ knows our suffering because He experienced it—and more. He will lift us from our sorrows just as He lifted us from an eternal death."

As my mom bore her testimony, a new picture of suffering replaced my former preoccupation with my mother and myself. It was a picture of the Savior in the Garden of Gethsemane, full of such anguish that He bled from every pore as He suffered for all, including my mother's physical agony and my own emotional pain.

"I realized then that I did not need tell my mother that it would be OK. We couldn't fix everything, but she was comforted by her knowledge that the Savior already had."4

. . . come into the fold of God, . . . be called his people, and . . . willing to bear one another's burdens, that they may be light; Yea, . . . are willing to mourn with those that mourn; yea, and comfort those that stand in need of comfort, and to stand as witnesses of God at all times and in all things, and in all places that ye may be in, even until death...5

So the next time you say to a suffering friend of yours that you feel his or her pain, you can do so with the confidence that, however sincere or otherwise your extension of sympathy might actually be, you are at least expressing a physiological possibility. Of course, given the findings of these studies it might be more technically accurate to say that plants and animals have stress and painful like reactions to their environment—in a way "just like us." However, no matter how another animal or a plant expresses it, the ability to experience someone else's stress or pain is a literal fact rather than a figurative expression.

The sin free innocent plants and animals living on this wonderful planet adjust instinctively to the unchanging natural laws of survival for the fittest. God's children are consciencely aware that their creation has been given the agency to choose for themselves the paths they will take. They also have been given special gifts from our Heavenly Father that can help them recognize and overcome life's sins and suffering through the atonement of Jesus Christ.

President Harold B. Lee taught: Every man has the privilege to exercise these gifts and these privileges in the conduct of his own affairs; in bringing up his children in the way they should go; in the management of his business, or whatever he does. It is his right to enjoy the spirit of revelation and of inspiration to do the right thing, to be wise and prudent, just and good, in everything that he does.6

Elder Bruce R. McConkie discussing "Agency or Inspiration," stressed our responsibility to do all that we can before we seek a revelation. He gave a very personal example. When he set out to choose a companion for eternity, he did not go to the Lord and ask whom he ought to marry. "I went out and found the girl I wanted," he said. "She suited me; . . . it just seemed . . . as though this ought to be . . . (Then) all I did was pray to the Lord and ask for some guidance and direction in connection with the decision that I'd reached."

Elder McConkie summarized his counsel on the balance between agency and inspiration in these sentences: We're expected to use the gifts and talents and abilities, the sense and judgment and agency with which we are endowed . . . Implicit in asking in faith is the precedent requirement that we do everything in our power to accomplish the goal that we seek . . . We're expected to do everything in our power that we can, and then to seek an answer from the Lord, a confirming seal that we've reached the right conclusion.7

1. *Laura Sanders. Mice smell, share each other's pain, Science News, 11-26-16 & Hal McDonald Ph.D., Time Traveling with Apollo, "I Feel Your Pain"*

2. *Science, Jose Feijo, Plants send out stress signals just like animals, a contributor to the study's research team out of Australia and a professor at the University of Maryland, 2015.*

3. *Mosia 3:7.*

4. *Catherine Matthews Pavia wrote in the April 2002 Ensign.*

5. *Mosiah 18:8-9.*

6. *Stand Ye in Holy Places, Salt Lake City: Deseret Book, 1974, p. 141-42.*

7. *Speeches of the Year, 1972–73, Provo, Utah: Brigham Young University Press, 1973, p. 108-113.*

25

INCUBATOR BABIES

Before Lucille Horn came to be under the care of Martin Couney, in 1920, the doctors who'd brought her into the world had provided a bleak prognosis. "They didn't have any help for me at all. It was just: you die because you didn't belong in the world," she later recalled. Horn had been born prematurely, weighing around two pounds; her twin had died at birth. Hospitals at that time did not treat such small babies, but her father knew someone who did. So, he bundled her up and took her to the only place he knew that might be able to care for her: a sideshow attraction at New York City's Coney Island, which featured babies in incubators.1

Preterm birth is when a baby is born too early, before 37 weeks of pregnancy have been completed. In 2016, preterm birth affected about 1 of every 10 infants born in the United States. Preterm birth rates decreased from 2007 to 2014, and CDC research shows that this decline is due, in part, to declines in the number of births to teens and young mothers. However, the preterm birth rate rose for the second straight year in 2016. Additionally, racial and ethnic differences in preterm birth rates remain.

A developing baby goes through important growth throughout pregnancy—including in the final months and weeks. Premature (also known as preterm) birth is when a baby is born too early, before 37 weeks of pregnancy have been completed. The earlier a baby is born, the higher the risk of death or serious disability. In 2016 the CDC stated that preterm birth and low birth weight accounted for about 17% of infant deaths. Babies who survive can have breathing issues, intestinal (digestive) problems, and bleeding in their brains. Long-term problems may include developmental delay (not meeting the developmental milestones for his or her age) and lower performance in school.2

Incubators were still relatively new by the time Couney set up at Coney Island. Developed for infants in the 1880s, in Paris, Couney first displayed incubators—with babies—at the Berlin Exposition in 1896. From there he traveled to more expositions, including an event in London in 1897 and the Pan-American Exposition in Buffalo in 1901. But in 1903 he settled in the U.S. to run his babies-in-incubators summertime sideshow, which would continue until the early 1940s.

The premise of the attraction was straightforward enough: pay an entrance fee to see something you wouldn't usually be able to see. What set Couney's sideshow apart was that his subjects were premature babies in incubators, (without the benefit of the mother's first milk (colostrum), receiving care that hospitals did not provide. The entrance fees he collected went toward his operating costs, including round-the-clock care and wet nurses. Couney did not charge the parents of his tiny patients.

Reporting in 1903, *The Brooklyn Daily Eagle* described the "seriousness and value of the system shown." A visit to Couney's showcase revealed rows of warmed, glass-fronted incubators supplied with filtered air, containing "little pitiful pinched looking waifs... the only things that indicate that they are alive are the healthy color of their little faces and the faint flutterings of movement which are perceptible on closer inspection."

In the book *The Strange Case of Dr. Couney: How a Mysterious European Showman Saved Thousands of American Babies* by Dawn Raffel, recently reviewed by *JSTOR Daily*, Raffel reports that Couney may not have actually been a doctor. He also seems to have been cognizant of the theater element of a good sideshow. On occasion, he reportedly dressed infants, as they grew, in too-large clothing; his nurses were known to have slipped a finger ring around the entire wrist of their tiny charges.

Speaking to the *New Yorker* in 1939, Couney explained, "all my life I have been making propaganda for the proper care of preemies, who in other times were allowed to die," he said. "Everything I do is strict[ly] ethical."1

During my veterinary school rotation assignment in the large animal clinics our group rotation was assigned to care for a premature critically ill foal. The large animal instructor gave us permission to transfer the horse to the small animal clinic where we were able to place it on oxygen, nutrient enriched intravenous fluids and kept it warm. Unfortunately, we did not have an incubator or any of the important first milk, colostrum, from the mother available, and the foal died several days later.

With a normal gestation period considered to be 345 days, a foal delivered before the 320th day is considered to be premature. Foals delivered early are vulnerable to infection that may be passed on from the mare or contracted through outside sources. In addition, organs and bones may be under-developed, leading to respiratory and cardiac problems, along with soft, weak bones that cause problems for the foal when it attempts to stand.

The cause of most premature foal deliveries is placental infection. Most placental infections are caused by bacteria ascending through the vagina and entering the uterus. In spite of the deaths and monetary costs connected with premature foals, little progress has been made in understanding how premature deliveries can be prevented or treated in a practical and economical way.3

For any new born foal receiving the first milk from their mother (colostrum) is extremely important.

Colostrum is the thick, sticky yellow fluid produced by the mammary gland of the mare during the last few weeks of pregnancy. It is comprised of carbohydrates, fats, proteins and electrolytes. Colostrum is rich in antibodies that are critically important for immune protection of the newborn foal. The process by which foals acquire antibodies from the colostrum of their dam is called 'passive transfer of immunity'.

The capacity of the small intestine to absorb and transfer antibodies is greatest during the first 6-8 hours after birth. It declines substantially after 12 hours and within 24 hours after birth the specialized intestinal cells are replaced by cells incapable of transferring antibodies. Consequently, ingestion of colostrum by the foal after 24 hours of age will not result in an increase in blood antibody levels.4

By one estimate, Couney saved the lives of 6,500 infants. His decades of caring for premature babies has been credited in the development of neonatal care in hospitals. But by the early 1940s, interest in Couney's exhibition had waned and hospitals were beginning to open units dedicated to the care of premature babies. Couney died in 1950, at age 80. At the time of his death he was reportedly broke, but he was memorialized in *The New York Times* as "the incubator doctor."

In 2015, two years before she died at the age of 96, Lucille Horn was asked by her daughter, as part of NPR's StoryCorps program, about being on display as a tiny infant. "It's strange," she said, "but as long as they saw me and I was alive, it was all right."1

Martin Couney may not have been a doctor and placed the preemie babies on display in a carnival environment for the wrong reason (money, fame etc.)—but he did the right thing. He saved upwards of 6,500 babies that were offered little to no hope of survival and popularized incubators enough to have hospitals take notice.

The Center for Disease Control reports that 1 out of 10 infants are born too early in this country. That means that before the use of incubators about 10% of all births would die.

I read somewhere comments on doing the right thing for the wrong reason. It went something like this: Doing something for others for your own personal gain? Are all actions created equal no matter any underlying intent by the person doing the good or bad action? Is it just as good for a person to inspire others because he gets acclaim for it as it is for the person who does it out of the goodness of his heart?

These questions are a little deep for my thought process. However, I know that many years ago our attempts to save the premature foal that died at Purdue University in the small animal clinic was not the right choice for our patient—but each of us caring for that horse gained experiences that helped us practice veterinary medicine with a better understanding of care for premature animals.

One can be confident they are doing the right things for the right reason if they remember, "Trust in the Lord with all you heart, and do not lean on your own understanding." Proverbs 3:5

You know in your heart what's right and wrong—
Do the right thing . . .
"but as long as they saw me and I was
alive, it was all right" Lucille Horn

1. *When Infants in Incubators Were a Side show Attraction, by Anika Burges, 09-27-2018.*
2. *CDC.*
3. *EQUIMED STAFF - 10/21/2014.*
4. *Animal Reproduction Systems, Patrick M. McCue, DVM, PhD, Diplomate American College of Theriogenologists, Colorado State University 200-2018.*

26

ENERGY USE AND AVAILABILTY

As Mark P. Mills explored in a previous paper, "The New Energy Economy: An Exercise in Magical Thinking" has many enthusiasts believing things that are not possible when it comes to the physics of fueling society, not least the magical belief that "clean-tech" energy can echo the velocity of the progress of digital technologies. It cannot.

This paper turns to a different reality: all energy-producing machinery must be fabricated from materials extracted from the earth. No energy system, in short, is actually "renewable," since all machines require the continual mining and processing of millions of tons of primary materials and the disposal of hardware that inevitably wears out. Compared with hydrocarbons, green machines entail, on average, a 10-fold increase in the quantities of materials extracted and processed to produce the same amount of energy.

This means that any significant expansion of today's modest level of green energy—currently less than 4% of the country's total consumption (versus 56% from oil and gas)—will create an unprecedented increase in global mining for needed minerals, radically exacerbate existing environmental and labor and the vulnerability of America's energy supply chain.

As recently as 1990, the U.S. was the world's number-one producer of minerals. Today, it is in seventh place. Even though the nation has vast mineral reserves worth trillions of dollars, America is now 100% dependent on imports for some 17 key minerals, and, for another 29, over half of domestic needs are imported.

Building wind turbines and solar panels to generate electricity, as well as batteries to fuel electric vehicles, requires, on average, more than 10 times the quantity of materials, compared with building machines using hydrocarbons to deliver the same amount of energy to society.

A single electric car contains more cobalt than 1,000 smartphone batteries; the blades on a single wind turbine have more plastic than 5 million smartphones; and a solar array that can power one data center uses more glass than 50 million phones.

Replacing hydrocarbons with green machines under current plans—never mind aspirations for far greater expansion—will vastly increase the mining of various critical minerals around the world. For example, a single electric car battery weighing 1,000 pounds requires extracting and processing some 500,000 pounds of materials. That's 20 times more than the 25,000 pounds of petroleum that an internal combustion engine uses over the life of a car. Averaged over a battery's life, each mile of driving an electric car "consumes" five pounds of earth.

Using an internal combustion engine consumes about 0.2 pounds of liquids per mile.

By 2050, with current plans, the quantity of worn-out solar panels—much of it nonrecyclable—will constitute double the tonnage of all today's global plastic waste, along with over 3 million tons per year of unrecyclable plastics from worn-out wind turbine blades. By 2030, more than 10 million tons per year of batteries will become garbage.

All machines wear out, and there is nothing actually renewable about green machines, since one must engage in continual extraction of materials to build new ones and replace those that wear out. All this requires mining, processing, transportation, and, ultimately, the disposing of millions of tons of materials, much of it functionally or economically unrecyclable.

A World Bank study noted what every mining engineer knows: "Technologies assumed to populate the clean energy shift . . . are in fact significantly more material intensive in their composition than current traditional fossil-fuel-based energy supply systems." All forms of green energy require roughly comparable quantities of materials in order to build machines that capture nature's flows: sun, wind, and water. Wind farms come close to matching hydro dams in material consumption, and solar farms outstrip both. In all three cases, the largest share of the tonnage is found in conventional materials like concrete, steel, and glass. Compared with a natural gas power plant, all three require at least 10 times as many total tons mined, moved, and converted into machines to deliver the same quantity of energy.1

Hydropower is a usable energy generated from water, whether it comes from turbines, dams or any other source. Construction costs up front are expensive, there are some adverse environmental impact considerations and there are limited areas where reservoirs can be constructed.

It is a renewable energy source, can help meet spike electricity demands, pairs well with other renewables, is inexpensive in the long run and produced domestically, and can be used for irrigation.

Biomass energy, sometimes known as 'bio energy', is the energy that is derived from organic matter of plants and animals. Biomass in the form of dead plants, trees, grass, leaves, crops, manure, garbage, animal waste can be a great source of alternative fuels that can be used to replace fossil fuels. Plants make use of a process called photosynthesis that converts energy from the sun into chemical energy.

This energy gets transferred to animals when they eat plants. When plants and animal waste are burned, the carbon dioxide and waste stored inside them are released back into the atmosphere. This is why biomass energy is said to be renewable.

Biomass energy is, perhaps, one of the more controversial types of alternative energy that is being used today. It helps reduce dependency on fossil fuels, considered to be carbon neutral, widely available, can be used in many forms, helps reduce waste and is less expensive than fossil fuels.

A concern for using biomass as a clean energy is the pollution created from burning natural materials. Incineration of some biomass creates pollution from different compounds produced that are comparable with coal and other types of energy resources. Primary concerns are the production of methane gases, which are also harmful to the Earth's ozone layer, and that it can attract unwanted pests (rats, flies) and spread bacteria and infection.

Wood is a major source of biomass energy. The desire to produce energy on a large scale can lead to deforestation and the loss of the beneficial natural ecology of the area, including droughts and loss of animal habitats. Governments are increasingly making efforts to match replanting with the rate of cutting down trees.

Building biomass plants, transporting and resource gathering expenses are much higher than fossil plants and will be continually needed every day. When you compare the process of biomass energy to fossil fuels, you find that the cost is actually much higher. Also, there is a solid contention against biomass in light of the fact that it causes crops to be planted with the aim of collecting for fuel in order to power the biomass plants.

By developing crops that are committed to delivering fuel that will, in the end, be used for biomass energy, we are utilizing land that may have been utilized for food sources. This practice is said to be causing some of the food deficiencies in specific parts of the world.

Using the process of liquification with NaOH or KOH of animal waste may become a viable way of helping solve the problem of air pollution, high energy needed for incineration, reduce some of the need for fertilizers that require energy to produce, and help remove the tons of animal carcasses into biogas and enriched fertilizer. The biogas (primarily methane) can be used to help meet the needs of natural gas to fuel electric plants.

Geothermal energy is a type of renewable energy taken from the Earth's core. It comes from heat generated during the original formation of the planet and the subsequent radioactive decay of materials. This thermal energy is stored in rocks and fluids in the center of the earth. There are many considerations that come with geothermal power.

It is a reliable source of power, installations do not require large land resources, energy production sources are limited, there are high initial investment costs, production of electricity has good longevity, but the plant area may develop some surface instability.

(In 2021, renewables make up 20% of electric generation—wind 9.2%, hydro 6.3%, solar 2.8%, biomass 1.3%, geothermal 0.4%)

Nuclear energy in modern power plants is created when an atom splits, becoming two separate, lighter atoms. The energy is released in the form of heat and it is then used to run steam turbines connected to alternators to produce electricity. The process that generates all of this energy is called nuclear fission.

These reactions are produced in nuclear reactors: safe and controlled environments created specifically for nuclear power plants. Uranium is the primary fuel used to facilitate the chain reaction and production of nuclear energy. This is because Uranium is one of the atoms with the largest nucleus and this facilitates the nuclear reaction.

Nuclear reactors have an expensive upfront cost, low operation costs, are built on a small land area, yield continuous reliable high-density energy, need to allow for radioactive waste disposal and the potential of catastrophic accidents.

The average age of nuclear reactors is approaching 40 years and experts say there are no technical limits to these units churning out clean and reliable energy for an additional 40 years. The last nuclear reactor built in the US was in 1995.

(In 2021, nuclear energy provided
20% of electric generation)

Coal energy is a non-renewable source of energy used to generate electricity. Coal is an affordable and number one source of energy for manufacturing plants and home appliances. There is an abundant supply of coal energy which is easy to extract and burn.

Coal offers continuous energy supply, is an efficient and predictable source of energy, there is an abundant supply, coal energy is more sustainable compared to other fossil fuels which will not last a century, cost-effective, it can be converted into a liquid or gas state.

Coal creates high levels of radiation that are 100 times that produced by a nuclear power plant, produce mercury, heavy metal, nitrous oxide and other pollutants which have a negative impact on the environment that can lead to the creation of acid rain, high levels of carbon dioxide which contributes to global warming, human air passageway inflammation and lung cancer, high levels of methane (which if technology becomes available this biogas can be an asset), and can cause underground burning that destroy local animal habitats and cause deforestation.

(In 2021, coal provided 22% of electric generation)

Natural gas (methane) emits less greenhouse gas and outdoor air pollution when burnt than other fossil fuels, is inexpensive as an energy source, widely available, can be turned on and ramped up to provide electricity very quickly to a power grid, biogas is renewable and there appear to be big reserves of gas to tap including beneath the ocean.

Mining natural gas can have negative environmental side effects, releases some green gases and emits air pollution when burnt.

Although oil use also has some disadvantages especially to the environment, you cannot survive without using it. After combustion, oil releases gases such as carbon dioxide and other greenhouse emissions. These gases are harmful to the ozone layer as their accumulation encourages its deterioration. Oil is used little for electricity production.

(In 2021, natural gas provided 38% of electric generation, petroleum provided 0.5%)

Lately:

When I get in our electric vehicle, I think of processing 500,000 pounds of material just to make the battery.

When I think about the year 1985, I spend less time thinking about how poor a wind turbine farm was for a retirement investment and more about the tons of noisy giant rotating blades that last for only about 20 years (that have killed uncountable birds, bats and insects), laying in piles somewhere on the ground waiting for the development of new technology so they can be recycled.

When I look at the solar panels on our roof, I'm reminded that by 2050 the quantity of worn-out solar panels, much of it nonrecyclable, will constitute double the tonnage of all today's global plastic waste.

I shudder when I hear our honorable governor of California telling us that he is stopping the building of more gas stations in our state, allowing only electric vehicles traveling on our highways by 2035 and in the next breath asks all electric car owners to not charge their cars during peak electricity use - so the power grid doesn't fail.

Thinking about an inefficient incandescent light bulb drawing 100W, that a car charger draws enough electricity to light about the equivalent of 72 of these light bulbs, run 5 hair dryers, or it can continuously run a bit less than two central AC systems.2

I think about my states electrical infrastructure being already challenged with frequent blackouts during peak use and I can only imagine what will happen when all these new electric cars are being charged using California's power grid (there are 17,765,625 vehicles registered and only 563,070 are electric—3.2%).

I don't look at or think much about our Tesla backup battery, we had attached to the side of our home four months ago, until we have a power outage. Unfortunately, in the last four months the power has failed six times in our home—one lasting over 24 hours. Primary inconveniences with the power out are: I have had to shut off my electric timer for the lights in our driveway because every time the power goes out the lights come on at random times of the day or night and there is no AC or heat available from the furnace. Will this become the sign of the times?

When I look as all the available energy options that can produce sustainable energy, my thoughts focus on the advantages of biomass and natural gas (methane). We flush tons of biomass down the toilet, bury or burn thousands of dead animals and release valuable methane gas as waste into the atmosphere.

I question the powers that be who spend millions of our tax dollars investing in foolishness like Solyndra to build solar panels in the United States, cash for clunkers that destroyed vehicles that were more efficient in total carbon use than the new greener ones being built, rebates and promotions encouraging us to purchase items that often are not cost or energy competitive, promote energy policies that force prices high enough to push customers into investing in inefficient renewable energy, etc.

I think of all the natural resources and what could be done if even a small fraction of the wasted dollars were spent pursuing the potential use of renewable energy produced every day by nature. The highly respected "Science" magazine I read seems to spend more time showing projections and consensus of opinions about how climate change may affect the world, which is questionable how much can be done, and doesn't present many studies on how we can benefit from better understanding how nature recycles energy. Science magazine discusses little about the increasing greening benefits of the earth we've experienced since the beginning of this last century—in October 2022 National Geographic Magazine noted, "Satellite images of the Alps show that the amount of vegetation above the tree line has increased by nearly 80% in less than 40 years…"

Someone said, "No one ever got off their horse and got into the newly developed automobile from government investing schemes, rebates or promotions. They got off their horse because the car filled the needs of travel much better than the horse." I read an article about the poor economic and environmental sense it makes adding wind turbines, solar panels and electric vehicles to our energy use equation.

However, his final comment was since there are so many government spiffs trying to get us into this habit, the economics makes sense—"I'm buying into it." So, I also did.

John Muir stated, "When one tugs at a single thing in nature, he finds it attached to the rest of the world." Tugging at the earth there is no energy system, in short, that is actually "renewable." All machines require the continual mining and processing of millions of tons of primary materials and the disposal of hardware that inevitably wears out. Compared with hydrocarbons, green machines entail, on average, a 10-fold increase in the quantities of materials extracted and processed to produce the same amount of energy.1

When we "tug" gently in relationships there is usually more sugar than vinegar to be found. Hopefully, man may learn to "tug" more gently, listening to the quiet voice of nature's way and side step the vinegar until the sugar is found.

1. *Mines, Minerals, and "Green" Energy: A Reality Check Report, Mark P. Mills, Senior Fellow, 07/2020.*
2. *How much electricity does an electric car use? Ted's energy tips, Posted on August 27, 2019.*

27

PLASTIC WASTE BECOMING A NATURAL RESOURCE

The disposal of plastics is a highly visible global problem—from the highest mountains to the deepest ocean trenches, waste plastic seems inescapable. In natural conditions, plastics are nearly indestructible, and yet they are discarded worldwide on a large scale: the world produces around 359 million tons of plastics each year. The environment cannot address their disposal at a speed fast enough to prevent harm to living beings.

This has led to a consensus that plastics are an unsustainable material. And yes, plastics are certainly an enormous problem, but they don't necessarily have to be. The main issue is not with plastic as a material, but with our linear economic model: goods are produced, consumed, then disposed of. This model assumes endless economic growth and doesn't consider the planet's exhaustible resources.

Most people believe that plastics recycling is severely restricted: that only a few types can be recycled at all. But there are many ways we could set plastics on a different lifecycle—and one that many have been working on is turning disused plastics into a hardy, reliable and sustainable building materials.1

Researchers at Argentina's National Agricultural Technology Institute crafted wooden, artificial nests for wild bees. Unlike bee species that have a large hive with queens and workers, wild bees burrow into nests to individually lay larvae. The constructed nests fit together like long rectangles with a narrow, hollow opening that allowed wild bees to crawl inside and fill it with cut leaves, twigs, and mud.

Sixty-three wooden nests were constructed, and three were found lined entirely with plastic. Similar in size and shape to a fingernail, the bits of plastic had been carefully cut by bees and arranged in an overlapping pattern in their nests. Based on the material, researchers think the plastic may have come from a plastic bag or film, which has a similar texture to the leaves bees typically use to line their nests.

Of the three plastic nests, one had not been finished, meaning the bee did not use it to lay her larvae, Science Alert reports. In the remaining two, one larva died and the other was not found, leading the researchers to believe it survived.

This new research, published in the journal Apidologie, documents the first-time bees have been seen making nests only out of plastic, but for years scientists have known bees were incorporating plastic into their building materials.2

The plants homes on Earth are adjusting to increasing amounts of microplastic materials accumulating in their environment. An intensive study by the American

Chemical Society in 2019 summed up their findings: In conclusion, our findings imply that pervasive microplastic contamination may have consequences for agroecosystems and general terrestrial biodiversity. Further studies on the potential effects of microplastics with regard to other plant species, particle types, and environmental conditions are required to further unravel the full extent of terrestrial environmental change potentially triggered by this class of anthropogenic particles.3

Plastics are strong, durable, waterproof, lightweight, easy to mold, and recyclable—all key properties for construction materials. All polymers are, technologically, 100% recyclable. Some of them have the perfect cradle-to-cradle lifecycle: they can be used again and again to produce the same goods.

Some plastics can be reused just as they are by shredding an object into flakes, melting it, and reusing. Examples of successful industrial recycling include PET, or poly(ethylene therephtalate), which is used to make soft drink bottles, and polystyrene. Also, any plastic waste can be shredded and used as filler for asphalt, or be pyrolysed—decomposed through heating—to produce fuel.

Recycled plastics may have lower mechanical properties compared to virgin plastics, because each time you melt and process a plastic, the polymeric chains degrade. But these properties can be recovered by mixing it to additives or virgin plastic, making it possible for the rest of recycled plastic to technically be reprocessed into new materials for different applications.

Currently researchers are adjusting the properties of plastic materials by a rotomolding process, a plastics molding technology that is ideal for making large hollow building materials. What is wanted is to use the maximum amount of recycled plastics in making these blocks. They are currently made of 25% recycled plastics and have performed extremely well in mechanical tests. The goal is to use as close to 100% recycled plastics in building materials.

Building materials made from recycled plastics are not yet widely used in the construction industry—prototypes have mainly been used for demonstrative installations. It will take political will and widespread environmental awareness to encourage more investment into the potential in plastics recycling.1

A Bogota-based company produces low-cost houses made of plastic; each one averages around 430 square feet. Since 2010, they have been building temporary and permanent homes, shelters, classrooms, community rooms and other buildings in Colombia.

Founded by Colombian architect Oscar Mendez, the company transforms the recycled plastic into Lego-like bricks that are easy to assemble and contain additives that make them resistant to fire and earthquakes. Its clients are the government, non-governmental organizations, foundations and private companies, who pay for housing solutions in the communities where the houses are built. Similar plastic home building production projects are occurring in Mexico and Argentina.4

In an effort to bring light to communities lacking electricity, one pioneering project is utilizing an unexpected tool: old plastic bottles. Liter of Light, a project of the Philippines-based nonprofit MyShelter Foundation, provides light to poor households around the world with limited or no access to electricity—by collecting plastic bottles, filling them with water and bleach, and sticking them into roofs. The bleach-filled bottles then refract the light from outdoors into the house, lighting up much like a lightbulb.

In poorer parts of the country you find houses that are so stuck together that they have no windows and an iron roof over head. No light can enter the homes even during the light of day.

But the bleach bottle lights—which were originally thought up by Brazilian mechanic Alfredo Moser, who worked with MyShelter to bring them to people worldwide—have a major downside: They only work when the sun is out.

To solve the problem, the group added a mechanism to have the bottles work at night as solar lamps. By slipping a test tube with a small LED lightbulb into the bottle, which in turn is hooked up to a mini-solar panel, the bottle can still refract outside light during the day, but then also be used as a lightbulb at night. The lights last for approximately five years. In addition to using the bleach bottle lamps and the nighttime solar bulbs, the group also converts kerosene lamps into solar lamps.

Since launching in 2012, Liter of Light has provided lights to 850,000 households across more than a dozen countries, including the Philippines, Egypt and Colombia. The plain bleach bottles represent about 5 percent of their lights, Diaz said, with the bulk being solar-converted bottles, kerosene lamps and streetlamps.5

It looks like there may be a time when plastics will not be the blessing/curse man fears. The day may be on the horizon when plastic is considered a safe reusable resource for many needs including a part of the environment's foundation for our plants, animals and, as long as they are built on a firm foundation, even humans can safely call their home.

Steven L. Taylor relates the following story: In 1976 my wife, Diane, and I, along with our two small children, traveled to Iran, where I had a contract through an American company to teach English to Iranian air force pilots. These pilots were in flight school being taught in English by American instructors to fly modern military aircraft. American-Iranian relations were very different then than they are today.

While in Iran we lived in Isfahan, an ancient city with beautiful mosques, bridges, fountains, and parks. We witnessed some of the amazing workmanship from the glory days of ancient Persia. These centuries-old treasures were obviously built on solid foundations.

During our stay in Isfahan we rented a house in a new, rapidly spreading area on the outskirts of the city called "the flats." Many of the houses there were being built quickly for rental to foreigners, particularly Americans, who were coming in large numbers to work on various projects going on in Iran at the time. The house we rented was brand new. It lacked some of the comforts and conveniences we were used to, but it had other luxuries that were new to us, such as beautiful chandeliers and marble floors.

One day while we were out walking in our neighborhood, we observed preparations being made to build a new house—workers were clearing the ground, moving rocks and piles of dirt. A day or two later we saw chalk lines on the ground showing where the walls were to be located, both exterior and interior. Within days, piles of mud adobe bricks appeared, and the walls began to rise on the bare ground where the chalk lines indicated. My wife and I asked each other, "Where is the foundation?"

Ironically, about this very same time, we began experiencing problems in our house. We could hear what sounded like water running in the house even when all of the faucets were turned off.

One day as my wife was eating lunch with the children in the kitchen, she heard a strange, loud noise. She turned and watched, in shock, as the floor in the large entry room adjacent to the kitchen caved in. Later, as I returned home to the scene, I also found that the wall of the garage had begun to disintegrate into oozing mud. A leak in the water pipe located in the dirt directly beneath the house was literally washing away the foundation of our house.

We were experiencing firsthand the problems of a house built on a sandy foundation. Though our house had many ornate features and fancy materials, its foundation was weak. We moved out, and, unfortunately, the landlord was left with a total disaster.6

Therefore, everyone who hears these words of mine and puts them into practice is like a wise man who built his house on the rock. The rain came down, the streams rose, and the winds blew and beat against that house; yet it did not fall, because it had its foundation on the rock. But everyone who hears these words of mine and does not put them into practice is like a foolish man who built his house on sand. The rain came down, the streams rose, and the winds blew and beat against that house, and it fell with a great crash. *Matthew 7:24-27.*

I remember in 1976 before we could move into our new home it was necessary to do an inspection to be sure it was considered earthquake safe. Most of the inspection time was spent under the crawl space looking for secure attachments on the foundation to the rest of the home.

I also remember jokes about a warm floor in one of or patient wards at Camden Pet Hospital. We proselytized many theories of what the previous owner or builders had buried under the foundation that would generate heat. Several years after I became owner the area was investigated. The jury was out and a leaking hot water pipe was discovered. All was repaired after removing the tile floor, breaking through the concrete, removing several wheel barrows full of mud, lost use of the room for a couple of weeks and an expense more than expected. Fortunately the building was built on a firm foundation and there was not more extensive underground damage - a plus was that the monthly energy bill was reduced.

Have you wondered about what happens to all the plastic stuff once you throw it away? While it's a common belief that most plastics end up in a recycling factory close to your locality, the reality is far from the truth. There are so many facets behind what truly happens to the plastics we leave behind.

With just 9% of the plastic getting recycled, most of it is ending up in lands and water bodies. This ends up harming the environment more. It's found that the huge majority of the plastic waste, which comprises about 79%

of the plastic produced, is lying around in the landfills and oceans.

Most of the plastic waste from the US are shipped to the poorest countries of the world. This is done because of cheap labor without any care about the consequence of public health and the environment.

Since some of these countries aren't adept at managing their local waste and as the volume of plastic waste is increasing, thousands of tons of plastic are getting stranded in the US.7

At least for now, plants and animals seem to be adjusting to the increasing amounts of plastic in their environment. Plastic waist is a crisis that technology stimulated by economics may one day produce a cradle to cradle 100% renewable resource. And, the poor countries where our plastic waste is being dumped and buried may get wealthy producing income from mining the plastic waste. The value of plastic waste may become a resource as important as coal, oil, gas and nuclear energy.

One day I may find myself building a new durable home with a firm foundation on the San Andreas Fault without concerns of ever having a termite problem, never needing to paint or reroof the structure, and that one day will be eco-friendly enough to be melted down and recycled into other uses for the benefit of man, plants and the animals. Much like concrete and asphalt is recycled today.

However, there may be one big potential drawback to my planned home: It was discovered by accident in 2017 when an amateur beekeeper and biologist for a Biological Research in Spain was tending to her hives that were plagued with wax worms. She placed them in a plastic bag, noticed later there were lots of holes in the bag, and found that they weren't only chewing—but there was a chemical breakdown of the plastic.

In a study published in the 2022 journal Nature Communications, researchers discovered that enzymes in the saliva of wax worms can readily degrade polyethylene, a common form of plastic used in bags and other packaging materials. They are moth larvae that live in the honeycombs of beehives and have two enzymes, or proteins that speed chemical reactions, in their saliva that break down the plastic (polyethylene) at room temperature within just a few hours, according to the study.

To the best of the researcher's knowledge, these are the first known animal enzymes with the ability to degrade plastic. This introduces possibly new solutions to the world's plastic pollution problem through "bio-recycling," in which organisms break down waste materials and create new products from them.

The new finding maybe a breakthrough because wax worms degrade plastic so quickly and without the need for extreme temperature conditions. Enzymatic breakdown may become a route for making use of polyethylene waste. One concern is that the wax worms produce carbon dioxide gas into the atmosphere, that is a green gas pollutant.

The finding could also be applied to large plastic waste management plants (located near greenhouses where the carbon dioxide gas produced could be used as a fertilizer) as well as contribute to the development of at-home kits that allow people to recycle their own plastic waste.8

One approach to recycling the wax worm larva, after their useful life span used for plastic enzymatic brake down of plastic, might be used along with other food waste for a protein source. It has been recently proposed that insect protein could be used to produce protein-rich feeds for aquaculture and livestock. Both the scientific community and the food and feed's industrial sectors have begun to reconsider the use of insects as feedstuff, based on food-waste recycling.

This approach actually has even greater potential, as insects could also be a rich source of protein for direct human consumption. So far, however, eating insects is not very popular in the West, despite the fact that humans in other cultures and regions consume about 1900 different insect species.

Using insects to feed animals seems to be much more acceptable for consumers. However, although this strategy holds great promise as a sustainable and environmentally friendly way of generating food and feeds from discarded food, it is severely hampered by existing EU legislation, which strictly bans the feeding of K3-food waste (any meat content) to livestock—including insects—and also bans insect meals in animal feeds other than pet-feed, and which has repercussions far beyond Europe.9

Although insects are becoming more accepted as potential protein sources for food and feed, the appearance of the insect may be off-putting due to associations of disgust. Edible insects are more likely to be eaten if they are processed into non-recognizable forms.

Thus, insects require the use of commercial processing methods that will render the protein suitable for food/feed formulation, while maintaining the safety, nutritional and sensory quality of the final product.

Common methods that can be used include lipid extraction, enzymatic proteolysis, commercial thermal processing (e.g. blanching, pasteurization, and commercial sterilization), low-temperature processing (refrigeration and freezing), dehydration, and fermentation technology. Each method has advantages and disadvantages that need to be carefully considered as not all processing methods and/or conditions apply to all edible insects or insect flours.10

So, what do you think about this scenario: What if the wax worm larva got out of my at-home plastic recycling kit and started dissolving holes in my durable home, built entirely with plastic waste, sitting on the San Andreas Fault. The potential for disaster could be worse than termites in a traditionally built wood constructed home; because—while I'm eating a protein rich meal that contains processed wax worms, the larvae could be busily engaged in dissolving away my home and destroying the "Whole Thing" -foundation and all...

Life is never easy—however, it's supposed to be worth it!
You Betcha . . .

1. *Why plastic waste is an ideal building material, Sibele Cestari, August 2020.*
2. *Researchers at Argentina's National Agricultural Technology Institute, 2017-2018.*
3. *Institute of Biology, Freie Universität Berlin. Leibniz-Institute of Freshwater Ecology and Inland Fisheries. Faculty of Forestry, University of Göttingen. Environ. Sci. Technol. 2019, 53, 10, 6044–6052.*

4. *Three Companies Building Houses Made of Plastic, Júlia Ledur.*

5. *Sarah Ruiz-Grossman, HuffPost, Liter of Light, July 2017.*

6. *Steven L. Taylor was assistant dean of the College of Life Sciences when this BYU devotional address was given on 22 June 2010.*

7. *Where Does All the Plastic Waste Go? Plastic Collectors of the World, Jun 29th, 2020 by Admin.*

8. *Wax Worm Saliva Is the Unlikely Hero of Fighting Plastic Waste, Their enzymes can break down plastic in a matter of hours, journal Nature Communications, by Jacquelyne Germain, intern Smithsonian, 2022.*

9. *Insect proteins- a new source for animal feed, The use of insect larvae to recycle food waste in high-quality protein for livestock and aquaculture feeds ...Science & Society, 2015.*

10. *Processing insects for use in the food and feed industry, Current Opinion in Insect Science, volume 48, 2021, Pages 32-36.*

28

ENERGY AND POOP

Have you ever wondered where most of the calories you eat eventually go? In most places I frequent in my environment the end products of digestion and metabolism ends up flushed down the toilet in the form of a semisolid mass called feces or a liquid called urine. It is estimated that the human race produces about 640 billion lbs. (290 billion kg) of feces per year, and about 3.5 billion gal. (1.98 billion liters) of urine. Divide by 7 billion if you'd like to get your own annual contribution to this heaping helping of yuck.

From the moment human beings began to congregate out of the state of nature, the problem has always been just what to do about all that biological refuse. In the developed world, the answer is familiar: Flush it away as fast as possible and try not to think about it. Disposal is a lot more difficult in the developing world where up to 2.4 billion people have no access to advanced sanitation and 1 billion have no facilities of any kind. Worse than difficult, the problem is dangerous, since human waste fouls water supplies, spreads infection and wrecks overall quality of life.

According to a United Nations think tank on water, environment and health, there may be a simple and profitable solution by turning human waste from a disposal problem to an energy resource.

Human feces ranges from 55% to 75% water. Much of the 25% to 45% that remains consists of gaseous methane produced by bacterial breakdown, and a solid residue which, if dried and concentrated, has an energy content similar to that of coal. This is a fuel that hardly needs to be sought or mined and is a renewal resource with a great energy potential that could help reduce the need for coal.

The U.N. report estimates that globally, human waste converted to fuel could have a value of about $9.5 billion. The amount of waste produced just by the 1 billion people with no sanitation facilities could be worth up to $376 million in methane production alone that could power 10 to 18 million households. The compressed, solid residue would produce the equivalent of up to 8.5 million tons of charcoal for industrial use. Their goal is to produce a simple, cost-effective approaches to enhance the development of needed energy resources, protect the environment and help reduce sanitation problems causing one-tenth of all world illnesses.

The energy-generating part of this equation involves solid waste only, but all that urine humans produce every year has a role too. According to a Swedish study, every 1,000 liters (264 gal.) of urine contains 600 g (.66 lbs) apiece of phosphorous and potassium and 900 g (1 lb.) of sulfur. Combining both solid and liquid waste, a single human produces 4.5 kg (9.9 lbs) of nitrogen per year, according to the World Health Organization. All of this could be recycled as nutrients for crops, increasing yields and helping to bring down both poverty and hunger.1

Historically, human excreta, 'nightsoils', were collected from towns and villages and spread in raw or composted form on fields in the surrounding farmland. This informal treatment is still practiced in some areas of China, South East Asia, Africa and Latin America, where municipal sewage works don't exist or are poorly functioning. In the 1850s, Europe's growing urban populations and the discovery of the link between raw sewage and cholera led to the implementation of large-scale sewage systems. These water-based systems combined all domestic waste, industrial effluent and road surface run-off. For the next century the resulting sewage sludge was disposed of in landfill and directly into the oceans. Eventually, in the 1970s, growing awareness of the environmental impact of sewage on aquatic life led to widespread bans on ocean dumping across the developed world. Since then, research, technology and regulation of wastewater management have progressed to a high standard.2

There are three stages of wastewater treatment, according to the New York City Department of Environmental Protection. During the first stage, all of the waste that accumulates in the city's pipes just sits in a tank for hours. This stage allows the solids to settle at the bottom of the tank. The water at the top of the tank is skimmed off and sent off to be processed and the poop remaining is called sludge.

The second step, called the activated sludge process, uses biology to make sure our poop is clean. Billions of microorganisms that are already in the poop breathe in oxygen and feed on pollutants such as nitrogen and phosphorous, cleaning the sludge in the process. These pollutants could otherwise cause massive algae overgrowth in waterways or react to form toxic compounds, like ammonia.

In the next tank, called a digester, low oxygen and hot temperatures (around 95 degrees Fahrenheit, or 35 degrees Celsius) create the perfect conditions for anaerobic bacteria, which thrive without oxygen. The anaerobes further break down the waste inside the tank, converting most of it into water, methane and carbon dioxide gas. Unlike anaerobe, most pathogenic organisms die in these inhospitable conditions.

The activated sludge process is incredibly effective and has been used in wastewater plants for over 100 years. In wetlands, rivers and streams, these same bacteria and biochemical processes have been purifying water for much longer.

At this final stage, the sludge is mostly liquid, so the next step is to dry it out as much as possible. A centrifuge operates like a dryer on its spin cycle, whirling that sludge around until centrifugal force removes most of the water. The dried-out sludge leftovers are called biosolids. Around 55% of the biosolids get used for agriculture, 17% are incinerated and the rest winds up in landfills.3

On farms throughout the U.S. you will find large ponds, called lagoons, full of cow or pig manure (poop) that resemble the storage tanks used in human waste water plants. This is the standard form of treatment for cattle and hog waste in parts of the country.

In the lagoon, bacteria go to work on the manure, breaking it down. The bacterial action releases a biogas that's 60% to 65% methane. On most farms, the energy from the gas is not used and just goes floating off into the air, contributing to the overheating of the planet. Methane is a greenhouse gas with a warming impact at least 25 times greater, per pound, than carbon dioxide.

Some farms trap the gas by using a blanket of rugged black plastic that covers the manure pond. The gas produced lifts the plastic layer, makes it bulge and creates enough pressure to be pumped out to processing stations where water vapor and carbon dioxide are removed.

What's left is almost pure methane, also called natural gas, ready to burn in any gas-fired home furnace or electric power plant. This basic idea of turning manure into energy is not new. Many farms are doing similar things, often using the biogas on-site to power a generator. Producers and energy companies are planning to build an infrastructure of pipelines that capture the methane gas from farms with miles of underground pipes, and feeding the biogas into existing natural gas pipelines. If no pipelines are close by, the gas may have to be trucked to its destination.4,5

Between two and ten years of age I learned a song in my church's Sunday school class called *Pioneer Children Sang As They Walked*. "Little pioneer children gathering berries for food; See the pioneer children hunting (buffalo added) chips for wood; Gladly helping each other, merry and happy were they..."6

Burning of animal waste for heat and fuel was used by early European settlers on the Great Plains of the United States with dried buffalo manure (called buffalo chips), the Pueblo Indians used dry animal dung , and in Peru, for several decades the Yavari steam ship used llama dung for fuel.

Dry animal dung was used from prehistoric times, including in Ancient Persia, Ancient Egypt and early modern England. In Equatorial Guinea archaeological evidence has been found of the practice and biblical records indicate animal and human dung were used as fuel.

In a district where wood is scarce, dung is the primary energy source available for heating and cooking. The difficulty of procuring firewood in Syria, Arabia, and Egypt has therefore made dung in all ages highly prized as a substitute. It was used for heating lime kilns, ovens, and for baking cakes, the even heat which it produced adapting it peculiarly for the latter operation.

Cows and camel's dung is still used for a similar purpose by the Bedouins, they even form a species of pan for frying eggs out of it; in Egypt the dung is mixed with straw and formed into flat, round cakes, which are dried in the sun. This use of dung for fuel by the ancient Israelites, however, is collected incidentally from the passage in which the prophet Ezekiel, being commanded, as a symbolical action, to bake his bread with human dung, excuses himself from the use of an unclean thing, and is permitted to employ cows dung instead (Eze 4:12-15).

This shows that the dung of animals, at least of clean animals, was usual, and that no ideas of ceremonial uncleanness were attached to its employment for this purpose. The use of cow dung for fuel is known to European villagers, who, at least in the west of England, prefer it in baking their bread "under the crock," on account of the long continued and equable heat which it maintains.

It is there also not unusual in a summer evening to see aged people traveling the green lanes with baskets to collect the cakes of cow dung which have dried upon the road. This helps out the ordinary fire of wood, and makes it burn longer. In many thinly wooded parts of south-western Asia, the dung of cows, camels, horses, asses, whichever may happen to be the most common, is collected with great zeal and diligence from the streets and highways, chiefly by young girls. They also hover on the skirts of travelers, and there are often amusing scrambles among them for the droppings of the cattle.

The dung is mixed up with chopped straw and made into cakes, which are stuck up by their own adhesiveness against the walls of the cottages, or are laid upon the declivity of a hill, until sufficiently dried. It is not unusual to see a whole village with its walls thus garnished, which has a singular and not very agreeable appearance to a European traveler. Towards the end of autumn, the result of the summer collection of fuel for winter is shown in large conical heaps or stacks of dried dung upon the top of every cottage. The usages of the Jews in this matter were probably similar in kind, although the extent to which they prevailed cannot now be estimated.7

Hopefully progress making animal excrement a valuable energy source will be adapted to human dung. It certainly is possible if a United Nations think tank on water, environment and health, report becomes reality and there is found simple and profitable solutions that can convert human waste from a disposal problem to an energy resource.

It will be interesting times if our clients are offered a credit on their next bill (like bringing in your old battery) for placing poop produced by their pet in a drop off box at Camden Pet Hospital for recycling -like aluminum cans.

My property contains two septic tanks that periodically fill with human excrement and need to be cleaned and the material removed by a truck. I would love to see the day when I hear an auctioneer's voice bidding up buyers to purchase my own family's contribution to the energy needs of the world.

An even better idea might be that during my family's annual 4th of July visit we might include a special family activity: My children and their seventeen kids could collect dung from my septic tanks, add chopped dry weeds collected from my field, mix it into cakes and place the stickie cow pie like material against the walls of my home to dry. They would then all be invited for a wonderful Thanksgiving feast in November that would be served after we stacked and covered the dried fuel stuck to my house. The stacked fuel (like kindling) would be saved for later sale or home use.

I can only imagine the energy that could be created from harvesting the available dung of the world.

There is one truism about all organisms. It's that they must both consume fuel and excrete waste. The problem will be here as long as we're here—so scientists have all the time they need to figure it out.1

ARTISTS TREAT FACTS AS STIMULI FOR IMAGINATION, WHERAS SCIENTISTS USE IMAGINATION TO COORDINATE FACTS.8

1. *Science, Environment, Jeffrey Kluger, How Poop Can Be Worth $9.5 Billion, 11/03/2015.*
2. *Human manure: Closing the nutrient loop, by Rachel Dring on 15 May, 2015 in Farming.*
3. *Everybody poops. But where does it go?, Isobel Whitcomb published January 25, 2020.*
4. *Big Companies Bet on Cleaner Power From Pig Poop Ponds, All Things Considered, Dan Charles, 11/11-2019.*
5. *For dairy farmers, this technology turns methane from cow manure into cash, Amy Mayer 07/21/2021, MarketPlace Morning Report.*
6. *Children's Songbook, "Pioneer Children Sang As They Walked," Church of Jesus Christ of Latter-day Saints, page 216, 1989.*
7. *From McClintock and Strong Biblical Cyclopedia + Wikipedia.*
8. *Arthur Koestler, Austrian novelist (1905-1983).*

29

OH, WHAT ABOUT PEE

Drinking or local application of human or animal urine for medicinal purposes has been practiced all over the world for millennia. Documented prescriptions in Europe originate from ancient Egypt, Greece and Rome. The use of urine and other excrements enjoyed popularity in mediaeval times. Ancient Indian yogic texts and ancient Chinese documents describe benefits of drinking one's own urine, and it can be assumed that people in Africa, the Americas and other parts of the world have traditionally used urine for various medical indications for a very long time.

The supposed indications for urine therapy, ancient or contemporary, are too numerous to recite. There is, it seems, virtually nothing urine won't cure.

Modern proponents use pseudoscience to explain the benefits of the various, mostly exaggerated, components of urine. Some hint at a conspiracy by the medical establishment and the pharmaceutical industry to keep the knowledge of the many fantastic healing properties of cheaply available urine a secret.1

The Ancient Roman's human waste was used daily for a variety of reasons, and urine was especially valued.

When left out for long periods of time, it transforms into a common ingredient ammonia. This was used as a disinfectant and in cleaning products. Roman launderers used urine to get stains out of fabrics. When urine changes into ammonia, it can neutralize dirt and grease, helps keep clothes white and brightens colors.

Besides cleaning clothes, the urine of both humans and animals was used as a teeth whitener and would rinse with it.

Urine was also used to tan leather, as urine can remove hair and flesh from animal hides. One could either pee on the leather or soak it in a large vat to get the job done. When this process was complete, feces (either dog or human) was used to soften it. The smell was so intense that tanneries were forced to the outskirts of town. It was common for public urinals to line the streets of Ancient Rome. Any passerby could relieve themselves, and the urine was then collected from this vessel and taken away.

Urine was valuable enough that its use became taxed. Around A.D. 70, Emperor Vespasian imposed a tax on the collection of urine from Roman sewage systems. Likewise, he is said to have built the first public toilet, and many urinals in Europe are still named after him.

It was mostly launderers and tanners who were paying this tax, as they were the biggest buyers of urine. Most Roman citizens were not a fan of it, including Vespasian's own son, Titus. Vespasian's response? "Pecunia non olet," Latin for "money doesn't stink." In other words, money is money, regardless of its origins. It's said that the Roman Colosseum was financed, in part, from this urine tax.2

There are long-famous reports about Siberian reindeer and man drinking their or the other's urine after eating a hallucinogenic fungus commonly known as fly agaric. This is the beautiful mushroom of fairy tales whose bright red cap is sprinkled with white spots.

The origins of its use as a hallucinogen by human beings is lost in the dawn of time. Archeological and ethnographic data have confirmed the early spread of this practice throughout Asia, Europe, and the Americas. It is told that shamans (a person regarded as having access to, and influence in, the world of good and evil spirits) used fly agaric when they entered a trance state during a ritual.

It is well known that the urine of humans who have eaten fly agaric becomes in itself hallucinogenic. Among some Siberian populations it was customary to drink the urine of those who had drugged themselves with the mushroom to attain an even greater degree of intoxication, reputedly more powerful than that achieved by eating the mushroom itself.

Even reindeer "go mad" for the urine of other reindeer or human beings who have ingested the hallucinogen. In fact, it would seem that the Siberian peoples discovered its inebriation properties by observing the behavior of the reindeer. Anytime these creatures scent fungus-rich urine in the vicinity, they make a mad dash for it, engaging in real battles among themselves as they vie for the position closest to the "golden shower."

When the snow in Siberia first begins to thaw, reindeer native to the region will hoof up fly agaric mushrooms sitting just below the surface of the snow. They have big red caps and the mushrooms are also known to cause visions.

The reindeer that eat them often run aimlessly, have random muscle spasms and make weird noises.

Not deterred, local herders wanted in on the action too, and they've found a way to do it without having to dig through frozen tundra. Herders will capture the reindeer, because the hallucinogen is voided unchanged in the reindeer's urine. So, they drink the urine or thaw the yellow ice and snow from the reindeer to get their own hallucination.3

Drinking urine for survival tends to worsen the chances for survival, even when no other fluid is available. It is reported that some people are sexually aroused by urine, which can include the drinking of their own or other people's urine. Urine practitioners claim anti-cancer therapy, camel urine is sold for prophetic medicine, COVID-19 treatment as well as I'm sure there are others currently using urine for various purposes.

The global system of food production is the largest human influence on the planet's natural cycles of nitrogen and phosphorus. How much crops can grow is limited by the amount of these two elements in the soil, so they're applied as fertilizers. But the majority of fertilizers are either made by converting nitrogen in the air to change methane into ammonia nitrogen that can be used by plants, which alone consumes 2% of the world's energy and relies heavily on fossil fuels, or by mining finite resources of phosphate from rocks.

A solution to this problem could be much closer than people realize. Most of the nutrients we consume in food are passed in our urine, because our bodies already have enough. But instead of being recaptured, these nutrients are flushed, diluted, and sent to wastewater treatment plants where they're scrubbed out, leaving effluents that can be safely released into the environment.

The most nutrient rich part of wastewater is human urine, which makes up less than 1% of the total volume but contains 80% of the nitrogen and 50% of the phosphorus. Recently it was discovered how to recycle this urine into valuable—and sustainable—farmland fertilizer.

You can capture urine with special toilets that separate it from feces after you flush. But because urine is mostly water, farmers would have to spread 15,000kg (33,069 pounds) of it just to fertilize a hectare (2.47 acres) of land. If there was a way to remove the water and extract just the nutrients, farmers would only need to apply 400kg (882 pounds) of it for the same effect.

Evaporating the water from urine is surprisingly difficult, as urine is a complex chemical solution. Almost all of the valuable nitrogen in urine is in the form of urea, a chemical that is used as the world's most commonly applied nitrogen fertilizer. But a fast-acting enzyme called urease is invariably present inside wastewater pipes and converts urea to ammonia. When exposed to air, the ammonia quickly evaporates, taking the nitrogen from the urine with it.

By increasing the pH of urine to make it alkaline ensures the urea doesn't break down. Using this technique, a process has been developed that can reduce the volume of urine and transform it into a solid fertilizer. The process is called alkaline urine dehydration.

Doing this is quite easy: you just fill a urine dryer with an alkalizing agent, connect it to your toilet, pee as usual into a urine collector and the urine is converted into dried fertilizer. A smart design could even make the dryer fit below the toilet so it doesn't take up a lot of bathroom space.

While electricity would be needed for evaporating the water, the dryer could be coupled with solar energy to take its energy use off the grid. It is estimate that it would cost just US $5 to supply an average family of four with a year's supply of alkalizing agent. The output from the dryer is a solid fertilizer containing 10% nitrogen, 1% phosphorus and 4% potassium—a similar combination to blended mineral fertilizers.4

When the Christmas season comes, I now think about eating fly agaric mushrooms, hallucinating Siberian reindeer and their herders drinking each other's urine, and how this parallels between the Santa story we all know about St. Nick and a Santa Christmas psychedelic mushroom story.

The main character, besides Santa, is the Amanita muscaria mushroom (fly agaric) also known as the "most sacred" and "holy mushroom." This mushroom is a psychedelic mushroom, or magic mushroom, and can be poisonous. It is the iconic fairy tale looking mushroom with a red cap that has white spots.

This story of Santa is from many years ago. Shaman (medicine men, magicians, or sorcerers) in Siberian and Artic regions who wore red robes with white ropes around the waist would give out gifts of dried mushrooms, usually psychedelic mushrooms. They would deliver these gifts around the time of the Winter Solstice. This time of year, there would often be snow blocking the door, so the Shaman would go through openings in the roof to deliver their gifts.

Are parts of this story starting to sound familiar? A man from the Arctic dressed in red and white clothing, bringing gifts near Christmas time, and dropping in through the roof . . .

These aren't the only parallels of the Santa story. The Amanita mushroom is found growing under pine trees, which is symbolized as the presents we put under the Christmas tree. The Shaman would dry the mushrooms by hanging them on tree branches, like how we hang ornaments on a tree.

Now let's talk about the reindeer, they're a big part of the Santa story. Reindeer in the wild have a liking to the Amanita mushroom and seek it out. When people eat the Amanita, they get a sensation of flying. So, the question is, do the reindeer also get this sensation, or is it that people see the reindeer when they're tripping and think the reindeer are flying? And Rudolph, the most well-known reindeer has a red nose, which some say looks like the Amanita mushroom on his nose.

Now this last point is a bit far-fetched, but some say that elves are the spirits that a Shaman encountered during a trip. Maybe the Shaman were high enough on the mushrooms that if they weren't there—they may have thought they saw elves.

Some think this connection between magic mushrooms and Santa is a bunch of hoopla, while others see a lot of merit to the story. While I was doing my research, I found a lot of information from professors and historians about Shaman and their traditions.

There is even a professor at Harvard who gathers his students each year for the Winter Solstice and discusses the magic mushroom Santa story. So now that you've heard the story, you'll have to decide for yourself—is it St. Nick or Santa of the psychedelics? Either way, this is an entertaining story to tell at the Christmas dinner table.

Merry Christmas to all and to all a good night!5

The story may be true about animals and man drinking urine, hallucinating from fly agaric during the winter solstice and fabricating over time the story about the jolly old man, Santa, who visits us on Christmas with gifts for all the good boys and girls.

However, to enter into the Christmas spirit, it is also important to remember the Christmas story of the birth of Christ. One should also remember that there really was a Santa Claus, the godly Saint Nicholas, who was willing to be imprisoned for his sincere Christian faith under Emperor Diocletian, who preached against pagan immorality of Diana worship, who stood for the Bible and doctrinal purity at the Council of Nicea, and who generously helped the poor, anonymously, so that the glory would go to God.6

As for using urine generated in my home to make fertilizer for my yard and garden, costing $5 a year for alkalizing agent, a drying box attached to my toilet and using my solar panels to dry the material—I don't think it's a fabricated story and is a good idea for us good boys and girls. My concerns are whether my wife would go for it and if it would come with a simple to understand booklet on how to care for the potently nasty thing. I would like it also to not cost too much of that -Pecunia non olet, Latin for "money (which) doesn't stink" I'm saving up for an electric car.

1. *The Golden Fountain Is urine the miracle drug no one told you about? Pan Afr Med J, 2010.*
2. *Read More: https://www.grunge.com/630800/how-ancient-romans-used-urine-for-tanning-leather/?utm_.*
3. *Animals and psychedelics, That Natural World and the Instinct to Alter Consciousness, Giorgio Samorini, 2000.*
4. *We found a way to turn urine into solid fertilizer—it could make farming more sustainable, Swedish University of Agricultural Sciences, 2020.*
5. *Megan Betcher at weeblly.com.*
6. *There Really is a Santa Claus, The History of Saint Nicholas…,William J. Federer, p 149, 2002.*

30

METHANE GAS

Some researchers consider methane to not only be one of the most hazards greenhouse gases but also an essential asset in the fight against climate change. They feel that it is important to banish the perception that the agriculture sector as one of the main contributors to pollution and start to understand that producers are key actors in the climate solution. Methane, emitted by cows and their manure, could also be a key to global cooling.

If methane is reduced it also reduces warming, the same is not true for other greenhouse gases. When you reduce other greenhouse gases you don't reduce warming, you just keep it stable. When you reduce methane, you can induce cooling and that makes agriculture part of the climate solution. Methane can be destroyed during the process of rusting, unlike carbon dioxide and nitrous oxide, which hang around in the atmosphere for thousands of years.

Ruminants are considered by many to be a miracle because they are capable of converting something undesirable such as weeds into consumer products. They're the only animals that can break down, digest the cellulose and make milk and meat from it. They use plant resources in the most efficient way possible to produce food that people desire.1

Each of those puffs coming out of a cow's plumbing, added together, can have a big effect on climate because methane gas is about 28 times more powerful than carbon dioxide at warming the earth. Since the Industrial Revolution, methane concentrations in the atmosphere have more than doubled, and about 20% of the warming the planet has experienced can be attributed to the gas.

There's about 200 times less concentration of methane in the atmosphere than carbon dioxide, the most abundant greenhouse gas. But methane's chemical shape is remarkably effective at trapping heat, which means that adding just a little more methane to the atmosphere can have big impacts on how much, and how quickly, the planet warms.

Methane is a simple gas, a single carbon atom with four arms of hydrogen atoms. Its time in the atmosphere is relatively fleeting compared to other greenhouse gases like CO_2 - any given methane molecule, once it's spewed into the atmosphere, lasts about a decade before it's cycled out. That's a blip compared to the centuries that a CO_2 molecule can last floating above the surface of the planet. But there are many sources of methane, so the atmospheric load is constantly being increased.

Today, about 60% of the methane in the atmosphere comes from sources scientists think of as human caused, while the rest comes from sources that existed before humans started influencing the carbon cycle in dramatic ways.

Most of methane's natural emissions come from a soggy source: wetlands, which includes bogs. Many microbes are like mammals in that they eat organic material and spit out carbon dioxide. But many that live in still, oxygen-deprived spots like waterlogged wetland soils produce methane instead, which then leaks into the atmosphere. Over all, about a third of all the methane floating in the modern atmosphere comes from wetlands.

There are a variety of other natural methane sources. It seeps out of the ground naturally near some oil and gas deposits and from the mouths of some volcanoes. It leaks out of thawing permafrost in the Arctic and builds up in the sediments under shallow, still seas; it wafts away from burning landscapes, entering the atmosphere as CO2; and it is produced by termites as they feed on woody waste or debris. But all of these other natural sources, excluding wetlands, only make up about 10% of the total emissions each year.

Today, human-influenced sources make up the bulk of the methane in the atmosphere. Cows and other grazing animals get a lot of attention for their methane-producing belches and releases. Such grazers host microbes in their stomachs that help break down and absorb the nutrients from plants containing cellulose. Those microbes produce methane as their waste which is released out of both ends of cows. Ruminants produce about 40% of the world's methane.

Agricultural endeavors release methane into the atmosphere. Rice paddies are a lot like wetlands: When they're flooded, they're filled with calm waters low in oxygen, which are a natural home for methane producing bacteria. Methane also leaks into the atmosphere at gas and oil drilling sites.

Worldwide, the energy sector contributes about a quarter of the annual methane in the atmosphere.

Microbes in landfills and sewage treatment centers produce about 14% of the methane gas released in the United States.

Under high pressure, like the pressures found deep at the bottom of the ocean, methane solidifies into a slush-like material called methane hydrate. Vast amounts of methane are "frozen" in place at the bottom of the sea in this chemical state, though the exact amounts and locations are still being studied. The hydrates are stable unless something comes along to disturb them, like a plume of warm water.

In the modern atmosphere, methane concentrations have risen by more than 150% since 1750. It's not clear whether this rise will continue.2

In Idaho ruminants graze on locally owned irrigated pastures and publicly owned mountain ranges controlled by the Bureau of Land Management (BLM). Range fed ruminants are transported in the spring from there winter home to summer pastures. I helped my Uncle Bud in the spring brand, vaccinate and dehorn his cattle and then truck them to the BLM range. The cattle in the fall were rounded up and transported back to winter at his ranch.

In those years I never heard the word methane or concern that it comes out of cattle when they chew their cud or defecated on the ground. According to the BLM there are still 155 million acres of public land used for livestock grazing.

Agricultural areas are divided into 3 categories: Arable land (28% of the global agricultural area), permanent crops (3%) and permanent meadows and pastures (69%) which account for the largest share of the world's agricultural area. Approximately 5% of grass-finished beef cattle remain on a pasture their entire lives. 26% of the earths terrestrial surface is used for livestock grazing.3

Ruminants release methane gas primarily from a large compartment in their stomachs that contain microbes who digest plant material. They have a four-chamber stomach, chew and swallow their food, regurgitate it back up, and then chew it again—called chewing their cud, and swallow it again. There are all types of ruminants grazing on the earth's terrestrial surface including parts of the arable land. Their manure drops off the animal, falling on the ground, is entrenched into the ground where it enriches soil fertility.

Methane gas buildup in the atmosphere from grazing animals is more difficult to address than ruminants (particularly cattle) that are concentrated in areas where feed is brought to them.1

At first glance, the idea of utilizing methane gas has considerable merit because it appears to offer at least a partial solution to the environmental crisis and the energy shortage. Especially where high levels of methane are produced.

Unfortunately, present-day large-scale methane generation requires rather high investments in money and management, which considerably reduces the idea's practicality. Basically, two things can be done: store the gas as it is produced or burn the gas to fulfill some energy requirement. In reality, a practical system would involve a combination of the two.

Methane does not liquefy at any pressure if the temperature is greater than -116 degrees Fahrenheit. It also has a relatively low heat value per unit volume because it does not liquefy like propane, at normal storage pressures and ambient temperatures. This makes its storage impractical in tanks like I have in my yard. They contain enough propane for heating, cooking, bathing etc. for my family and are usually filled twice during the winter.

Another important factor is the strength required in the walls of a tank in which gas is stored at very high pressures. For pressures greater than about 1000 psi, storage tanks more than a foot or so in diameter must have extra wall thickness, which makes such storage for methane impractical.

The other obvious alternative to storage of methane is to use it as it is generated. The easiest way to accomplish this is to burn the gas as it flows from the digester gas generator. Obviously, this isn't efficient use of the gas unless the flame is used to fulfill a heat requirement. The most frequently proposed use is home heating with the methane gas.4

Nitrogen gas fixation by nature into nitrogen that can be used by plants for fertilizer occurs by atmospheric lightening and ultra violet light, soil microorganisms (90%) that are free living or blue green type algae bacteria, or nodular producing symbiotic bacteria that invade leguminous plants and cereal grasses.

In 1963 I did a high school science fair project on the nitrogen cycle (see photo below). My father did graduate work on nitrogen fixation in bacteriology and we had a fun family project. Speaking for myself during presentation of my (our) project without Pops around was a bit of an embarrassing experience. This was my first introduction into the complexities of the workings of nature.

It has been estimated that almost half the people on the Earth are currently fed as a result of synthetic nitrogen fertilizer. Methane gas is used to produce products that combine with nitrogen making it available as a plant fertilizer.

Rapid population growth, rising meat consumption, and the expanding use of crops for nonfood and nonfeed purposes increase the pressure on global food production. At the same time, the excessive use of nitrogen fertilizer to enhance agricultural production poses serious threats to both human health and the environment. To achieve the required yield increases and make agriculture more sustainable, intensified breeding and genetic engineering efforts are needed to obtain new crop varieties with higher photosynthetic capacity and improved nitrogen use efficiency.5

Increasing numbers of pig and cattle feed lot lagoons of manure are using methane trapping techniques and feeding the biogas methane into existing natural gas pipelines for use as a fuel. Add that to toilets that catch urine and form a dry fertilizer that has 10% nitrogen, 1% phosphate, and 4% potassium, and overtime human and animal waste may become a valuable renewable resource that is not just looked at as a polluter of our environment.

The average person produces 0.6–1.8 liters of intestinal gas each day. It's the by-product of a digestive system at work. In fact, farting (flatus) is healthy and good for your body. All of this gas and air builds up in your digestive system. Some of it is absorbed naturally, but the remaining gas needs to be released in some way - either as flatulent or a burp. Gases released contain tiny amounts of hydrogen, carbon dioxide and methane with smelly hydrogen sulfide and ammonia.7

I'm a little embarrassed to admit it but in my early years my friends and I tested flatulent gas for combustion ability. We lifted our rears towards the sky and lite a match above the emitted gas. The air would light up for a brief moment like a cigarette lighter. I also recalled what branding cattle with a hot iron burning hair and flesh smelled like when my friend left his shorts off before trying the experiment.

My grandson shared with me a video showing him and his friends learning about methane gas. One night they lit a piece of paper stuffed into a container with gasoline and watched it slowly descend into a man hole. The sudden force from a blast of accumulated methane gas deep in that hole caught a friend by surprise and his face and arms also had the smell of burning hair and flesh. Luckily, he was young, quick, closed his eyes and was not leaning down any closer to the man hole.

There are a lot of good potential uses for wasted combustible gases produced in our environment. As energy becomes more in demand, scarce and expensive, capturing of these resources from man, animals and the environment will become more common place—even using chicken manure.

In 2022 the Reverend Amos C. Brown was exploring ideas with Elder Jack N. Gerard on the topic of "overcoming attitudes and actions of prejudice so that we can become one in Christ begins with humility before God, better communication, greater understanding, and a willingness to work together."

Towards the end of the conversion Elder Gerard asked "Are there any universal principles that you would share for how individuals can make a difference in their communities in overcoming racism and prejudice, no matter where they are in the world?

Reverend Brown: I don't mean to make it simplistic, but it is simple. Do unto others as you would have them do unto you. We reap what we sow. Injustice anywhere, as Dr. (Martin Luther) King said, gets around to affecting all of us everywhere. It is like the ripples of the waves. When you throw a pebble in the water, there are ripples. We ought to be about making positive ripples.

As I recall, Howard Washington Thurman once told a story about his mother, who lived in a community in which this White woman didn't like the fact that she had a Black neighbor. And she would be mean to Mrs. Thurman. But Mrs. Thurman kept on going to church, rearing her children, being kind to everybody.

One day, (Howard's) mother told him to get ready to go with her next door to see this lady who was ill. (Mrs. Thurman) cooked a bowl of soup, and they went over to the house. The lady said to her, "Oh, you didn't have to do all of this." And Mrs. Thurman said, "No, but the love of Jesus told me I had to do it."

And then she said, "Howard, go back over to the house and get those roses I left on the table." He came back with these beautiful red roses. And the sick woman said, "Oh my. What florist did you buy those roses from?" And

Mrs. Thurman said: "I didn't buy those roses from any florist. When you were unkind to me, you would throw the chicken manure from your chicken coop over into my yard. But you didn't know that while you were throwing the chicken manure, God was preparing the soil for me to grow my roses."

So that's what we've got to do in the midst of evil. Take the manure but have the faith in God to use it to grow a garden of roses. That's what we have to do. Be kind, do the right thing, and love and respect all people. They are God's opportunity for you to touch their messy situations and leave them better than they were before.8

Yup, in the midst of energy shortages (evil), take the wasted energy of the world (methane), have faith in finding a way to use it to care for our necessities of life, do the right thing for the (earth), receive God's opportunities of love He gives us to help others take care of messy situations (challenges facing mankind) and leave the world a better place than we found it.

1. *Methane emissions from cattle, an asset in curbing climate change, Online News, Alexander Prieto, 04/05/2022.*

2. *Cows and bogs release methane into the atmosphere, but it's by far mostly human activity that's driving up levels of this destructive greenhouse gas, Alejandra Borunda, National Geographic, 01/23/2019.*

3. *Land Use, Hannah Ritchie & Max Roser, September 2019.*

4. *Generating Methane Gas From Manure, Charles D. Fulhage, Dennis Sievers and James R. FischerDepartment of Agricultural Engineering, University of Missouri.*

5. *Science, Plant Science, P 386, July 2022.*
6. *We found a way to turn urine into solid fertilizer—it could make farming more sustainable, Swedish University of Agricultural Sciences, 2020.*
7. *Google search.*
8. *Amos C. Brown of the Third Baptist Church of San Francisco, California, USA, a longtime advocate of civil rights in the United States and a member of the board of the National Association for the Advancement of Colored People (NAACP).*

31

CARBON DIOXIDE

Carbon dioxide (chemical formula CO_2) is a chemical compound made up of molecules that each have one carbon atom covalently double bonded to two oxygen atoms. It is found in the gas state at room temperature. In the air, carbon dioxide is transparent to visible light but absorbs infrared radiation, acting as a greenhouse gas.

It is a trace gas in Earth's atmosphere at 417 ppm (about 0.04%) by volume, having risen from pre-industrial levels of 280 ppm. Burning fossil fuels is the primary cause of these increased CO_2 concentrations and also a concerned primary cause of global warming and climate change. Carbon dioxide is soluble in water and is found in groundwater, lakes, ice caps, and seawater. When carbon dioxide dissolves in water it forms carbonic acid (H_2CO_3), which causes ocean acidification as atmospheric CO_2 levels increase.

As the source of available carbon in the carbon cycle, atmospheric carbon dioxide is the primary carbon source for life on Earth. Its concentration in Earth's pre-industrial atmosphere since late in the Precambrian has been regulated by organisms and geological phenomena. Plants, algae and cyanobacteria use energy from sunlight to synthesize carbohydrates from carbon dioxide and water in a process called photosynthesis, which produces oxygen as a waste product.

In turn, oxygen is consumed and CO2 is released as waste by all aerobic organisms when they metabolize organic compounds to produce energy by respiration.

CO2 is released from organic materials when they decay or combust, such as in forest fires. Since plants require CO2 for photosynthesis, and humans and animals depend on plants for food, CO2 is necessary for the survival of life on earth.

Carbon dioxide is 53% more dense than dry air, but is long lived and thoroughly mixes in the atmosphere. About half of excess CO2 emissions to the atmosphere are absorbed by land and ocean carbon sinks. These sinks can become saturated and are volatile, as decay and wildfires result in the CO2 being released back into the atmosphere. CO2 is eventually sequestered (stored for the long term) in rocks and organic deposits like coal, petroleum and natural gas. Sequestered CO2 is released into the atmosphere through burning fossil fuels or naturally by volcanoes, hot springs, geysers, and when carbonate rocks dissolve in water or react with acids.

CO2 is a versatile industrial material, used, for example, as an inert gas in welding and fire extinguishers, as a pressurizing gas in air guns and oil recovery, and as a supercritical fluid solvent in decaffeination of coffee and supercritical drying. It is also a feedstock for the synthesis of fuels and chemicals. It is an unwanted byproduct in many large scale oxidation processes used in manufacturing, for example, in the important production of acrylic acid (over 5 million tons/year) which is vital for many manufacturing processes.

The frozen solid form of CO_2, known as dry ice, is used as a refrigerant and as an abrasive in dry-ice blasting. It is a byproduct of fermentation of sugars in bread, beer and wine making, and is added to carbonated beverages like seltzer and beer for effervescence. It has a sharp and acidic odor and generates the taste of soda water in the mouth, but at normally encountered concentrations it is odorless.[1]

In the Cretaceous period, 100 million years ago give or take a few tens of millions, Earth was a very different place than today. Flowering plants and trees had only recently evolved to coexist with conifers, ferns, cycads, and other groups, while a diverse array of dinosaurs was the dominant form of megafauna on land. The global climate in which these plants and animals lived was also very different: warmer, steamier, and virtually devoid of ice.

Today, Earth is markedly cooler than the Cretaceous, and ice sheets and glaciers still cover large portions of the poles. Yet we know conditions are changing. The planet is already about 1°C warmer than it was during preindustrial times because of anthropogenic emissions of greenhouse gases like carbon dioxide (CO_2), and many governments are working to limit further warming to no more than 2°C (or even 1.5°C) above preindustrial levels.

Meanwhile, Earth scientists are critically evaluating the possibility and consequences of scenarios in which radiative forcing (the surplus in the amount of solar energy Earth absorbs compared to what it radiates back into space) drives temperatures beyond those targets. What will happen, they ask, if atmospheric CO_2 levels (pCO_2)—about 280 parts (0.0280%) per million by volume (ppmv) in the preindustrial era and more than 415 ppmv (0.0415%) now—reach 800–1,300 (0.130%) ppmv and the atmosphere warms as much as 5°C by 2100? The ensuing climate change would raise sea levels and could produce drastic shifts in the hydrologic cycle that would exacerbate hazards like drought, floods, fire, and extreme temperatures—all of which could severely affect ecosystems and humans around the world.

The Cretaceous period is an archetypal example of a greenhouse climate. Atmospheric pCO_2 levels reached as high as about 2,000 (0.200%) ppmv, average temperatures were roughly 5°C–10°C higher than today, and sea levels were 50–100 meters (115—330 feet) higher. These conditions resemble the most extreme scenario that the IPCC has predicted could occur by the end of this century, with pCO_2 levels greater than 1,200 (0.120%) ppmv and global temperatures roughly 4°C higher.

The Cretaceous represents the last gasp of dinosaurs' dominance in Earth's ecosystem; in addition, it was a time of rapid evolutionary turnover and proliferation of mammals, birds, and angiosperms (flowering plants). For decades, the scientific community has been thoroughly engaged in understanding Cretaceous climate, especially how events such as the Chicxulub asteroid impact and Deccan volcanism contributed to evolution and to the extinction of non-avian dinosaurs and other biomes.

Despite this intense interest, we still lack long and continuous continental geological records of the Cretaceous. Currently a scientific drilling project in China is in the process of retrieving that continuous history of conditions from Earth's most recent "greenhouse" period.2

During the Triassic period the earliest dinosaurs were found and the climate was supposedly the harshest. The world was hot and mostly desert, and the only vegetation grew at the coastal areas. The continents were joined to form the super-continent Pangaea, and most dinosaur species were small and light-weight; the types you might expect to find in a harsh desert climate.

Toward the end of the Triassic there was apparently a shift in climate temperature. Carbon dioxide levels increased for no apparent reason, and the resulting heat caused a mass extinction, or so scientists believe. The Pangaea continent also began to split apart.

During the Jurassic because of the increased greenhouse effect, the amount of global rainfall increased, making more of the world into tropical swamps and jungles. The increased amount of vegetation supported the bigger dinosaur species. The amount of oxygen in the atmosphere seems to have increased at this time, allowing plants and animals alike to grow much bigger than they can today.

During the Cretaceous period the continents continued to drift apart, and more temperate regions formed at the poles. These areas were filled with coniferous trees, while deciduous trees and plants grew closer to the equator. The biggest and most popular dinosaur species apparently lived at this time, the continents became recognizable as the ones existing today, and their climates were quite different.

Dinosaurs covered the globe, from the tropics to the temperate zones at the far north and south. Scientists have always assumed that the dinosaur age was very hot and humid, but recent findings have revealed that the earth may have only been a few degrees warmer than it is today.

The climate warmed and cooled back then as it does today. Some areas became more like our present-day temperate zones, with more coniferous forests, while the equator remained tropical, or dried out and became desert. Dinosaurs have been found in all these environments, showing that they adapted well to their world the way animals do today. If they lived today, dinosaurs would live in warm, moist climates like central Africa and the Amazon basin in South America.3

Photosynthesis is the process which involves a chemical reaction between water and carbon dioxide (CO_2) in the presence of light to make food (sugars) for plants, and as a by-product, releases oxygen in the atmosphere. Carbon dioxide currently comprises 0.04 percent (400 parts per million) of the atmospheric volume. It is a colorless and odorless minor gas in the atmosphere, but has an important role for sustaining life.

Plants take in CO_2 through small cellular pores called stomata in the leaves during the day. During respiration at night (oxidation of stored sugars in plants producing energy and CO_2) plants take in oxygen (O_2) and give off CO_2, which complements during the day the photosynthesis when plants take in CO_2 and give off O_2.

The CO_2 produced during the night's respiration is always less than the amount of CO_2 taken in during photosynthesis. So, plants are always in a CO_2 deficient condition, which limits their potential growth.

Photosynthesis utilizes CO_2 in the production of sugar which degrades during respiration and helps in plant's growth. Although atmospheric and environmental conditions like light, water, nutrition, humidity and temperature may affect the rate of CO_2 utilization, the amount of CO_2 in the atmosphere has a greater influence.

Variation in CO_2 concentration depends upon the time of day, season, number of CO_2-producing industries, composting, combustion and number of CO_2-absorbing sources like plants and water bodies nearby. The ambient CO_2 (naturally occurring level of CO_2) concentration of 400 parts per million can occur in a properly vented greenhouse. However, the concentration is much lower than ambient during the day and much higher at night in sealed greenhouses. The carbon dioxide level is higher at night because of plant respiration and microbial activities.

The carbon dioxide level may drop to 150 to 200 parts per million during the day in a sealed greenhouse, because CO_2 is utilized by plants for photosynthesis during daytime. Exposure of plants to lower levels of CO_2 even for a short period can reduce the rate of photosynthesis and plant growth.

Generally, doubling ambient CO_2 level (i.e. 700 to 800 parts per million) can make a significant and visible difference in plant yield. Plants with a C3 photosynthetic pathway (geranium, petunia, pansy, aster lily and most dicot species) have a 3-carbon compound as the first product in their photosynthetic pathway, thus are called C3 plants and are more responsive to higher CO_2 concentration than plants having a C4 pathway (most of the grass species have a 4-carbon compound as the first product in their photosynthetic pathway, thus are called C4 plants).

An increase in ambient CO_2 to 800-1000 ppm can increase yield of C3 plants up to 40 to 100 percent and C4 plants by 10-25 while keeping other inputs at an optimum level. Plants show a positive response up to 700 to 1,800 parts per million, but higher levels of CO_2 may cause plant damage.

A major effect of CO_2 supplementation is the rapid growth of plants because of enhanced root and shoot growth. The enhanced root system allows greater uptake of nutrients from the soil. It is recommended to increase fertilizer rate with increasing CO_2 level.

Since CO_2 is a free and heavy gas, it stays at a lower level in the greenhouse. Carbon dioxide produced by plants at night is depleted within a few hours after sunrise, thus proper ventilation integrated with horizontal airflow fans just above the plant can help in distributing available CO_2 at least to the ambient level. Another natural way of increasing CO_2 in the greenhouse is through human respiration. Humans also exhale CO_2 during respiration like plants. People working in the greenhouse for pruning, irrigation and other operations can increase CO_2 levels.

Increasing CO_2 levels in nurseries can also be obtained by vaporizing compressed CO_2, the combustion of hydrocarbon fuels (propane or methane), organic waste decomposed in plastic containers, fermentation using sugar solution and yeast, sublimation (turning to gas) of dry ice and the chemical reaction of baking soda with acid (mostly acetic acid—vinegar like products).4

Carbon dioxide is often measured in indoor environments to quickly but indirectly assess approximately how much outdoor air is entering a room in relation to the number of occupants. CO_2 can be measured with relatively inexpensive real-time digital air monitoring equipment. CO_2 measurements have become a commonly used screening test of indoor air quality because levels can be used to evaluate the amount of ventilation and general comfort.

The Minnesota Department of Labor and Industry Rule states that "outside air shall be provided to all indoor workrooms at the rate of 15 cubic feet per minute per person." These rates of ventilation should keep carbon dioxide concentrations below 1000 ppm and create indoor air quality conditions that are acceptable to most individuals.

At high levels, the carbon dioxide itself can cause headache, dizziness, nausea and other symptoms. This could occur when exposed to levels above 5,000 ppm for many hours. At even higher levels of CO_2 can cause asphyxiation as it replaces oxygen in the blood-exposure to concentrations around 40,000 ppm is immediately dangerous to life and health. CO_2 poisoning, however, is very rare.

Carbon dioxide is not generally found at hazardous levels in indoor environments. The MNDOLI has set workplace safety standards of 10,000 ppm for an 8-hour period and 30,000 ppm for a 15-minute period. This means the average concentration over an 8-hour period should not exceed 10,000 ppm and the average concentration over a 15-minute period should not exceed 30,000 ppm. It is unusual to find such continuously high levels indoors and extremely rare in non-industrial workplaces.5

The irony is almost perfect: a chemical that threatens the planet because of its overabundance in the atmosphere is in dangerously short supply as a commodity. Shortages of industrial carbon dioxide have emerged periodically over the last couple of years, but the problem has blown up again in Europe, largely due to the war in Ukraine and President Vladimir Putin's decision to cut supplies of natural gas to Europe, which sent the price of that fuel soaring.

A lot of CO_2 is made as a by-product in large factories that make chemical fertilizer and these factories use a lot of natural (methane) gas, both as an energy source and a raw material. Several factories across Europe that make both fertilizer and liquid CO_2 have either shut down entirely, or reduced their production significantly.

In the U.K., this is having a big impact on food and drink businesses. Nick Allen, CEO of the British Meat Processors Association, said the U.K. meat industry depends on plentiful supplies of CO_2.

It's extremely important in the pig and poultry sector. It's the only way we can humanely stun and slaughter pigs and poultry.[6]

In the past most pigs and chickens were stunned for slaughter by electricity. The pigs had electric probes placed on their bodies, the current turned on and rendered unconscious for slaughter. Chickens were shackled, hung upside down and their heads placed under water where an electric current stunned them before their heads were cut off. It has been determined that stunning by CO_2 is much more humane.

An excerpt from U.K.'s Welfare of animals (Slaughter or Killing) regulations states: "Pigs led to be slaughtered pass through a series of automatic gates, with pressure sensors to prevent crushing, to move the pigs forward and then load them into the gas system. This avoids the need for handling by staff and also the need for handling aids. The gas machine consists of a number of gondolas which rotate down into a chamber and then rotate up to the top to release the stunned/killed animals.

Once in a gondola the animals are lowered into the chamber. Since carbon dioxide is heavier than air, the maximum concentration is at the bottom. However, the gas should be of a suitable concentration to take effect on the animals as soon as they are lowered into it. It is a legal requirement that no more than 30 seconds must elapse after a pig has entered the chamber before it is in a gas concentration of 85% or more. (Note: atmosphere CO2 is 0.041%).

U.K. law requires that pigs are not removed from the system until they are dead or irrecoverably stunned. To ensure that animals cannot return to consciousness, a dwell time of two and half minutes is required. It is important that pigs show no corneal reflex after exiting the system."[7]

My thoughts:

1-Atmosphere CO2 levels as a fertilizer for plants is deficient and prevents plants from reaching their full growth and production potential. Plants show increased growth rates when CO2 atmospheric levels are increased up to 700 to 1,800 parts per million (ppm). Atmospheric air contains 417 ppm and in a closed greenhouse drops down at night to 150-200 ppm. Nurseries add CO_2 gas into their green houses to stimulate growth in their plants.

The Cretaceous period is an archetypal example of a greenhouse climate. Atmospheric CO_2 levels reached as high as about 2,000 (0.200%) ppm. It is predicted under the most extreme scenario for climate change that CO_2 levels could reach greater than 1,200 ppm by the end of the century.

2- During the Jurassic (and into the Cretaceous period) because of the increased greenhouse effect, the amount of global rainfall increased, making more of the world into tropical swamps and jungles. The increased amount of vegetation supported the bigger dinosaur species. The amount of oxygen in the atmosphere seems to have increased at this time, allowing plants and animals alike to grow much bigger than they can today.

3-Dinosaurs covered the globe, from the tropics to the temperate zones at the far north and south. Scientists have always assumed that the dinosaur age was very hot and humid, but recent findings have revealed that the earth may have only been a few degrees warmer than it is today.

4-At high levels, the carbon dioxide itself can cause headache, dizziness, nausea and other symptoms. This could occur when exposed to levels above 5,000 ppm (1,200 ppm predicted by the end of the century) for many hours. It is unusual to find such continuously high levels indoors and extremely rare in non-industrial workplaces.

Is it possible that climate change is just a phase in the earth cycle that will result in fertile valleys above the tree lines in the mountains, plentiful water supplies, fast growing productive plants, higher oxygen levels increasing the size of plants and animals, the ocean rising by 115 to 330 feet, plenty of CO2 to fill the food, drink and animal stunning needs; and, the earth resembling descriptions of the Garden of Eden in the Bible?

I don't want to go too far with this. I suspect the oceans would rise by 115 to 330 feet, weeds would grow faster than the crops, the animals would still be eating each other, narcissist individuals would still have to do their dominate thing and their still would be plenty of work keeping us busy. At least there wouldn't be any dinosaurs—however, the higher oxygen levels in the atmosphere might lead to some awfully big beasts of prey.

Oh, by the way. My city of San Jose is 28 feet, and I guess my home is about 100 feet, above sea level. I would hope the ocean would rise slow enough and would not be another issue needed to contend with.

1. *Wikipedia.*
2. *An Unbroken Record of Climate During the Age of Dinosaurs, A scientific drilling project in China has retrieved a continuous history of conditions from Earth's most recent "greenhouse" period that may offer insights about future climate scenarios, 2021.*
3. *Act For Libraries.org. enchantedlearning.com/subjects/ dinosaurs/dinofossils/locations, en.allexperts.com/q/ Paleontology-Dinosaurs-1571/climate-dinosaur-times. htm, environment.gov.au/heritage/places/national/ dinosaur-stampede/lark-quarry/environment.html.*
4. *Greenhouse Carbon Dioxide Supplementation, Oklahoma State University Extension, 2017.*
5. *Minnesota Department of Public Health, indoor air.*

6. *Fizzling out: a shortage of carbon dioxide hits U.K. food and drink industry, Market Place Morning Report, Stephen Beard, Oct 11, 2022.*

7. *The Welfare of Animals (Slaughter or Killing) Regulations 1995 (as amended) HMSO 1995 Regulation (EC) No. 853/2004 - 'H2' HMSO 2006.*

32

CARP

On April 6, 2022, the Illinois Conservation Foundation inducted Bettu DeFord into its hall of fame for raising public awareness about the dangers of Asian carp. The recognition was given for her big heart, love for the environment, and starting a weird fishing tournament that is won by someone brandishing a big dip net and, as likely as not, wearing a hockey mask. She started the Redneck Fishing Tournament on a channel of the Illinois River in Bath, Illinois, in 2005.

The tournament doesn't allow poles and hooks. Instead, contestants arm themselves with the nets and go out in motorboats. The noise of the motors prompts silver carp, a kind of Asian carp, to leap out of the water. Once airborne, they are scooped up in nets. Trouble is, silver carp get big. An average one measures 24-39 inches, but they get considerably bigger—up to 55 inches—and can weigh 100 pounds. A fish like that flying through the air can hurt you. Bruises and broken noses are commonplace, hence the hockey masks and other protective gear. In keeping with the redneck theme, many teams go shirtless and wear overalls. Pair that with a hockey mask, a football helmet, or, like one year, a Darth Vader costume, and you've got a look that folks remember.1

However, impressive acrobatics aren't what make this invasive fish such a threat. As the Asian carp chomps its way through U.S. waterways, the danger is its appetite. Originally imported in the early 1970s to clean up algae on catfish farms and sewage lagoons, Asian carp soon escaped—likely during flooding. They have spent the last 40 years infiltrating Midwest rivers right up to the edge of the Great Lakes, wreaking havoc on native fish populations and ecosystems along the way.

Of the seven Asian carp species that have been introduced to the U.S., two cause the most chaos: the bighead carp and the silver carp. These destructive algae gorgers graze constantly, scooping up plankton that support fish that people actually want to eat.

But plankton aren't the only green stuff these fish are devouring: They're also slurping up money.

Sport and commercial fishing in the Great Lakes is a $7-billion-a-year industry; carp are a looming threat to the economic security of the entire region. They're yet another drain on the Great Lakes, which already struggle with 180 invasive species.

And it's not just the U.S. that's under siege. Australian waters are overrun with common carp, which wreak their own environmental havoc. In Asia, where carp are a natural part of the ecosystem, the fish has long been a popular dish and the Chinese have been aquafarming them since 3500 B.C. But, plunked in unfamiliar settings, the massive creatures adapt easily, quickly outbreeding and out-eating the competition.2

My first exposure to carp was a friend of mine wanting me to go bow and arrow night fishing in the Blackfoot Reservoir in southeastern Idaho. He told me that the fish came close to the shallow water near the shoreline, would make a ripple in the full moon lit water in the shape of a "V" and shooting an arrow in front of the ripple would often hit the carp.

The second exposure was when my wife and I were looking for a home for her parents. We looked at a house in a beautiful country area near Lake Lowell (constructed in 1909) in the Nampa area of Idaho. Unfortunately, we were informed that the area had a mosquito problem, in the summer Cyanobacteria (blue-green algae) produces smelly toxins in the water that are harmful to people, pets and livestock and that the lake is over run by carp. Boise Idaho's KTVB reported in September 2022 that the fish competes with native fish's diet of plankton, stirs the water and forms a chocolatey brown silt that has health effects on the bass, crappie, blue gill and catfish that live in the lake. Also, when other fish are spawning, carp eat the eggs.

The Idaho Department of Fish and Game recommended paying commercial fishermen to remove an estimated 1.3 million carp, about 5 million pounds, of invasive carp from Lake Lowell. The carp could be sold as food in China or India, or ground into fertilizer. Fish and Game has considered options for removing carp including an aquatic pesticide called rotenone.

Rotenone has historically been used by indigenous peoples to catch fish. Typically, rotenone-containing plants in the legume family, Fabaceae, are crushed and introduced into a body of water, and as rotenone interferes with cellular respiration, the affected fish rise to the surface in an attempt to gulp air, where they are more easily caught. Rotenone has been used by government agencies to kill fish in rivers and lakes in the United States since 1952. Lake Lowell first struggled with an Asian carp invasion in 1955 and Rotenone was used in the 1960's to kill the carp and the native fishes rebounded.

The preferred method was subsidized fishing. Few people in the U.S. eat carp, because it's bony and considered a "trash fish," but it could be sold to India and China, where it's a popular dish. Further, rendering plants in the U.S. buy carp to make fertilizer and fish meal.3

Asian carp from the Tennessee River have invaded the Kentucky and Barkley lakes resulting in fisherman incentives offered by the Tennessee Wildlife Resources Agency to catch and produce pet food or fertilizer from the fish. During the years of 2018 to 2021 there were more than 10 million carp harvested.

Just looking at the population of carp removed from the Kentucky and Barkley lakes in three years, 10 million, it is unbelievable how many invasive carp are living in the waters of America. Below are some calculations that puts the crisis into a little more perspective: The average body weight of a steer ready for slaughter is 950 pounds, a Holstein milk cow 1300 pounds and a Holstein bull 2400 pounds. Harvested Asian carp are 24-29 to 55 inches in length and may weigh as much as 100 pounds.

If I use the low average figures of 1000 pounds for a Holstein cow and 20 pounds for the average harvested carp, that means for every cow there are 50 carp to equal 1000 pounds; 10 million carp body weight would equal 200 million pounds or 200,000 Holstein cows each weighing 1,000 pounds.

These figures represent only three years of Asian carp removal in two lakes. The fish is boney, not eaten by many in the US and the economics of shipping to foreign markets makes it restrictive.

Just imagine the tonnage of carp needed to be disposed of if all the infested lakes and rivers in the US were harvesting these fish. I foresee that proper disposal of Asian carp will be a major challenge in the near future and part of the solution could be the use of the liquification process described by Barnyard Technologies.

Barnyard Technologies states that they have a method for the sterilization of organic waste by adding NaOH and/or KOH to the waste and processing it into a sterile, pathogen-free, homogenous, aqueous solution that is suitable for land application or mixing into manure retention vessels prior to land application of the mixture.

The methods provide for the disposal of large volumes of animal by-products and/or dead or diseased animals, provide a processing method that destroys any actual or potential pathogens associated with the dead or diseased tissues, and further provide alternative methods for the safe, effective, and economical treatment and disposal of large volumes of such wastes. A further advantage is that the end product is suitable for land or municipal sewage system disposal and optionally can be mixed directly into manure lagoons to adjust the pH of the manure slurry, prior to land application of the mixture, thereby decreasing or eliminating the need for liming applications normally associated with land-based disposal of anaerobically fermented agricultural and municipal wastes.4

I would suspect that the Asian carp would dissolve much more quickly than the hide, hair and the density of a cow weighing 1000 pounds.

Body liquification (Aquamation) is available for humans in several states. The process is basically the same process that happens in nature when an animal dies and its body broken down into the basic elements (…dust thou art, and unto dust shalt thou return, Genesis 3:19). It works faster than nature, uses less energy, doesn't pollute the atmosphere and kills all potentially life-threatening pathogens.

Aquamation dissolves a body, DNA and all, in a vat of liquid that is a relatively unharmful solution of slightly alkaline water that can be neutralized and returned to the earth. The chemical process behind aquamation is called alkaline hydrolysis, which involves sticking a body into a solution of potassium hydroxide and water that's heated to about 200 degrees Fahrenheit, a slightly lower temperature than boiling, and waiting for it to dissolve.

Potassium hydroxide, often referred to as potash or lye, is a common chemical used in manufacturing soft soap and biodiesel. Its defining quality is that it's chemically alkaline, which means that it's packed with oxygen-hydrogen pairs known as hydroxide groups. In strong enough concentrations, hydroxides can dissolve organic solids into liquids; it's essentially the same process I used to unclog hair and debris from a bathroom drain with a strong solution of sodium hydroxide ($NaOH$).

In aquamation, raising the temperature and pressure helps the process move along faster. Usually, it takes about four hours to dissolve a skeleton. By the end of the process, the only solid thing that's left is a pile of soft bones (potassium hydroxide won't eat through calcium phosphate) that gets crushed into a sterile powder for family members of the deceased to take home.

Human composting often called Natural Organic Reduction (NOR) is a method in which unembalmed remains are processed and turned into soil. The body is broken down with organic materials like wood chips and/ or straw for several weeks inside of an enclosure until it becomes soil.

A funeral home uses a "vessel", is a steel cylinder that is 8 feet long and 4 feet tall. The metal container is then monitored by a computer and staff as the deceased decompose into soil with the help of wood chips, alfalfa, and straw. The organic materials create an environment for microbes and microorganisms that help the decomposition process. There are no fossil fuels or gas involved and the process uses 1/8th the energy expended for a traditional burial or cremation. The process makes approximately a cubic yard of soil, or about enough to fill a truck bed.

Not everyone is a candidate for the decomposition process. Bodies that have been embalmed cannot be decomposed in a vessel because it has disturbed the natural decomposition process. Diseases like tuberculosis or those who have undergone treatments like radiation treatments a month before passing are currently not eligible for the process according to state safety regulations. This is largely to ensure that the resulting soil doesn't have harmful pathogens, and it is always tested once the decomposition has been completed.

It looks like my family will have four options on how they'll take care when Pops is gone:

1- Burial near a cemetery stone, that has my name, date of birth but no deceased date, where their mom is buried,

2- Cremation with parts of me polluting the atmosphere and a small ern's worth of ash left for memories,

3- Liquification with most of me being poured down the drain and the bones remaining crushed into dust and carefully boxed up for safe keeping,

4- or have the remains of my body mixed in wood chips, alfalfa and straw, slowly being eaten by the microbiome that was living with me at the time of death—then presenting the family with a truck bed full of compost probably destined to help keep the roses in bloom.

During a discussion about Asian carp with Iva, a past colleague of mine from Czech Republic, she mentioned that her family has a carp for Christmas instead of turkey. In Eastern Europe, the traditional Christmas dish is not turkey or duck; instead taking center stage on most Christmas Eve dinner tables is an oily freshwater fish: carp.

The carp typically arrives at the table after having spent two to three days in the family bath tub. Carp are bottom feeders, so spending a few days in clean water is supposed to make the fish taste fresher. However, most people aren't thinking of these logistics when they plop their fish into the tub—they do so in order to uphold old traditions. Children have fun playing with the fish, and the anticipation for Christmas builds as the fish swims around in circles. If families need to use the tub, they simply move the carp into a bucket, bathe, then move the fish back in!

Strong Catholic traditions in Eastern European countries brought about the carp tradition hundreds of years ago. Fish became popular for Christmas Eve dinner during the 13th century, because Catholics considered fish as a fasting food, and Christmas Eve was the last day of the Advent fast. The history of eating fish on Christmas Eve (or as many Slovaks say, 'Generous Day') is entirely due to the fact that Catholics couldn't eat meat during the fast.

So, due to the medieval pope's decision that fish isn't meat, Catholic people began eating carp every year for Christmas Eve dinner. If you find yourself walking around the city center of Prague on December 22 or 23, don't be surprised to see several vendor stalls set up selling carp in transparent bags to families who take it home to put into the tub. However, many families today don't wish to keep the carp in the bathtub for days, so they elect to buy a dead carp from the stalls instead and place it in the freezer or the fridge for a day or two instead of the tub.5

Even though many in our country dislike turkey for Christmas dinner, I'm doubtful that there will ever be a movement big enough to reduce the Asian carp population by replacing it for turkey dinner even with the encouraging blessings given by a modern-day pope.

I also am very doubtful that when my time comes that I won't be buried in the cemetery with my deceased date written and only a dash between the two dates representing what I did with my life. I guess that's better than being poured down a sewer, vaporized into the sky or having the children trying to decide what to do with a pile bones or compost.

On October 04, 2022 I received this email . . .

Hi Dr. Hoge,

It is so good to hear from you! I may be somewhat happy but not so much wealthy or wise. As always you wrote a fascinating article with some dark humor there.

I just have to laugh when I am thinking about 10 years back when my American ex boyfriend did come to visit my parents to the Czech Republic and for this special occasion my mom made fried carp with potato salad - our greatest feast. But in his mind he had to wonder why are they making me eat this trash fish and he certainly did not seem as thrilled from this meal as my family and I were. And probably did not help when my parents started talking about how sometimes people end up in an ER on Christmas Eve due to accidentally swallowing one of these very sharp tiny almost invisible carp bones. But it is actually really delicious meal, at least for some of us:)

I am glad everything is well at work and looking forward to read another research article from you.

Best,
Iva

1. *Redneck Fishing Tournament Founder Inducted into Illinois Conservation Foundation Hall of Fame Founder Betty DeFord was honored on April 6 for raising awareness about the dangers of invasive carp, Bill Heavey, 2022.*

2. *Science Natural Science, Invasive Species: Why Are Asian Carp a Problem? Meghan Holmes April 28, 2021.*

3. *Carp for sale? Idaho Fish and Game considers paying fisherman to remove carp in Lake Lowell, Nate Green, 2011.*

4. *Classification: Fertilizers from human or animal excrements, e.g. manure, applicant/assignee Barnyard Technologies, LLC, 2013.*

5. *Here's Why Eastern Europeans Celebrate Christmas with Carp, Tayler Geiger, Freelance Travel Writer, 12/14/2017.*

33

ALKALINE HYDROLYSIS AS AN ENERGY SOURCE

The disposal of animal manure and animal carcasses and other potentially pathogenic wastes and by-products of animal production and processing has always presented challenges. Modern agricultural techniques that involve confinement of farm animals have further increased the environmental problems associated with animal waste disposal. These problems are encountered in all types of animal production, including, for example, hog farming, feedlot cattle farming, poultry farming and many others. The problem is particularly prevalent among that portion of the agricultural industry that pertains to confined animal feeding operations, such as those typically used for dairy, poultry and swine production. In particular, the storage and treatment of manure and the management, processing and disposal of manure is one of the most difficult, expensive and potentially limiting problems facing the agricultural industry.

One major trend in the livestock industry is the movement to larger buildings and larger manure waste stored in retention pits, ponds or lagoons located near the property where the manure is generated. In one common method of operation, manure handling in confined animal feeding operations consists of a mechanical system that flushes the animal manure slurry from the animal holding area to storage, before ultimately being applied as fertilizer or in conjunction with irrigation. The basic function of the lagoons is to store and treat high-strength liquid waste, such as the wastewater, livestock manure, etc., to control unwanted odors and to process the waste for ultimate recycling in the environment. Manure from these lagoons often is used to irrigate agricultural crops, typically after being mixed with four to five parts of fresh water for every one part of recycled water.

Animal manure contains high amounts of nitrates and salts, as well as other compounds such as pharmaceuticals, much of which derives from the animal feed. These contents make manure and its effluent undesirable for contact with fresh water sources, such as rivers and underground aquifers, and difficult to treat or remove, once they contaminate fresh water. Although many of these components of animal manure are valuable nutrients that can be highly useful as soil amendments, for safety and to comply with various regulations, raw animal manures normally are processed and preferably should be sterilized, before being applied to agricultural soils or crops, particularly if intended for human or food-animal consumption.

To maintain soil pH for optimal agriculture plant growth, the need for lime (calcium carbonate) application is increased, when livestock manure is land-applied, due to the acidic pH of the manure itself. Furthermore, when subjected to the effects of anaerobic bacteria, the need for liming is significantly increased. This is because during storage, in the absence of oxygen, the manure slurry proceeds through the four stages of anaerobic digestion: 1) hydrolysis, 2) acidogenesis, 3) acetogenesis and finally, 4) methanogenesis (methane gas production). Throughout these stages the acidity of the manure slurry increases as a by-product of the anaerobic digestion process. Thus, relatively more lime ultimately is required to neutralize the acidity of anaerobically digested manure that has been stored.

Another major animal waste disposal challenge in agriculture pertains to the disposal of animal carcasses and other potentially pathogenic waste and by-products of animal production and meat processing. Each year millions of animals, including, but not limited to mammals, birds, fish and invertebrates are killed by natural disasters, such as floods and hurricanes (dairymen brothers lost 550 dairy cows from hurricane Ian. Each cow weighs about 1000 pounds and costs $2000.00 apiece to replace), man-made disasters, such as oil and chemical spills, or by diseases. Additionally, many animal-based agricultural activities, such as commercial egg production, meat and poultry processing and commercial fishing and fish farming regularly produce large volumes of animal carcasses and animal by-products that must be disposed of safely and quickly.

In some instances, animal tissues to be disposed of are classified as regulated medical waste. Regulated medical waste, pathologic wastes and chemotherapeutic wastes, generally are separated from other contaminated components of medical waste and usually can only be treated and disposed of by incineration. With the development of the Clean Air Act, currently, all pathologic wastes and chemotherapeutic wastes must be incinerated.

The most common method currently in use for disposal of large volumes of animal carcasses and animal by-products is burial, however, incineration and rendering also play a role. Burial isolates the animal tissue underground, but traditional disposal by burial and composting does not destroy some of the most resistant pathogens and may result in further spread of disease. Furthermore, burial leads to decomposition of the animal tissue and an attendant environmental degradation and risk of contamination and further spread the disease.1

The state of Massachusetts Mortality Management regulations for livestock demonstrates how complicated it is to legally bury and decompose animal carcasses. "Burial must be no less than 6 feet deep with a minimum of 30 inches of soil cover, be in well drained soils and be at least 2 feet above the highest groundwater elevation, be at least 100 feet from a private well, 200 feet from a public well, 50 feet from an adjacent property line, 500 feet from a residence and more than 100 feet from a stream, lake or pond, and burial cannot be in a wetland, floodplain or shoreline area.

Before composting check with proper authorities to be sure a permit is not required. As an underlying layer, or substrate, use a mixture of hay, manure and bedding with moisture content between 40 to 50 %, turn to aerate to help reduce odor, and the substrate should have a 25:1 ratio of carbon to nitrogen.

Construct a windrow 10 feet wide by 4 feet deep of the dry manure and bedding mixture. Locate it on a solid spot where the ground slopes 1 to 2%, site it lengthwise with the slope of the land so runoff and snow can't puddle, orient the windrow north to south so that only one end faces a cold exposure.

Once you've placed a carcass (might want to puncture the rumen on cattle to avoid a gas buildup and possible explosion), cover it with at least 2 feet of the same manure and bedding mixture that is underneath the carcass. Maintain a stockpile of the material for covering. Carcasses can be added anytime but should be spaced about 4 feet apart.

The pile must heat up for proper composting. Use a compost-style dial thermometer, ideally with a 30 inch long probe, to monitor the temperature. Temperatures around the carcass will rise to 150 to 160 degrees. Monitor temperatures every two to three weeks. When temperatures fall to 110 to 125 degrees, stir the material with a bucket loader, allowing oxygen to re-activate the composting.

Left untouched, under summer temperatures, an adult carcass (1,500-pound cow) will compost in five to six months. Stirring the mix and covering the carcass again can accelerate the time.

When you see no more soft animal parts, you can spread the compost or leave it in place. Bones, which degrade very little, can be pulverized to spread on fields, creating good fertilizer. Or they can be left in the pile."[2]

Here are some figures that bring a little more perspective as to the scope of labor and expense involved in processing and disposing by burial of animal carcasses in the United States:

There approximately 74 million head of swine weighing between 300-700 pounds (average market average weight 280#'s). Assuming the average body weight of 300#s for each carcass X's 74 million head ='s 22 billion pounds X's 6.8% (the number of deaths from suckers to adults), leaves *1.5 billion pounds of deceased pig being raised on farms per year.*

Slaughter weight to mature cattle weigh from 950 to 2,400 pounds body weight. There are very few formal studies that focused on this, but in some states there is a mortality rate of greater than 10%. In 2019 there were 94.8 million head minus 10% loss rate. Assuming an average body weight of 900#s for each carcass X's 9.48 ='s *8.5 billion pounds of deceased cattle being raised on farms per year.*

In 2019 there were 608,400 sheep and lambs lost from the recorded 5.2 million in the US. Adult body weight ranges from 80 to 400 pounds. Assuming the average body weight of 100#'s X's 608,400 sheep ='s *60.84 million pounds of deceased sheep being raised on farms per year.*

In 2021 there were about 2.12 adult and kid goats (weighing between 44 & 300 pounds) of which 9.8% were lost to nonpredator and predators in the US. Assuming the average weight of 100#'s for each carcass ='s 207,760 Goats or *20.78 million pounds deceased goats being raised on farms per year.*

Incineration is one disposal method that offers the advantage of destroying some or, in some cases, all pathogens present in animal tissues. However, incineration of large volumes of animal material generally is performed in open trench fires or air curtain burners and, under such open-air conditions, produces significant air pollution and the possibility of airborne spread of pathogens not destroyed by combustion.

Incineration of large amounts of animal carcass, food and other wastes creates secondary environmental pollution and potentially toxic effects. It also requires large amounts of fuel to generate the high temperatures necessary to destroy animal tissue, as well as large areas of land, where the open burning can take place.

Rendering is a method of cooking animal tissues to reduce their volume before burial or other land-based disposal and also is impractical in situations where large numbers of animals must be processed quickly. Rendering requires large, fixed facilities such that the animal material usually must be transported to the rendering facility before processing. Moreover, the high temperature and pressure needed for inactivation of some pathogens are not readily achievable using standard rendering or animal waste recycling equipment. Also, high temperature treatments tend to produce unwanted by-products, such as carcinogens, di-amino acids and volatile odors. Furthermore, special risk materials generally are prohibited for use as a feedstock for rendering plants.

There presently exists a need for technologies that safely eliminate the health and environmental risks of infectious or potentially infectious organic materials by a processing method that destroys or otherwise neutralizes any actual or potential pathogens associated with the dead or diseased tissues. The technology also needs to eliminate the negative impacts of contamination, pollution and odors associated with traditional methods of rendering, burial and burning. A further need exists for efficient methods for processing and disposal of large volumes of animal by-products and/ or dead or diseased animals. There is further a need for alternative methods for the safe, effective, and economical treatment and disposal of large volumes of such wastes, as well as other agricultural wastes, including manure produced in association with large animal production facilities, as well as a need for methods to minimize liming applications normally associated with land-based disposal of anaerobically fermented agricultural and municipal waste.

Barnyard Technologies states that they have a method for the sterilization of organic waste includes the steps of introducing an organic waste material for disposal into an unpressurized reaction vessel, adding NaOH and/or KOH plus water to the vessel, heating the vessel to a temperature below but near the boiling point of the resulting solution, and holding the temperature for at least 16 hours, while agitating the contents of the vessel, thereby producing a sterile, pathogen-free, homogenous, aqueous solution that is suitable for land application or mixing into manure retention vessels prior to land application of the mixture.

By using the alkaline hydrolysis effluent as an energy source in an anaerobic digester, the first stage of the anaerobic digestion process (hydrolysis) can be accelerated, reducing the overall time from hydrolysis to methanogenesis (methane gas production) for potential heat or electricity production, thereby producing the same amount of energy in a shorter period of time.

The system thus provides a novel solution to numerous problems in modern agriculture. The methods provide for disposal of large volumes of animal by-products and/or dead or diseased animals, provide a processing method that destroys any actual or potential pathogens associated with the dead or diseased tissues, and further provide alternative methods for the safe, effective, and economical treatment and disposal of large volumes of such wastes. A further advantage is that the end product is suitable for land or municipal sewage system disposal and optionally can be mixed directly into manure lagoons to adjust the pH of the manure slurry, prior to land application of the mixture, thereby decreasing or eliminating the need for liming applications normally associated with land-based disposal of anaerobically fermented agricultural and municipal wastes.

They foresee large dairy, beef, poultry and swine production centers being located near their waste with easy access to the waste from animal carcasses and other potentially pathogenic waste and by-products of animal production and meat processing, the millions of animals, including, but not limited to mammals, birds, fish and invertebrates that are killed by natural disasters, such as floods and hurricanes, man-made disasters, such as oil and chemical spills, or by diseases. Also, other agricultural activities, such as commercial egg production, meat and poultry processing and commercial fishing and fish farming that regularly produce large volumes of animal carcasses and animal by-products which must be disposed of safely and quickly.1

Someday in areas that large numbers of livestock are confined there may be ready access to roads and railroad tracks for distribution of supplies and products that include onsite electricity and natural gas lines. The addition of alkaline hydrolyses capabilities would make it possible to receive, process and mix the aqueous solution of animal carcass digestion in with manure lagoons. Lagoons would be capable of capturing methane gas during the manure digestion process that could be processed and used to provide energy for the production center and the excess energy would be released into natural gas lines.

Recently, the world's largest pork producer and a major public utility announced they would team up to turn hog manure from North Carolina swine farms into energy, they billed their new partnership as a win-win for both the companies and the climate. With a $500 million commitment and a recently minted joint venture called Align RNG, Smithfield Foods and Dominion Energy set out to capture the methane emitted from giant hog manure "lagoons," convert it into biogas—what the industries dub "renewable natural gas"—and inject that biogas into pipelines to heat homes and buildings.

Similar alliances are emerging around the country as the livestock industry comes under increasingly critical scrutiny for its greenhouse gas emissions, and utilities and power companies attempt to meet climate-related commitments. To name only two recent examples, Duke Energy announced in July that it will collaborate with dairy farmers in the Southeast. In September, Chevron announced a project with California Biogas and the state's dairy farmers.[3]

Capturing biogas (methane) could help reduce the need for fossil fuels and help reduce the greenhouse gases of methane and carbon dioxide. Maybe some of the methane gas produced from manure will find itself helping man explore Mars.

One of the trickiest things to get right in space flight is the chemical properties of the propellant, and there's a dizzying array of recipes. First you start with a liquid fuel that reacts with oxygen—of which there are several choices. Some require a second fuel that acts as an oxidizer, and then you need to get the ratios right. The desired mix depends on the properties and parameters around your craft and mission—different needs demand chemical fine-tuning in the substances that propel them.

After a century of rocket fuel research that has looked at everything from RP-1 (kerosene) to hydrogen to paraffin, the industry is turning to a surprising new source—methane natural gas. One of the most abundant chemicals on our planet, methane is finally enjoying the spotlight. And it could take us to Mars.

Methane engines can be designed to run at much higher, more efficient pressures than kerosene. Those efficiency savings mean significant cost savings, making space travel far cheaper. With a higher specific impulse, the quantity of methane required for lift off is less, meaning smaller fuel tanks. There is also easier storage of the fuel before launch, and simpler and lighter fuel pumps on the rocket itself. Methane also pressurizes itself in its tanks by a process called autogenous pressurization, which means complex and heavy systems pressurization systems can be dispensed with.

Producing methane as a rocket fuel is far easier than refining kerosene for RP-1. Getting all the gunk out of jet fuel is hard enough, but RP-1 needs even more work. The RP-1 grade of kerosene rockets run on is made in small, high price batches where methane rockets can readily use industrial grade LNG (liquid natural gas).

One major downside of swapping to methane fuels is a painful initial cost for the launch facilities, as they'll need expensive new equipment to be able to support methane-fueled rockets.

Once Martian colonists reach the red planet, they'll find an atmosphere that's over 95 percent carbon dioxide and plenty of underground water—both key ingredients in making methane and oxygen. With the right technology, a colony could potentially become self-sufficient in its own heating and power needs and—given enough volume—fuel its own return trip back to Earth, maybe even further into the solar system thanks to highly re-usable engines. Mars becomes not just a destination, but potentially a stopover.[4]

1. *Classification: Fertilizers from human or animal excrements, e.g. manure, applicant/assignee Barnyard Technologies, LLC, 2013.*

2. *Livestock and Poultry Environment Stewardship (LPES), Curriculum. Mortality Management, MA Dept. of Agriculture Resources, updated April 2020.*

3. *Pulitzer Prize-winning, nonpartisan reporting on the biggest crisis facing our planet, As the Livestock Industry Touts Manure-to-Energy Projects, Environmentalists Cry 'Greenwashing' by Georgina Gustin, December 7, 2020.*

4. *Why the next generation of rockets will be powered by methane, People & Industry, 07/03/2019.*

PART II

THOUGHTS SHARED
WITH FAMILY
AND FRIENDS

PART II

34

WHERE ARE YOUR
ACRES OF DIAMONDS?

I became a stock holder in Camden Pet Hospital, Inc in 1977, with a loan agreement from the two other stock holders (Jack Hylton DVM and Patrick Baymiller DVM) and in 1982 purchased the building on 4960 Camden Avenue with a loan agreement to Dr. and Mrs. Walter G. Hoge MD. The interest rates in the 1980s were high at the time and my debt load was heavy.

One day a real estate broker approached me about my property that was located near an on ramp going onto Highway 85 and near the just finished Highway 87 (September 1, 1993) that goes north to downtown San Jose. He mentioned that he had a plan that would set me up economically for the rest of my life. The plan including "tearing down the small building and replacing it with a several story business building." The property was zoned commercial and it would be my own personal "Gold Mine," This would truly be a fine decision for my family and theirs for time and near all eternity.

A collection bag containing traces of moon dust that was used by astronaut Neil Armstrong on the Apollo 11 mission was sold at auction to an unidentified buyer for $1.8 million (July 2017). The bag had a long journey even after returning from the moon: After languishing for years in a box at the Johnson Space Center in Houston, Texas, the bag (labeled "Lunar Sample Return") vanished at some point. It was later found in the garage of the manager of a Kansas museum, who was convicted after its theft in 2014.

It was seized by U.S. Marshals and put up for auction three times before Nancy Carlson, a Chicago, Illinois-area attorney, bought it in 2015 for $995.00. Sent to NASA for authentication, the agency fought to keep it after discovering lingering traces of moon dust—and that it had belonged to Armstrong.

Her attorney sued to get it back, and won—but the increased interest in the bag led her to put it up once for auction with Sotheby's in New York City in 2018, where it fetched 1.8 million dollars.1

In this life what fame or fortune will you seek by using your talents and gifts? If you happen to be as fortunate as the Chicago attorney, how will you manage your "gold mine?" I would like to share a story of failure, success and how a man used his talents to successfully reach a goal of helping others have the opportunity to succeed in their lives:

One of the most interesting Americans who lived in the 19th century was a man by the name of Russell Herman Conwell. He was born in 1843 and lived until 1925. He was a lawyer for about fifteen years until he became a clergyman.

One day, a young man went to him and told him he wanted a college education but couldn't swing it financially. Dr. Conwell decided, at that moment, what his aim in life was, besides being a man of cloth—that is. He decided to build a university for unfortunate, but deserving, students. He did have a challenge, however. He would need a few million dollars to build the university. For Dr. Conwell, and anyone with real purpose in life, nothing could stand in the way of his goal.

Several years before this incident, Dr. Conwell was tremendously intrigued by a true story—with its ageless moral. The story was about a farmer, Ali Hafid, who lived in Africa and through a visitor became tremendously excited about looking for diamonds. Diamonds were already discovered in abundance on the African continent and this farmer got so excited about the idea of millions of dollars worth of diamonds that he sold his farm to head out to the diamond line. He wandered all over the continent, as the years slipped by, constantly searching for diamonds, wealth, which he never found. Eventually he went completely broke and threw himself into a river and drowned.

Meanwhile, the new owner of his farm picked up an unusual looking rock about the size of a country egg and put it on his mantle as a sort of curiosity. A visitor stopped by and in viewing the rock practically went into terminal convulsions. He told the new owner of the farm that the funny looking rock on his mantle was about the biggest diamond that had ever been found. The new owner of the farm said, 'Heck, the whole farm is covered with them' - and sure enough it was. The farm turned out to be the Kimberly Diamond Mine . . . the richest the world has ever known. The original farmer was literally standing on 'Acres of Diamonds' until he sold his farm.

Dr. Conwell learned from the story of the farmer and continued to teach it's moral. Each of us is right in the middle of our own 'Acre of Diamonds', if only we would realize it and develop the ground we are standing on before charging off in search of greener pastures.

Dr. Conwell told this story many times and attracted enormous audiences. He told the story long enough to have raised the money to start the college for underprivileged deserving students. In fact, he raised nearly six million dollars and the university he founded, Temple University in Philadelphia, has at least ten degree-granting colleges and six other schools.

Doctor Russell H. Conwell talked about each of us being right on our own 'Acre of Diamonds', he meant it. This story does not get old . . . it will be true forever . . . Opportunity does not just come along, it is there all the time - we just have to find it.2

Before diamonds were discovered at the site of the Kimberley mine, two Dutch pioneers, Johannes Nicholas and Didrik Arnoldus De Beers had established a farm there. When diamonds were found in 1866, the discovery set off a diamond rush and diamond prospectors from many countries flocked to the area. The De Beers brothers eventually sold their property.

Between 1871 and 1914 some 50,000 miners had excavated 22.5 tons of rock, producing a total weight of 2,722 kilograms of rough diamonds—14,504,566 carats. In 1888, Cecil John Rhodes and Charles Rudd took over the mines and set up a new company—De Beers

Consolidated Mines Ltd. Today, De Beers remains the dominant company in the diamond market, owning 70% of the mines in South Africa and producing 40% of the world's rough diamonds.

When the pit mining became dangerous and unprofitable, the kimberlite pipe (named after the city of Kimberley) was bored to a depth of 1,097 meters, and the underground mine operated until 2005.

In later years, some claimed that the Kimberley 'Big Hole' was the largest hole ever dug by human hands. But when the claim was investigated, the Big Hole lost out to the Jagersfontein Mine.

Originally, the Big Hole had been dug 240 meters deep but was partly filled in, leaving a depth of 215 meters—only 175 of which are still visible due to the fact that water has partially filled the pit. In 2006, De Beers invested some $7.7 million in developing the Big Hole as a tourist site and diamond mining museum.

Discussing the Acres of Diamonds story Scott Aughtmon stated, "I want to share with you the moral that I think Dr. Conwell totally missed. Don't get me wrong. I think the moral that he came up with is a powerful one: we all are surrounded by opportunities that we are blind to.

But I think the moral I found hidden in the story might be an even more powerful one. Let me explain. As I was writing out the story of Ali Hafed for you I was struck by this statement…

Ali Hafed owned a very large farm. He had orchards, grain-fields, and gardens. He had money saved away at interest and he was a wealthy and contented man. That is, he was until one day when a Buddhist priest came to visit.

Ali Hafed was ALREADY a wealthy man! And he was very content! This isn't the story of a poor man! That's an important distinction!

Do you remember what sent him on the journey in the first place? If you don't, here it is again…

And when Ali Hafed heard all about diamonds and how much they were worth, he went to bed that night feeling like a poor man.

He hadn't lost anything, but he felt poor because he was discontented, and discontented because he was afraid he was poor. Do you now see the moral to this story that Dr. Conwell totally missed? He was right. We are surrounded by opportunities that we are clueless about. We need to open our eyes and pay attention, so we don't miss out on them.

But the fact that Dr. Conwell forgot to remind us about is this one that's even more pitiful: we are already wealthy and we've forgotten this fact! You and I will become much more content and satisfied in life the moment we begin to focus on all the wealth that we have, instead of all that we don't have.

What? You don't feel wealthy? Maybe you've forgotten the treasures that are more valuable than any acres of diamonds or mines filled with gold:

- Friends
- Family
- Health
- A chance to live one more day

And any of us in the U.S. who still don't feel wealthy have forgotten this fact: America's Poor Still Live Better Than Most Of The Rest Of Humanity.

When we remember this overlooked moral to the story, we'll be more content because we'll be working from a place of contentment instead of desperation.3

The real estate investor finished his pitch. I looked at him and as I recall said, "I want to practice veterinary medicine, I have a place where I can sink roots for my family and the families who will come my way, yes I have a growing family and am deep in debt from my business and home but I forsee my happiness to come from the experiences and joy I anticipate by staying right here for the rest of my career."

I must tell you that I have not received a "Gold Mine"—I have received "Acres of Diamonds" of choice memories and relationships that give me joy and contentment as I enter my final years.

May our "aim in life" be to use our gifts and talents as President Hinckley admonished: "I wish to be up and doing. I wish to face each day with resolution and purpose. I wish to use every waking hour to give encouragement, to bless those whose burdens are heavy, to build faith and strength of testimony."4

1. *Science, 07-27-2017, Vol 357 Issue 6349, p 337.*
2. *Written by Earl Nightingale.*
3. *Myth of Better Content: Surprising Lessons from "Acres of Diamonds," By Scott Aughtmon, 05/04/2016.*
4. *Ensign, Mar. 2008, 26-27.*

35

POLIO AND THE IRON LUNG

On a hot summer day in 1952, Paul Alexander of Texas was not feeling well. His neck and head hurt and he was running a high fever. Within days, the six-year-old boy (he was born the same year I was) could not move, speak or even swallow: he had contracted polio. Today, though almost completely paralyzed from the neck down, Alexander - who is now 75 years old - is alive and well, thanks to the large steel ventilator that has enabled him to breathe for nearly seven decades. He is one of the last people to use an iron lung, a device that was a common sight in polio wards at the peak of the epidemic.

Poliomyelitis kills by suffocation by attacking motor neurons in the spinal cord, weakening or severing communication between the central nervous system and the muscles. The ensuing paralysis means that the muscles that make it possible to breathe no longer work. Polio existed in isolated outbreaks around the world for millennia, but it didn't become epidemic until the 20th century—helped, ironically, by improvements in sanitation. Poliovirus enters the body through the mouth, via food or water, or unwashed hands, contaminated with infected fecal matter.

Until the 19th century, almost all children would have come in contact with poliovirus before the age of one, while they still enjoyed protection from maternal antibodies transferred from mother to baby during pregnancy. However, as sanitation improved, children were less likely to come into contact with poliovirus as babies; when they encountered it as older children, their immune systems were unprepared.

At its peak in the 40s and 50s, the virus killed or paralyzed at least 600,000 people annually worldwide. 1952 saw the largest single outbreak of polio in US history—mostly in children. In places where outbreaks occurred, families sheltered in fear at home with the windows shut. All kinds of public gathering places closed. Human interactions were laced with uncertainty.

According to the historian of New York University David Oshinsky, some people refused to talk on the phone out of concern that the virus could be transmitted down the line. During the first major outbreak in New York in 1916, 72,000 cats and 8,000 dogs were killed in one month after a rumor went around that animals transmitted the disease (they don't). By the 1940s, parents had their children perform "polio tests" every day during the summer - touch their toes, tuck their chin to their chests, checking for pain or weakness - while insurance companies sold "polio insurance" to parents of new babies.

Before the arrival of a vaccine in 1955, what made polio so terrifying was that there was no way of predicting who would walk away from an infection with a headache, and who would never walk again. "Back then, it affected business and travel," says Stacey D. Stewart, current president and CEO of the March of Dimes. "People didn't know how the virus was transmitted. They lived in a state of fear. Pools were closed. Businesses were affected because people didn't want to be out in public."

President Franklin D. Roosevelt, who had himself essentially lost the use of his legs after a polio infection in 1921, when he was 39, launched the National Foundation for Infantile Paralysis, a charitable organization, in the late 1930s. Later renamed the March of Dimes, the foundation took the lead in efforts to fund research at a time when the National Institutes of Health was in its infancy. "Roosevelt's passion for finding a solution - a cure, a vaccine - made polio a priority coming from the very top leader of this country," says Stewart. "People across the country felt like they were called to duty. It was a call to action, like the war effort." An army of volunteers for the March of Dimes, largely mothers, went door to door, distributing the latest information about polio and the effort to stop it; they also asked for donations. As little as a dime would help, they said. And the dimes and dollars poured in, Oshinsky says, handed to the volunteers, or inserted into cardboard displays at store checkout counters or placed in envelopes sent directly to the White House.1

No device is more associated with polio than the tank respirator, better known as the iron lung. Physicians who treated people in the acute, early stage of polio saw that many patients were unable to breathe when the virus's action paralyzed muscle groups in the chest. Death was frequent at this stage, but those who survived usually recovered much or almost all of their former strength. Nothing worked well in keeping people breathing until 1927, when Philip Drinker and Louis Agassiz Shaw at Harvard University devised a version of a tank respirator that could maintain respiration until a person could breathe independently, usually after one or two weeks. The machine was powered by an electric motor with two vacuum cleaners. The pump changed the pressure inside a rectangular, airtight metal box, pulling air in and out of the lungs. Inside the tank respirator, the patient lay on a bed (sometimes called a cookie tray) that could slide in and out of the cylinder as needed. The side of the tank had portal windows so attendants could reach in and adjust limbs, sheets or hot packs. The National Foundation for Infantile Paralysis began mass distribution of tank respirators in 1939. In 1959, there were 1200 people using tank respirators in the United Stated; in 2004, there were 39. *Wikipedia etc.*

Instead of being imprisoned by the iron lung that keeps him alive, Paul Alexander has used it as a springboard to thrive. He graduated with honors from high school, then received a scholarship to Southern Methodist University, and graduated in 1984 with a Juris Doctor from the University of Texas, and practiced as a Lawyer.

In 2020, Alexander wrote a book about his experience, *"Three Minutes for a Dog: My Life in an Iron Lung."* It took him five years to do it, writing every word himself with a pen attached to a stick he held in his mouth. He stated in a recent video, "I wanted to accomplish the things I was told I couldn't accomplish and to achieve the dreams I dreamed." At a time when disabled people were less often seen in public—the Americans with Disabilities Act, which banned discrimination, wouldn't be passed until 1990—Paul was visible. Over the course of his life, he has been on planes and to strip clubs, seen the ocean, prayed in church, fallen in love, lived alone and staged a sit-in for disability rights. He is charming, friendly, talkative, quick to anger and quick to make a joke. At 74, he is once again confined to the lung full-time.1

The Salk vaccine by injection was ready for experimental testing in 1954, the years-long campaign of information and donations to the polio eradication effort made anxious Americans feel they were invested in a solution. So confident was the public in the research leading up to the polio vaccine that the parents of 600,000 children volunteered their own offspring as research subjects. Studies showed the vaccine to be safe and effective in 1955, and church bells rang. Loudspeakers in stores, offices and factories blared the news. People crowded around radios. There was jubilation and people couldn't wait to sign their kids up for a shot.

Other than temporarily halting of vaccinations in 1955 resulting from one defective batch of vaccines resulting in 40,000 polio cases, 200 left with varying degrees of paralysis and 10 deaths—that same year the mothers and fathers jumped right back in following the tragedy, once again signing permission slips and lining their kids up to get their polio shot. It was widely understood and accepted that the risks of polio were a much greater threat than the risks of the vaccine.

Even as Salk's vaccine was being tested, Albert Sabin was developing a vaccine with an attenuated virus. Sabin argued that his vaccine would provide long-term immunity and also would have the benefit of conferring "herd immunity." Individuals who have received this vaccine shed weakened virus in their fecal waste; this gives others a partial exposure to the weakened virus, boosting their immune system. He isolated strains of each of the three types of the virus that would stimulate the production of antibodies, but weren't strong enough to lead to the disease itself.

Following meticulous experiments on thousands of monkeys and hundreds of chimpanzees, Sabin tested the three strains on himself and other volunteers. On October 6, 1956, Sabin announced that his vaccine was ready for mass testing. However, at this time most the public and most of the scientific community in the U.S. still backed Salk's vaccine. By the time Sabin's vaccine was ready to undergo field trials, most American children had received Salk's vaccine and were, therefore, immune to polio.

Searching for a population that had not received Salk's vaccine, Sabin and his team decided to run field trials in the regions then known as the U.S.S.R. and the Belgian Congo. Polio's dangers were such that the Americans and Soviets were willing to trust one another in testing Sabin's vaccine, even at the height of the Cold War.

In the mid-1950s, Sabin carried out his first experiment (that I can find) with a live, attenuated (weakened) oral vaccine on 30 adult male volunteer inmates of the Chillicothe Federal Reformatory. Volunteers for this experiment were given $25 and promised free days, a total of 30 men, all consenting adults, were chosen for this study. Early testing saw four cases of paralytic polio develop in 4 million tests in Canada. In 1960, Sabin described, in an article published in JAMA, Live, an orally given poliovirus vaccine, the results obtained with his newly developed trivalent oral vaccine to 26,033 children from a city of 100,000 people in South America. Because the strains developed by Sabin provided good antibody levels and were less neurotropic for monkeys, they were selected and licensed between 1961 and 1963 in the United States for widespread application. *Wikipedia etc.*

A blogger wrote, "When I was in the second grade (1950? 1951) my father, who was principal had everyone in school vaccinated. Sugar cubes were used. I was told this wasn't possible. Was it? - I suspect that you may be off a bit in the year(s) you mentioned, in the question. It had to have been a bit later than 1950, or 1951. But it most certainly happened. Yes, in the very late 1950s and the very early 1960s, sugar cubes and also "drops" were used, as an oral vaccine for polio. (Note - Sugar cubes were still being widely used in the 1970s, and the 1980s and the 1990s)."2

Because of the discrepancy of when the Sabin polio vaccine was licensed (1961-1963) in the United States, when I recalled getting my oral vaccine several years before entering high school in 1960, four individuals I asked living in California (one stated 1957) and three relatives from Idaho all stating having receiving the sugar cube oral vaccine before 1960—it leads me to believe we were all chosen "Polio Volunteers" as non-consenting children, did not receive $25 (I would have preferred silver dollars), and did not get any free days from school (unless we got sick from the vaccine).

I remember in the mid 1950's lining up with my classmates and instead being given a vaccine injection receiving a sugar cube to prevent polio as a "Polio Pioneer." I did get a certificate card with the date 1954 on it, but not a written date (like I did for each date I received four COVID-19 vaccines), and I didn't realize that I was most likely a "polio volunteer" until researching Paul Alexander's use of the iron lung for 69 years of his life and finding my "POLIO PIONEER" card.

I do remember a lady, Donna Carson, who lived down the street from my home that lived most of her days and all her sleeping life in an iron lung. My father was assigned to visit her as a Home Teacher to watch over and help her family and report any special needs to their bishop (the leading authority in a religious congregation, called a ward, consisting of approximately 500 individuals). Being an MD, dad was able to give advice and assistance others in our congregation were not equipped to offer. Home Teachers visited their assigned families in pairs (called companions) and needless to say I had the opportunity to visit Donna Carson with my father. I remember at my age how uncomfortable I felt listening to the iron lung, watching her struggle to breath and speak, and how her hand was withered and placed in a way to hold a tube that she placed in her mouth to receive air when not in the iron lung.

She was raised in the small town of Blackfoot Idaho and in 1955 at the age of 23 received a call to go on a mission. Donna was undecided as to whether she should go because she had just become engaged to be married. She talked to her fiancé, the stake president (religious leader over several wards), she and her family fasted and prayed, and she received a definite answer that she should go. On April 13, 1955 she left Blackfoot to serve a mission in the Boston MA area. She had been there for 4 months when she became ill from what turned out to be polio.4

Elder Clark G. Gilbert stated, "Brothers and sisters, in this Church, we believe in the divine potential of all of

God's children and in our ability to become something more in Christ. In the Lord's timing, it is not where we start but where we are headed that matters most. We all have different intercepts in life - we start in different places with different life endowments. Some are born with high intercepts, full of opportunity. Others face beginning circumstances that are challenging and seem unfair. We then progress along a slope of personal progress. Our future will be determined far less by our starting point and much more by our slope. Jesus Christ sees divine potential no matter where we start. He saw it in the beggar, the sinner, and the infirm. He saw it in the fisherman, the tax collector, and even the zealot. No matter where we start, Christ considers what we do with what we are given. While the world focuses on our intercept, God focuses on our slope. In the Lord's calculus, He will do everything He can to help us turn our slopes toward heaven. I recently had a conversation with a nationally prominent educator who was inquiring about the success of BYU–Pathway education program. He was bright and his inquiry was sincere, but he clearly wanted a secular response. I shared with him our retention programs and mentoring efforts. But I concluded by saying, "These are all good practices, but the real reason our students are progressing is because we teach them their divine potential. Imagine if your whole life, you were told you could never succeed. Then consider the impact of being taught that you are an actual son or daughter of God with divine possibility." He paused, then replied simply, "That's powerful."3

During a discussion a book written about her challenges Donna Carson stated, "First of all I must tell you that I give thanks every day for this privilege of having polio. I don't think of it as a tragedy, for there is only tragedy in sin. I think of it as a very special way to obtain the schooling that I needed. It has been a tremendous experience and the blessings I have received can't even be numbered. The author says that 'we only advance through suffering'. This is so true. It is through sorrow and suffering, toil and tribulation, that we gain the education that we came here to acquire... Being human we would like to eliminate the sorrow, distress, pain and mental anguish from our lives so that we might have continual ease and comfort, but if we did this we would be closing the doors on our greatest friends.

The sufferings of our Savior were part of His education. In Hebrews 5:8 it says, 'Though He were a son, yet learned He obedience by the things which He suffered.' I think of Paul and the thorn in his flesh and how it kept him humble. Perhaps if I were completely well and lovely to look at like I would be, and free from the things that make me humble, I would very probably lose my reward... I have felt that the Lord must be very mindful of me to 'crush' me like He did and then remold me into what he wants me to be. It is like having a second chance and—OH MY—I surely hope I don't 'muff' it this time...

About a year ago they had a reunion for a few of us who went to school together. This one girl remarked to another that she thought it was terrible to expose me to their life when they had everything and I had nothing. It made me feel very sad to think that her vision was so limited. True, they have a lot of things that I don't have but on the other hand I have so much that they don't have...

I know that this has been so much harder on my family than on me. You can imagine how you would feel to see someone you loved lying helpless in bed. It would practically tear your heart out*. (The Lord blesses her with strength each day to go on). Whenever I think of this I think of the scripture, 'Greater love hath no man'. I have seen her so sick that she couldn't hardly get her head off the pillow and yet she would come in here to care for me. Sometimes lying right down on the floor or sometimes crawling to get me taken care of. Imagine a person being so sick and thinking of some else's comfort. Yes, my folks have given up so much for my benefit and happiness. *I am gaining so much and my lovely mother is getting so worn out."4

When Franklin Roosevelt started a foundation to fight polio, Comedian Eddie Cantor came up with the "March of Dimes", asking people to mail a dime to the White House. They were soon overwhelmed with 2,680,000 dimes mailed to them, literally truckloads, mostly from children. These dimes went directly to research that resulted in the Polio vaccine. This is why Roosevelt is on the U.S. dime. Jonas Salk (1914 - 1995) decided not to patent his 1955 Polio Vaccine so that it would be affordable for millions of people who couldn't afford it. As a result, he lost out on an estimated 7 billion dollars.1

"Today there are those who have met disaster which almost seems defeat, who have become somewhat soured in their natures; but if they stop to think, even the adversity which has come to them may prove a means of spiritual uplift. Adversity itself may lead toward and not away from God and spiritual enlightenment; and privation may prove a source of strength if we can but keep the sweetness of mind and spirit." *David O. McKay, Treasures of Life, pp. 107–8.*

1. *The man in the iron lung, Paul Alexander, by Linda Rodriguez McRobbie, The Gardian, 2020.*
2. *Bruce Spielbauer - Updated April 23, 2020 by Robert Hampton, MD, Emory University (1976) & Richard Smith formerly pharmacist & ENT surgeon.*
3. *Becoming More in Christ: The Parable of the Slope, Elder Clark G. Gilbert, Of the Seventy, October 2021. 4-Donna Carson 1932—1991, "To Every Thing there is a Season and a Time to every Purpose under the heaven" Humpherys 1991.*

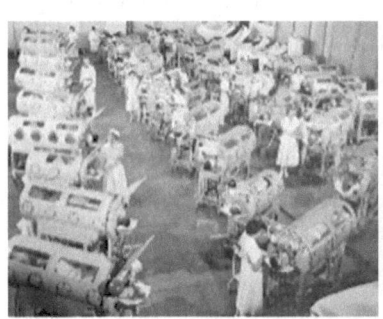

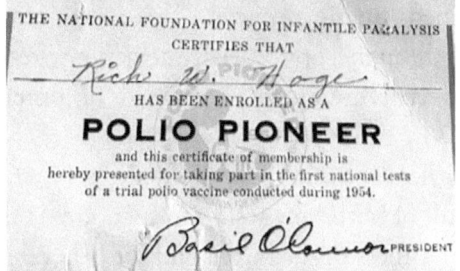

36

MAKING THE SALE

Fundamentally, the concept of business has remained constant for thousands of years. Firms produce goods and services to turn a profit. It sounds simple enough. However, one of the challenges businesses have faced since the beginning of time is how to ethically influence the buyer to purchase their goods and services.

A morally responsible businessperson wants to solve a problem for their customers. In other words, they don't lie, cheat, or otherwise deceive their customers to get them to buy something that they know doesn't work. Customers trust businesses to give them good information to make an informed buying decision. This information can be delivered through copy, social interactions, testimonials, video, advertisements, or a myriad of other delivery methods.

Regardless of the delivery method, the buying decision is the result of both how well information was transferred from the business to the buyer, and the believability of the information. If a company does a poor job of educating a customer about the reasons they should purchase a specific item, the customer simply won't purchase the item.

Once a consumer believes that a product can help them obstacles to the purchase often become of less concern and logically or not the consumer must have it. They have become what is known as "Hot" customers with a burning desire to buy.

A "hot" consumer only needs information that allows them an experiential opportunity to "try it out and got to have it moment." Sometimes, this is as easy as getting the product in the hands of the consumer. Automobile dealerships allow customers to take cars home. Software and application companies give users free trials. Stores have "sample" items on the shelves for people to play with. Most vitamin, food and pain supplement testimonials on TV or the radio have a bottle free offer. Amazon not only makes it easy to place a product in our hands but has a convenient no charge return policy.

By allowing the consumer the opportunity to try the product out, the companies are reducing the perceived risk associated with user experience. In addition, there is evidence that physically holding products can create a sense of psychological ownership, making people more likely to purchase. Also, how many of us have gift cards or unused purchased items in our home that will probably never get used?1

In 1985 I purchased my own personal windmill in southern California. High taxes, tax credits offered, interest rates on the loans I held on my home and business, the pride of owning a windmill that I could visit with my family during trips to Disneyland, cost discount from $275,000 to $250,000, financing and protecting the environment all pushed my hot button. At the time I could not think of a reason why this wasn't a great purchase for my financial, family and the earths environment's needs. My accountant advised me that a person shouldn't invest in anything they are not familiar with. In spite of the accountants concerns I signed the paper work and headed home with a beautiful photo of my windmill to display on the family wall. Tax credits to help reduce the financial burdens of the day and an income flow from the windmill farm for my retirement—who could ask for anything more?

One year my tax credits were challenged by the State of California because many of the windmills failed and the owners abandoned them. I was allowed to keep my credits because I had paid for a damaged blade to be repaired and the machine was still in production.

The leased land where the windmill farm was located went bankrupt, foreclosure occurred and my windmill became 3696 shares of stock in a new corporation. The corporation has over the years been invested in Mexico and Tehachapi wind energy projects. I receive a yearly statement, vote as a shareholder, and inconsistently receive a yearly dividend check for $3696.00 from my $250,000.00 investment. No one has ever shown an interest in buying Oak Creek Holdings or my shares of stock.

I was introduced and heavily encouraged by a friend to buy some penny shares of stock in a new phone company. Eventually the stock sold for $5 a share and it received awards at electronic shows. The stock was projected to reach $100.00 before making a public offering. I went from a lukewarm to a hot button buyer.

I had fantasies of donating a good portion of the projected twenty-five million dollars (approximately

250,000 shares of stock) to my universities and favorite charities. Instead, I now periodically receive notices from the state of Utah about a fraud case against the individual who was "making us millions" from his technology/phone company. In this hot button experience I will not receive any tax credits, an occasional $3606.00 dividend or a photo of my investment. I currently have a pile of stock certificates and warrants, that I've invested into it nearly the cost of the windmill, that will most likely have no value and be placed in my home Museum of Shame.

Writing scientific articles during my college years was done under the guidelines of a professor specializing in my area of studies using the scientific method. This method presents a question about how an observed process or condition occurs, doing background research, presenting a hypothesis or theory about how it works, testing the theory, analyzing the testing data, drawing conclusions and sharing the results with others in a publication where interested parties are encouraged to verify or dispute the findings. They contain a "nothing but the facts," neatly arranged, short and concise article with an introduction, body containing the research, and a conclusion stating the value of the study and recommendations for further investigation.

Doing research in graduate school and as a veterinary student increased my enthusiasm about learning how the biological processes work. The professors helped guide and direct my thoughts and the investigations we pursued. Overall, I had wonderful experiences doing and publishing research.

Shortly after the passing of my kid's mom I wrote a story about two of my Labrador Retrievers and a fantasy trip to McEaster Valley in the Sierra Mountains. The story was about tales I told my young children at night while they were laying on my bed. I wrote it on typing paper and gave it to them for Easter. There were a few comments and I'm not sure any of my five children read it.

Several years later I was traveling with my second wife Shauna and her mother to Utah on Memorial Day to pay our respects to our ancestors. In the car Shauna read Easter: McEaster Valley to her mom and she insisted that I have the book published and was persistent until I got it done.

I recently was encouraged by a publisher to re-do Easter: McEaster Valley and I had them publish a new book called THOUGHTS ON MY THOUGHTS: The TALES That Wagged This Veterinarian. I'm satisfied that the books accomplished my goal of telling experiences about my life that my progeny may find of value in the future. I'm convinced that if I had written a life's stories journal it would rarely if ever be read.

Until publishing these two books I had no idea how great an author I am. I have been bombarded on my phone, text and emails concerning the placement of ads about the books in major magazines and newspapers, radio interviews available, creation of a web site, filming a you-tube documentary, creating a screen play for a movie, attending book fairs, and the list goes on.

They really know how to stimulate a person's ego and pride with dreams of recognition, fame and fortune. They use your hot button to influence the purchase of services that are most likely of little to no promotional or economic value. There is importance in stroking you with an air of brilliance and importance - to feed their profit center. I can testify from personal experience raising children that if they push long and hard enough you will succumb and participate in the success of their profit center.

Ultimately, the goal is to get a consumer to buy something that they need but don't have, or to get rid of something they have, but don't need or want.1

The experience reminds me of a trip to Mexico on my honeymoon at the age of 21. Walking through Tijuana my new bride and I were approached by a young man about drugs available we could drink, smoke or inject into ourselves. We declined and he proceeded to tell me that he had a sister at home for me that was a virgin waiting for me. I held my wife's left hand up for him and said we were just married. He said, "Oh I see that what you want is a divorce. Come with me and we can take care of this for you."

Another experience was with my brother-in-law on a beach in Mexico. He was being hounded by people selling everything from Chiclet's gum to blankets. Finally, he pulled out all the money he had in his pockets and threw it on the ground stating, "That is all I have. It's yours. Take it and go away and leave me alone!"

Unfortunately, there are book publishers that offer you services that are little or nothing of what you need except to publish your book. Like a child many use every means available to have you participate in services that you do not need or want. Yes, I have been pushed to the point of emptying some of my pockets mostly to just be left alone and not have to empty my text or phone messages so often. Has it worked—No!

Life is pretty much like a cafeteria line. We are offered many choices, both good and bad. Our goal is to be in tune with what is best for our family. The decision of buying a windmill had value even though I'm receiving very little income from it in my later years. The spending of unnecessary money with book publishers at my age has little consequence on my financial wellbeing. The stock purchases of the cell phone company that is in the courts as a fraud case fortunately was not bought with money I absolutely needed to have.

Ultimately, the goal is to get a consumer to buy something that they need but don't have, or to get rid of something they have, but don't need or want.1

It's a good thing that I have all my retirement funds under the care of reputable firm. Of the three investments I mentioned there isn't a good, better or best choice. Thy all kind of stink.

The only regret I have about not having the money I dreamed about from two of these investments is: I will not be able to afford the ATM machine I wanted to have at my grave site.

I wanted to record messages for my children and grandchildren that would be heard on a scheduled basis, getting all my children together often, and distribute my inheritance to them on a regular basis.

Imagine your family coming together on a monthly basis, having a retinal scan ID, listening to a few words of wisdom by yours truly and then have your inheritance distributed to them by your ATM machine after they inserted their ID card. If anyone did not show up the funds would be added equally among the participating family members and distributed the next month.

Your family would need to live fairly close to each other, your grave site would be visited and hopefully cleaned more often and there wouldn't be any big hunks of money available at your death to encourage greed and fighting among your offspring.

I think an ATM machine would show my family how responsible I am as a father and businessman. It would help keep the family together and solve the problems of inheritance money getting in the way of their relationship. Also, if I were stingy enough on the funds given out on a monthly basis the machine would always have money available so none of my children would ever starve.

1. *Psychology, Adopted from Dr. Ari Zelmanow, The ProfessorOfPersuasion.com, 02-05-2016.*

37

PLIMSOLL LINE

Syracuse, Sicily, (then a Greek seaport, now part of Italy), 287 B.C.–212 B.C. The Wise One. The Master. The Great Geometer. These were a few of the nicknames given to the Greek mathematician Archimedes, a man who forgot to stop for meals when he was hard at work on a mathematical problem. He often gave advice to the ruler of Sicily, King Hiero II, who was his friend.

One day, Hiero II asked Archimedes to help him solve a problem. Hiero II had hired a goldsmith and had given him a block of gold weighing a specified amount to use to make a gold crown. When the crown was finished, Hiero II weighed it. It weighed the same as the gold block the king had given the goldsmith. Yet Hiero II had a sneaking feeling that the goldsmith had cheated him and had used silver as well as gold in the crown—and kept the unused gold for himself.

How could this be proved without spoiling the crown? Archimedes mulled over the problem. It was still on his mind one day as he stepped into his bathtub. Water splashed over the edge of the tub as Archimedes settled into it. As the water dripped, a realization popped into the great mathematician's mind: the water he splashed out of the tub when he got in was equal to the volume taken up by his body.

At that moment, Archimedes knew he had the key to Hiero II's dilemma. Supposedly, more water splashed on the floor as he leaped out of the tub and, without even stopping to grab a towel, dashed out of the house. He ran down the street, shouting "Eureka!" which means "I have found it" in Greek.

No doubt the citizens of Syracuse wondered what the great mathematician had lost as he bolted through the town. His mind, perhaps? Archimedes was quite sane, even though he was forgetful about ordinary things such as towels and clothes.

But what did the water in the bathtub have to do with whether Hiero II's crown was pure gold or a mixture of silver and gold? Well, Archimedes knew that a piece of gold weighs more than a piece of silver the same size. According to legend, Archimedes weighed the king's crown. Then he got a piece of pure gold that weighed the same amount as the crown. He placed the gold into a bowl of water, measured how much it made the water rise, and took the gold out. Next, he put the crown into the water and saw that it made the water rise higher than the piece of gold had.

Why? Because this crown was larger than one made of pure gold. The goldsmith had to make the crown larger when he substituted silver for some of the gold so that it would weigh the same as a pure gold crown. But the silver-gold crown took up more space in the bowl and made the water rise higher.

Because Archimedes took a bath, the dishonest goldsmith was now in hot water!

Archimedes had discovered the principle of buoyancy of objects when placed in water. That's why a coin when thrown in the sea will sink like a stone, but a steel ship will float. Two objects can have the same mass, yet one might sink while the other one will float. This happens when one has the mass spread out more, taking up more space for the water to push against. To test this idea of buoyant force, get a piece of clay or play dough about the size of a golf ball. Work it into different shapes, testing each shape to see if it sinks or floats.1

In the 19th Century working on a merchant ship was a dangerous business. In 1876 the Board of Trade recorded that 856 British merchant ships were lost within ten miles of the British coast, in conditions that were no worse than a strong breeze. Successive governments and greedy ship owners did little to protect the lives of seamen.

Step forward Bristol hero Samuel Plimsoll (1824-1898), the sailor's friend, a philanthropist whose tireless campaigning saved hundreds of lives and whose work is still remembered today in a safety marker simply called the Plimsoll Line.

Plimsoll moved as a child to Sheffield and then Cumbria, leaving school at an early age to become a brewery clerk and then manager. In 1853 he moved to London and became a coal merchant, a business which left him destitute and instilled a huge sympathy for the struggles of the poor.

Despite his problems he picked himself up and was soon campaigning against overloaded and unseaworthy merchant vessels, known as "coffin ships". As a youth in

England, Plimsoll was fascinated with watching ships load and unload their cargoes. He soon observed that, regardless of the cargo space available, each ship had its maximum capacity. If a ship exceeded its limit, it would likely sink at sea.

The public supported his campaign but he faced ridicule and obstruction from the powerful ship owners of the time, and the government. In 1871 a huge gale off the coast of Bridlington, resulted in Plimsoll's call for change to be taken seriously. In 1872 he published a work entitled Our Seamen, in 1873 a Royal Commission was appointed to look into Plimsoll's suggestions and two years later a government bill was introduced, which he agreed to accept.

A year later the Merchant Shipping Act was introduced, giving strong powers of inspection to the Board of Trade and introducing a mark onto the hull of all ships to ensure they were not overloaded - the Plimsoll line.2

(Different conditions of water for sailing)
A—B Line showing even load front to back.
TF&F Lines Fresh water & Tropical Fresh water.
W&WNA Winter & Winter North Atlantic.
T&S Tropical & Summer water.

Like ships, people have differing capacities at different times and even different days in their lives. In our relationships we need to establish our own Plimsoll marks and help identify them in the lives of those around us. We need to monitor the load levels and be helpful in shedding or at least readjusting some cargo if we see ourselves or others sinking. Then, when the ship is stabilized, we can evaluate long-term what has to continue, what can be put off until another time, and what can be put off permanently.

Friends, sweethearts, spouses and those we are in close contact with in our community need to be able to monitor each other's stress and recognize the different tides and seasons of life.

We owe it to each other to declare some limits and then help jettison some things if emotional health and the strength of relationships are at risk. Remember, the principle of pure love "beareth all things, believeth all things, hopeth all things, endureth all things," and helps others do the same.3

2,000 Years Later Modern historians note that there are some things wrong with the Archimedes story. Nobody knows for sure whether Archimedes ran through Syracuse naked, for one thing. More important, the difference in the amount of water displaced by a pure gold crown and a silver gold crown is so small that it couldn't have been measured using the tools that existed in Archimedes' time. Also, water would cling to objects as they were taken out, which would distort the results.

But even if the story is wrong in its details, Archimedes' principle has remained true for the past 2,000 years. Scientists today call Archimedes' discovery the Archimedes

Principle. It states that an immersed object is "pushed up" or buoyed up by a force equal to the mass of liquid it displaces. What does this mean? Liquids push up against the bottom of objects. This is buoyant force.

Archimedes died during the siege of Syracuse, when he was killed by a Roman soldier despite orders that he should not be harmed. Unlike his inventions, Archimedes' mathematical writings were little known in antiquity. Mathematicians from Alexandria read and quoted him, but the first comprehensive compilation was not made until c. 530 AD.

The oldest authority for the naked-Archimedes eureka story is Vitruvius, a Roman writer, who included the tale in his introduction to his ninth book of architecture sometime in the first century B.C. Because this was nearly 200 years after the event is presumed to have taken place, the story may have been improved in the telling.1

The truth is that Archimedes did discover the principle of buoyancy of objects when placed in water, Samuel Plimsoll watching ships load and unload their cargoes observed that, regardless of the cargo space available, each ship had its maximum capacity and if it exceeded its limit, it would likely sink at sea, and Jeffrey R. Holland gave good advice on how to keep our boats afloat during stresses in our life's experiences. These are all Eureka's—hope you can find yours too . . .

1. *Scientific American, The famed mathematician made many important scientific contributions. Was this exclamation really one of them?, David Biello, December 8, 2006 + others.*

2. *What is a Plimsoll line?, A commercial ship is properly loaded when the ship's waterline equals the ship's Plimsoll line, 2008 + others.*

3. *How do I Love Thee?, Jeffrey R. Holland, BYU 1999-2000 Speeches, 158-62 (generalized to include more than just spouses).*

38

RECOGNIZING GREATNESS

A man sat at a metro station in Washington DC and started to play the violin; it was a cold January morning. He played six Bach pieces for about 45 minutes. During that time, since it was rush hour, it was calculated that 1,100 people went through the station, most of them on their way to work.

Three minutes went by, and a middle-aged man noticed there was musician playing. He slowed his pace, and stopped for a few seconds, and then hurried up to meet his schedule.

A minute later, the violinist received his first dollar tip: a woman threw the money in the till without stopping and continued to walk.

A few minutes later, someone leaned against the wall to listen to him, but the man looked at his watch and started to walk again. Clearly, he was late for work.

The one who paid the most attention was a 3-year-old boy. His mother hurriedly tugged him along, but the kid stopped to look at the violinist. Finally, the mother pushed hard, and the child continued to walk, turning his head all the time. This action was repeated by several other children. All the parents, without exception, forced them to move on.

In the 45 minutes the musician played, only 6 people stopped and stayed for a while. About 20 gave him money, but continued to walk their normal pace. He collected $32.17. When he finished playing and silence took over, no one noticed it. No one applauded, nor was there any recognition.

No one knew this, but the violinist was Joshua Bell who is one of the most talented musicians in the world. Washington Post writer Gene Weingarten in 2007 enlisted Joshua, a winner of the Avery Fisher Prize for outstanding achievement in classical music who regularly undertakes over 200 international engagements a year, to spend part of a morning playing incognito at the entrance to a Washington Metro station during a morning rush hour. He was playing some of the most intricate pieces of music ever written on a violin he purchased for $3.5 million dollars.

Three days earlier, Bell had played to a full house at Boston's Symphony Hall, where fairly good seats went for $100. But, on this day he collected just $32.17 for his efforts, contributed by a mere 27 of 1,097 passing travelers. Only seven people stopped to listen, and just one of them recognized the performer.

Mark Leithauser a senior curator at the National Gallery who oversees the framing of the paintings thinks he has some idea of what happened at that Metro station: "Let's say I took one of our more abstract masterpieces, say an Ellsworth Kelly, and removed it from its frame, marched it down the 52 steps that people walk up to get to the National Gallery, past the giant columns, and brought it into a restaurant. It's a $5 million painting. And it's one of those restaurants where there are pieces of original art for sale, by some industrious kids from the Corcoran School, and I hang that Kelly on the wall with a price tag of $150. No one is going to notice it. An art curator might look up and say: 'Hey, that looks a little like an Ellsworth Kelly. Please pass the salt.'" Leithauser's point is that we shouldn't be too ready to label the Metro passersby unsophisticated boob. No one is going to notice it. An art curator might look up and say: 'Hey, that looks a little like an Ellsworth Kelly. Please pass the salt.1

The miracles of Jesus are proposed miraculous deeds attributed to Jesus in Christian and Islamic texts. The majority are faith healings, exorcisms, resurrections, and control over nature. In the Synoptic Gospels (Mark, Matthew, and Luke), Jesus refuses to give a miraculous sign to prove his authority. In the Gospel of John, Jesus is said to have performed seven miraculous signs that characterize his ministry, from changing water into wine at the start of his ministry to raising Lazarus from the dead at the end.

For many Christians and Muslims, the miracles are actual historical events. Others, including many liberal Christians, consider these stories to be figurative. Since the Enlightenment, many scholars have taken a highly skeptical approach to claims about miracles (Wikipedia).

How many that witness a blessing or healing do not notice the event, think how was that done, or feel touched by the moment and then go on about their business? Christ performed great miracles and experienced rejection by most the people and was hung on a cross. Even when one "feels the spirit", unless someone has a need and is earnestly looking for answers, they usually "get over it" and go about their business of living an unchanged life.

I recently was visiting with the son of the veterinarian who owned Camden Pet Hospital when I joined the practice in 1976. Dick mentioned that when he was working with severely burned victims knowing they were going to die, they all were seeking God for answers and became believers. Much like the comment that there are no soldiers in a fox hole that don't believe in God during enemy fire. When fear fades, so does belief.

My dog, Maui, and I take walks early in the morning on a regular basis. Three months (January 2013) ago I set a goal to walk at least 1000 miles in a 12-month period. My theme has become the song I'm Gonna Be (500 miles) by the Proclaimers, "But I would walk 500 miles, And I would walk 500 more, To be your man, who walked 1000 miles to fall down at your door."

During our walks in the dark I notice items on the road that shine and get my attention. Looking several feet down the road fallen leaves or drips of asphalt on the pavement are most noticed. Close up items such as glass, wrappers, pieces of metal, money etcetera are more easily seen. All items on the road have had or still have value to someone.

Of all the items I've noticed during my walks I have stopped to pick up only 3 dimes, 3 pennies, one nickel, a small magnet, a watch battery, and a washer. The washer was the brightest and the nickel the most difficult to see. As to value the battery when new was the most valuable and the washer the least. The $.38 currently is of the most value—unless I find myself needing a washer of this size, to help bolt something together "right now."

I have saved these items as a reminder to me that brightest, shiniest, and the most attractive items found in the world may not always be of the most value. So far, I've been paid close to a penny for each ten miles walked. Who could ask for anything more? And, the beat-up magnet may someday hold a picture of my grandchildren on my refrigerator door (March 2013).

A person who is said to possess greatness stands apart from others in some way, usually by the size or originality of their vision and their ability to manifest that vision. And yet those who recognize that greatness, whether they display it themselves or not, also have greatness within them; otherwise, they could not see it in another. In many ways, the achievements of one person always belong to many people for we accomplish nothing alone in this world. People who display greatness rely upon others who are able to see as they do, to listen, encourage, and support. Without those people who recognize greatness and move in to support it, even the greatest ideas, works of art, and political movements would remain unborn.

We are all moved by greatness when we see it, and although the experience is to some degree subjective, we know the feeling of it. When we encounter it, it is as if something in us stirs, awakens, and comes forth to meet what was inside us all along. When we respond to someone else's greatness, we feed our own. We may feel called to dedicate ourselves to their vision, or we may be inspired to follow a path we forge ourselves. Either way, we cannot lose when we recognize that the greatness we see in others belongs also to us. Our recognition of this is a call to action that, if heeded, will inspire others to see in us the greatness they also possess. This creates a chain reaction of greatness unfolding itself endlessly into the future.

Ultimately, greatness is simply the best of what humanity has to offer. Greatness does what has not been done before and inspires the same courage that it requires. When we see it in others, we know it, and when we trust its presence in ourselves, we embody it.2

I have to admit that if Joshua Bell were playing his $3.5 million dollar violin in the Washington Metro station during rush hour that I may have paused a few seconds wondering what he was up to. I probably would not leave a tip or have any idea he was one of the most talented musicians in the world or that anyone had ever paid that much for a violin.

I have to admit that I would not have suspected, especially an abstract painting, hanging in a restaurant would be worth $150 let alone $5 million.

Last night my wife and I attended, with friends who provided the tickets, an opening season hockey game at the San Jose Shark Arena. The first forty-five minutes were spent honoring retired hockey players and giving special recognition to a gentleman by the name of Doug Wilson. He is a member of the Hockey Hall of Fame, was the Sharks captain 1991-1993 and general manager from 2003-2022. His entire family was present, they placed a pendant bearing his initials and achievements high in the rafters in a permanent location, and he gave an impressive speech.

Not a follower of hockey and having only attended a handful of games in my life, I was unable to recognize his greatness because I haven't followed the game close enough to appreciate the effort and talent needed for such an achievement. I am sure my daughter Kara and her husband, who have played and coached on recreation hockey teams, would have found the event to be a special moment in their lives.

A note of interest: *The Washington Post* won a Pulitzer Prize in the feature writing category for Gene Weingarten's April 2007 story about this experiment, based in part on the article's originality. Weingarten was therefore quite surprised at finding out in mid-2008 that his concept wasn't quite so unique. The very same experiment had been tried by another journalist 77 years earlier:

The similar event was initiated by the *Chicago Evening Post* in May 1930 with violin virtuoso Jacques Gordon outside a subway station. He played for 45 minutes dressed as a beggar and received $5.61. The real surprise is that he played two of the same songs Joshua Bell played. When Bell was asked if he knew of Gordon he replied that he had not heard about the stunt - but he knew Gordon because he had played the same Strad that Gordon had once owned. For 11 years, Bell's fingers held the same ancient wood.1

Value is in the eyes of the beholder . . .

*May we always be on the lookout for true enduring values,
"...If there is anything virtuous, lovely, or of good report
or praiseworthy, we seek after these things." Joseph Smith*

1. *Pearls Before Breakfast: Can one of the nation's great musicians cut through the fog of a D.C. rush hour? Let's find out, By Gene Weingarten' Washington Post, 2007.*
2. *The Greatness of others...in ourselves, Madisyn Tyler; July 16, 2013.*

39

MARSHMALLOWS—
TEST OF BEHAVIOR

I was Cub Master in a troop of approximately twenty active youth between the ages of seven and eleven. My primary responsibility was to act as a ring leader and keep the boy's attention for an hour learning social skills and about the "golden rule." The theme of the meeting was reverence. I discussed how of all the snowflakes ever formed on the earth there has never been two created the same. Just as snowflakes, none of God's children are the same and we should have reverence and respect for everyone. At the end of the meeting the Cub Scout and his family made snowmen with marshmallows and all sorts of candy decorations. Funny thing - even the snowmen all looked different.

Thinking about children, learning behavior and marshmallows, I would like to share with you some research called, "The Marshmallow Test". PD50021388_000_0In the 1960s, a professor at Stanford University began a modest experiment testing the willpower of four-year-old children. He placed before them a large marshmallow and then told them they could eat it right away or, if they waited for 15 minutes, they could have two marshmallows. He then left the children alone and watched what happened behind a two-way mirror.

Some of the children ate the marshmallow immediately; some could wait only a few minutes before giving in to temptation. Only 30 percent were able to wait.

It was a mildly interesting experiment, and the professor moved on to other areas of research, for, in his own words, "there are only so many things you can do with kids trying not to eat marshmallows." But as time went on, he kept track of the children and began to notice an interesting correlation: the children who could not wait struggled later in life and had more behavioral problems, while those who waited tended to be more positive and better motivated, have higher grades and incomes, and have healthier relationships.

What started as a simple experiment with children and marshmallows became a landmark study suggesting that the ability to wait—to be patient—was a key character trait that might predict later success in life.

Waiting can be hard. Children know it, and so do adults. We live in a world offering fast food, instant messaging, on-demand movies, and immediate answers to the most trivial or profound questions. We don't like to wait. Some even feel their blood pressure rise when their line at the grocery store moves slower than those around them.1

Patience - the ability to put our desires on hold for a time—is a precious and rare virtue. We want what we want, and we want it now. Therefore, the very idea of patience may seem unpleasant and, at times, bitter. From that experience, patience (is) far more than simply waiting for something to happen—patience requires actively working toward worthwhile goals and not getting discouraged when results didn't appear instantly or without effort.

There is an important concept here: patience is not passive resignation, nor is it failing to act because of our fears. Patience means active waiting and enduring. It means staying with something and doing all that we can— working, hoping, and exercising faith; bearing hardship with fortitude, even when the desires of our hearts are delayed. Patience is not simply enduring; it is enduring well!

Impatience, on the other hand, is a symptom of selfishness. It is a trait of the self-absorbed. It arises from the all-too-prevalent condition called "center of the universe" syndrome, which leads people to believe that the world revolves around them and that all others are just supporting cast in the grand theater of mortality in which only they have the starring role.

The ability to delay gratification and resist temptations has been a fundamental challenge since the dawn of civilization. It is central to the Genesis story of Adam and Eve's temptation in the Garden of Eden. Self-control is crucial for the successful pursuit of long-term goals. It is equally essential for developing the self-restraint and empathy needed to build caring and mutually supportive relationships. It can help people avoid becoming entrapped early in life, dropping out of school, becoming impervious to consequences, or getting stuck in jobs they hate. It is the "master aptitude" underlying emotional intelligence, essential for constructing a fulfilling life.2

Discussing resisting temptations and delaying or avoiding temptations, Doctor Mischel wrote, "I once had the pleasure participating with Thomas Schelling, a Nobel laureate in economics, in a seminar on self-control. He wrote this summary of the dilemmas created by a weakness of will: How should we conceptualize this rational consumer whom all of us know and who some of us are, who in self-disgust grinds his cigarettes down the disposal swearing that this time he means never again to risk orphaning his children with lung cancer and is on the street three hours later looking for a store that's still open to buy cigarettes; who eats a high-calorie lunch knowing that he will regret it, does regret it, cannot understand how he lost control, resolves to compensate with a low-calorie dinner, eats a high-calorie dinner knowing he will regret it, and does regret it; who sits glued to the TV knowing that again tomorrow he'll wake early in a cold sweat unprepared for that morning meeting on which so much of his career depends; who spoils the trip to Disneyland by losing his temper when his children do what he knew they were going to do when he resolved not to lose his temper when they did it?"3

At the end of the Cub Scout meeting, the families made snowmen with marshmallows and all sorts of candy decorations. Funny thing: Like the snowflakes and children all being different, the snowmen they made also were all different. But guess what? Instead of only 30% of the Cub Scouts being able to resist eating a marshmallow in 15 minutes, 100% of the Cub Scouts did not eat any of the marshmallows they were given to make their snowmen. However, I'm not sure how many marshmallows were consumed from the bag of extra marshmallows sitting on the table next to their activity.

1. *"The Marshmallow Test, Walter Mischel, 2014, p6, 13-14.*
2. *Continue In Patience, April 2010, Dieter F. Uchtdorf, General Conference, April 2015.*
3. *Jonah Lehrer, "Don't! The Secret of Self-Control," New Yorker, May 18, 2009, 26–27.*

40

(FUN)AMBULISM'S
IN OUR LIVES

In November 2014 a seventh-generation aerialist and member of the Flying Wallenda circus family, walked 94 feet on a tightrope between two Chicago skyscrapers. He was blindfolded, 600 feet in the air. The stunt was broadcast live—but with a 10 second delay, in case he fell. He didn't, of course, and the jaunt added two new Guinness World Records to the nine he already holds.

The Wallendas are among the most high-profile acrobats today, and they're part of a long tradition of highwire daredevils.

Funambulism dates back at least to Ancient Greece—that's where the name comes from: funis means "rope" and ambulare means "to walk." In both Ancient Greece and Ancient Rome, tightrope walkers were revered, but their work was not considered "sporting" enough to be part of the Olympic Games. Instead, it often became the providence of jesters and other entertainers.

In 5th-century France; tightrope-walkers were forbidden to come near churches, and since near churches was where most of the fairs were held, this was effectively a ban on tightrope-walking. But things seem to have gotten back on track by the 1300s; during the lavish coronation of Queen Isabeau in 1389 Paris, an acrobat carrying candles "walked along a rope suspended from the spires of the cathedral to the tallest house in the city." This trend continued; there were tightrope walkers at the coronation of Edward VI in Westminster in 1547, and at the occasion of Philip of Spain's arrival in London to meet Queen Mary in 1554. In Venice in the mid-16th century, the annual Carnival gained a new opening tradition—Svolo del Turco (Flight of the Angel)—when a Turkish acrobat walked on a rope strung between the bell tower of the St. Mark's Church and a boat docked on the Piazzetta.

During the late 1600s in England, tightrope walkers began to be associated with a disreputable element, including pickpockets, streetwalkers, and conmen. In his early-1700s song collection "Pills to Purge Melancholy," Thomas D'Urfey wrote: "In houses of boards men walk upon cords / An easy as squirrels crack filbords / The cut-purses they do bite, and rob away."

The 1800s brought acrobats and other similar performers indoors as business - and showmen opened more permanent circus venues. Also, many funambulists desired to walk across Niagara Falls. The first to do so was Jean François Gravelet, known as the Great Blondin, who was the most famous wire-walker of the time.1

What Happens to Your Body When You Walk on a Tightrope? It's more than just an insane amount of courage that gets people on the tightwire. Joseph Gordon-Levitt playing the part of Philippe Petit in "The Walk" by Sony Pictures describes his experience:

You are on a rooftop, looking across empty air 1,350 feet above the ground. Your foot dangles over the ledge and touches a steel cable just centimeters wide. As you shift your body forward, hands gripped tight around a balancing pole, you find yourself suspended over a gut-wrenching void. Now what?

Acrophobics would surely hope to wake from this nightmare in a cold sweat. But for seasoned tightrope walkers, the dizzying feat can be accomplished if you understand the physics of the human body.

"Posture is the absolute most important thing," says Sonja Harpstead, a tightrope instructor at Circus Warehouse in New York City. The key to balancing on a tightrope is to lower the body's center of gravity toward the wire. Just as it's harder to topple a stout vase than a tall slim one, a human is less likely to fall if the bulk of their mass is closer to the ground—or, in this case, the wire.

Amateurs often try to accomplish this shift by leaning forward. That may lower your overall mass, but it also interferes with your sense of location in space. Then, it's hello pavement.

Harpstead instead instructs her students to stand up straight and lower their hips by bending their knees. This brings a person's center of gravity closer to the wire while allowing them to keep their bearings.

At the same time, a tightrope walker has to remember that the wire itself tends to rotate. Each step along the cable invites it to spin underfoot, potentially throwing the walker off balance. To keep from falling, the walker must increase something called rotational inertia—effectively, positioning the body so that it fights against the wire's want to rotate.

As any child on the playground knows, the best way to improve your balance on a cylindrical object is to stick out your arms horizontally. This spreads out your mass and improves your ability to fight rotational forces, giving you enough time to correct your motions if you start to slip. Many tightrope walkers boost this effect by carrying a long balancing pole.

For his daredevil walk between the Twin Towers of the World Trade Center in 1974, currently depicted in the Joseph Gordon-Levitt vehicle "The Walk", French high-wire artist Philippe Petit carried a 26-foot balancing pole he crafted for the act. "After a few steps, I knew I was in my element and I knew the wire was not well rigged (we had some tremendous problem during the whole night of rigging) but it was safe enough for me to carry on," says Petit in an episode of the PBS series "American Experience." "And then, very slowly as I walked, I was overwhelmed by a sense of easiness, a sense of simplicity."

Says Harpsted, "The pole increases your rotational inertia so that each tiny little movement you do does more, and in general the little bit of wiggle that happens in your personal body means less in relation to the whole system." As an added bonus, the ends of the pole bend down, helping to lower the walker's center of gravity even more.

The state of the wire itself can also play a role in the walker's ability to successfully cross it. In the ideal scenario, the wire would be infinitely taut, says Paolo Paoletti of the University of Liverpool's School of Engineering. The more slack in the wire, the more likely it is to undulate under your feet as you take each cautious step, making it harder to balance.2

In the 1800s there was also a young man that one day would be remembered as the leader that helped preserve the Union during the Civil War and beginning the process (Emancipation proclamation) that led to the end of slavery in the United States. Even though Abraham Lincoln's feet were always on the ground his life seemed to be as one walking a tightrope and being a (fun)ambulist for him was mostly not fun. A professional tightrope performer may come to an end by failing once - Abe was fraught with enduring many.

By studying Lincoln's own letters and the observations of his friends and associates, historians have concluded that Lincoln battled with chronic depression for much of his life. In fact, it wasn't something Lincoln hid from his friends or the public. Even amidst the enthusiasm and excitement of the 1860 Republican convention in Illinois, an observer called Lincoln "one of the most diffident and worst plagued men I ever saw." He had spells that his friends described as "melancholy," sometimes spoke of suicide and described the world as "hard and grim."

In 1841, Lincoln sought a doctor's help for his depression. It isn't known what type of treatment he received, but he later told his law partner, "I am now the most miserable man living... Whether I shall ever be better I cannot tell; I awfully forebode I shall not." According to Joshua Wolf Shenk, author of Lincoln's Melancholy, at times Lincoln's behavior exhibited many of the symptoms of a major depressive episode, including change in appetite, fatigue, feelings of worthlessness and thoughts of suicide.

Fortunately for Lincoln and the country, he learned to defeat depression and he maintained a healthy attitude about it. "A tendency to melancholy….," he wrote in a letter to a friend, "let it be observed, is a misfortune, not a fault." The unfortunate stigma surrounding depression and mental illness that exists today was not as prevalent in Lincoln's day.

In fact, Lincoln's depression may have actually aided his election to president. Lincoln's melancholy made him more approachable and sympathetic to the public. It may have made him a better man and even played a role in his success. Below are some of the coping methods Lincoln employed to defeat his own depression, and they can still be effective today:

- Since Lincoln's depression included frequent thoughts of suicide, he was always aware of his mortality. It became important to him that he accomplish something of importance before he died. And focusing on a higher purpose gave him a reason to live even when he felt as if we wanted to die.
- He also had a witty sense of humor. Telling funny stories and making jokes seemed to give him relief from his sadness. Lincoln said, "If it were not for these stories—jokes, jests, I should die; they give vent—are the vents of my moods and gloom."
- Lincoln found joy and had a love of learning and reading, which he used as a distraction from his

melancholy. He especially loved Shakespeare and poetry. Though Lincoln had very little formal education, he always enjoyed reading and was said to have walked miles as a young man to borrow a book.

- Despite attaining the country's highest office, Abraham Lincoln had a sense of humility and did not have a problem with ego. He was open to learn from others and even appointed former adversaries to positions on his cabinet. His belief in a higher power gave him the ability to let go when his sense of responsibility became too great. "I have been driven many times upon my knees by the overwhelming conviction that I had nowhere else to go," Lincoln once said. "My own wisdom and that of all about me seemed insufficient for that day."3

Charles Blondin, was born on 28 February 1824 in France. At the age of five, he was sent to Lyon's gymnastic school and, after six months of training as an acrobat, made his first public appearance as "The Boy Wonder." His superior skill and grace, as well as the originality of the settings of his acts, made him a popular favorite.

Blondin went to the United States in 1855. He was encouraged by William Niblo to perform with the Ravel troupe in New York City and was subsequently part proprietor of a circus. He especially owed his celebrity and fortune to his idea to cross the Niagara Gorge (on the Canada–US border) on a tightrope, 1,100 ft long, 3.25 inches in diameter and 160 ft above the water, near the location of the current Rainbow Bridge. This he did on 30 June 1859, and a number of times thereafter, often with different theatrical variations: blindfolded, in a sack, trundling a wheelbarrow, on stilts, carrying a man (his manager, Harry Colcord) on his back, sitting down midway while he cooked and ate an omelet, drank a beer pulled up on a rope from the Maid of the Mist, riding a bicycle across, or standing on a chair with only one of its legs balanced on the rope.

In Civil War days President Abraham Lincoln was "At the White House one day when some gentlemen were present from the West, excited and troubled about the commissions or omissions of the Administration. The President heard them patiently, and then replied: "Gentlemen, suppose all the property you were worth was in gold, and you had put it in the hands of Blondin to carry across the Niagara River on a rope, would you shake the cable, or keep shouting out to him, 'Blondin, stand up a little straighter—Blondin, stoop a little more—go a little faster—lean a little more to the north—lean a little more to the south.' No, you would hold your breath as well as your tongue, and keep your hands off until he was safe over. The Government are carrying an immense weight. Untold treasures are in their hands. They are doing the very best they can. Don't badger them. Keep silence, and we'll get you safe across."

What if Blondin were carrying all your fortune, a family member, your best friend or even you across the Niagara Gorge on his back "would you shake the cable, or keep shouting out to him, 'Blondin, stand up a little straighter— Blondin, stoop a little more—go a little faster—lean a little more to the north—lean a little more to the south.'?" I think not. I suspect we would do as Lincoln stated, "No, you would hold your breath as well as your tongue, and keep your hands off until he was safe over."4

These days, most people have some kind of online presence whether it takes the form of a personal Twitter feed, MySpace or LinkedIn account, or Facebook page, or posted comments and reviews on products, news articles, company websites, or on their or other people's social media pages.

Using the internet to vent unkind words about someone that has let you down, discussing another's weaknesses or shortcomings, being critical concerning the way another has resolved an issue, or accusations (true or false) cannot easily be retracted or forgiveness given. Unfortunately, the words my mother taught me, "Sticks and stones may break my bones - but names will never hurt me" are not true when using social media. They can hurt you and those you should care about. They may even destroy a reputation, family relationship, result in loss of a job or in suicide and the words are out there for the ones we care the most about to read.

Marvin J. Ashton stated, "None of us need one more person bashing or pointing out where we have failed or fallen short. Most of us are already well aware of the areas in which we are weak. What each of us does need is family, friends, employers, and brothers and sisters who support us, who have the patience to teach us, who believe in us, and who believe we're trying to do the best we can, in spite of our weaknesses. What ever happened to giving each other the benefit of the doubt? What ever happened to hoping that another person would succeed or achieve? What ever happened to rooting for each other?"

Perhaps the greatest charity comes when we are kind to each other, when we don't judge or categorize someone else, when we simply give each other the benefit of the doubt or remain quiet. Charity is accepting someone's differences, weaknesses, and shortcomings; having patience with someone who has let us down; or resisting the impulse to become offended when someone doesn't handle something the way we might have hoped. Charity is refusing to take advantage of another's weakness and being willing to forgive someone who has hurt us. Charity is expecting the best of each other."5

Life is like walking between two tall buildings on a tightrope. For some, the rope is wide enough and the walk is easy. For others, it's narrow and hard and maybe there's a strong wind blowing through their days. - Walter Dean Myers

1. *An Abridged History of Funambulists, by Oriana Leckert, 11/05/2014 & Wikipedia.*

2. Overcoming. Katie Nodjimbadem, Science-Nature, Smithsonian Magazine, 10/13/2015

3. Obstacles: How Abraham Lincoln Defeated Depression, by Elizabeth Street, Family Living, Inspiration Jan 6, 2015.

4. *Francis Carpenter, Six Months at the White House, p. 257-258.*

5. *Marvin J. Ashton, "The Tongue Can Be a Sharp Sword", Ensign, May 1992, P 19.*

41

IN SPITE OF IT ALL

Nicholas Yung considered himself a lucky man. A German who immigrated to the United States in 1848, Yung had worked hard to carve out a living for himself and eventually prosper as the owner of a mortuary in San Francisco. The business allowed him and wife Rosina to purchase a modest lot on the top of California Street Hill, where they built a quaint, cottage-style home and planted a beautiful garden. Every day, California sunlight and fresh air would stream in through their windows.

Yung had no reason to believe that anything could interrupt his idyllic life, or that any one person could somehow deprive him of the beautiful days he had worked so hard to enjoy. But Yung also hadn't accounted for Charles Crocker, a very rich and very petty man who would eventually become both his neighbor and the bane of his existence. With enough lumber to build a 40-foot-tall, blighting fence around much of Yung's property, Crocker and his spite fence became a legendary revenge tale, a tourist attraction, and a lesson in the danger of escalating tempers.

At 6 feet tall and 300 pounds, Charles Crocker cut an imposing figure. He had filled his bank account by being one of the "Big Four" barons behind the building of the Central Pacific Railroad. By the 1870s, he could afford whatever he desired. And what he wanted was to loom over San Francisco like a gargoyle.

Crocker and his wealthy partners began scouting California Street Hill for its scenic views and proximity to the city's financial district. One of his "Big Four" associates, Leland Stanford—former governor of California and future founder of Stanford University—suggested that the area would make for a beautiful residential plot if a cable car could bring residents up and down the hill.

Stanford arranged to have one installed, and soon a group of wealthy men, including Crocker, were buying up all the homes on their chosen blocks. By the time Crocker was finished, he had erected a 12,000-square-foot mansion. With its new, wealthy inhabitants, California Street Hill was renamed Nob Hill.

As the project neared completion in 1876, there was one nagging detail: Nicholas Yung was reluctant to sell his space on the northeast corner of the block. His cottage was dwarfed by the mansions going up, but he had come to enjoy the neighborhood. There are varying accounts of what happened next. In the end it appears that Yung wanted $12000 for the property and Crocker balked, spewing profanity and walking away from negotiations.

With one or both men causing acrimony, the end result was that Yung was not moving. Crocker's workers were busy razing the entire block, creating a steamroller of activity that should have seen them swatting Yung's cottage down like a cardboard box. In an ominous sign of his frustration,

Crocker ordered his workers to arrange their dynamite blasts so that rock debris would pelt Yung's house.

If the goal was to drive Yung away, it had the opposite effect. Yung doubled down, refusing to move. Crocker refused to raise his offer. The two men were at a stalemate. Although Yung's obnoxious negotiating methods didn't make him blameless, it was Crocker who had the means to provide a real disruption.

At a reported cost of $3000, Crocker had his workers construct a wooden fence on his land that towered over three sides of Yung's home. With its 40-foot-tall panels, the enclosure acted like a window shade, blotting out the sun and cool air and immersing Yung in darkness.

While Crocker gleefully had gardeners decorate his side with ivy, Yung saw his beautiful garden wilt. Despite the obvious interruption of Yung's environment, Crocker's "spite fence," as the papers came to call it, was perfectly legal.

Without other recourse, Yung threatened to install a flagpole that would fly a skull and crossbones, an act of defiance that might help blight Crocker's view; he also wanted to place a coffin on his roof, ostensibly for advertising his business, but clearly to agitate Crocker as well. He had some members of the media on his side, who condemned "Crocker's Crime" and criticized the financier for using his immense wealth to bully a family of more modest means. The San Francisco Chronicle later called it a "memorial of malignity and malevolence." Tourists would take the cable car and ride up to Nob Hill just to gawk at the massive fence. But Crocker wouldn't budge.

In October 1877, the pro-labor Workingmen's Party of California (WPC) organized a protest rally near Crocker's home to condemn his hiring of Chinese immigrant and admonished Crocker to tear down the "spite fence." If Yung harbored any hope that some vigilante justice would resolve the situation, it never came to pass. He and his family threw in the towel and moved out—but they still refused to sell the land to Crocker.

Crocker may have thought the feud would end with Yung's death in 1880. It didn't. His widow, Rosina, continued to rebuff offers to sell the now-vacant land, which was slowly becoming a place for empty cans and other garbage. After Crocker passed away in 1888, his heirs were just as unsuccessful in persuading Rosina to let the land go. In 1895, she tried to appeal to the city's Street Committee, arguing that the fence was a nuisance and rendered her property worthless.

When Rosina died in 1902, the rivalry appeared to die with her. Her four daughters finally gave in to Crocker's descendants in 1904, selling the land—said to be worth $80,000—for an undisclosed sum. With no more neighbors to spite, the fence was torn down in 1905.1

Discussing spiteful behavior Natalie Angier mentioned that after decades of focusing on such staples of bad behavior as aggressiveness, selfishness, narcissism and greed, scientists have turned their attention to the subtler and often unsettling theme of spite—the urge to punish, hurt, humiliate or harass another, even when one gains no obvious benefit and may well pay a cost.

Psychologists are exploring spitefulness in its customary role as a negative trait, a lapse that should be embarrassing but is often sublimated as righteousness, as when you take your own sour time pulling out of a parking space because you notice another car is waiting for it and you'll show that vulture who's boss here, even though you're wasting your own time, too.

Evolutionary theorists, by contrast, are studying what might be viewed as the brighter side of spite, and the role it may have played in the origin of admirable traits like a cooperative spirit and a sense of fair play.

The new research on spite transcends older notions that we are savage, selfish brutes at heart, as well as more recent suggestions that humans are inherently affiliative creatures yearning to love and connect. Instead, it concludes that vice and virtue, like the two sides of a V, may be inextricably linked.

Taking the increasingly popular approach of applying game theory to probe human social behavior, a computer model of virtual players challenging each other to single rounds of the famed ultimatum game.

According to the rules, Player A decided how a pot of money was to be shared with Player B: half and half, say, or 80 percent for A and 20 percent for B. If B consented to the split, both received the agreed-upon portion; if B rejected the offer, neither player received anything.

The contestants were assigned one of four predetermined strategies, from the easygoing approach of "when you're Player A, you share 50-50, but when you're Player B you accept any offer, no matter how stingy" to the spiteful "when you're A, you make a stingy offer, but when you're B you spurn a stingy offer." The researchers then allowed the players to coalesce into mock societies, and they were startled by the results.

Although groups of excessively spiteful or selfish players quickly collapsed, and rigidly fair-minded societies were readily destabilized by influxes of selfish exploiters, the flexible sharers not only proved able to coexist with the spiteful types, but the presence of spitefuls had the salubrious effect of enhancing the rate of fair exchanges among the genials.

Their conclusion was it looked like fairness is acting as a defense against spite.2

The Yung/Crocker feud would ultimately prove pointless. In 1906, an earthquake and related fire swept through San Francisco, gutting the Crocker mansion and neighboring buildings. In a strange twist, rather than rebuild, the family decided to donate the block to charity.

Towering over San Francisco's Nob Hill neighborhood, the iconic Grace Cathedral is hard to miss. Known as much for its "Gates of Paradise" as for its breathtaking murals and labyrinths, the cathedral is one of the largest Episcopalian churches in the United States. Painstakingly built brick by brick, mural by mural, over the course of 37 years, the church is both a tourist landmark and a symbol of hope and resurrection, thanks to its storied history.

Grace Cathedral traces its roots to Grace Church, a small parish that was built during California's Gold Rush in 1849. The 1906 earthquake completely destroyed the original structure. The Crocker family, an influential family in San Francisco at that time, donated their Nob Hill land for the construction of the present structure. The building of Grace Cathedral began in 1927 but it was only in 1964 that the intricate structure, with all its gorgeous details, was fully completed. The landmark event was celebrated with a sermon by Martin Luther King Jr., which was attended by nearly 5,000 people.

An old legend tells of a wise grandfather teaching his grandson about the importance of making good choices. "A fight is going on inside me," he explained to the boy. "It's a terrible fight between two wolves. One is evil: he is anger, spitefulness, greed, selfishness, resentment, lies, and pride." The other," he continued, "is good: he is fairness, joy, peace, love, hope, humility, truth, and faith. The same fight is going on inside you—and inside every other person as well."

The grandson listened intently and asked, "Which wolf will win?"

The grandfather answered simply, "The one you feed."

According to Natalie Angier's studies it looks like fairness is acting as a defense against spite. Therefore, why can't the human animal just save a lot of unhappiness and choose to feed the good?

Why feed the bad and live a miserable life? Eastern European folk tale tells how ridicules and silly spiteful hate can go - when a genie offers to grant a man's wish as long as his hated neighbor gets double the prize; the man says, "Put out one of my eyes.".

It seems best to "remove ourselves from people who spark darkness to explode. Spite and malice don't reflect light well." *DNC* - For, in the end "you will find the roots of the good and the bad, the fruitful and the fruitless, all entwined together in the silent heart of the earth." *Kahlil Giban, 1883-1931 from Lebanon.*

In or around 1956, California put a law on the books prohibiting the construction of fences meant for the express purpose of irritating neighbors and/or obstructing their views. Most states cap the height of a fence at 6 feet for similar reasons.

Visiting San Francisco many years ago I purchased an "authentic rail section and cable" from one of the old San Francisco cable lines. Holding it in my hands I ponder if this section was laid during the spiteful Crocker/Yung years. Giving you a chance of touching history - below is a photo of my find.

1. *The Man Who Built a 40-Foot Spite Fence Around His Neighbor's Home, By Jake Rossen, Updated 07/05/2021.*
2. *Spite Is Good. Spite Works, By Natalie Angier, 03/31/2014.*

42

A LIFE CHANGING MOMENT

A devout Mormon sent by the church on a mission, he settled in Fatuvalu, a traditional village on the northern coast with fewer than 200 people. One day, a high chief named Aumalosi came to visit from nearby Letui village. The chief, who didn't speak English, sat down in Paul's hut and began uttering what seemed like strange noises, breaking down the Samoan language syllable by syllable and gesturing for Paul to repeat them. The chief came back day after day, month after month, walking the 4 miles each way, and the syllables turned into long passages. Paul learned that Aumalosi was reciting local proverbs and excerpts of speeches from high chiefs.

One afternoon when Aumalosi arrived at Paul's hut, the young American was prone on his mat, very sick. By then, Paul could speak enough Samoan to apologize for being unable to do the lesson. "I didn't come for the lesson," Aumalosi replied. He emptied the contents of a woven coconut-leaf basket onto the mat: condensed milk, tinned peaches, gingersnap cookies, and other imported delicacies, "perhaps you are sick because you are not used to our food," he said. Aumalosi had gone to the local district store and spent all his money on food the American could eat.

I have spent much of the last 40 years trying to pay back the contents of that coconut basket," Paul, now 63, says. The unorthodox path inspired by this quest includes-incongruously-establishing a national park, launching a cosmetics line (NuSkin—proceeds go to his nonprofit Seacology), and earning international acclaim for his contributions to medicine.

Paul has degrees in philosophy, botany, ecology, biology and while at Harvard pursued a degree in ethno-botany, a field that requires expertise in plant science, anthropology, and languages (he speaks more than a dozen), a field that requires expertise in plant science, anthropology, and languages (along with the faith that people who lived off the same land for thousands of years must know something about their environment). Quickly becoming a star in the field, he taught for 14 years at BYU, until the king of Sweden appointed him to a prestigious chair at Uppsala University. Today he makes his home in Jackson, Wyoming, where he and his team at the Institute for EthnoMedicine conduct ground-breaking research in an unassuming residential cabin.

In 1985, back in Samoa doing research, Paul watched as a healer brewed a tea from the bark of the mamala tree and used it to treat hepatitis. Paul sent the tea to researchers at the National Cancer Institute, who found that its powerful antiviral qualities could relieve the infection in T cells. It became one of the leading drugs used to treat HIV/AIDS, and Paul negotiated a deal to ensure that part of the profits go to the Samoan people. He then worked with the U.S.

Congress and the government of American Samoa to create the United States' 50th national park.

In the late 1990s, Paul Alan Cox, Ph.D. and his colleagues, began traveling to the Pacific island of Guam to interview Chamorro villagers who were suffering from a disease that was similar to Parkinson's, ALS (Lou Gehrig's disease) and Alzheimer's disease. The mysterious illness was first noticed by the U.S. military in the 1950's. Yet 20 years of research didn't turn up any clues. Researchers discovered that cycad seeds, used to make flour for tortillas by the Chamorro people and eaten by flying foxes, another staple of the Chamorro diet, contained the neurotoxin BMAA.

Researchers pursued the neurotoxin as the trigger and eventually found that it was also present in cyanobacteria in harmful algae blooms, also known as blue-green algae. Other studies have found BMAA can accumulate in fish and shellfish in South Florida and other areas where algae blooms are present, potentially entering the human food chain.

For now, Cox says that the research offers hope for people concerned about neurodegenerative diseases: "We have discovered that chronic exposure to an environmental toxin triggers Alzheimer's-type pathology in the brain," he told CBS News. "Thus, people can reduce their risk of disease simply by avoiding exposure to cyanobacteria in harmful algal blooms or contaminated foodstuffs."

In 1988, he brought his wife and four young children to Samoa. They stayed for a year, living without plumbing or electricity in a fale, or thatch hut. They were supposed to blend in, but while they were there the villagers faced a terrible dilemma: The government required the island to build a new school, whose construction would cost $50,000. The only way to pay for the school was to sell their 30,000-acre forest to loggers. Paul convinced the chiefs to halt the logging while he made a quick trip back to the states to raise money. The school was built and in 1997 the forest preserved. Cox subsequently helped to create an additional 20,000 acre rainforest preserve in Tafua, also on the island of Savai'i.

Much to his dismay, the grateful people of Savaii declared him a chief, a title that comes with the name Nafanua, after a goddess who first saved the island's forest. In 1997, the Nafanua published a page-turning book about the experience titled, appropriately, Nafanua. The same year he was awarded the Goldman Environmental Prize, known the "Green Nobel," and "Heroes of Medicine." It reads:

"The Goldman Environmental Prize honors grassroots environmental heroes from the world's six inhabited continental regions: Africa, Asia, Europe, Islands & Island Nations, North America, and South & Central America. The Prize recognizes individuals for sustained and significant efforts to protect and enhance the natural environment, often at great personal risk. The Goldman Prize views "grassroots" leaders as those involved in local efforts, where positive change is created through community or citizen participation in the issues that affect them. Through recognizing these individual leaders, the Prize seeks to inspire other ordinary people to take extraordinary actions to protect the natural world." The prize is also known as the "Green Nobel" and it was awarded to them in 1997.1&2

In October 1995 Paul Cox gave a speech at Brigham Young University entitled "Seeing with New Eyes." He mentioned that he had been traveling three hours from Provo into the west desert at Fish Springs to study the pollination of a little aquatic plant, Z. palustris. One day while he was walking next to a canal that runs along a path near Heritage Halls on the BYU campus and he relates, "Wouldn't it be grand if (this plant) grew right here in this ditch? I thought to myself. I glanced toward the canal and there it was. I couldn't believe it. …Although my discovery of Z. palustris in the Heritage Halls ditch led to some very interesting biology, I still must confess to feeling silly. No, I didn't feel silly about jumping in the ditch—any of my Biology-130 students would have done precisely the same thing. What I felt silly about was that I had not previously noticed Z. palustris in that ditch before, although I had walked hundreds of times along that path. I had viewed the ditch but had never before truly seen it."3

Amy E. Herman teaches "The Art of Perception," a course to help FBI agents, police, Fortune 500 CEOs, emergency room doctors and many others become more effective in their jobs and their lives by improving their ability to observe. That includes taking them to museums to stare at paintings but also much more. When asked her how we all can develop this skill and how it can help us improve our lives she comments…"our brains actually process only a small amount of what our eyes see. It has to be this way- if the brain analyzed every last visual detail, we would be overwhelmed every time we walked down a city street. But sometimes our minds miss things that turn out to be important, and this problem is only growing worse. distraction dramatically reduces the brain's ability to process visual information. Thanks to devices such as smartphones, many of us are more distracted than ever."4

Mike Singletary, Chicago Bears football player and coach of the Los Angeles Rams, made the following quote on "life-changing moments": "Because too many times in life there's just one person that I met, just one thing that I heard, one movie that I saw, one song that was sung, that changed my life. So, I'm always trying to stay awake to be in the moment, and capture the moments when they come, because they come and go all the time."5

I have a feeling that if I were to ask Paul Cox what was one of his "life-changing moments" he would mention a Samoan chief, struggling with a foreign language and a coconut-leaf basket full of food a young American man was used to eating. Another might be finding that "little aquatic plant", he was traveling three hours back and forth to study, growing in a canal on BYU's campus.

Paul Alan Cox's and his staff's comments on research involving human trials investigating prevention and treatment of early onset ALS patients:

…"Will the critics be convinced? I could have the angel Gabriel come in and they still won't be convinced," Paul replied. Still, the proof-gathering continues. The Food and Drug Administration approved a human trial in 2012 to test the safety of L-serine for ALS patients. (The FDA saw little risk since L-serine has been a part of the human diet for millennia—one of the key advantages of ethnobotany.) Next will come a phase two trial to determine whether L-serine relieves symptoms in early-onset ALS patients. If that works (and there is no guarantee), then Paul will ask the FDA to recommend L-serine as a supplement for patients.

After that: a trial with hundreds of patients, "and probably some pharmaceutical company will license the patent," he says. Meanwhile, you can buy L-serine on Amazon. I asked Sandra whether their team takes it, and she walked me back to an alcove with a sink, a stove, and a large tub of sparkling white powder. Heating up a tea kettle, she stirred a spoonful of L-serine into a coffee cup and handed it over. It tasted like aspartame. "We're all taking it," she said…"1

1. *Southwest Airlines, The Magazine, Sept 2016.*
2. *Paul Alan Cox, Science Algae Bloom Linked to Alzheimer's, By Amy Kraft, CBS News, January 21, 2016.*
3. *Paul Alan Cox, Dean of General and Honors Education at Brigham Young University, October 10, 1995.*
4. *Bottom Line Personal, Amy E. Herman teaches, President of the "The Art of Perception." Seeing with New Eyes.*
5. *brainquote.com.*

43

BILLY GRAHAM'S RULE & VICE PRESIDENT PENCE

What an age to be alive! The internet has broken out into a feverish and wildly entertaining debate over, of all things, the fallen nature of man. What prompted all of this was a profile of the vice president's wife, Karen Pence, in *The Washington Post*, that included this detail about the vice president: In 2002, Vice President Mike Pence told the Hill that he never eats alone with a woman other than his wife and that he won't attend events featuring alcohol without her by his side, either. CBN News also stated in a recent interview that Mrs. Pence mentioned, "that her husband told her to make Jesus her 'number one' and not him." Also, I noted that he followed the Billy Graham Rule. When I read this article, I thought Bravo...this is a man that doesn't want to even appear that he is not faithful to his wife or family; and, if there would be any accusations of the appearance of impropriety there would be at least two present to testify of the truth (John 8:17).

During all my callings in the Scouting program or my faith I have always been admonished to have at least one adult companion with me when visiting a single person's home, activities with the youth, interviewing for merit badges etcetera. To work with the Scouts and church youth groups we even have to go through a training program to help keep the young folks safe. At work I also use the "at least two present or the office door open" policy when only one person is in the room with me.

Instead of the responses I expected from Mr. Pence's pledge to his "wife with me policy" I noted: "A new and juicily detailed *Washington Post* profile of the second lady dredged up a 2002 interview with then-Congressman Mike Pence that revealed something so grotesque you won't be able to look away: He declined to dine alone with women other than his wife, and avoided events without her if alcohol was being served. Nonetheless, the practice described by Pence in that 2002 interview is clearly illegal when practiced by a boss in an employment setting, and deeply damaging to women's employment opportunities. So why can't Mike Pence be alone with women, or be around alcohol when women are present and Mrs. Pence isn't? Because he might rape them?"

The Billy Graham Rule

On October 24, 1948, Billy Graham began a series of evangelistic meetings in Modesto (Spanish name means modesty), California—about 90 miles east of San Francisco. Graham was a couple of weeks shy of his 30th birthday. He was with his close friends and associates, George Beverly Shea (age 39), Grady Wilson (age 29), and Cliff Barrows (age 25). They were lodging at a motel on South Ninth Street in

Modesto. In November, Graham initiated discussion with the men about problems they had witnessed among other evangelists, actions that had undermined the integrity of the gospel message, revealed hypocrisy, and ruined lives.

Graham recounts the story in his autobiography: "One afternoon during the Modesto meetings, I called the team together to discuss the problem. Then I asked them to go to their rooms for an hour and list all the problems they could think of that evangelists and evangelism encounter. When they returned, the lists were remarkably similar, and in a short amount of time, we made a series of resolutions or commitment among ourselves that would guide us in our future evangelistic work. In reality, it was more of an informal understanding among ourselves - a shared commitment to do all we could do to uphold the Bible's standard of absolute integrity and purity for evangelists.

The first point on our combined list was money. Nearly all evangelists at that time, including us, were supported by love offerings taken at the meetings. The temptation to wring as much money as possible out of an audience, often with strong emotional appeals, was too great for some evangelists. In addition, there was little or no accountability for finances. It was a system that was easy to abuse and led to the charge that evangelists were in it only for the money... In Modesto we determined to do all we could to avoid financial abuses, to downplay the offering and depend as much as possible on money raised by the local committee in advance.

The second item on the list was the danger of sexual immorality. We all knew of evangelists who had fallen into immorality while separated from their families by travel. We pledged among ourselves to avoid any situation that would have even the appearance of compromise or suspicion. From that day on, I did not travel, meet or eat alone with a woman other than my wife. We determined that the Apostle Paul's mandate to the young pastor Timothy would be ours as well: "Flee . . . youthful lusts" (2 Timothy 1:22).

Our third concern was the tendency of many evangelists to carry on their work apart from the local church, even to criticize local pastors and churches openly and scathingly. We were convinced, however, that this was not only counterproductive but also wrong from the Bible's standpoint. We determined to cooperate with all who would cooperate with us in the public proclamation of the Gospel, and to avoid an antichurch or anti-clergy attitude.

The fourth and final issue was publicity. The tendency among some evangelists was to exaggerate their successes or to claim higher attendance numbers than they really had. This likewise discredited evangelism and brought the whole enterprise under suspicion. It often made the press so suspicious of evangelists that they refused to take notice of their work. In Modesto, we committed ourselves to integrity in our publicity and our reporting. So much for the Modesto Manifesto, as Cliff [Barrows] called it later years. In reality, it did not mark a radical departure for us; we had always held these principles. It did, however, settle in our hearts and minds, once and for all, the determination that integrity would be the hallmark of both our lives and our ministry."[1]

Are we at risk of "falling into immorality" and having infidelity destroy our personal lives?

-King David was a mature man, knew God well and had pretty much everything a person could desire in his kingdom. However, in the spring when kings go out to battle he stayed home, during an idle moment he noticed Bathsheba bathing, took a second look and had her come to him. She conceived, notified David and he arranged for her husband (Uriah) to come from battle and be with her. He came but would not stay with her and David made arrangements for him to be at the forefront of the battle where he was killed. 2 Samuel 11:1-27.

-The Lord appeared to King Solomon and gives him his wish to have a wise and an understanding heart. The Queen of Sheba sought after him for his knowledge and he built the first temple in Jerusalem. Yet, his sins included idolatry, marrying foreign women, and ultimately turning away from God, and led to the kingdom's being torn in two during the reign of his son Rehoboam.

According to a survey of 191 CDFA professionals from across North America, the three leading causes of divorce are "basic incompatibility" (43%), "infidelity" (28%), and "money issues" (22%). "Emotional and/or physical abuse" lagged far behind (5.8%), and "parenting issues/arguments" and "addiction and/or alcoholism issues" received only .5% each.2

Number of marriages: 2,015,603, Marriage rate: 6.1 per 1,000 total population. Number of divorces: 746,971 (45 reporting States and D.C.). Divorce rate: 2.7 per 1,000 population (45 reporting States and D.C.)3

It is a most fearful fact to think of, that in every heart there is some secret spring that would be weak at the touch of temptation, and that is liable to be assailed. Fearful, and yet salutary to think of; for the thought may serve to keep our moral nature braced. It warns us that we can never stand at ease, or lie down in this field of life, without sentinels of watchfulness and campfires of prayer.4

IT IS EASIER TO AVOID TEMPTATIOIN THAN RESIST IT . . .

1. *Mike Pence and the 'Billy Graham Rule.'*
2. *From August 1 to 29, 2013, (Certified Divorce Financial Councilors).*
3. *Sources: National Marriage and Divorce Rate Trends pdf icon [PDF—48 KB] (data shown are provisional 2019).*
4. *E.H. Chapin, Living words.*

44

THE LEGEND OF THE WALDORF ASTORIA

When it re-opened in 1931, New York's Waldorf Astoria was the largest hotel in the world. The lobby of the second edition of the building (the first was built in 1893) was an Art Deco masterpiece with a ceiling so magnificent, it has been the subject of numerous Hollywood productions. In October 2014 the hotel went into the hands of China-based Anbang Insurance Group for a stunning $2 billion, making the Waldorf the most expensive hotel ever sold. This hotel is noted for inventing room service and there is a legend known as the Waldorf Principle about how selfless service to others will one day return benefit to you. The anecdote tells the rise of the Waldorf Astoria's first ever manager, George C. Boldt.

Many years ago, on one stormy night, an elderly man and his wife entered the lobby of a small hotel in Philadelphia. Running from the raging tempest outside, the couple was desperate for an overnight shelter. "We'd like a room, please," the husband requested the front desk clerk. The younger man looked down at the list of reservations and frowned—all the rooms were taken. But with a winning smile he carefully explained: "I can't send a nice couple like you out in the rain. Would you perhaps be willing to sleep in my room? It's not exactly a suite, but it will make you folks comfortable." The stunned couple was hesitant. "Don't worry about me, I'll make out just fine," the clerk assured them. After a good night's rest the husband, while paying the bill next morning, told the clerk: "Finding people who are both friendly and helpful is rare these days. You are the kind of manager who should be the boss of the best hotel in the United States. Maybe someday I'll build one for you." The clerk smiled and bade the couple goodbye.

Two years later, the clerk received a letter recalling the storm and how gracious his gesture was towards the couple. But also enclosed was a one-way ticket to New York along with a note asking the young man to leave for the city immediately. The couple received him in New York and after a short exchange of pleasantries the husband took the clerk to Park Avenue and pointed towards a towering new building. As he pointed, the elderly man said: "That is the hotel I'd like you to manage." The clerk was Boldt and the elderly gent was William Waldorf Astor. The building he pointed to was the Waldorf Astoria, in all its glory. Boldt soon went on to redefine hospitality. He introduced room service, abolished the segregated ladies' entrance, had his senior staff inspect the lobby round-the-clock and placed ashtrays at strategic locations, while insisting that all guests must be treated to fresh flowers and a copy of the day's newspaper in their rooms. "Make the Waldorf so comfortable they will never go to another place," he was once quoted as saying.1

In his book *Authentic Happiness*, professor Martin Seligman tells a wonderful story about visiting a good friend in the hospital. The friend Mr. Miller, was in a coma, but Seligman spent a long time simply sitting next to his bed and occasionally holding his hand. Then an orderly came into the room. The orderly proceeded to take out pictures from his bag and hang them on the walls around the patient's bed. Seligman asked him what he was doing. "My job? I'm an orderly on this floor," he answered. "But I bring in new prints and photos every week. You see, I'm responsible for the health of all these patients. Take Mr. Miller here. He hasn't woken up since they brought him in, but when he does, I want to make sure he sees beautiful things right away." This hospital orderly, wrote Seligman, "did not define his work as the emptying of bedpans or the swabbing of trays, but as protecting the health of his patients and procuring objects to fill this difficult time of their lives with beauty. He may have held a lowly job, but he crafted it into a high calling."

Similarly, this is what Amy Wrzesniewski a professor of business at New York University, discovered when she interviewed cleaners at a hospital. Although she found that many only regarded their work as a job, many others saw the greater good in what they did. These people saw their work as vital in contribution to the wellbeing of sick people and considered their work as a calling. That was the motivation in the workplace.2

When the judgement day arrives and our lives are reviewed, we will probably be judged in large measure on whether we were kind to other people, not by the wealth, social status and material things we accumulated. The judgement will be based on what was in our hearts and what we did for others. The great principle taught by the Savior was one of service and unselfish concern for our fellow man. The ability to be the servant and not the served requires a peace of mind, an understanding of that which is of greatest worth. It is an attitude that comes from within the soul. At any given time, we may lose our strength, our money, every single possession, but we will never lose the happiness in our lives if we serve our fellow man.

Rev. Theodore Hesburgh of Notre Dame has suggested three qualities intimately associated with service to others: First, compassion—the human quality of sensitivity, to suffer with those who suffer, to be moved, to reach out, to understand. Second, commitment—without which we are likely to live for ourselves alone, and that is a poor and valueless life indeed. Third, consecration—a quality with religious connotations. But the qualities of compassion and commitment are difficult to achieve unless buttressed by religious motivation to help us overcome the urge for personal selfishness and self-centeredness. That's what the Lord is telling us when He says we have to lose our lives to find them.3

Much of the Woldorf Astoria legend story is actually true. Boldt did manage a tiny hotel and yes, he's the man who 'invented' room service. But in an obituary of Boldt, published in 1916, the New York Times finally revealed the true story. Turns out Boldt and his wife gave up their rooms at a resort for relatives of the Astoria's and their sick child. The child soon recovered and later, the relatives persuaded millionaire Astor that Boldt was the man he was looking for, to manage his new hotel in New York—the Waldorf Astoria. Making the Waldorf Principle almost 90 per cent true. So, George C. Boldt did set the gold standard of hospitality. His is also a tale from the earliest days of earnest industry, filled with near-legendary levels of humility and unselfish concern for his fellow man.1

One achieves great things not just through service, but through extraordinary service. When someone goes out of their way to help you it makes all the difference in the world.

"No one has ever become poor by giving."4

1. *Tags: travel, sunday chronicle, lifestlye Fact or fiction: The legend of Waldorf.*
2. *Martin E. P. Seligman, Ph. D., Authentic Happiness, Pages 166-167.*
3. *Music & the Spoken Word, December 11, 1983, Broadcast Number 2,834.*
4. *Anne Frank, The Diary of a Young Girl, (1929-1945).*

45

CAN WE ONLY IMAGINE

Bart Millard's dad wasn't always a monster. In fact, Arthur Wesley Millard Jr. was a beloved high school football hero, one of only two All-Americans from his rural Texas town of Greeneville, about 45 miles northeast of Dallas. Everyone called him "Bub," and even though he was a big bear of a guy, he was more teddy than grizzly. Until the accident.

While flagging cars for the Texas highway department, Arthur Millard got hit by a diesel truck, a collision that put him in a coma for eight weeks. When he regained consciousness, "Bub" was a different guy. His attitude and temperament darkened. Combative with orderlies, crude with nurses, Arthur Millard eventually was restrained.

Tension in the house grew, and six years later Bart's mother with two sons divorced. Now three years of age Bart lived with his mother. But, after his mother decided to move out of town with her third husband, Bart and his older brother moved in with their dad when he was in third grade.

Arthur began spanking Bart first with only a few pops on the bottom. But punishment became longer and more intense. Bart often felt like his dad was taking out anger and frustration that had nothing to do with his children's behavior. If dad got cut off in traffic, Millard might get a beating. If the Dallas Cowboys lost, another beating.

The whippings came as often as three or four times a week, and the boy lived in constant fear, and yet... Eventually, after the beatings, Millard's father would hoist the boy onto his lap, apologize for losing his temper and hold him while the two watched TV. "While I didn't always understand the severity of the punishment versus the actual crime," Millard wrote in his book, "I still always savored those moments of father-and-son intimacy." Millard said he sometimes would intentionally set off his father so his dad would get the paddle. "Because I knew then that afterward, we could then cuddle up and watch TV together."

One day at school, Bart signed his father's name to a notification that the boy made honor roll and handed in the form. Millard usually wanted to avoid most contact with his dad, even if it was good news. But Millard was pretty bad at forgery. The teachers thought it was so cute the boy signed his dad's name that they called his father at work to tell him. The father laughed it off on the phone, but he felt embarrassed. And that infuriated the big man.

Millard's father rushed home to lie in wait for his younger son. Right after the boy walked through the sliding glass door, he felt the sting of the razor strap on the back of his legs. The whipping continues for several minutes. "All of a sudden, I'm like, 'He's gonna kill me,'" Millard said. "He beat me all the way through the house. Everything on me hurt so badly I couldn't lay on my back."

The boy cried in the dark in his room for hours, until his dad exploded through the door, flipped on the light and shouted, "It's about time you stop crying!" Then his father stopped: He saw the dark welts and the deep purple and black bruises on his boy's back. "That's the first time I heard my dad cry." The worst beating was the last.

After that, Arthur Millard, afraid of what he might do next, sent his younger son to live with his mother and her new husband in San Antonio, Texas. But father and son stayed in touch and at the end of sixth grade Millard moved back in with his dad. The two occasionally clashed and got into a handful of physical altercations, but there were no more beatings.

That didn't stop Arthur from doing something his son thought was far worse than the beatings. Millard's dad found out his son, one night in seventh grade, got drunk at a party. The dad's reaction? Total apathy, from that point on. "He said, 'Do what you want, I don't care anymore.' He never let up from that." The two hardly spoke to each other. Millard could disappear for days at a time, and his dad wouldn't say a word about it. And that stung more than the razor strap. "That is the most painful thing he's ever done in my life."

"Sad? Yes. But true." A child trauma expert at Vanderbilt University said that it's not unusual for children to crave attention and love from abusive parents. Clinical psychologist Jon Ebert - who has never met Millard and has no firsthand knowledge of the situation - said it's what makes childhood trauma so complicated. "Most trauma experts would hear this description, and it wouldn't be surprising," Ebert said. "It highlights how attachment trumps all. That need to be loved and taken care of is so strong in a child that a child is willing to endure and even blame themselves."

Harm is any detrimental effect of a significant nature on the child's physical, psychological or emotional wellbeing. Physical abuse happens when a child has been hurt or injured, and it is not an accident. Physical abuse does not always leave visible marks or injuries. Child sexual abuse happens when an adult, teenager or child uses their power or authority to involve another child in sexual activity. Emotional abuse happens when a child is treated in a way that negatively impacts their social, emotional or intellectual development. Neglect happens when a child's basic needs are not met, affecting their health and development.1

Experiencing domestic and family violence can also lead to emotional harm. A child who experiences violence at home is at greater risk of not having their basic needs met, including their protection and care needs. In 2019 Child Maltreatment reported by the Department of Health & Human Services reported the number of children who received a child protective services investigation response was 3,476,000 and victims was 656,000 (rounded). 84.5% suffered a single type of maltreatment, 61% were neglected only, 10.3% were physically abused and 7.2% were sexually abused only. More than 15.5% were victims of two or more maltreatment types. A national estimate of 1,840 children died from abuse and neglect at a rate of 2.50 per 100,000 children in the population.2

Millard turned to his local church youth group to fill the void, a group his dad called "cultish." Two years later, Millard's dad, 44, was diagnosed with pancreatic cancer, a disease that would prove to be fatal four years later. It was a rocky four years, but their relationship got smoother as his dad got sicker. Eventually, his dad told Millard he was proud of him, told the teen to chase his dreams of being a singer. The old man had even set it up so Millard would get $600 a month for 10 years to support those dreams.

Bart's father often fell asleep reading the Bible, no longer deriding his son's involvement in church, even shocking his son one night by asking him, "Can I pray for you?" That sent Millard's faith into hyperdrive. "If the gospel could change that guy," Millard figured, "the gospel could change anybody." Millard and his father became friends, chatting for two hours each night as the teen administered a treatment through his dad's IV. They talked about what would happen after Arthur died, who Millard should or shouldn't be dating, all sorts of things. Arthur Millard died Nov. 11, 1991, with both of his sons by his side.

And that's the first time Millard got mad at God. "I finally got the dad I wanted, and he left." At the gravesite, Millard's grandmother, a woman of faith, said, "I can only imagine what Bub's seeing now." Millard became obsessed with the phrase I can only imagine, toyed with it for years and finally wrote the song "I Can Only Imagine" in 1998.

The physical scars have faded, and Millard, 45, lead singer of the popular Christian band Mercy Me, eventually found peace with his father shortly before his father died. In fact, it was his father's death that launched Millard's musical success. His band had its first breakthrough with the song Millard wrote about his father dying. He said he got his dad's last $600 check the week the song hit No. 1 on Christian radio charts.1

Corrie ten Boom, a devout Dutch Christian woman, found such healing despite having been interned in concentration camps during World War II. She suffered greatly, but unlike her beloved sister Betsie, who perished in one of the camps, Corrie survived.

After the war she often spoke publicly of her experiences and of healing and forgiveness. On one occasion a former Nazi guard who had been part of Corrie's own grievous confinement in Ravensbrück, Germany, approached her, rejoicing at her message of Christ's forgiveness and love. "How grateful I am for your message, Fraulein, he said. To think that, as you say, He has washed my sins away! His hand was thrust out to shake mine, Corrie recalled. And I, who had preached so often . . . the need to forgive, kept my hand at my side.

Even as the angry, vengeful thoughts boiled through me, I saw the sin of them . . . Lord Jesus, I prayed, forgive me and help me to forgive him. I tried to smile, [and] I struggled to raise my hand. I could not. I felt nothing, not the slightest spark of warmth or charity.

And so again I breathed a silent prayer. Jesus, I cannot forgive him. Give me Your forgiveness. As I took his hand the most incredible thing happened. From my shoulder along my arm and through my hand a current seemed to pass from me to him, while into my heart sprang a love for this stranger that almost overwhelmed me.

And so, I discovered that it is not on our forgiveness any more than on our goodness that the world's healing hinges, but on His. When He tells us to love our enemies, He gives, along with the command, the love itself." Corrie ten Boom was made whole.3

"Please remember tomorrow, and all the days after that, that the Lord blesses those who want to improve, who accept the need for commandments and try to keep them, who cherish Christlike virtues and strive to the best of their ability to acquire them. If you stumble in that pursuit, so does everyone; the Savior is there to help you keep going. If you fall, summon His strength. Call out like Alma, 'O Jesus, . . . have mercy on me.' He will help you get back up. He will help you repent, repair, fix whatever you have to fix, and keep going. Soon enough you will have the success you seek. 'As you desire of me so it shall be done unto you,' the Lord has declared."4

"Our birth is but a sleep and a forgetting; The soul that rises with us, our life's star, Hath had elsewhere its setting. And cometh from afar; Not in entire forgetfulness, And, not in utter nakedness, But, trailing clouds of glory do we come From God, who is our home." *William Wordsworth, "Intimations of Immortality.*

"And so, I discovered that it is not on our forgiveness any more than on our goodness that the world's healing hinges, but on His. When He tells us to love our enemies, He gives, along with the command, the love itself." *Corrie Ten Boom.*

"I can only imagine what my eyes will see when Your Face is before me..." Song—I Can Only Imagine.

1. *USA Today 2018/03/20.*
2. *2019 Child Maltreatment reported by the Department of Health & Human Services.*
3. *Corrie ten Boom, The Hiding Place (1971), 215.*
4. *Tomorrow the Lord Will Do Wonders among You, Elder Jeffrey R. Holland, April 2016.*

46

WALMART CASHIER STEPS IN

When a Walmart cashier in Burton saw a customer get turned away from the store's nail salon, she took matters into her own hands. "I was like making sandwiches and I was watching her like," Tasia Smith said of the scene Thursday that brought her to tears.

She works at the Subway inside the Burton Walmart on Court Street. That's where she captured a photo, which has since gone viral, of Walmart cashier Ebony Harris skipping her break to paint customer Angela Peters' nails.

"I just wanted to post it for awareness and appreciation, because people needed to know what was going on with the business and Ebony deserved all the appreciation she could get," Tasia said. Harris said she watched the nail salon, located just a few feet over, refuse to do Peters' nails because her hands shake quite a bit due to cerebral palsy. So, she decided to do something about it.

"I just wanted to make her day special. I didn't really want her day to be ruined. That's why I did it. And plus she's a sweetie," Harris said. Together, the two picked out some polish and relaxed in the seating area at Subway for a manicure. "And you know, she moved her hands a little bit and she kept saying she was sorry. And, I told her don't say that. I said you're fine," Harris said.

It was a simple act of patience and kindness that's still making Angela smile. "I thought that was so nice of her and I already felt comfortable with her because, like I said, I shop at Walmart a lot," Peters said.

Harris has no qualms with the nail salon, but she hopes her actions inspire others to treat people with disabilities the way they would want to be treated themselves. "We're not trying to bash the nail salon. We're not trying to make them lose customers, make them look bad," she said. "But maybe spread awareness that no matter the person, who they are, what color they are, disability, whatever, they're people too. She's a girly girl. She's just like you, me, Tasia, my daughter, anybody. She wants to look pretty, you know, and so why can't she?"

Sitting next to her new friend at her store inside Collette's Vintage and Antique Mall, Peters said she's grateful not only for Harris' help, but a beautiful manicure too. "I'm like wow. These are amazing!" she said. "I told her she's a blessing to us, to anybody, not just me. She makes me look at life and appreciate it much more than, you know, what I have been," Harris added.

The three plan to continue their friendship, already scheduling a dinner at Peters' favorite restaurant in town. To check out Angela's business, stop by Collette's Vintage and Antique Mall or the Davison Farmer's Market on Saturdays. It's called 'Heavenly Poems For You'.1

Compassion for others is vital to our well-being. To feel for others, to "walk in their shoes," and to help when help is needed is the source of true happiness in life. The more we nurture such compassion, the more generosity of spirit we feel. Though we may doubt our own abilities, if we are watchful we'll find that we can all help others in our own way. Few stories illustrate this so well as Aesop's tale of the lion and the mouse. You know the story. When a mouse accidentally wakes a sleeping lion, the lion threatens to eat him. But the mouse pleads for his life, promising that someday he will return the kindness and help the lion. The great lion scoffs at the idea that a little mouse could help him but, nonetheless, lets the mouse go.

Sometime later, the lion gets caught in a net. He tugs and pulls with all his might to free himself, but the ropes are too strong. The mouse hears the lion's loud roar and comes running. He starts gnawing at the ropes with his sharp teeth and finally sets the humbled and grateful lion free.

This fable brings to life the importance of doing what we can to bless others, even if our abilities seem insignificant to some—even ourselves.

The well-known poet Emily Dickinson wrote:

> If I can stop one Heart from breaking
> I shall not live in vain
> If I can ease one Life the Aching
> Or cool one Pain
> Or help one fainting Robin
> Unto his Nest again
> I shall not live in Vain

What could be more gratifying than using our God-given talents to help another in distress? In the end, touching another's life for good is what brings joy and meaning to our days2

From one of Angela Peters books, 'Heavenly Poems for You': May I share this with you: "Who is Angela Peters?—"I was born three months early with Cerebral Palsy at Hurley Hospital in Flint, Michigan. Cerebral Palsy is a medical condition that makes your muscles contract constantly, except for when you are sleeping.

I tried taking the medications that will allow the muscles to loosen up when I was younger but the side affects were tremendous. There is now new technology that a pump can be implanted into the body which will distribute medicine when needed.

After careful thought I decided against the pump. I have learned over time that the only part of my body that is really tight are my hips. The alternative to taking medication is to exercise daily. If a person with Cerebral Palsy does not exercise enough their muscles contract and stay tight and the result would be the inability to move that part of your body."

1. *Walmart cashier steps in when nail salon refuses wheelchair-bound woman By Ann Pierret , Posted: Fri 6:22 PM, Aug 03, 2018, Updated: Tue 5:06 PM, Aug 07, 2018, BURTON (WJRT) (8/3/2018) - A simple act of kindness is making a big impact.*
2. *Music & The Spoken word, Touching a Life for Good, Sept 17, 2006, Program #4020, The Complete Poems of Emily Dickinson,* ed. Thomas H. Johnson (1960), 433

SOMETIMES

SOMETIMES WE MUST BE IN CERTAIN
PLACES BEFORE WE CAN MOVE FORWARD

WE MUST WALK WITH GOD FOR
GOD TO BLESS OUR LIFE

SOMETIMES WE CAN CRY BECAUSE
WE REGRET LIFE CHOICES

SOMETIMES WE NEED TO REMEMBER
WHERE WE WERE WHEN WE
WALKED AWAY FROM GOD

SO WE WILL ALWAYS LET GOD
HOLD OUR RIGHT HAND

SOME DAY WE WILL SEE BRIGHTER DAYS

GOD WILL TAKE US TO GREAT PLACES IN LIFE

IF WE ALWAYS WALK IN HIS WAYS

*Angela Peters: Author, business owner
& exceptional women…1*

47

THINGS OF MY SOUL

During idle conversation I mentioned the jack-o-lantern sweat shirt a staff member, Alysa, often wears to work. I jokingly asked if she were going to were Christmas clothing in December and she said that she didn't believe in Santa Clause. So, I made it my business to "in a fun way" change her mind about the spirit of good old Saint Nick and we celebrate him along with the birth of Jesus Christ. Right after Thanksgiving I gave her a book about the history of the history of Saint Nicholas and the traditions of Christmas.1

Each day I worked in December dressed in a different Christmas attire and made it a point to visit Alysa at the front desk, discuss my gig for the day and ask if she was enjoying the book.

My wife Shauna and I attended the 2021 Camden Pet Hospital annual staff noon lunch and Christmas Party on Tuesday the 21st along with our staff of 15. Respecting the Covid-19 pandemic the hospital was still only offering curb service, there were employees that had not yet been vaccinated and we all wore masks while at work.

However, during lunch staff dogs roamed the area socializing one with another and begging for food, the masks came off and stayed that way the rest of the day. As lunch was finishing and hospital gifts were being shared, Shauna and I slipped away and dressed up in whole body hooded Christmas costume pajamas with HO-HO written on the rear, KISS ME on the front, with hoods pulled over our heads and a bow of mistletoe hanging over our foreheads we sang "Kiss me once, Kiss me twice and Kiss me once again," as we danced down the hallway hand in hand into the lunch room.2

Not respecting the CDC's suggestions for social distancing, I dangled the mistletoe hanging over my forehead near my colleagues, and I passed out the gifts Shauna and I had prepared for the staff.

Along with my behavior discussed above at the Christmas party I had further breached social distancing by targeting Alysa and placing a Christmas hat on her head and I telling the hospital staff that I had not believed in Christmas until my grandfather and I had an experience that made believers out of us.

That this experience was later made into a song by a famous veterinarian, Elmo Shropshire. I then pushed a button on the hat and flashing lights came on, the tip of the hat wagged back and forth and the words rang out "grandma got run over by a reindeer and as for me and grandpa we believe."3

Two days later during Christmas Eve Shauna and I were visiting her children and our friends in Idaho. BeBe our Winchester Terrier went with us and, other than keeping masks over our mouth and nose to help avoid the COVID-19 pandemic, the December 23rd flight from

San Jose to Boise check in, departure time and flight were a breeze.

Christmas Eve Shauna and I were enjoying the decorations and atmosphere in the homes of her children. I was interrupted by a call from Nancy, the office manager at Camden Pet Hospital. I expected a Merry Christmas and how was your flight call but the words spoken were, "I need to inform you that a staff member has called in sick and is Covid positive."

I felt my stomach tighten and my mind flashed with thoughts of the number of people that may have been exposed by us during our trip from San Jose to Boise Idaho. The next two days it took before we could be tested were filled with "what ifs." If we were positive, had we exposed Shauna's children, would we get sick and need care away from home, would we need to change our flights home, would we be able to socialize in the community or with our friends?

Waiting for testing in the critical care medical facility sitting near others that were ill or waiting for testing, I wondered if they were of any risk from us or if we were at risk from them. Fortunately, all three tests were negative.

According to the Greek Orthodox history, the first recorded Santa Claus' parents received him as their son after many years of prayer, similar to Abraham and Sarah of the Bible. They considered this child a direct gift from God with a special calling to help people. They therefore named him "Nicholas," which meant in Greek "victor or hero of the people." Nicholas' uncle was the bishop of the town and noticed that his personality was one that he may be called to the service of God. He entered the monastery and was ordained a minister.

Nicholas' parents died while he was on a pilgrimage of a plague leaving him a substantial inheritance. He was generous in distributing it to the poor and needy, feeding the hungry, clothing the naked and ransoming those taken captive by debt to money lenders.

Nicholas was most remembered for helping the family of a nobleman of Patara who had gone bankrupt. Ruthless creditors not only took the nobleman's property, but threatened to take his three beautiful daughters as well. The father's only hope was to marry off his daughters quickly before the creditors could take them, thereby saving them from a life of white slavery and prostitution. Unfortunately, he did not have enough money for the girl's dowries, which were necessary for them to marry. Nicholas heard of this dilemma and late one night threw a bag of gold in the family's window to save the eldest daughter from the fate of an outcast. The news spread across town and she was soon lawfully married. Shortly thereafter Nicholas did the same, rescuing the second daughter. Finally, then Nicholas threw the bag of gold in to save the third daughter, which supposedly landed in one of her stockings set out by the fireplace to dry, the father ran outside and caught him.

Nicholas, who wanted the glory to go to God alone, made the father swear with an oath not to reveal where the gifts came from while Nicholas was living. This was the basis for the later tradition of secret gift-giving on the anniversary of Nicholas' death. The tradition of Christmas balls used for decorations are in remembrance of the three round bags of gold given to a family in need.1

Shauna and I had some fun with Alysa and she seemed to enjoy the Christmas party. My real intent was to bring out how Christ is the "reason for the season" because his Father gave Him as a gift to help us find the way back into our Heavenly-Father's presence. And, that Saint Nicholas gave us the gift of an example of how to love our fellow man as ourselves through his generous giving of his love, time, and talents. Nicholas gave the lessons temporal blessings—Christ the spiritual blessings.

The description of Nicholas' life experiences helped me appreciate why he and Jesus Christ share a common holiday together: "Saint Nicholas strove to be an example to the believers, in word, in conversation, in love, in spirit, in faith, and in purity. He was humble of spirit and forgiving, shunning all vainglory. All day long he spent in labor proper to his office, listening to the requests and needs of those who came to him. The doors of his house were open to all. He was kind and affable to all, to orphans he was a father, to the poor a merciful giver, to the weeping a comforter, to the wronged a helper, and to all a great benefactor. Nicholas lived through the persecutions of Diocletian, the last Roman emperor who persecuted Christians in the early part of the 4th century. Under the threat of imprisonment and even death, Nicholas continued to proclaim the Good News of God's love through Jesus Christ. And he suffered for it. His sufferings are often compared to what the Apostle Paul went through before he was martyred. Fortunately, Saint Nicholas did not suffer such a fate."[1]

1. *There Really Is a Santa Claus—The History of Saint Nicholas & Christmas Holiday Traditions" by William J. Federer.*
2. *It's Been a Long, Long Time by Harry James.*
3. *Grandma Got Run Over by a Reindeer by Elmo & Patsy.*

48

WISH I MAY AND WISH I MIGHT CHANGE THINGS I CAN'T

The widow, Dominique Luzuriagas, of slain NYPD Detective Jason Rivera delivered a heart-wrenching eulogy Friday January 28, 2022 morning during her husband's funeral. Dominique Luzuriaga said she and her husband, Jason Rivera, met in elementary school.

I would say good morning to you all. But in fact this is the worst morning ever. I can't believe I'm standing in front of thousands of people in the cathedral we planned to visit later this year. All of this seems so unreal. Like I'm having one of those nightmares that you never thought you'd have.

Friday morning, we were together eating breakfast and drinking some Starbucks… just like every other morning before work… (except) This Friday was different. We had an argument, you know it's hard being a cop's wife sometimes. It's hard being patient when plans were canceled or we would go days without seeing each other or when you'd have to write a report that would take forever because you'd have to voucher so many things, so you did OT. Or when you had a bad day at work because an EDP (emotional disturbed person) drove you nuts but you always reminded me that it was going to be all right, that we were going to get through it . . . "You would drive me home and say goodbye with three kisses, all the time, and texted me when you were eighty-four (in a meeting). That was our routine.

This Friday, we were arguing because I didn't want you to use your job phone while we were together. You were so mad that you took your LeBron jersey down, gave me your chain and put the lotions I gave you for your ashy hands in the bag and said, 'Here, take them.' We left your apartment and because I didn't want to continue to argue, I ordered an Uber. You asked me if you are sure 'that you don't want me to take you home, it might be the last ride I give you.' I said no and that was probably the biggest mistake I ever made.

Later that day, I received the call I wish none of you that are sitting here with me will ever receive. I had gotten a notification from the Citizen app, which was my central. And I saw that two police officers were shot in Harlem. My heart dropped. I immediately texted you and asked you, 'Are you okay? Please tell me you're okay. I know that you are mad right now but just text me, you're okay, at least tell me you're busy.' I get no response. We used to share locations on Find My iPhone and when I checked yours, I see that you're at Harlem Hospital. I thought maybe you were sitting on a perp (person who committed a crime) but still, nothing. I called and then called again and then called one more time and this time, I felt something wasn't right. I messaged PO Kadavid and Joe because I know they were your friends from the 32 and I get no response. Then I get a call asking if I'm Jason's wife. And then I had to rush to the hospital.

Walking all those steps seeing everybody staring at me was the scariest moment I've experienced. Nobody was telling me anything. Dozens of people were surrounding me and yet I felt alone. I couldn't believe you left me. Seeing you in a hospital bed wrapped up in sheets, not hearing you when I was talking to you broke me... I asked why. I said to you, 'Wake up, baby, I'm here.' The little bit of hope I had that you would come back to life just to say goodbye or say 'I love you' one more time has left. I was lost. I'm still lost. Today I'm still in this nightmare that I wish I never had. Full of rage and anger, hurt and sad. Torn. Although I gained thousands of blue brothers and sisters, I'm the loneliest without you. I know you're looking at me and beside me telling me I can do this. And I'm trying, trust me I am. I didn't prepare for this. None of us did." 1

Often, we regret and brood about past decisions, what we should or shouldn't have done. Or we think of what we should now be doing and are not doing, of what we would like to learn, and it makes us uneasy. We regret misunderstandings, words we wish we hadn't said, words we wish we had said, mistakes we have made, people we have offended, opportunities gone by, errors and carelessness that could have been avoided, places we might have gone, things we might have been.

The past has its place and is valuable for lessons learned. The present also has its place, and what we cannot change should not now needlessly keep us from looking and moving forward. Nothing lost or left behind should keep us from now becoming what we can become, from learning what we now can learn.

There are new decisions every day, every hour, and reasons to improve and to repent. Whatever we are, wherever we've been, each day we have some opportunity to determine direction.

Each day we need to win, or keep, and certainly to deserve the love of loved ones; each day to be more patient, more pleasant, more understanding. If there have been loved ones neglected, unreconciled differences, unspoken gratitude, unacknowledged debts, we ought to do now what we should do. If there has been within something that has soured us, we well would turn now to sweetening ourselves, for we hurt ourselves as well as others when we live below the level of our possibilities.

Whatever the past or its meaning, or its length, or its losses, or its lessons learned or left unlearned, we go on from where we are, wherever we are, and become what we can become; with work, repentance, improvement; with faith in the future.2

I have imprinted in my mind the guilt and regret I felt for not being home during the passing of my kid's mom, Sheryl. Even though she was receiving in home hospice care from colon cancer, her care nurse and I expected she would be fine during the time I flew to Arizona to assist my youngest son Jeremy during his shoulder surgery.

During his surgical recovery the nurse kept asking Jeremy what level of pain he was having. He kept giving them a high number and they would give him more pain medication through his IV. At this time, I received a call, from family watching over Sheryl, that she had passed.

I called my son Chris, who was living in Arizona, and he arranged flights home that day for his family, Jeremy and me. Doctor's orders were that Jeremy was not to fly in an airplane for a few days. The memory I have during the flight home was constantly trying to control my son enough to prevent casting suspicion that he was over dosed on something.

It wasn't until after sleeping many nights in the room in which Sheryl passed and spending lots of time at the office doing busy work that I was able to start emotionally healing and going forward with my life.

A portion of a letter written to my children shortly after her death reads, "I'm sure you knew that Sheryl was a person that could not say goodbye. She told me that she stayed away from those about to say goodbye because she didn't want to become emotional and she always wanted to have hellos.

When she died, I felt very bad that I was in Arizona with Jeremy when he had his shoulder operated on. I had discussed leaving her with Hospice. They said that she was in good flesh, not dehydrated and felt that she would be fine for another week or two. After I got home and spent some time thinking about it, I realized that Sheryl being as private as she was and that she didn't like to say goodbyes probably had chosen this moment in time to leave."3

Often, we regret and brood about past decisions, what we should or shouldn't have done.

Often leading to self-searching of the events we can't change . . . Whatever the past or its meaning, or its length, or its losses, or its lessons learned or left unlearned, we go on from where we are, wherever we are, and become what we can become; with work, repentance, improvement; with faith in the future.2

1. *The widow, Dominique Luzuriagas, of slain NYPD Detective Jason Rivera delivered a heart-wrenching eulogy Friday January 28, 2022 morning during her husband's funeral.*
2. *Richard L. Evans, 04/23/1946, Program #3940, Music and the Spoken Word.*
3. *Walter R. Hoge, Your Mother Sheryl 2003.*

49

ORANGE FOR CHRISTMAS

As a young child Christmas morning came very early for me. Christmas Eve visions of the toys and gifts Santa was expected to leave on a chair where a large stocking with my name on it had been attached with a safety pin and the wrapped gifts with my name on them under our Christmas tree kept me awake tossing and turning late into the night. The chair and Christmas tree were all conveniently located next to my parent's upstairs bedroom.

I would awaken well before my brother and sisters while it was still dark. I would sneak upstairs quietly taking a Santa gift from the chair and quietly descend down the stairs and into my shared bedroom with my younger brother. I would then go into the closet, close the door and turn the light on. I looked at the gift from Santa and then returned the treasure to its rightful place on the chair and repeat the process. It wasn't long before I heard, "Rich, get back in bed! We'll call down the stairs when it's time to get up."

I took those words seriously because one Christmas while living in the Wilcox Apartments when my older sister, Bobbie, and I were very young, we were attempting to water the decorated Christmas tree and it fell over. Christmas morning came as usual until a knock came at the door. There was Santa, he came into the house, discussed the "knotty and nice" story and asked our parents to put the gifts away until we had time to have a family council with them and showed penitence.

In the toe of our stockings was always a large orange. I didn't pay much attention to it until I had gone over all of Santa's gifts, opened the presents from under the tree and eaten the breakfast my mother insisted us having before we started in on too many goodies. I do remember how bad the orange tasted if I had eaten sweets before and was very good if I cleansed my taste buds first with salty foods, like potato chips, before eating the orange. Being born in the '40s I don't remember oranges or bananas being present on a regular basis and didn't know why they were a tradition in our home. However, when my children were still at home there was always a large orange placed in the toe of their stockings that were placed on a chair the night before Christmas.

A child today would probably be disappointed by the goodies found in the Christmas stockings of the past. Some of the best present-day stocking stuffers may be considered an electronic or game (even our pets and newborns get in on the action now!), but in the past, stocking stuffers were more like candies, nuts, and fresh oranges, all of which were considered to be a real treat at the time.

The holiday tradition may have started during the Great Depression, a time when many families couldn't afford to buy holiday's presents and gifted these sweet and hard-to-come-by fruits instead.

Waking up on Christmas morning and finding a fresh orange in your stocking was considered a luxury. For some families, especially ones that lived in cold areas, oranges were an exotic treat. Tobias Roberts, a writer for the Huffington Post, recalls his Midwestern grandmother's fascination with the fruit. "As a child, every Christmas she would find an orange in the toe of her stocking; a mysterious fruit brought all the way from some exotic warm place called Florida," he wrote. "It was special and unique, because of its rarity and because of the natural limitations that made oranges a scarce commodity in Michigan." Eating this tropical fruit was a fun way for kids to celebrate the holidays.1

Sometimes it is easy to forget the true meaning of Christmas. The busy traditions of the season and the appealing advertisements for material goods can leave the pure and simple truths far, far behind.

Jake was nine years old with tousled brown hair with blue eyes as bright as a heavenly angel. For as long as Jake could remember he had lived within the walls of a poor orphanage. He was just one of ten children supported by what meager contributions the orphan home could obtain in a continuous struggle seeking donations from townsfolk. There was very little to eat, but at Christmas time there always seemed to be a little more than usual to eat, the orphanage seemed a little warmer, and it was time for a little holiday enjoyment. But more than this, there was the Christmas orange!

Christmas was the only time of year that such a rare treat was provided and it was treasured by each child like no other food admiring it, feeling it, prizing it and slowly enjoying each juicy section. Truly, it was the light of each orphan's Christmas and their best gift of the season. How joyful would be the moment when Jake received his orange!

Unknown to him, Jake had somehow managed to track a small amount of mud on his shoes through the front door of the orphanage, muddying the new carpet. He hadn't even noticed. Now it was too late and there was nothing he could do to avoid punishment. The punishment was swift and unrelenting. Jake would not be allowed his Christmas orange! It was the only gift he would receive from the harsh world he lived in, yet after a year of waiting for his Christmas orange, this was to be denied him.

Tearfully, Jake pleaded that he be forgiven and promised never to track mud into the orphanage again, but to no avail. He felt hopeless and totally rejected. Jake cried into his pillow all that night and spent Christmas Day feeling empty and alone. He felt that the other children didn't want to be with a boy who had been punished with such a cruel punishment. Perhaps they feared he would ruin their only day of happiness. Maybe, he reasoned, the gulf between him and his friends existed because they feared he would ask for a little of their oranges.

Jake spent the day upstairs, alone, in the unheated dormitory. Huddled under his only blanket, he read about a family marooned on an island. Jake wouldn't mind spending the rest of his life on an isolated island, if he could only have a real family that cared about him. Bedtime came, and worst of all, Jake couldn't sleep. How could he say his prayers? How could there be a God in Heaven that would allow a little soul such as his, to suffer so much all by himself? Silently, he sobbed for the future of mankind that God might end the suffering in the world, both for himself and all others like him.

As he climbed back into bed from the cold, hard floor, a soft hand touched Jake's shoulder, startling him momentarily and an object was silently placed in his hands. The giver disappeared into the darkness, leaving Jake with what, he did not immediately know! Looking closely at it in the dim light, he saw that it looked like an orange! Not a regular orange, smooth and shiny, but a special orange, very special. Inside a patched together peal were the segments of nine other oranges, making one whole orange for Jake! The nine other children in the orphanage had each donated one segment of their own precious oranges to make a whole orange as a gift for Jake.[2]

Sharing what we truly value is the true spirit of Christmas. Our Heavenly Father gave us His beloved Son. May we, like the children in the orphanage, find ways to share His love with others less blessed.

1. *Christmas Traditions Around the World, 11/10/2021 Country Living US.*
2. *Christmas Oranges was written by Linda Bethers in 1999. She is an elementary school librarian in Utah. The book was just 13 pages. It was reprinted in 2002 and expanded to 32 pages.*

50

CHURCH AND
CHRISTMAS BELLS

Bells are first mentioned in the Old Testament during a description of the high priest's robe. Exodus instructs that "bells of gold" were to be attached to the hem of the high priest's robe so that the people could hear the high priest as he entered and exited the Holy of Holies (Exodus 28:31-35). The Holy of Holies was the most sacred space in the Old Testament Tabernacle and Temple, housing such items as the Ark of the Covenant. Biblical law allowed only the high priest to enter the Holy of Holies and only one time a year, on the Day of Atonement, to make offerings to atone for the sins of God's people.

If the high priest did not precisely follow biblical law in how he purified himself, dressed, and acted in relation to his duties within the Holy of Holies, God would strike him dead (Leviticus 16).

Because only the high priest could enter the Holy of Holies and because that holy sanctuary was covered by a thick veil, a tradition emerged that the high priest wore a rope around his foot or waist in case he were to die while in the Holy of Holies. In such an instance, the people outside the Holy of Holies would be alerted to the high priest's death upon noticing that the bells of his hem had stopped jingling. The deceased high priest would then be pulled out of the holy space by the rope tied around his foot or waist.

Whether this tradition is grounded in truth or not, we can see that as early as Old Testament days, the sound of bells ringing meant good news for God's people because the jingling indicated that the people's sins had been atoned for in a way acceptable to God.

The use of bells in churches dates back to 400 AD when an Italian bishop named Paulinus of Nola introduced bells as part of Catholic church services. In 604 AD, Pope Sabinian officially sanctioned the ringing of church bells during worship. Specifically, Pope Sabinian introduced the custom of ringing church bells during the celebration of the Eucharist and to announce times of daily prayer called the canonical hours.

By the early Middle Ages, church bells were common in Europe. As church bells became more common elsewhere in the world, their importance grew as church bells became used as a form of mass communication to convey religious and secular information or to summon people across large areas.

For example, in 18th century America, church bells rang not only as a part of worship, but also to alert communities of important events such as the end of a war, of emergencies such as a fire, or of an important community gathering. In small villages, church bells also rang to announce deaths to solicit prayers for the deceased's soul, and rang in a kind of Morse code that the hearers knew how to decipher. When a death was announced by church bells, the age of the deceased was sometimes rung as well. In sparsely populated villages, such death knell rings could effectively identify who had just died.

Today, certain Christian denominations use large and small bells as part of their worship. These churches ring large bells from steeples or bell towers either by means of a bell-ringer who stands in the towers and pulls on ropes attached to the bells, or by automatic bell ringing equipment. Some churches also ring small bells inside the church at particular intervals during worship. Churches such as those of the Anglican, Catholic, and Lutheran denominations ring bells to signal that Mass (Catholic) or service (Protestant) is about to begin, mark each hour from early morning to the late evening to remind those hearing the bells of God's daily presence in our lives, and announce that three specific daily prayer times have been reached - 6 a.m., 12 p.m., and 6 p.m. - during which the faithful are encouraged to unite in prayer, such as the Lord's Prayer or the Angelus. They are also used to honor a special occasion taking place at the church, such as a wedding or funeral, highlight a specific stage of a church service, such as when handbells are rung during a Catholic Mass to draw attention to the priest's elevation of the consecrated Host and Precious Blood during the Eucharistic Prayer. They welcome Christmas day and Easter day with a "joyful noise" (Psalm 100) and accompany the singing of hymns, as seen during services that include handbell choirs.

There is also a belief among some Christians that the ringing of church bells drives away demons. This belief may be rooted in ancient pagan celebrations in which bells were rung to drive out evil spirits. The people believed that they could use bells to frighten away evil spirits. Bells were a simple form of noisemaking. They could be easily obtained or made and everyone knew how to use them. Many people thought that as winter began, evil spirits would come to harm them. So, during the dark days after the harvest or the hunt, people would engage in ceremonies to keep bad things from happening to them while they waited for Spring and warmer days.

The tradition of using noisemakers like bells during these times carried over into the celebration of Christmas. But instead of making noise to keep away evil things, people made noise to celebrate something happy. In many villages, there was a church and most churches had a bell. When something important was happening—such as remembering the birth of Jesus Christ—they would ring the bell.

For millions around the world, it is a time of great joy as we celebrate the birth of Jesus together.

Moreover, it is a time when we reflect on the year past and count our many blessings as we celebrate with joy the birth of God's precious Son. Though for many, this time of the year brings sorrowful memories. We remember a loved one who died or a friend who lost their battle against cancer. Perhaps this time of year causes us to reflect on a tragedy that struck out of nowhere.

Such was the case in 1861 for Henry Wadsworth Longfellow. Longfellow lived in Cambridge Massachusetts with his wife and five children. The first shots of the civil war pitting the north against the south rang out in April 1861. In July, Henry's wife, Frances, was burned to death in an accidental fire started by some hot wax. In trying to put out the fire that engulfed Frances, Henry himself suffered severe burns. At Christmas, the year of Frances' death, Henry grieved for his wife as he wrote in his journal, "How inexpressibly sad are all holidays."

A year later, at Christmas in 1862, Henry was still grieving for his beloved Frances. He wrote in his journal, "A merry Christmas say the children, but that is no more for me." The following year, Henry's son, Charles, ran off and joined the Union army. Henry received a letter on December 1, 1863, that Charles was badly wounded in battle when a bullet passed through his shoulder and injured his spine.

His wife died in a tragic fire. Henry suffered disfiguring burns in the vain attempt to save her life. His son was severely injured in battle. The civil war raged on. On Christmas morning 1863, Longfellow heard the church bells ringing. Listening to the church bells, Longfellow wrote a poem reflecting on the tragedy of war and the despair in his life. Yet, while he was in the midst of his sorrow, Longfellow expressed hope for the future. He titled his poem simply, Christmas Bells. The poem was actually about the tragic heartbreak one felt during the civil war.

The famous Christmas hymn I Heard the Bells on Christmas Day began from the poem Christmas Bells written by Henry Wadsworth Longfellow. Christmas bells are remembered in classic holiday songs such as "Jingle Bells", "Silver Bells", and "Christmas Bells are Ringing". Bells make a happy sound and are enjoyed in "ringing out the old and ringing in the new" each season as has been done in times past.

You might hear this saying at Christmas: "Every time a bell rings, an angel gets his wings". Most people remember this saying from the movie "It's a Wonderful Life". But over a hundred years ago, this was a very common saying amongst kids. Back in those days, kids believed that making noise was just a part of Christmas. And bells were an easy way to make that noise.

Bells were inexpensive musical instruments that people could take with them caroling or wassailing and almost every family had one or more. Bells also provided a bright and cheery sound and were acceptable to parents as proper tools to celebrate and make noise at Christmas.

Bells play an important part in other areas of celebrating Christmas. Some people probably picture Santa's reindeer with bells draped over them for decoration. Santa might also use bells to help find the reindeer in the dark or in the fog or snow. And bells have always had a place in Christmas songs.

In 2016 our family took a Christmas Cruise to Mexico. The atmosphere was wonderful for the occasion and I have memories and photos of the family I will never forget. In the family room of our home is a picture of the entire family on the ship's stairway all formally dressed, except for me, for the ship's special evening sit down dinner. I was dressed in a Christmas suit with shoes that blinked red and green along the outer soles. As I walked through the ship a small group of women asked to have a picture taken with me and what surprised me was all the different perfume smells women mist upon themselves. As I walked through the lounges men would notice my blinking shoes and shout out cool dude type language my way. During the dinner a man came over to our table and asked me to shut off my blinking shoes. He said that blinking lights had caused him to have seizures in the past—I obliged.

We found a private area where each family presented a different daily activity surrounding family and Christmas. During one activity, each family received a silver bell with a red bow attached and engraved on it "Christmas 2016." We discussed the importance of our families, those we miss who are no longer with us, read a story by Abby Westover about Christmas bells and "how every time a bell rings, and angel gets its wings, and rang our bells to make sure all or deceased family members would be sure and get their wings.

> "Then pealed the bells more loud and deep:
> "God is not dead, nor doth He sleep; for Wrong
> shall fail, and Right prevail, with peace on earth,
> good will to men!" *Henry W. Longfellow*

Biblestudytools.com, New International Version. Crosswalk. com, "The One Time Bells Are Mentioned in the Bible," Dec. 19, 2017, Clint Archer. Biblestudytools.com, Easton's Bible Dictionary's definition of "bell." Patheos.com, "Why Do Churches Have Bells?" Oct. 28, 2016, Jack Wellman. American Heritage, "The Sound of Bells," June 1964, Eric Sloane. Olean Times Herald, "Rev. McDowell: The history and significance of church bells," Aug. 1, 2014, Rev. Dan McDowell. Poem Christmas Bells written by Abby Westover.

51

SUPERHEROES

I recently attended my grandson Graham's baptism shortly after he was eight years of age. He and his father, who has the authority, stepped into a fount filled with water and was completely submerged after the words, "Having been commissioned of Jesus Christ, I baptize you in the name of the Father and of the Son and of the Holy Ghost, Amen." Two witnesses confirmed that Graham had been completely submerged under the water. This emersion signified our death and coming out of the water representing being cleansed of our sins and pure as a newborn child. The baptism is often referred to as "born again."

A short time later, his father and several others in authority placed their hands on his head and blessed him with the "Gift of the Holy Ghost" and pronounced a blessing admonishing him to keep the covenants he had made before his baptism and to seek out guidance from the Godhead throughout his life.

During the next Sabbath Day I sat by Graham, as well as the rest of the congregation, and we renewed those covenants made before our baptism by partaking of the sacrament. The sacramental prayer states that we will be reminded of the body and blood of Jesus Christ that was given up so that all mankind will have the opportunity to live once again with Him through the process of the resurrection. The specific things that we renew in the name of our Eternal Father's son, Jesus Christ, are: . . . "witness unto thee, O God, the Eternal Father, that they are willing to take upon them the name of thy Son, and always remember him, and keep his commandments which he has given them, that they may always have his Spirit to be with them." (Book of Moroni 4:3, Doctrine and Covenants 20:77).

I don't remember being born, baptized or receiving the Gift of the Holy Ghost. However, I do remember how, on my birthday each year, my mother would tell me how wonderful a baby I was and her waiting until I was six months of age so my sister and I could travel with her on a ship to Germany. My father was serving in the army there just after WW II.

I vividly remember two times when I strongly felt having His Spirit to be with me. When I was participating in the ordinance of preforming baptisms for the dead as a teenager in the Idaho Falls temple, I felt the warmth and calming reassurance that there is a hereafter to this life and that I have a Father in Heaven who knows me, cares about me and if I am doing His will that I can receive promptings directly from Him or the Holy Ghost.

As a high school student on a Spanish class trip to Mexico I learned how direct promptings from the spirit can occur. We boarded a bus in Salt Lake City and while making the long drive there and back, several of us paired off with girls. Things got a little too comfortable and I remember starting to enter a hotel room and seeing my mother's face in front of the door. I immediately left the area and later I was belittled by my friends because of my choice. But, I have never lived to regret the "promptings" of the Spirit who was with me at that time.

Throughout my life I have found the God head to be three superheroes that have off and on truly saved my day. They are out there waiting to counsel and guide us, we need to live by their rules (like love the Lord your God with all your heart and with all your soul and with all your strength and with all your mind,' and, Love your neighbor as yourself. Luke 10:27) to receive inspiration and knowledge. They don't necessarily give us what we want— but give us what we need and we have to rely on faith, hope and their charity when we are lacking in the first two. They don't tend to use a mighty sword of destruction—they usually communicate with a whisper or feeling that we need to be tuned in to recognize.

Final Boss has investigated why superheroes are so much a part of our lives: Since long before they hit our screens, we've been obsessed with superheroes. The Golden Age of comics kickstarted our fascination and since then, we've been hooked. Regardless of who you are, where you come from or what your upbringing, chances are you have a soft spot for at least one superhero. We all have one that resonates with us - not necessarily because we feel we're similar in any way, more because we admire their values, what they stand for and the way they live their lives. But does it go deeper than that?

To understand why we love superheroes and to explore what effect they have on us, I contacted Dr Oliver Sindall, Chartered Clinical Psychologist at Sindall Psychology.

Dr Sindall specializes in working with children and adolescents. Based on his experience of how children relate to superheroes (along with his own love of them), Dr Sindall has applied his knowledge of the published work to help us understand why do we love superheroes? Why are they so important to us?

Why do you think superheroes have been so consistently popular over the decades? The book Our Superheroes, Ourselves by Robin S. Rosenberg identified a number of factors to help try and understand our fascination with superheroes. As a Clinical Psychologist I think four of those factors are key to the consistent popularity of superheroes:

Our childhood is when our imaginations are the most unfiltered and limitless, when anything feels possible. Therefore, as adults, superhero stories allow us to reconnect with that developmental stage when we could really shut out our external reality and go on an amazing adventure.

The formula for a good superhero story is always familiar. The hero saves the day, while overcoming moral, physical and emotional challenges. All of this allowing them to develop into a stronger/better character, "With great power comes great responsibility." The familiarity of this narrative is comforting. In the chaos of the world around us, people are not always looking for just escapism; they want to experience some element of certainty and predictability. Superhero stories are like a rollercoaster; thrill rides, with lots of ups and downs, but you know everything will be alright in the end.

There are so many different looks, personalities, emotions, triggers, backstories, strengths, weaknesses and ways in which they save the day! If we can see ourselves in these traits then we can identify with them. We are then drawn in by how they are able to triumph over the challenges they face. Also let's not forget that with every superhero comes a superpower that we crave, based on our own psychological fears and/or desires.

As a Psychologist I often find this idea resonates the most. In 'analyzing' myself I am aware of how my early fascination with superheroes relates to being bullied as a child, and from my work, I know that this is very common. We have all experienced something where we wished we had been rescued. This ranges from the extreme of severe trauma, to the bullies in the playground or workplace. Superhero stories show this wish coming true over and over again.

The power of 'The Rescuer' is not just felt on an individual level, but across society as a whole, which makes it one of the most influential factors in the superhero's consistent popularity. Just look at Batman, Superman and all the characters of comics' 'Golden Age' (1938-1949). They were created at the time of world wars and failing economies, and the more recent surge of Superhero blockbuster films has followed wars in the Middle East, 9/11 and a general increase in global terrorism.

Superheroes are given a traumatic past because we need to see that the challenges and stresses of life cannot prevent us from becoming a better version of ourselves. The pain of loss and trauma can be transformed into a new life, or to work towards a higher purpose.

Given the increasing popularity in 'origin' stories, I would argue that many of us have an increasing need to immerse ourselves in, and identify with, the most challenging and traumatic elements of our superhero's past. This connection and familiarity with a character's journey makes their rise to superhero status all the more powerful, and we can begin to imagine how we might overcome and rise from our own traumatic experiences.

There is something undeniably special about superheroes, and the psychology behind them is fascinating. What might seem a trivial past-time for kids might actually be helping them to persevere during trying times, or turning them into the solid, dependable adults they'll one day be. But our love for superheroes doesn't die during adulthood—we need them now as we needed them then, to be our anchors and to remind us what really matters.1

A man, who many recognize as a prophet and whose people were to them living in an Apocalyptical time, around 400-420 AD did not think the end of the world was coming. He wrote about a record of his people on metal that he predicted would be preserved and found before the second coming of Christ.

What has caught my attention are his comments, found in a book about these records published in March 1830, concerning worldly events that would occur at the time his people's record would be found. To me his comments seem to fit very closely with the current conditions we are living in and the need for superheroes to help "save our day."

- "It shall come forth in a day when it shall be said that miracles are done away."
- "And it shall come in a day when the blood of the saints (I would include this to mean all who

worship their God) shall cry unto the Lord, because of secret combinations and the works of darkness."

- "Yea, it shall come in a day when the power of God shall be denied."

- ". . . and churches become defiled and lifted up in the pride of their hearts . . ."

- "Yea, it shall come in a day when there shall be heard of fires, and tempests, and vapors of smoke in foreign lands, and there shall also be heard of wars, rumors of wars, and earthquakes in divers places."

- "Yea, it shall come in a day when there shall be great pollutions upon the face of the earth;"

- ". . . there shall be murders, and robbing, and lying, and deceivings, and whoredoms, and all manner of abominations;"

- ". . . When there shall be many who will say, Do this, or do that, and it mattereth not, for the Lord will uphold such at the last day."

- "Yea, it shall come a day when there shall be churches built up that say: Come unto me, and for your money you shall be forgiven of your sins."2

We all go through phases of our lives where we wish we could be saved. It may be a relationship, an addiction, health issues, temporal, mental, emotional or spiritual. We play the "what if" game—spending too much time worrying about issues that we can do nothing about or will never occur. We often look for superheroes, in name only, that present themselves with the intention of "saving our day" when in reality they are attempting to build their power and fortune at the expense of those around them.

The warriors of America's armed forces are living superheroes that risk their lives in the name of justice and freedom around the world, defending these principles whenever they come under attack.

Serving their country many of them pledge themselves to be ennobled by Paul's lesson to the Ephesians: they figuratively strap their loins with truth; put on the breastplate of righteousness; stand tall in the shoes of the gospel of peace; wield the shield of faith; wear the helmet of salvation; and brandish the sword of the Spirit. Ephesians 6:11-13

They know that to be truly victorious they need to "be strong in the Lord, and in the power of His might. Put on the whole armor of God, that ye may be able to stand against the wiles of the Devil. For we wrestle not against flesh and blood, but against principalities, against powers, against the rulers of the darkness of this world, against spiritual wickedness in high places." Ephesians 6:10-12

If you've been in the military or worked for the Defense Department, you know what a challenge coin is. They've been an American military tradition for a century, meant to instill unit pride, improve esprit de corps and reward hard work and excellence.

The coins represent anything from a small unit to the offices of top leaders, such as the defense secretary. There are also coins made for special events, anniversaries and even nonmilitary leaders.

Many service members and veterans proudly display challenge coins at their desks or homes, showing off the many missions they've been on, the top leaders they've met and the units for which they've worked.

There are no written records found about challenge coins in the National Defense University, Pentagon librarians and historians, as well as those with the U.S. Army Center of Military History and the Naval History and Heritage Command. This is probably because the challenge coin tradition didn't start as an officially sanctioned activity.

The most well-known story that the internet produced linked the challenge coin tradition back to World War I. As the U.S. started building up its Army Air Service, many men volunteered to serve. One of those men was a wealthy lieutenant who wanted to give each member of his unit a memento, so he ordered several coin-sized bronze medallions to be made.

The lieutenant put his own medallion in a small leather pouch that he wore around his neck. A short time later, his plane was shot down over Germany. He survived but was captured by a German patrol, who took all of his identifiable items so he would have no way to identify himself if he escaped. What they didn't take was the small pouch with the medallion.

The lieutenant was taken to a small town near the front lines of the war. Despite his lack of ID, he managed to find some civilian clothing and escaped anyway, eventually stumbling into a French outpost. Wary of anyone not in uniform, the French soldiers didn't recognize his accent and immediately assumed he was an enemy.

They initially planned to execute him, since they couldn't ID him. But the lieutenant, remembering he still had the small pouch around his neck, pulled out the coin to show the soldiers his unit's insignia. One of the Frenchmen recognized that insignia, so he was spared.

Instead of being executed, the lieutenant was given a bottle of wine, probably as a form of reparation for his initial treatment. When he finally made it back to his squadron, it became a tradition for all service members to carry a unit-emblazoned coin at all times, just in case.3

A true story or not, challenge coins offer comfort to the brave men and women who fight righteously against the world-rulers of darkness and the hosts of wickedness. One of the more popular coins produced is the "Put on the Whole Armor of God" pledge.

An ancient superhero who lived during the first century BC according to the Book of Mormon was Captain Moroni. He was an important Nephite military commander who was first mentioned in the Book of Alma as "the chief captain over the Nephites." He is presented as a righteous and skilled military commander. Among his accomplishments were his extensive preparations for battle and his fierce defense of the right of the Nephites to govern themselves and worship as they saw fit.

According to the Book of Mormon, Moroni was "only twenty and five years old when he was appointed chief captain" of the Nephites. The appointment came in response to a looming war with several sects that included Nephite dissenters. The Lamanite army attacked the Nephites in the land of Jershon and the battle ended on the banks of the river Sidon.

In this war, Moroni set to work readying the Nephite people with body armor for the first time. He sent spies to investigate the Lamanites' weaknesses, and then he led his troops with the plan to surround those of the Lamanites.

Moroni's overriding objective was to defend his people and their right to worship their God as they pleased.

Ultimately, Moroni met that objective, which resulted in keeping many of the Lamanites from ever coming to combat against the Nephites again.

Moroni introduced to the Nephites revolutionary strategies in military tactics, safety, and precaution. He kept the people physically safe while he prayed, guiding and leading his armies by divine intervention.

He was also known by his people for his firm ideology and integrity and his constant willingness to support the causes of personal freedom gaining the people's trust.

Moroni is associated with the "title of liberty", a standard that he raised to rally the Nephites to defend their liberties from a group of dissenters who wanted to establish their leader as a king. Moroni was so angry with Amalickiah's dissension and wicked influence that he tore his coat and wrote upon it, "In memory of our God, our religion, and freedom, and our peace, our wives, and our children." With those words, he rallied his people to defend their families and their freedom and drive out the armies of Amalickiah. Moroni put to death any dissenters who did not flee and would not support the cause of freedom, and his "title of liberty" was raised over every Nephite tower.4

I place Fred Rogers in my category of superhero in our modern times. My medical doctor father called him a savior to many of the home from school latch key children who watched TV waiting for their parents to come from work. Most programs were entertaining and kept children busy but Mister Rogers' Neighborhood was something special in the way it helped children prepare for adult life.

Mister Rogers' Neighborhood emphasized young children's social and emotional needs, focused on the child's developing psyche and feelings and sense of moral and ethical reasoning, as well as early childhood education concepts. As the Washington Post noted, Rogers taught young children about civility, tolerance, sharing, and self-worth "in a reassuring tone and leisurely cadence." He tackled difficult topics such as the death of a family pet, sibling rivalry, the addition of a newborn into a family, moving and enrolling in a new school, and divorce. For example, he wrote a special segment that dealt with the assassination of Robert F. Kennedy that aired on June 7, 1968, days after the assassination occurred. I remember sitting down with my grandchild and watching Mister Rogers technique explaining how a goldfish breathes. I came away with ideas about how I might do a more effective job reaching out to the cub scouts in my troop.

Fred Rogers mentioned that when he was a boy and would see scary things in the news, his mother would say to him, "Look for the helpers. You will always find people who are helping." To this day, especially in times of "disaster", I remember my mother's words and I am always comforted by realizing that there are still so many helpers—so many caring people in this world.

Roger's biographer Maxwell King Wrote, "Whenever a great tragedy strikes such as war, famine, mass shootings, or even an outbreak of populist rage, millions of people turn to Fred's messages about life. Then the web is filled with his words and images. With fascinating frequency, his written messages and video clips surge across the internet, reaching hundreds of thousands of people who, confronted with a tough issue or ominous development, open themselves to Rogers' messages emphasizing the values of patience, reflection, silence in a noisy world, quiet contemplation, of simplicity, of active listening and the practice of human kindness.5

My favorite superhero as a child was Mighty Mouse: Mister Trouble never hangs around, when there is a wrong to right, though we are in danger, never despair and don't worry at all. Here I come, to save the day. That means that Mighty Mouse is on his way to join the fight, on the sea or on the land, he gets the situation well in hand. Here I come to save the day—that means Mighty Mouse is on his way!

With Mighty Mouse available to save my day and my dog Judy to hug and cry on when the need arose; somehow, I made it through childhood without feelings that I was damaged goods.6

1. *The Psychology of Superheroes: Why We Love Them and How They Help, By Final Boss, October 2020.*
2. *Book of Mormon, Mormon Chapter 8, pages 481-484.*
3. *The Challenge Coin Tradition: Do You Know How It Started?, OOD News, by Katie Lange, 2017.*
4-5. *Wikipedia.*
6. *Mighty Mouse Song Lyrics.*

52

AM I MISSING ANYTHING

It was Christmas Eve; and, as usual, George Mason was the last to leave the office. He walked over to a massive safe, spun the dials, and swung the heavy door open. Making sure the door would not close behind him, he stepped inside. A square of white cardboard was taped just above the topmost row of strongboxes. On the card a few words were written. George Mason stared at those words, remembering….. Exactly one year ago he had entered this self-same vault. And then, behind his back, slowly, noiselessly, the ponderous door swung shut. He was trapped—entombed in the sudden and terrifying dark. He hurled himself at the unyielding door, his hoarse cry sounding like an explosion. Through his mind flashed all the stories he had heard of men found suffocated in time vaults. No clock controlled this mechanism; the safe would remain locked until the next day when it was opened from the outside. He was trapped and not sure if he would live to see the next day.

Bronnie Ware an Australian palliative nurse has counseled the dying in their last days and revealed the most common regrets we have at the end of our lives. She spent several years caring for patients in the last 12 weeks of their lives. She recorded their dying epiphanies in a blog called Inspiration and Chai, which gathered so much attention that she put her observations into a book called *The Top Five Regrets of the Dying*. Ware writes of the phenomenal clarity of vision that people gain at the end of their lives, and how we might learn from their wisdom. "When questioned about any regrets they had or anything they would do differently," she says, "common themes surfaced again and again." Here are the top five regrets of the dying, as witnessed by Ware:

1. I wish I'd had the courage to live a life true to myself, not the life others expected of me: "This was the most common regret of all. When people realize that their life is almost over and look back clearly on it, it is easy to see how many dreams have gone unfulfilled. Most people had not honored even a half of their dreams and had to die knowing that it was due to choices they had made, or not made. Health brings a freedom very few realize, until they no longer have it."

2. I wish I hadn't worked so hard: "This came from every male patient that I nursed. They missed their children's youth and their partner's companionship. Women also spoke of this regret, but as most were from an older generation, many of the female patients had not been breadwinners. All of the men I nursed deeply regretted spending so much of their lives on the treadmill of a work existence."

3. I wish I'd had the courage to express my feelings: "Many people suppressed their feelings in order to

keep peace with others. As a result, they settled for a mediocre existence and never became who they were truly capable of becoming. Many developed illnesses relating to the bitterness and resentment they carried as a result."

4. I wish I had stayed in touch with my friends: "Often they would not truly realize the full benefits of old friends until their dying weeks and it was not always possible to track them down. Many had become so caught up in their own lives that they had let golden friendships slip by over the years. There were many deep regrets about not giving friendships the time and effort that they deserved. Everyone misses their friends when they are dying."

5. I wish that I had let myself be happier: "This is a surprisingly common one. Many did not realize until the end that happiness is a choice. They had stayed stuck in old patterns and habits. The so-called 'comfort' of familiarity overflowed into their emotions, as well as their physical lives. Fear of change had them pretending to others, and to their selves, that they were content, when deep within, they longed to laugh properly and have silliness in their life again."1

When physical or emotional illness strikes, our immediate need is to be healed. Whether it's a scraped knee or a broken heart, a serious disease or a deep sadness, what we long for, first and foremost, is freedom from pain. We simply want to be healed. Some ailments are overcome easily, and we can get on with life without much trouble. Some sicknesses of the body or mind are more difficult to manage, and healing may take years. And then there are chronic illnesses that are simply incurable and can make life seem almost unbearable. But even in the most trying circumstances, there is a source of relief that is available to all. When the body cannot readily respond to our best healing efforts, there is a balm that can provide peace of mind and hope of heart.

Many, despite their personal burdens, have found that peace and hope as they reach out in service to others. One woman undergoing treatment for cancer made head scarves as a gift for women who, like her, had lost their hair. A man who came frequently to the hospital for chemotherapy brought doughnuts to share with those he met. These simple acts of kindness brought cheer and optimism to both givers and receivers.

After years of health and vigor, a young woman was given a medical diagnosis that meant a drastic change in her capacity and lifestyle. Besides physical pain, she now faced anxiety and fear as she worked to cope with her new reality. But she found she could turn to three sources for healing: her family and friends, her God, and herself. Her family and friends helped her relieve stress and reassured her that she would be OK. She also turned to God, spending meaningful time developing her spiritual life and strengthening her faith in His love and influence. Finally, this brave young woman began to treat herself with greater compassion and to care for herself in a way that contributed to her feelings of self-confidence and well-being.2

A client of mine, Mrs. Mackey, lived in an environment of financial difficulties, had a relative living in her home increasing the stresses in her life, and was battling terminal cancer. She was always a delight to visit with. She spent time with neighborhood children and read them stories. I got the impression that she often served as a parent when the parents were away or unable to work with their kids.

Mrs. Mackey also made hand tied quilts that she gave away to people with more needs (in her opinion) than hers. I once insisted on giving her some money to buy material for the quilts. In return she surprised me with one of the quilts that I hold special and have used over the years to keep my legs and arms warm in the evenings.

We had a stray cat dropped off at Camden Pet Hospital with wounds from what was suspected to be a car accident. The cat had a brain injury and circled continuously when walking. We decided to keep it as a hospital cat but Mrs. Mackey insisted on adopting her. She always wanted to help anyone in any way she could. She was convinced that she was going to survive cancer and each day to her was a present (gift). I've learned from her how I should overcome the anxieties and fears that come my way.

The cat eventually improved enough to take care of itself and until Mrs. Mackey passed, often in severe pain from the cancer in her chest and arm muscles, she continued to read to the children and tie her quilts. Recently my wife tied quilts intended to be donated for those less fortunate than we are. I couldn't help but think of what Mrs. Mackey must have been going through when my wife mentioned how tying the quilts made her arms and hands sore.3

When Mrs. Mackie passed I wrote, "Dear Mrs. Lois Mackie Family and Friends: I would like to take a moment to let you know how wonderful a person Lois was. Every time she came into my hospital she brought with her a smile, optimism, love and energy. No matter what her trials she was "getting better and life was wonderful." The last time I saw her she mentioned that she was "cured one more time by the grace of God and that he still had things she needed to accomplish before it was time for her to go home." She also always stated how she kept my monthly letters so that she could read them to her "children friends."

On my couch is a blanket Lois made for me. Pretty much all my five children and thirteen grandchildren plus my wife, some friends and I have warmed ourselves with that blanket one time or another. I have other blankets but I have left only this one in my family room because every time I see it laying there it reminds me of the shoulder and upper body muscle problems Lois had and the pain she must have gone through to make the many blankets she did for other's comfort.

She reminds me a lot of my ninety-two-year-old mother. The last day I saw her she said that she was getting a little better each day, she was happy and told my family that she had friends to visit with over lunch. Mom passed just a few days later.

Lois loved her pets and I will always remember her tortoise that hibernated in her closet each winter and after waking up in the spring she would bring it in to see me for its physical exam and a B-complex injection. Those visits stopped when the tortoise became so heavy that she couldn't lift it into the car. And, it seemed to get along just fine without annual physical exams and injections.

She had been touched by the Spirit and knew that "God is our refuge and strength..." Psalm 46:1. May the depth of your faith and the love of those who share your loss comfort you at this time of sadness and celebration of her life. With Sympathy and Prayers.4

Then realization hit George Mason. No one would come tomorrow—tomorrow was Christmas. Once more he flung himself at the door, shouting wildly, until he sank on his knees exhausted. Silence came, high-pitched, singing silence that seemed deafening. More than thirty-six hours would pass before anyone came - thirty-six hours in a steel box three feet wide, eight feet long, and seven feet high. Would the oxygen last? Perspiring and breathing heavily, he felt his way around the floor. Then, in the far right-hand corner, just above the floor, he found a small circular opening. Quickly he thrust his finger into it and felt, faint but unmistakable, a cool current of air. The tension release was so sudden that he burst into tears.

But at last he sat up. Surely he would not have to stay trapped for the full thirty-six hours. Somebody would miss him. But who? He was unmarried and lived alone. The maid who cleaned his apartment was just a servant; he had always treated her as such. He had been invited to spend Christmas Eve with his brother's family; but the children got on his nerves and expected presents. A friend had asked him to go to a home for elderly people on Christmas Day and play the piano - George Mason was a good musician. But he had made some excuse or other; he had intended to sit at home, listening to some new recordings he was giving himself.

George Mason dug his nails into the palms of his hands until the pain balanced the misery in his mind. Nobody would come and let him out, nobody, nobody, nobody... Miserably the whole of Christmas Day went by, and the succeeding night. On the morning after Christmas the head clerk came into the office at the usual time, opened the safe, and then went on into his private office. No one saw George Mason stagger out into the corridor, run to the water cooler, and drink great gulps of water. No one paid any attention to him as he left and took a taxi home.

Then he shaved, changed his wrinkled clothes, ate breakfast and returned to his office where his employees greeted him casually. That day he met several acquaintances and talked to his own brother. Grimly, the truth closed in on George Mason. He had vanished from human society during the great festival of brotherhood; no one had missed him at all. Reluctantly, George Mason began to think about the true meaning of Christmas. Was it possible that he had been blind all these years with selfishness, indifference, pride? Was not giving, after all, the essence of Christmas because it marked the time God gave His son to the world?

All through the year that followed, with little hesitant deeds of kindness, with small, unnoticed acts of unselfishness, George Mason tried to prepare himself. Now, once more, it was Christmas Eve. Slowly he backed out of the safe, closed it. He touched its grim steel face lightly, almost affectionately, and left the office. There he goes now in his black overcoat and hat, the same George Mason as a year ago. Or is it? He walks a few blocks, flags a taxi, and is anxious not to be late. His nephews are expecting him to help them trim the tree. Afterwards, he is taking his brother and his sister-in-law to a Christmas play.

Why is he so happy? Why does this jostling against others, laden as he is with bundles, exhilarate and delight him? Perhaps the card has something to do with it, the card he taped inside his office safe last New Years' Day. On the card is written, in George Mason's own hand: "To love people, to be indispensable somewhere - that is the purpose of life. That is the secret of happiness."5

President Gordon B. Hinckley stated, "Sometimes in our day, as we walk our narrow paths and fill our little niches of responsibility, we lose sight of the grand picture. When I was a small boy, draft horses were common. An important part of the harness was the bridle. On the bridle were blinders, one on each side. They were so placed that the horse could see only straight ahead and not to either side. They were designed to keep him from becoming frightened or distracted and to keep his attention on the road at his feet.

Some of us do our work as if we had blinders on our eyes. We see only our own little narrow track. We catch nothing of the broader vision...Each of us has a small field to cultivate. While so doing, we must never lose sight of the greater picture, the large composite of the divine destiny of our work. It was given us by God our Eternal Father, and each of us has a part to play in the weaving of its magnificent tapestry. Our individual contribution may be small, but it is not unimportant..."6

Do we passively let life take its course, allowing one day to flow into the next, without a sense of purpose? Dr. Patricia A. Boyle and her colleagues recently conducted a study indicating that having a mission in life can "help stave off cognitive decline and promote a broadly healthier, longer life." When you set and pursue meaningful goals, you help your brain, your body - your life. There are so many ways to add purpose to life. And it doesn't need to be anything grandiose. "The first step," Dr. Boyle explains, "is to think about what is important to you, what energizes and motivates you, what gives you the sense that life is meaningful."

Some volunteer to help those in need. Some become mentors, sharing their wisdom and experience. Others focus on self-improvement, learning a new language or a new skill. One young man spends months training guide dogs for the visually impaired. A busy young mother finds a few minutes each morning to think of ways she can influence her children for good. A grandma who can no longer write calls her friends and extended family members on special occasions.

Each, in his or her own way, finds purpose. And although life can be demanding and tedious at times, when we decide to live with purpose, the quality of our life improves. We don't just float; we sail purposefully to our destination.7

1. *Bronnie Ware, The Top Five Regrets of the Dying, 2012.*

2. *Music & The Spoken Word Broadcast, June 23, 2019, 4,684.*

3. *Walter R. Hoge, 2021.*

4. *Walter R. Hoge, September 21, 2014.*

5. *The Man Who Missed Christmas, Reverend J. Edgar Park 1879-1956.*

6. *Teachings of Presidents of the Church: Gordon B. Hinckley.*

7. *Thomas S. Monson, "The Race of Life," Ensign 05/2012, 92, Diane Cole, "Why You Need to Find a Mission, "Wall Street Journal, 01/11/2013, Music & the Spoken Word #4363.*

53

WHERE DO I WANT TO BE GOING?

Ben Carson said of himself, "I was the worst student in my whole fifth-grade class." One day Ben took a math test with 30 problems. The student behind him corrected it and handed it back. The teacher, Mrs. Williamson, started calling each student's name for the score. Finally, she got to Ben. Out of embarrassment, he mumbled the answer. Mrs. Williamson, thinking he had said "9," replied that for Ben to score 9 out of 30 was a wonderful improvement. The student behind Ben then yelled out, "Not nine! ... He got none ... right." Ben said he wanted to drop through the floor.

Ben Carson's mom grew up with 24 children in a foster home, had only a third-grade education, and could not read. She was thirteen years old when she met and married Robert Carson, a twenty-eight-year-old minister. The couple moved to Detroit and had two sons together. Later Sonya discovered that her husband was a bigamist with another secret family. Ben was eight years old and his brother, Curtis, was ten when their parents divorced.

Sonya Carson moved her sons to Boston where she lived with her sister for a short time. Later, she returned to the ghettos of Detroit and worked in as many as three jobs at a time to support herself and her boys. There were days when she left before the boys woke up and was unable to return home until late that night. Nonetheless, she was fiercely self-reliant and had a firm belief that God would help her and her sons if they did their part.

One day a turning point came in her life and that of her sons. It dawned on her that successful people for whom she cleaned homes had libraries—they read.1

Whatever your mind can conceive and believe, your mind can achieve. Napoleon Hill published a book in 1937 during the Great Depression called *Think and Grow Rich*. It gives direct, simple, even brilliant advice on implementing Seventeen Principles of Success. With it, he encourages us to focus our ideas & enthusiasm into a comprehensive and coherent plan for prosperity. This book remains the biggest seller of Napoleon Hill's books. BusinessWeek magazines Best-Seller List ranked it the sixth best-selling paperback business book 70 years after it was published. His book is the result of more than twenty years of study of many individuals who had amassed personal fortunes.

While the book's title and much of the writing concerns increasing income, the author proclaims that his philosophy can help people succeed in any line of work, to do and be anything they can imagine if they can put in perspective what they want out of life. "If you would plant for days, plant flowers. If you would plant for years, plant trees. If you would plant for eternity, plant ideas!"2

Napoleon's 17 Principles of Success are the essence of the action and attitudes of everyone who has ever had a lasting accomplishment. If you make them your actions & attitudes, you will realize every one of your worthwhile goals:

* Develop Definiteness of Purpose - "If you have a strong purpose in life, you don't have to be pushed. Your passion will drive you there."—*Roy T. Bennett.*
* Assemble an Attractive Personality - Personality has power to uplift, power to depress, power to curse, and power to bless. *Paul P. Harris.*
* Use Applied Faith - Faith is taking the first step even when you don't see the whole staircase.—*Martin Luther King, Jr.*
* Go the Extra Mile - Only those who go the extra mile can find out how far they can go. *Author?*
* Create Personal Initiative - Initiative is doing the right thing without being told. *Victor Hugo.*
* Build a Positive Mental Attitude - A strong positive mental attitude will create more miracles than any wonder drug. *Patricia Neal.*
* Control Your Enthusiasm - I do have a childlike enthusiasm at times. I certainly enjoy life and get pleasure sometimes in childish things. *Brian Baumgartner.*
* Enforce Self-Discipline - With self-discipline most anything is possible. *Theodore Roosevelt.*
* Think Accurately - Fast is fine, but accuracy is everything. *Wyatt Earp.*

* Control Your Attention - Smart people focus on the right things. *Jensen Huang.*
* Inspire Teamwork - Unity is strength... when there is teamwork and collaboration, wonderful things can be achieved. *Mattie Stepanek.*
* Learn from Adversity & Defeat - In prosperity, our friends know us; in adversity, we know our friends. *John Churton Collins.*
* Cultivate Creative Vision - You never have to change anything you got up in the middle of the night to write." *Saul Bellow.*
* Maintain Sound Health - I believe that the greatest gift you can give your family and the world is a healthy you. *Joyce Meyer.*
* Budget Your Time & Money - Everything in life... has to have balance. *Donna Karan.*
* Use Cosmic Habit-force - Faith gives you an inner strength and a sense of balance and perspective in life. *Gregory Peck.*3

When Ben was in the fifth grade and came home with an unsatisfactory report card, Sonya knew she needed to ask God for the wisdom she needed to help her boys.

After work Sonya Carson went home and turned off the television that Ben and his brother were watching. She said in essence: You boys are watching too much television. In your free time you will go to the library, read two books a week and give me a report.

The boys were shocked. Ben said he had never read a book in his entire life except when required to do so at school. They protested, they complained, they argued, but it was to no avail. Then Ben reflected, "She laid down the law. I didn't like the rule, but her determination to see us improve changed the course of my life." Sonya began applying her life motto of "Learn to do your best and God will do the rest."

A devout member of the Seventh Day Adventist Church, Sonya believed in the power of God and knew that education was the road to success for her sons. Ben Carson was receiving an award when he quoted these words his mom often said to him: "Bennie, if you can read, honey, you can learn just about anything you want to know." Sonya's limiting her sons' television viewing to two programs a week and visits to the public library changed their lives.

Each week the boys were required to check out and read two library books. Sonya required her boys to write a book report on one of those books each week and she would use a highlighter pen to grade those reports. Later both boys realized that their mom had not read those reports she had graded. Sonya was not able to read.

And what a change it made. By the seventh grade Ben was at the top of his class. He went on to attend Yale University on a scholarship, then Johns Hopkins medical school, where at age 33 he became its chief of pediatric neurosurgery and a world-renowned surgeon. How was that possible? Largely because of a mother who, without many of the advantages of life, magnified her calling as a parent.

We might all ask ourselves: do our children receive our best spiritual, intellectual, and creative efforts, or do they receive our leftover time and talents, after we have given our all to our outside pursuits? In the life to come, I do not know if titles such as religious leader, lawyer, doctor, president or CEO will survive, but I do know that the titles of husband and wife, father and mother, will continue and be revered, worlds without end. That is one reason it is so important to honor our responsibilities as parents here on earth so we can prepare for those even greater, but similar, responsibilities in the life to come.1

The Seventeen Principles of Success in one way or another help us prepare and sustain joyfully happy careers and lives. In my life enthusiasm and appreciation for the complexity of animal life, staying healthy, sinking roots and staying in one area to practice veterinary medicine, establishing a close relationship with many pet owner families, and avoiding financial or marriage difficulties have helped me be successful and stay interested in practicing well into my seventies.

Hardly a day goes by that I don't visit with a client that we have special memories and the work helps keep up my brain plasticity. Most of my children and grandchildren do not live in the area. However, many of my client families are still nearby and help me have a "wonderful day in my neighborhood" on a regular basis.

When it's all said and done is it the titles, fame or fortune that really matters in this life. In 1965 David O. McKay shared his vision on what will be discussed in our "God talk" with our Father in Heaven after we slip through the veil into eternity.

A group of brethren in the Physical Facilities Department of the Church were doing some work outside the Hotel Utah apartment of President David O. McKay. As President McKay stopped to explain to them the importance of the work in which they were engaged, he paused and told them the following:

Let me assure you, Brethren, that someday you will have a personal priesthood interview with the Savior, Himself. If you are interested, I will tell you the order in which He will ask you to account for your earthly responsibilities.

* First, He will request an accountability report about your relationship with your wife. Have you actively been engaged in making her happy and ensuring that her needs have been met as an individual?
* Second, He will want an accountability report about each of your children individually. He will not attempt to have this for simply a family stewardship but will request information about your relationship to each and every child.
* Third, He will want to know what you personally have done with the talents you were given in the pre-existence.
* Fourth, He will want a summary of your activity in your Church assignments. He will not be necessarily interested in what assignments you have had, for in his eyes the home teacher and a mission president are probably equals, but He will request a summary of how you have been of service to your fellowmen in your Church assignments.
* Fifth, He will have no interest in how you earned your living, but if you were honest in all your dealings.

*   Sixth, He will ask for an accountability on what you have done to contribute in a positive manner to your community, state, country and the world.4

May we be able to meet these tests with affirmative answers and receive a loving welcome home from the Lord, who we hope will say, "Well done, thou good and faithful servant."

It is my fervent desire that each of us will use our God-given intelligence to gain the knowledge, wisdom, and understanding in our hearts to meet life's tests and trials and to endure to the end.

May each of us use our gifts and talents to protect, love, and lift others in a caring way is my prayer, in the name of Jesus Christ. Amen.5

Progress towards success begins with a fundamental question: Where am I going?

1. *Ben Carson, Gifted Hands: The Ben Carson Story (1990) & Tad R. Callister, Sunday School General President, "Parents: The Prime Gospel Teachers of Their Children, Ensign, November 2014.*

2. *asquare.buzz.*

3. *Napoleon Hill published a book in 1937 during the Great Depression called Think and Grow Rich.*

4. *Notes of Fred A. Baker, Managing Director, Department of Physical Facilities, 1965.*

5. *speeches.byu.edu/talks/Robert-d-hales, understanding-heart.*

54

DO YOU DESERVE A CERAMIC OR STYROFOAM CUP?

I heard a story about a former Under Secretary of Defense who gave a speech at a large conference. He took his place on the stage and began talking, sharing his prepared remarks with the audience. He paused to take a sip of coffee from the Styrofoam cup he'd brought on stage with him. He took another sip, looked down at the cup and smiled. "You know, he said, interrupting his own speech. I spoke here last year. I presented at this conference on this stage. But last year, I was still an Under Secretary. I flew here in business class and when I landed, there was someone waiting for me at the airport to take me to my hotel. Upon arriving at my hotel there was someone else waiting for me. They had already checked me into the hotel, so they handed me my key and escorted me up to my room. The next morning, when I came down, again there was someone waiting for me in the lobby to drive me to this same venue that we are in today. I was taken through a back entrance, shown to the greenroom and handed a cup of coffee in a beautiful ceramic cup."

"But this year, as I stand here to speak to you, I am no longer the Under Secretary, I flew here coach class and when I arrived at the airport yesterday there was no one there to meet me. I took a taxi to the hotel, and when I got there, I checked myself in and went by myself to my room. This morning, I came down to the lobby and caught another taxi to come here. I came in the front door and found my way backstage. Once there, I asked one of the techs if there was any coffee. He pointed to a coffee machine on a table against the wall. So, I walked over and poured myself a cup of coffee into this here Styrofoam cup." He then raised the cup to show the audience.

"It occurs to me, he continued, the ceramic cup they gave me last year…it was never meant for me at all. It was meant for the position I held. I deserve a Styrofoam cup. This is the most important lesson I can impart to all of you. All the perks, all the benefits and advantages you may get for the rank or position you hold, they aren't meant for you. They are meant for the role you fill. And when you leave your role, which eventually you will, they will give the ceramic cup to the person who replaces you. Because you only ever deserved a Styrofoam cup."[1]

The comments made above by Simon Sinek reminded me of the movie "All About Schmidt" (Jack Nicholson - 2002) in which Warren Schmidt is retiring from his position as an actuary with "Woodmen of the World", an insurance company in Omaha, Nebraska. As he leaves work for the last time the office staff seems agreeable that they would be glad to have him drop by the office at his convenience. After the retirement dinner, Schmidt finds it hard to adjust to his new life, feeling useless. One day Schmidt revisits his young successor to offer his help, but the offer is politely declined. As he leaves the building, Schmidt sees the contents and files of his office, the sum of his entire career, set out for garbage collectors.

I couldn't help but place myself in Schmidt's situation. For the first time in my life I was faced with the thoughts that this could be me in a few years and how would I "handle" this change in my life. From as long as I can remember the animal kingdom has been a part of me. As a child you would find me spending hours on a ditch bank or the Snake River (Idaho) catching small minnows, snails, tadpoles, frogs, etcetera, bringing them home and placing them in an aquarium . Later I raised pigeons, cattle, pigs, horses, rabbits and had two special white rats (in time there became many rats—Mom took most of them to Idaho State University, she said to "get them an education") and a bum lamb named Agatha. I spent my summers working on farms.

In high school I took courses in agriculture (even though I was raised a city boy), joined the "Future Farmers of America" and later enrolled at the University of Idaho in the animal science department, and then graduate school and veterinary school at Purdue University. I came to the realization that if I retired and found my life away from the animal kingdom I might crash in a bigger way than Schmidt did. I have now practiced for nearing 50 years and have never felt burned out (however - worn out many times). My kid's mom used to have to work out a "vacation with the family" behind my back. I would be told by the receptionist that I had been blocked out of the appointment book and I might as well check the agenda my family had scheduled for me.

Wilford Andersen commented, When I was called to serve as a General Authority, President Uchtdorf reminded me of some timely advice he had received at the time of his call. "Brother Andersen," I was told, "as a General Authority, people will be very kind to you. They will compliment you on your service and tell you how much they like your conference talks. But when they do, just don't inhale."

Compliments can be like a drug. If we are not careful, they can cloud our judgment and create in us an ungodly desire for more and more praise and credit. And if our friends don't give us the credit we so richly deserve, we risk rotator cuff injury from trying to pat ourselves on the back.

Like our ancient adversary, we whisper to ourselves that we deserve the credit, for surely we have done it. And thus we can behold how false, and also the unsteadiness of the hearts of the children of men; yea, we can see that the Lord in his great infinite goodness doth bless and prosper those who put their trust in him. Yea, and we may see at the very time when he doth prosper his people, yea, in the increase of their fields, their flocks and their herds, and in gold, and in silver, and in all manner of precious things of every kind and art; . . . yea, and in fine, doing all things for the welfare and happiness of his people; yea, then is the time that they do harden their hearts, and do forget the Lord their God, and do trample under their feet the Holy One—yea, and this because of their ease, and their exceedingly great prosperity."2

As I ponder Schmidt's dilemma, the comments of Wilford Andersen, and my attempts to prepare to leave a wonderful long career - there is one thing that I do know. If I were going down in an airplane and seeing my life coming to an end my thoughts would be concerning the welfare of my family; and, the hopes that they found their experiences being a part of my life uplifting and one where they felt my love and concern for their wellbeing. And, especially that they knew that I would much prefer a Styrofoam cup where ever they might find me (especially, working with the animals). "Then Peter opened his mouth, and said, Of a truth I perceive that God is no respecter (*gives special consideration*) of persons."3

KING, PAUPER, RICH, OR POOR—"THE POSITION(S) WE HOLD IN THIS LIFE MAY INCLUDE A CERAMIC CUP...LET US REMEMBER THAT ONE DAY IT WILL BE REPLACED BY STYROFOAM IN THIS LIFE OR WHEN WE ENTER THE NEXT..."

1. *"LEADER'S ONLY EAT LAST", Simon Sinek, 'The Ceramic Cup', p67-68.*
2. *WILFORD W. ANDERSEN, of the Seventy, November 7, 2017.*
3. *Acts 10:34.*

55

CAUSING HURT TO
THOSE WE LOVE

In bygone days there lived a King, who was very fond of hunting. The King had a Falcon, which he counted among his chief treasures. This Falcon the King always fed from his own hand, and always carried on his own wrist when he went on the hunt.

One day, when the court was out a-hunting, a deer ran across their path and the King started in pursuit. Some of the royal party followed, but none of them could ride as well and as fast as the King. Through some accident the King did not overtake the deer, and became separated from his companions. Hot and thirsty from his long ride, he dismounted to find some water.

For a long time he sought in vain, but at last came to the foot of a hill, where a small stream was trickling down over the rocks. The King took a drinking-cup from his sash and held it beneath the stream, catching the water drop by drop. As soon as it was full, he raised the cup to his lips, and was just about to drink when the Falcon flew up, hit the cup, and upset it.

"You awkward bird!" exclaimed the King, and began once more patiently to fill the cup from the stream. A second time the King raised it to his lips, and a second time the Falcon flew against it, knocking it from the King's hand. The thirsty King could no longer control his rage. He threw the Falcon to the ground with such force that he killed it instantly.

Just then one of the attendants rode up, and, hearing that the King was thirsty, drew out his flask to give the King to drink. But the King shook his head. "I have set my heart," he said, "on drinking from this stream which runs down the mountain-side; but it takes a long time to fill a cup drop by drop here at the bottom. Go therefore to the top of the hill, and bring me down a cup of water from the source of this spring."

The attendant did as the King commanded, but returned with his cup empty. "Your Majesty," he cried, "you have been perilously near death. At the source of the spring lies a dead dragon, whose poison has polluted the entire stream. Will your Majesty not drink of the water in my flask?"

He held out the cup, and as the King drank, the tears rolled down his face. "Alas, why does the King weep?" asked the attendant, in great alarm.

The King picked up the dead bird. "This Falcon, the dearest of all my treasures," he said sadly, "saved my life twice, and I, by my own act of anger, killed it with one cruel blow!"1

It's impossible to go through life without causing hurt to those people we love. We may have to do this for their own good—for instance, when we need to be firm with a child who we believe is engaged in destructive behaviors. We may inflict pain on another person when we need to do what is right for us, such as leaving a relationship.

Most of us feel bad about inflicting pain and might stay in situations way too long for fear of hurting our loved ones. But some people go through life causing a great deal of hurt to other people, including romantic partners and even their own children. They might even fall under the label of narcissistic or borderline personality types. Claire Jack, PhD shares some of the reasons why people repeatedly hurt other people.

- Some people have low empathy for others. They have a hard time "walking in someone else's shoes" and cannot see other people's perspectives. They're actually unaware of the hurt they cause other people and things that hurt you might not hurt them.

- When people don't like themselves, no matter how good of a front they put on, they are likely to project this self-dislike onto others. Particularly if this self-dislike stems from abusive behavior which they have experienced in their past. They may be driven by a desire to hurt you in the same way they have been hurt, to bring you down and cause you pain in the same ways they have experienced it.

- When people place a low value on themselves, which is essentially what low self-esteem is, they may be unaware of how hurtful their actions are to other people. Let's say it's your turn to host your mother for Christmas and it's important to you and your family to do so. Your mother, however, doesn't value herself and doesn't know how important it is so she makes arrangements to visit your sister for the third time in a row. Your mother's low self-esteem means that she has a very different perspective from you on how important her presence is and causes you deep hurt in the process.

- Often, people hurt others unintentionally - but sometimes, people deliberately set out to hurt others. If your partner puts you down in front of others, it may make her feel superior. If she criticizes you, name calls, or puts down your achievements, it may make her feel like she has power within the relationship. He or she may want you to be in a weakened position so that he or she can become dominant within the relationship and create a power imbalance which is in their favor. Hurting others can be part of a strategy to weaken you.

- Some people enjoy the process of hurting other people. Again, this usually stems from a deeply disturbed and potentially abusive childhood. They may be acting out things which have taken place in their own life, this time with them as the abuser, and may experience a thrill from hurting you. Inflicting pain on you may be a distraction from their own pain, a way of "getting even" for things which have happened to them and a way to feel something deeply in a way which makes sense to them, given their past experiences.

They attracted you because you're easily hurt. This can be a hard pill to swallow, but we don't choose people by accident. Subconsciously, we choose people who fit in with our unconscious understanding of their world. If your partner is someone who inflicts hurt on other people for all the above reasons, they may have chosen you because they see you as someone who will respond appropriately to their behavior. Just as your partner might repeatedly attract people who he can hurt, you might be attracted to relationships in which you are hurt. If you grew up with a parent who was abusive towards you, whether emotionally or physically, you may be attracted to a partner who acts in the same way.2

There were many reasons I was attracted, pursued and asked Sheryl to marry me. I was never told why she found me attractive enough to put up with my behavior or be willing to enter a relationship that would include my willingness to care for and protect her and a future family. I did however find out very early in my marriage that there were definite things she expected from me.

On my wedding night we uncorked the champaign bottles given by friends to help reduce the pain of our first night together and poured them down the drain. She then took a wash cloth and with warm water and soap showed me how to wash my pimpled face.

Attending college at the University of Idaho we were socializing among married couples and showing off I boasted a challenge before the group—"I bet I can make Sheryl angry in less than five minutes." It took much less than that. I lived to regret the intentional hurt I caused her and embarrassment each of us felt in front of our friends.

Still in our first year of marriage Sheryl invited my cousin Tom over for dinner. We were visiting and Sheryl kept reminding us the dinner was ready and about to be ruined. Finally trying to show my stupidity and be funny I said to my cousin, "I guess the dinner is ruined and not fit to eat." I then threw it in the sink.

I also learned that year a phrase that I should not use unless I was prepared for a quick explosive response. The phrase, "If I were you I would." Her response was "you're not me and don't you ever forget it!"

I can only imagine confessing these sins to Dr. Clair Jack and the guilt I would feel as she pointed out the pain I inflicted on my wife during our early marriage. She might have counselled Sheryl by saying, "(he) may have inflicted enough pain on (you and you need to) do what is right for (you by) leaving (the) relationship."

I'm sure the marriage was successful primarily because when Sheryl had had enough of my foolishness she fought back in ways only a women knows. I was pretty well tamed and trained by the time our children joined the scene.

Thirty years ago, Elder Robert D. Hales as a branch president, said, "I was interviewing a man and his wife. The wife was tearing down her husband: he had not been the provider she had expected; he had not been the companion she had dreamed about before her marriage; they could not communicate together without arguing and attacking one another.

Her husband loved her, and yet she hurt him. There were tears in his eyes as he absorbed the verbal abuse. I couldn't take any more as a twenty-one-year-old branch president, and asked, "Why do you hurt this person who loves you the most? Why do you hurt a husband who would do anything to help you?"

Her answer startled me. 'Oh, I guess we argue and injure those we love because we can hurt them the most.'

I have never forgotten that incident. There is truth in that example. We can't hurt a stranger as much as we can a loved one. We know just what to do to hurt our companions, parents, or brothers and sisters. We know where they are vulnerable. We know how they can be hurt the most by our actions. To many it seems to be a test of faith in life to be wounded by those closest to us. Of Jesus it is said in Zechariah that when asked where he had received the wounds in his hands, he would say that he "was wounded in the house of [his] friends." (Zech. 13:6.) Isn't it true that God, our Father, and his Son grieve when we sin? When we fail to be obedient and accept the atoning sacrifice of our Lord, aren't we hurting Him who loves us most?"3

Contemplating thoughts about hurting most the ones we love I was carried back to Mr. and Mrs. Edge. I say Mr. and Mrs. because I never heard Mrs. Edge call her husband anything but Mr. Edge. They had a cute little white dog I helped care for and before I got to know them they looked like a happy aging couple with English accents caring for themselves as best they knew how.

Mr. Edge was shorter than his wife and it was obvious that he worshiped her. Watching him trying to care for her every need reminded me of a servant caring for royalty as a red carpet was rolled out before her and he tended to her desires. She played the part by constantly saying Mr. Edge do this or that, Mr. Edge did this or that and Mr. Edge did not do this or that. To me he was more like an indentured servant than a part of the royal family.

One day I heard her voice at the grocery store barking out her to do list at Mr. Edge. When I turned into the grocery isle they were in I saw her directing Mr. Edge up a ladder to retrieve an item he couldn't reach.

At work one day I received a call from Mrs. Edge. She was very distraught and spoke in a near whisper. As I remember her words, "Dr. Hoge, I don't know what I am going to do. Last night Mr. Edge was making a lot of noise in the dark of our bedroom. I told him that I could not sleep, shut up and be quiet so I could sleep. After a few minutes all was quiet. Today when I awoke, I found him dead laying on the floor next to my bed. I'm lost, don't know what to do and miss him so much."

When Sheryl was fighting terminal colon cancer, I asked her why she had never shared intimate inner thoughts with me. She replied, "When you don't let a person know your inner thoughts they can't hurt you." I don't need Dr. Clair Jack's council to answer why I wasn't able to share a closer relationship during our marriage.

1. *Maude Barrows Dutton, The Riverside Readers, page 60, 1912.*
2. *Psychology Today, Claire Jack, PhD, Posted August 10, 2020.*
3. *Your Sorrow Shall Be Turned to Joy, Robert D. Hales, of the Seventy, Oct 1983 Conference.*

56

IVAN GARDNER AND LETTER FROM HOWARD H. HARRINGTON

Ivan Gardner was a successful business man, seemed to care about all those around him, a leader in his faith, had a smile that radiated from his face and he bonded a friendship with me that lasted until he passed in 1991. He loved to make caramel popcorn, ate onion sandwiches, loved taking his children and grand kids to Disneyland, at Christmas time liked reading the first Christmas story while his offspring reenacted it and enjoyed watching the livestock in his corral and the crops in his field grow. The only off-colored word I remember him using, and he often did so, was the word "crrrap." Another often used phrase was, "Let me ask you a question?" The question was a way of finding out what your thoughts were so he could interject what he felt about the subject.

Working for him, he tolerated the damage I caused to a grain combine, a main line to an irrigation system and others I don't recall. Probably the biggest mistake I made involved a hired hand named Carlos Medina.

Ivan's son Lance remembers him as being about 19 or 20 with a wife Juanita and a new baby. They lived in a house that was on the farm in Rising River in the Rose Idaho area. Carlos moved irrigation pipes on that farm, 6-8 lines morning and evening every day except Sunday. He also worked throughout the day. He only worked for his Dad one or perhaps two summers. One winter he and his family went to Texas or Oklahoma and he sent word back that he would not be returning because he had gotten a job with the railroad. He was a great worker and just a good person.

Carlos and I were assigned to spray a patch of potatoes that were set apart as a project for Lance. Instead of spraying the DDT insecticide on the field, the potatoes were sprayed with a weed killer called 2-4 D. They were being grown for the R.T. French Company in Shelley Idaho. That spring they offered to their contract growers an acre of potatoes for one of their children over a certain age and below a certain age. The idea was to give that child the experience of keeping the records that go along with growing a crop. Every step in the production cycle was to be recorded and the amount of time it took. The mistake Carlos and I made became immediately obvious because the odor in the field was not DDT.

Although a mistake was made the crop did not suffer much and the end results were better than knobby potatoes. Lance remembers that he got a check for $300.00 as a prize for having the second-best crop. "I did score 100% on the weed control portion of the experience. They may not have been the best crop ever but they were surely one of the most weed free crop we ever had."

Lance Gardner mentioned that "his Uncle Morris and Ivan farmed together some. The farm where he lived was developed by his dad and Uncle Morris. They removed the sagebrush and were the first farmers to produce a crop on that farm.

They mainly helped one another with potato harvest. In the days when we had school kids come and pick potatoes, working together ensured both that they had a crew and would get the potatoes harvested.

In those days they had to wait for a killing frost to kill the potato vines before they could even start harvest. They purchased their first potato harvester together. This machine did away with the use of school kids and pickers. The only pickers now needed were clod pickers because the early harvesters did not eliminate dirt from getting into the truck like the machines of today. There was always plenty of dirt that had to be scraped out of the potato cellar after every truck load.

I remember Dad telling us that he decided while he was milking the cows for his father that if he ever became his own boss there would be no milk cows. Grandpa Gardner argued with Dad about not having milk cows. He felt that a farmer could not make enough money just raising crops to support a growing family. There was also an argument about raising sugar beets. Dad never raised them either. His money crops were the potatoes he raised for the R.T. French Company under a contract.

Dad never minded the early hours that he had learned to accept while growing up. One of the issues that he discussed a little one time was the odor that a dairyman has on his hands. Dad's comment was that you could not ever get rid of that odor as long as you were milking cows. The nature of the job had you washing the cow's teats twice each day to ensure that the manure was gone and the teat was clean enough to put the automatic milker on. Instead of milk cows, Dad had beef calves that he purchased and feed every winter. He enjoyed watching them grow."1

When Ivan was a boy he contracted undulant fever (brucellosis) most likely from drinking unpasteurized milk, cheese or ice cream. At the time, there were no antibiotics available to treat the disease. He told me the need to be up early in the morning and available in the early afternoon to milk cows was restrictive when it came to other things that needed to be done on the farm.

Lance mentioned that the undulant fever surely had some bearing on the choice to not have milk cows. He also wrote that he does not remember undulant fever being talked about or even discussed other than letting the family know about how sick he got and how long it took to recover. Ivan's family never used raw milk. The milk his children received growing up was always heat treated, pasteurized, to kill infectious bacteria and homogenized to keep the fat gathering on top, make it look more appealing and increase the shelf life - by breaking up the fat particles enough to disperse them throughout the milk.

Brucellosis is found globally and is a reportable disease in most countries. The disease causes flu-like symptoms, including fever that comes and goes, weakness, malaise and weight loss, and person-to-person transmission is rare.

People all over the world, in every culture and clime, pursue greatness. The desire to succeed and excel is as universal as it is natural. But what is true greatness? How do we know when we have achieved it? Some might say that greatness happens in rare, extraordinary moments when someone of unusual ability rises above his or her peers. Howard W. Hunter, himself a great man and beloved spiritual leader, offered a different definition of greatness when he said, "To do one's best in the face of the commonplace struggles of life—and possibly in the face of failure—and to continue to endure and to persevere in the ongoing difficulties of life when those struggles and tasks contribute to others' progress and happiness, . . . this is true greatness." Such greatness—far from being unusual or exceptional—can be found all around us, though it sometimes goes unnoticed. It is evident in the humble heroes who consistently do the right thing, even when no one is watching.2

Letter written to Ivan Gardner's family from Howard H. Harrington June 23, 1995 (Ivan Gardner passed 1991)

To the Gardner Family in the memory of my special friend Ivan Gardner:

The company of Rocky-Mountain Machinery Co. (Blackfoot Idaho) is my brain child, and I started organization of the firm in 1963. By spring of 1964 we were under way with business and signed our first dealer contract with John Deere Company on April 19, 1964. It was a really big undertaking for a guy that was a high school dropout and whose job experience consisted of several years of truck driving and a couple of years of selling farm machinery for Lockwood Corporation and Dahlman Manfacturing Company. Both manufactured potato harvesting and potato handling equipment. The year 1964 was a good year for me to start a small business, mainly because the fall of 1964 brought good potato prices that really gave me and the general economy of our area a shot in the arm. We were riding high and our business really started to grow. 1965 saw us have some real sound growth in our business in spite of the fact that there were eight other competitive dealerships in our trade area.

Even though we were grossly under financed, this growth would continue on through the spring and summer of 1966. However, the fall of that year would burst our business bubble and put a strangle hold on the economy that would have some difficult and long lasting effects. On the 14th day of October of that year, following some rainy weather, we would be hit by an extremely hard frost. So hard in fact that a large portion of the crops in Bingham County would never be harvested at all and the potatoes would suffer the most. A lot of potatoes that were harvested after the frost were stored with those harvested prior to the frost and the results were horrible.

It was a complete loss of crop for some farmers. The spring of 1967 would find us in the grip of an agricultural recession. Many of our customers could not make their payments and our sales of equipment would fall to a near zero. In fact, one customer alone would have the bank foreclose on him and the results would cost our company nearly $100,000.00. By the fall of 1967 I would stand the pressure no more. I had literally reached the end of my rope and had decided to contact John Deere Co. and advise them that we were bankrupt. The letter that I was sending them would serve as an official notice of our closure. This took place on a Saturday afternoon in late November. In as much as this was a Saturday in the winter, our place of business was closed and I was there alone pondering our fate and future.

As I sat there, a knock came to the back door of my little office and who should be there but my friend Ivan Gardner. He was in need of a five gallon can of hydraulic oil. I quickly found it for him. However, after he had made his purchase, instead of leaving, he had sensed my despair and sat down across the desk from me and asked what was troubling me. I put my head in my hands and cried as I told him of our financial plight, of the letter to John

Deere Co. and of my decision to close our business. I poured my heart out to him along with my tears. As I quit sobbing and regained my composure to some degree, Ivan would put his arm around my shoulder and with a display of gentle compassion, would teach me one of the greatest sermons I have ever heard in my life. I will never forget the lessons he taught me that day.

Of course, I cannot quote him verbatim, but the massage is as clear in my mind today as it was 29 years ago. He simply told me this. Tough times never last but tough people will. Then he took me by the hand and led me outside of the office. He pointed to the sky, to the mountains and the valley itself and said, "this world we live in and see every day is simply the handy work of our God. But when we look in the mirror, we see a son of God. As a son of God, you were never put on earth to fail but to learn, to grow, and to succeed at all things in life. And, as a son of this same God, you are indeed entitled to inspiration from Him." He went on to tell me that as long as I would keep God on my side it would never ever matter who or what was against me. Then he reassured me that we needed each other and that I was not in this struggle alone. The farmers needed me just as well as I needed them and if I would simply keep trying, that in due time all would work out for the best. Then he took the hand written letter that I had prepared to mail to John Deere Company and tore it to bits and tossed it into the waste basket.

Time, or course, has proven that he was correct in all of his statements. My business, to this day, has remained a good solid business, in no small part, to the special encouragement from Ivan Gardner.

Throughout the years of my life, I have sat at the feet of great men in the business world as well as religion experts and have been taught by many motivational speakers. But none have ever touched me quite like the words of wisdom and encouragement of this great man to a brother like me in great need of his help. I miss him, and even now as I write this, tears come to my eyes as I think of him. You, members of his family, surely you must realize that you are indeed a blessed generation, if for no other reason than the fact that the blood of Ivan Gardner, a great man, runs through your veins. You have been taught concepts by him that will serve as a guide to you forever.

Signed by
Howard H. Harrington

Ivan's daughter, Sheryl, and I became friends during our sophomore year in high school. I found Ivan easy going, very likable and a parent figure that helped me get through some difficult teenage years. I worked on his farm during my high school and part of my college education.

I enjoyed the cool dewy mornings working in the fields, his wife's wonderful lunches that were prepared for the crew and the Q and A sessions we had driving together back and forth from the farm.

I drove Sheryl and friends just under 600 miles back and forth to the University of Idaho in Moscow. Ivan would always fill my trunk with frozen meat from a steer he had slaughtered. He was not pleased having his daughter so far away from home and would give me a look (both before and after we were married) that burned into my brain that he expected me to respect and care for her as her father had.

Sheryl did not have financial difficulties while attending college. If money got tight she had a father that took care of it. During our marriage she did not want her children to go bare foot or without food. I did not want to not be able to meet payroll, pay for drugs and supplies, or mortgage payments. There were times she didn't watch her budget and over spent. When the cows of debt came home our relationship was not the best.

Just as we were leaving for a Gardner Family vacation to Rocky Point in Mexico, I opened a credit card bill that to me was a whooper. In Rocky Point I confronted Ivan and asked him how he could have raised a child so poorly equipped at balancing a budget? He said to me, "I raised her this way so you would be successful." I was furious and could barely contain myself from making comments that would have damaged our relationship.

I carried the issue home with me and confronted my accountant. He gave me the option of taking away her checking account and credit cards or building a backup emergency business account. If I made the first choice I would mostly likely lower Sheryl's self-esteem, strain our relationship and may end up with ½ the assets of Camden Pet Hospital and be looking for another chick to bed down with.

I chose number two and when she came forward on bended knee from debt, I had a slush (at least hidden from her) fund available to take care of my needs and she appreciated rather than despised me.

Thanks to Ivan and the mother of my children, many years later when my son Jeremy purchased half of my corporation, I gave myself a $250,000.00 bonus as I moved that emergency fund into my private account.

The only time I recall Ivan displaying anger was when he and his wife, Jean, were driving my children, Brad and Jana, from Idaho to California. Brad didn't remember much about the event—here is Jana's recollections:

"I remember we were coming home from Idaho. I think Brad and I got to stay alone with Grandpa and Grandma for a week or so, and they were driving us home. Brad and I were in the backseat of whatever luxury sedan they owned at the time. I remember crying and whining about whatever Brad was doing to me (Brad was called Mr. Maytag in our family—the agitator). It could have been a number of things—teasing, giving me a dead leg, not sharing…he was pretty ruthless back then. I was surprised when Grandpa abruptly pulled over to the side of the road and got out of the car. I remember him walking around to the back of the car. He proceeded to take Brad out of the car and spank him with his shoe. Right there on the side of the freeway!

I felt guilty for making Grandpa mad enough to hurt Brad like that. Although, he probably deserved it. The teasing and tattling had probably been going on for quite a while before Grandpa finally pulled over. I don't think he would've done that if Brad hadn't forced his hand…or in this case his shoe."3

Previous to the above event I was spanking Brad with my bare hand on his cloths covered derriere. With large droplets of tears in his eyes, he cried out, "If it makes you feel any better just keep spanking me!"

After this event I never had the heart to spank another one of my children.

> *"As a son of God, you were never put on earth to fail but to learn, to grow, and to succeed at all things in life. And, as a son of this same God, you are indeed entitled to inspiration from Him." Ivan Gardner.*

> *"Success is little more than a chemical compound of man with moment." Philip Guedalla (1889-1944).*

1. *Lance Gardner, personal communication, April 10, 2022. Lance also stated, "The Howard Harrington letter always brings tears to my eyes (me too). I never knew about this (letter)until one day after dad had passed away Howard took me into his office and shared it with me. We are very fortunate to call this wonderful man our father."*

2. *What is True Greatness? -Lloyd D. Newell, Broadcast Number 4,522 Music & the Spoken Word, Sunday, May 15, 2016.*
3. *Text message, Janalyn Hart, 04/12/2022.*

57

SOME SURPRISING GEOLOGY OF JOSEPH SMITH'S SEER STONE

There has been a flurry of articles over the last several years regarding the translation process of the Book of Mormon, and in particular the use of "seer stones". On August 4th of 2015, The Church of Jesus Christ of Latter-day Saints released its latest volume of the Joseph Smith Papers Projectwhich included photos of the brown seer stone that Joseph Smith used in the translation process of the Book of Mormon.1

Numerous articles have been written on the topic, and I will not attempt to duplicate those efforts. What I would like to share are just a few things that I *haven't* seen published, which some may find quite fascinating. Genesis Stones and Blue-Green Algae.

When I get curious about something, I sometimes like to go down deep to the foundations and see what they're built upon. Then I can work my way up to the details. For Joseph's brown seer stone, that means geology. As soon as I saw the pictures, I wanted to know what kind of stone it was. I didn't know if I would find any answers, but I decided to make a little effort and the first rock shop I could get to answer the phone was one in southern Utah.

I asked if they had a tenured geologist there that could identify a stone for me. "I haven't worked here that long," the guy who answered the phone said, "but I'm a geologist and I can probably help you." I asked him if he had seen anything about the 'seer stone' picture that the LDS Church had released and if from the picture he could tell me what kind of stone it was and where it came from. "OH YEAH!" he said. "In fact, we've been waiting for someone to call, because it's actually pretty cool. You're the first one."

Suffice it to say, he had my attention. The first thing he told me is that the stone is almost definitely banded-iron jasper. He then told me that it has a nick-name: Genesis Stone. It turns out that banded-iron jasper is a "secondary" or "trace" fossil (rocks that are evidence of life, but don't contain any primary evidence, such as bones). They are evidence of one of the very first forms of life on earth: photosynthetic cyanobacteria, also known as blue-green algae.

He explained that about 2.5 billion years ago, the earth's atmosphere was inhospitable to almost all forms of life now in existence. As algae started to create oxygen in the earth's atmosphere, it reacted with plentiful iron in the earth's acidic ocean. These iron deposits then oxidized. In layman's terms…the oceans rusted. As the iron deposits became oxidized, they fell out of dilution with sea water and accumulated as sediment on the ocean floors. This process seemed to occur in waves, hence causing the formation of the sedimentary rock known as banded iron jasper. The ribbons you see in the seer stone are those iron layers on top of more common shale. The "Genesis" name comes from the implications that the stone attests in regards to the 2nd day of creation.

I also learned that when this process of the earth's atmosphere becoming more oxidized began, there was still one massive Pangaea or super-continent. I was told that, without getting too much into the theories of super-continent drift and plate tectonics, I should just take their word that most continents just have one banded iron jasper deposit, all stemming from one original deposit. In North America, that area is in a rough oval spanning parts of Wyoming and Minnesota. It doesn't come *anywhere near* upstate New York, where Joseph originally found the seer stone down 15 feet or so in a well he was digging.

So how did it get there? The experts told me that judging by the egg-like shape, as well as the way it appeared to be polished and its distant location from the deposit area, it was probably a "gastrolith", also known as a "gizzard stone". Banded-iron jasper is rare enough on its own, but a gizzard stone is one that a dinosaur inadvertently digests, and then when it dies and decays, the stone returns to the environment. The time spent inside the dinosaur would actually aid in digestion, as well as polish the stone's edges in a manner slightly differently than it would if it were smoothed out in a stream or on a beach.

So, millions of years ago, a dinosaur near Wyoming/Minnesota probably ate a rock, traversed to upstate New York, and died. Glaciers and erosion could easily account for the 15' depth. Normal banded-iron jaspers are actually found on the surface, and have more of a wind-blasted look, with flat surfaces and polygonal angles. I was told a smooth egg-shaped banded-iron jasper stone like Joseph's was an almost impossibly rare find. In fact, as far as I can tell, it is the only banded-iron jasper gizzard stone in existence.

Beginning about 1.8 billion years ago, atmospheric conditions were such that banded-iron jasper ceased to form in the oceans. From this time forward, earth had an oxidized atmosphere which allowed oxygen-breathing life to begin, and all the iron in the oceans had oxidized. Therefore, all rocks of this type are at least as old as that.

It is undisputed that Joseph did in fact come into possession of an incredibly rare rock that was formed and prepared long before it was actually needed. The provenance of ownership from Joseph to the LDS Church is pretty clear, and its exact look and features were described by witnesses long before almost anyone had even explored the banded iron jasper deposit areas out west. He could not have known how rare it was, but what he could have known is that no one had ever seen anything like it. It was unique.

Wanting one of my own, I could only find a single vendor that offered them, and his selection was sparse. Despite their rarity, for one reason or another, the world does not place a lot of value on banded-iron jasper. I believe there are a number of interesting takeaways in the geology of Joseph's brown seer stone, and if anything, it offers evidence that the Lord knows the end from the beginning, and that by small and simple things are great things brought to pass.2

Banded iron formations (also known as branded ironstone formations or BIF's) are distinctive units of sedimentary rock that are almost always of Precambrian age. A typical BIF consists of repeated, thin layers of iron oxides, either magnetite (Fe3O4) or hematite (Fe2O3) alternating with bands of iron poor shale and chert. Most Wyoming BIF are aged as old as 2.5 billion and some are as "young" as 1.8 billion. Due to the extreme age of these formations, almost all BIF have undergone some faulting, fracturing, folding, compaction, veining, intrusions and metamorphism. Although all BIF formations are probably metamorphosed to some degree, their general character is still sedimentary.

The conventional concept is that the branded iron layers were formed in sea water as the result of oxygen released by photosynthetic cyanobacteria (blue green algae), combining with dissolved iron in Earth's oceans to form insoluble iron oxides, which precipitated out, forming a thin layer on the substrate, which may have been anoxic mud (forming shale and chert).

Each band is similar to a varve, to the extent that the banding is assumed to result from cyclic variations in available oxygen. For reasons largely unknown, this was a periodic process resulting in the alternating bands of iron oxide and shale. The periodic process might have been due to seasonal fluctuations or storm surges or other hypothesis.

It is assumed that initially the Earth started out with vast amounts of iron dissolved in the world's acidic seas. Eventually, as photosynthetic organisms generated oxygen, the available iron in the Earth's oceans was precipitated out as oxides. At the tipping point where the oceans became permanently oxygenated, small variations in oxygen production produced pulses of free oxygen in the surface waters, alternating the pulses of iron oxide deposition.

Since the origin of the iron layer is derived from a living organism, the photosynthetic bacteria, BIF actually qualifies as a trace fossil. Some of the oldest fossils known to man just predate banded iron formations. Bacteria are believed to be the earliest life forms on Earth and eventually the oxygen producing varieties formed the BIF and helped transform the Earth.

The conditions to form BIF, dissolved iron and episodic oxygenation, existed early in Earth's history and then once the Earth's oxygen levels stabilized the conditions for banded iron formation all but ceased to exist.3

The physical Creation itself was staged through ordered periods of time. In Genesis and Moses, those periods are called days. But in the book of Abraham, each period is referred to as a time. Whether termed a day, a time, or an age, each phase was a period between two identifiable events—a division of eternity:

* In period one included the creation of atmospheric heavens and physical earth, culminating in the emergence of light from darkness.
* In period two, the waters were divided between the surface of the earth and its atmospheric heavens. Provision was made for clouds and rain to give life to all that would later dwell upon the earth.
* In period three, plant life began. The earth was organized to bring forth grass, herbs, trees, and vegetation—each growing from its own seed.
* Period four was a time of further development. Lights in the expanse of the heaven were organized so there could be seasons and other means of

measuring time. During this period, the sun, the moon, the stars, and the earth were placed in proper relationship to one another. The sun, with its vast stores of hydrogen, was to serve as a giant furnace to provide light and heat for the earth and life upon it.

* In period five, fish, fowl, and "every living creature" were added. They were made fruitful and able to multiply—in the sea and on the earth—each after its own kind.

* In the sixth period, creation of life continued. The beasts of the earth were made after their kind, cattle after their kind, and everything which "creepeth upon the earth"—again, after its own kind. Then the Gods counseled together and said: "Let us go down and form man in our image, after our likeness . . .

"So the Gods went down to organize man in their own image, in the image of the Gods to form they him, male and female to form they them." Thus, Adam and Eve were formed. And they were blessed to "be fruitful, and multiply, and replenish the earth, and subdue it: and have dominion over the fish of the sea, and over the fowl of the air, and over every living thing that moveth upon the earth."

* The seventh period was designated as a time of rest.4

Joseph Smith's Seer Stone: "The stone found by Joseph Smith measuring, 5.5 by 3.5 by about 4 cm. This stone matches some descriptions of the seer stone used by Joseph Smith during the translation of the Book of Mormon. One contemporary observer remembered Smith's seer stone as an 'oval-shaped, chocolate-colored stone, about the size on an egg, only flatter.' According to David Whitmer, Joseph Smith gave the seer stone he used in the translation to Oliver Cowdery after the translation was completed.

Shortly after Cowdery died in 1850, his brother-in-law Phineas Young acquired the stone from Cowdery's widow, Elizabeth Whitmer Cowdery. Brigham Young apparently acquired the stone from his brother Phineas, and it remained in his possession throughout his life. Young, who apparently did not have any seer stones other than those that had belonged to Smith, stated in 1853 that he had 'Joseph's 1st Seer Stone, which I (h)ad from O(liver) C(owdery).

Zina Diantha Huntington Young, a plural wife of Brigham Young, bought two seer stones from his estate, and she and her daughter Zina Young Williams Card then donated them to the president of the Church of Jesus Christ of Latter-day Saints. The box in which the stone pictured here is stored contains a handwritten note, on which is written the name of Zina Williams Card. The box and the note link the stone to Card, and through her, to the history of the stone used by Joseph Smith to translate...5

For millennia, many people throughout the world have accepted the idea that physical objects can be used for sacred purposes. The Bible affirms that God worked through objects such as the rod of Aaron, a brass serpent, and the ark of the covenant. Jesus later healed a blind man by applying spittle to the man's eyes. The Book of Mormon describes a sacred purpose for specially designated stones. In one passage, the brother of Jared asked the Lord to touch 16 small stones, which were "white and clear, even as transparent glass" (Ether 3:1). After the Lord's finger touched the stones, they provided light for the Jaredites as they journeyed across the ocean. Another verse speaks of sacred stones that "shall magnify to the eyes of men these things which ye shall write" (Ether 3:24). In Joseph Smith's day, some individuals claimed that they had a gift to "see," or receive divine or supernatural messages, through seer stones. These beliefs came from the Bible and from European cultural traditions brought to early America by immigrants. Joseph Smith and his family accepted these beliefs, and Joseph occasionally used stones he located in the ground to help neighbors find missing objects or search for buried treasure.

When Joseph Smith received the golden plates in 1827, he also received a translation instrument with them, "two stones in silver bows" used by "'seers' in ancient or former times" (Joseph Smith—History 1:35). This instrument was referred to in the Book of Mormon as the "interpreters." During the translation of the Book of Mormon, Joseph Smith apparently used both of these instruments—the interpreters and his seer stone—interchangeably. They worked in much the same way, and the early Saints sometimes used the term "Urim and Thummim" to refer to the seer stone as well as the interpreters.

The Prophet also received several of the revelations found today in the Doctrine and Covenants by means of these instruments of revelation. As Joseph became more experienced in spiritual matters, he eventually started receiving revelation without these aids.6

So, Joseph Smith's Seer Stone that aided in the translation and revelation of scriptures came from a rock that was created 1.8 million years ago and was shaped and smoothed in the gizzard of a dinosaur. If so, I believe since seer stones and dinosaurs have made great books and movies in the past that there are a number of interesting takeaways in the future about the geology of Joseph's brown seer stone.

I have purchased some BIF stones. They are all different ruff shapes and sizes, have milk or dark chocolate colored sediment lines between a dark gray material and most of them attract magnets. I have placed them in my safe, some in my museum collections and in the future my offspring will probably find no use for them as they try to decide what to do with my estate.

However, if the science holds true, branded-iron jasper stones may set the stage for a great leap in helping understand the history of the earth and just maybe shed more light into the lives of dinosaurs. Who knows, BIF stones may end up on necklaces, rings, bracelets and other fine jewelry. If nothing else, this information offers a little more evidence about how the Lord knows the end from the beginning, and that by small and simple things are great things brought to pass.2&7

1. *Revelations and Translations, Volume 3: Printer's Manuscript of the Book of Mormon.*
2. *Christopher Kirkland, Meridian Magazine, April 12, 2018.*
3. *ReallyOldRocks.com. PO Box 376 Lander, WY 82520*
4. *Genesis 1 & 2, Moses 2 & 3, Science Magazine VOL 363 ISSUE 6423, 01/11/2019 and VOL 371 ISSUE 6534 03/12/2021.*
5. *The Joseph Smith Papers, Revelations and Translations, Vol 3, Part 1, Printer's Manuscript...xx-xxi.*
6. *"Book of Mormon Translation," Gospel Topics, topics. lds.org, Richard E. Turley, Robin E. Jensen, and Mark Ashurst-McGee, "Joseph the Seer", Oct. 2015, 48–55, "Seer stone," josephsmithpapers.org and "Joseph Smith's Seer Stones", MH Mackay & NJ Frederick, 2016.*
7. *Thoughts from Walter R Hoge.*

58

ARE WE NEAR APOCALYPTIC TIMES?

The year 2020 is turning out to be one that most of us will remember for the rest of our lives. The pandemic COVID-19 virus has been filled with tragedy and limited our life style; cities have been held hostage by unhappy demonstrators; wildland fires and smoke have caused financial stress, loss of loved ones and other health issues. Hurricanes and tornados are battering our gulf coast and the mid and eastern United States, and a few earth quakes have added to the mix.

My daughter in law mentioned recently that we must be truly living in the last days and the earth may soon be set to be destroyed. The Four Horsemen of the Apocalypse were on their way. The Four Horseman commonly identified as Pestilence (or Conquest), War, Famine, and Death, whose arrival heralds the end of the world, as described in the biblical book of Revelation. To top it off our president, his family and White House staff (including the vice president) have been infected with the corona virus. Thankfully the potential for a serious crisis seems to be avoided. Unfortunately, during the pandemic of 1918 President

Woodrow Wilson was not so lucky and the consequences of him getting the virus most likely helped set the stage for World War II and the United States Government finding the need to pass the 25th Amendment to the constitution.

The 1918 influenza pandemic killed an estimated 50 to 100 million people worldwide—including some 675,000 (approximately 654 deaths per 100,000 population compared to as of October 2020 COVID-19's 67 deaths per 100,000) Americans—in just 15 months. But Woodrow Wilson's White House largely ignored the global health crisis, focusing instead on the Great War enveloping Europe. Wilson wanted the focus to remain on the war effort. Anything negative was viewed as hurting morale.

In private, the president acknowledged the threat posed by the virus, which struck a number of people in his inner circle, his oldest daughter and multiple Secret Service members. Even the White House sheep came down with the flu and Wilson himself contracted the disease shortly after arriving in Paris in April 1919 for peace talks aimed at determining the direction of a post-World War I Europe.

At a decidedly inopportune moment the president was suddenly taken violently sick with the influenza at a time when the whole of civilization seemed to be in the balance. The staff downplayed the president's illness, telling reporters that overwork and Paris' "chilly and rainy weather" had sparked a cold and fever. Wilson began to show signs of severe disorientation. At one point, the president became convinced that he was surrounded by French spies. Something queer was happening in his mind.

Wilson's bout of influenza weakened him physically . . . at the most crucial point of the war negotiations. Days after coming down with the flu, an exhausted Wilson conceded to the other world leaders' demands, setting the stage for what historians believe was a settlement so harsh and onerous to Germans that it became a provocative cause of revived German nationalism ... and, eventually, a rallying cause of Adolf Hitler. Whether Wilson would have pushed harder for more equitable terms if he hadn't come down with the flu is, of course, impossible to discern. The illness certainly drained his stamina and impeded his concentration, in addition to affecting "his mind in other, deeper ways."

Six months after he came down with the flu, Wilson suffered a debilitating stroke in October 1919 that left him paralyzed on his left side and partially blind. Instead of disclosing her husband's stroke, his second wife First Lady Edith Wilson hid his life-threatening condition from politicians, the press and the public, embarking on a self-described "stewardship" that was more accurately a secret presidency.

The first lady was able to assume such broad power due to a lack of constitutional clarity regarding the circumstances under which a president is considered incapacitated. A clearer protocol was only established with the ratification of the 25th Amendment in 1967. Edith continued, for all intents and purposes, to serve as the nation's chief executive until her husband left office in March 1921. The weakened president died three years later, on February 3, 1924.1

Is 2020 the year when The Four Horsemen of the Apocalypse will swarm the earth spreading death and destruction? Or are we just a little "scared to death?" I read a book, called *Scared to Death,* several years ago that "...

tells the inside story of each of the major scares of the past two decades, showing how they have followed a remarkably consistent pattern. It analyzed the crucial role played in each case by scientists who have misread or manipulated the evidence; by the media and lobbyists who eagerly promote the scare without regard to the facts; and finally, by the politicians and officials who come up with an absurdly disproportionate response, leaving us all to pay a colossal price" for making a "so what" into a crisis.2

Let me share a few statistics that may help ease your mind about 2020:

- Chances of dying of COVID-19: All ages is less than one percent (0.64%) & over 65 years of age is 5.6%.
- There is little year to year upward change in the total death rate in the US per 100,000 population: 2017 (858), 2018 (868), 2019 (872) & 2020 (888).
- Chances of dying between 1847-1868 as pioneers moving west. Handcarts 4.7%, Wagons 3.5%, Willie & Martin companies 16.5%, and staying behind in the Illinois area 2.9%.
- Wildland fires (CA, WA & OR) statistics recorded since 1983. Years where more than 10 million acres burned were 2006, 2015 and 2017. So far this year, Sept 18th, these states have had 4.7 million acres burn.
- Hurricanes: Most extreme season was 28 storms in 2005. In the worst category (5) six occurred in a twenty-year period (1980's—1990's) and ten have occurred from the year 2000 through 2020.

- Earthquakes: There were 12,980 in 2019 and 10,876 in 2020. The ten worst earthquakes ranged from 1906 to 2011 and ranged from 8.6 to 9.5 on the Richter scale.

Polls, reported by Wikipedia, conducted in 2012 across 20 countries found over 14% of the people believe the world will end in their lifetime, with percentages ranging from 6% of the people in France to 22% in the US and Turkey. So is the Apocalypse going to occur in our lifetime and there is no hope except to hunker down in our homes and wait for the destroying angles to appear?

A man, who many recognize as a prophet and whose people were to them living in an Apocalyptical time, around 400-420 AD did not think the end of the world was coming. He wrote about a record of his people written on metal that he predicted would be preserved and found before the second coming of Christ.

What has caught my attention are his comments, found in a book about these records published in March 1830, concerning worldly events that would occur at the time his people's record would be found. To me many comments seem to fit very closely with the current conditions we are living in? Let me share his comments just before he buried this ancient record:

- "It shall come forth in a day when it shall be said that miracles are done away."
- "And it shall come in a day when the blood of the saints (I would include this to mean all who

worship their God) shall cry unto the Lord, because of secret combinations and the works of darkness."

- "Yea, it shall come in a day when the power of God shall be denied."

- ". . . and churches become defiled and lifted up in the pride of their hearts . . ."

- "Yea, it shall come in a day when there shall be heard of fires, and tempests, and vapors of smoke in foreign lands, and there shall also be heard of wars, rumors of wars, and earthquakes in divers places."

- "Yea, it shall come in a day when there shall be great pollutions upon the face of the earth;"

- ". . . there shall be murders, and robbing, and lying, and deceivings, and whoredoms, and all manner of abominations;"

- ". . . When there shall be many who will say, Do this, or do that, and it mattereth not, for the Lord will uphold such at the last day."

- "Yea, it shall come a day when there shall be churches built up that say: Come unto me, and for your money you shall be forgiven of you sins."3

In the children's classic *The Secret Garden,* author Frances Hodgson Burnett tells the story of the orphan, Mary Lennox, who is taken to her uncle's house, where she meets her cousin, Colin, who is a recluse. Even though there is nothing wrong with him, he is paralyzed by the fear he will become a hunchback if he lives, and he has convinced himself that he will soon die. Mary Lennox is a lonely child who is determined not to be interested in anything.

One day while walking on her uncle's estate, she stumbles upon the key to the entrance of a garden enclosed by a high wall. Once she enters the garden, a transformation takes place. In working to restore the garden to its former grandeur, she experiences a freshening of her spirit. Colin is coaxed from his gloomy room into the garden, and the author writes this commentary:

"So long as Colin shut himself up in his room and thought only of his fears and weakness and his detestation of people who looked at him and reflected hourly on humps and early death, he was a hysterical half-crazy little hypochondriac who knew nothing of the sunshine and the spring and also did not know that he could get well and could stand upon his feet if he tried to do it. When new beautiful thoughts began to push out the old hideous ones, life began to come back to him, his blood ran healthily through his veins and strength poured into him like a flood. ... Much more surprising things can happen to anyone who, when a disagreeable or discouraged thought comes into his mind, just has sense to remember in time to push it out by putting in an agreeable determinedly courageous one.

Two things cannot be in one place. *'Where you tend a rose, my lad, A thistle cannot grow.'*"

"major scares . . . followed a remarkably consistent pattern . . . scientists have misread or manipulated the evidence, the media and lobbyists eagerly promote the scare . . . and finally, the politicians and officials come up with an absurdly disproportionate response,

leaving us all to pay a colossal price" for making
a "so what" into a crisis." Scared to Death

. . . don't allow ourselves to get paralyzed into a stupor of
inactivity by our sorrow and pain (or fear). 'Where you tend
a rose, my lad, A thistle cannot grow.' The Secret Garden

Apocalypse? Only God knows when
and He isn't talking...YET

1. *Historian John M. Barry, author of The Great Influenza: The Story of the Deadliest Pandemic in History, By Meilan Solly, Smithsonianmag.com 10/02/2020, & Public domain via Wikimedia Commons.*
2. *"Scared to Death", Christopher Booker & Richard North, 2007.*
3. *Book of Mormon, Mormon Chapter 8, pages 481-484 and "Superheroes."*

59

THOUGHTS ON THE THOUGHTS OF ANCIENT GREAT THINKERS

Moses ben Maimon, commonly known as Maimonides and also referred to by the acronym Rambam, was a medieval Sephardic Jewish philosopher who became one of the most prolific and influential Torah scholars of the Middle Ages. In his time, he was also a preeminent astronomer and physician. Born in 1135 or 1138, he worked as a rabbi, physician, and philosopher in Morocco and Egypt. He died in Egypt on December 12, 1204, whence his body was taken to the lower Galilee and buried in Tiberias.

During his lifetime, most Jews greeted Maimonides' writings on Jewish law and ethics with acclaim and gratitude, even as far away as Iraq and Yemen. Yet, while Maimonides rose to become the revered head of the Jewish community in Egypt, his writings also had vociferous critics, particularly in Spain. Nonetheless, he was posthumously acknowledged as among the foremost rabbinical decisors and philosophers in Jewish history, and his copious work comprises a cornerstone of Jewish scholarship. He is sometimes known as "ha Nesher ha Gadol" (the great eagle) in recognition of his outstanding status as a *bona fide* exponent of the Oral Torah. The Oral Torah includes all the 24 books, from the Book of Genesis to the end of the of Tanakh (Chronicles), and it can even mean the totality of Jewish teaching, culture, and practice, whether derived from biblical texts or later rabbinic writings.

Aside from being revered by Jewish historians, Maimonides also figures very prominently in the history of Islamic and Arab sciences and is mentioned extensively in studies. He influenced prominent Arab and Muslim philosophers and scientists. He became a prominent philosopher and polymath in both the Jewish and Islamic worlds.

In his commentary on the Mishnah (tractate Sanhedrin, chapter 10), Maimonides formulates his "13 principles of faith". They summarized what he viewed as the required beliefs of Judaism. (to me, many of these principles of faith are similar to the 13 Articles of Faith written by Joseph Smith):

1. The existence of a creator. (*A of F:1,5,8,9,11*)
2. God's unity and indivisibility into elements—there is no one like Him. (*A of F:1*)
3. God's spirituality and incorporeality. (*A of F:5,9*)
4. God's eternity—the first and the last. (*A of F:1*)
5. God alone should be the object of worship. (*A of F:1,9*)
6. Revelation through God's prophets are true. (*A of F:5,9*)
7. The preeminence of Moses among the prophets. (*A of F:8*)

8. That the entire Torah (*both the Written and Oral law*) are of Divine origin and were dictated to Moses by God on Mt. Sinai. (*A of F:8*)

9. The Torah given by Moses is permanent and will not be replaced or changed.

10. God's awareness of all human actions and thoughts. (*A of F:2,3,5,13*)

11. Reward of righteousness and punishment of evil. (*A of F:2,13*)

12. There will be a coming of the Jewish Messiah. (*A of F:1,10*)

13. The resurrection of the dead. (*A of F:3*) *Wikipedia*

One thing that caught my eye when reading about Maimonides was his writing about the Parable of the Palace and *how it made me think of the similes of Lehi's vision of the tree of life (I Nephi:8-11)*:

As quoted from the *Guide of the Perplexed, Chapter 51* . . . "does not contain any additional matter that has not been treated in the [previous] chapters of this treatise. It is a kind of conclusion, and at the same time it will explain in what manner those worship God who have obtained a true knowledge concerning God; it will direct them how to come to that worship, which is the highest aim man can attain, and show how God protects them in this world till they are removed to eternal life.

I will begin the subject of this chapter with a simile. A king is in his palace, and all his subjects are partly in the country, and partly abroad. Of the former, some have their backs turned towards the king's palace, and their faces in another direction; and some are desirous and zealous to go to the palace, seeking "to inquire in his temple," and to minister before him, but have not yet seen even the face of the wall of the house. Of those that desire to go to the palace, some reach it, and go round about in search of the entrance gate; others have passed through the gate, and walk about in the ante-chamber; and others have succeeded in entering into the inner part of the palace, and being in the same room with the king in the royal palace. But even the latter do not immediately on entering the palace see the king, or speak to him; for, after having entered the inner part of the palace, another effort is required before they can stand before the king—at a distance, or close by—hear his words, or speak to him.

I will now explain the simile which I have made. The people who are abroad (*pride of those in great and spacious building, fountain of filthy water*) are all those that have no religion, neither one based on speculation nor one received by tradition. Such are the extreme Turks that wander about in the north, the Kushites who live in the south, and those in our country who are like these. I consider these as irrational beings, and not as human beings; they are below mankind, but above monkeys, since they have the form and shape of man, and a mental faculty above that of the monkey.

Those who are in the country, but have their backs turned towards the king's palace, (*dark and dreary world*) are those who possess religion, belief, and thought, but happen to hold false doctrines, which they either adopted in consequence of great mistakes made in two their own speculations, or received from others who misled them. Because of these doctrines they recede more and more from the royal palace the more they seem to proceed. These are worse than the first class.

Those who desire to arrive at the palace (*wondering in strange roads, lost their way or tasted of the fruit but were ashamed from being scoffed at*), and to enter it, but have never yet seen it, are the mass of religious people; the multitude that observe the divine commandments, but are ignorant.

Those who arrive at the palace, but go round about it (*Laman & Lemuel, mist of darkness*), are those who devote themselves to the study of the practical law; they believe traditionally in true principles of faith, and learn the practical worship of God, but are not trained in philosophical treatment of the principles of the Law, and do not endeavor to establish the truth of their faith by proof.

Those who undertake to investigate the principles of religion, have come into the antechamber (*pride—mist of darkness*); and there is no doubt that these can also be divided into different grades.

But those who have succeeded in finding a proof for everything that can be proved, who have a true knowledge of God, so far as a true knowledge can be attained, and are near the truth, wherever an approach to the truth is possible, they have reached the goal, and are in the palace in which the king (God) lives (*partook of the fruit of the tree and stayed faithful to the fountain of living water, word of God and love*)."

Maimonides described the coporeal world as constituted of matter and form; matter he resolved into the ultimate elements of fire, air, water and earth, the proportions into which these elements combine determining the character of specific objects. The total universe, he described, as consisting of three strata (compare them to Joseph Smith's understanding of the three degrees of glory):

1. The first strata, the "intelligences" which are forms without matter, act upon the world of matter to shape its destiny (These are they whose bodies are Celestial, whose glory is that of the sun, even the glory of God, the highest of all, whose glory the sun of the firmament is written of as being typical—D&C 76:70).

2. The second strata, the realm of corporeal beings, constitutes a solid globe containing nine spheres, one within another, and like the Intelligences, they are not destructible (And again, we saw the terrestrial world, and behold and lo, these are they who are of the terrestrial, whose glory differs from that of the church of the Firstborn who have received the fulness of the Father, even as that of the moon differs from the sun in the firmament—D&C 76:71).

3. The third strata consists of transient things such as the bodies of men, plants, animals, and minerals. The ruling power in creation, as he phrased it, "emanates from the Creator and is received by Intelligences according to their order; from the Intelligences part of the good and the light bestowed upon them is communicated to the spheres, and the latter being in possession of the abundance obtained of the Intelligences, transmit forces and properties unto the beings of this transient world (And again, we saw the glory of the telestial, which glory is that of the lesser, even as the glory of the stars differs from that of the glory of the moon in the firmament. These are they who received not the

gospel of Christ, neither the testimony of Jesus. These are they who deny not the Holy Spirit…These are they who received not of his fulness in the eternal world, but of the Holy Spirit through the ministration of the terrestrial—D&C 76:81-86).

Last: thoughts I would like to share with you from Maimonides teachings:

"We must bear in mind that all such religious acts as reading the Torah, praying and the performance of other precepts, serve exclusively as the means of causing us to occupy and fill our mind with the precepts of God and free it from worldly business; for we are thus as it were communion with God and undisturbed by any other thing. If we, however, pray with the motion of our lips…but at the same time think of our business…we are like those who are engaged in digging the ground or hewing wood in the forest, without reflecting on the nature of those acts, or by whom they are commanded, or what is their object."

"You must know that even if you were the wisest man in respect to the true knowledge of God, you break the bond between you and God whenever you turn your thoughts entirely to the necessary food or necessary business."

Please note the above thoughts were written
sometime before 1204 AD.

As I have been reading the writings of Maimonides and some of the other ancient great thinkers that lived before and after the birth of Christ. I find it interesting these writers in depth and heavy discussions of such things as the quest for truth, the nature of God and how we should think of Him, Angels, miracles, religion and culture, revelations, Christianity and Jewish/Islam, problems with evil, ethics and others. It's amazing to me how through their study, discussions, prayer and being quickened by the Spirit how close they came to many of the truths about God and His teachings as we understand them.

Fortunately for all of us we now have access to a testimony of truths about our Heavenly Father's plan obtained recently from visual encounters, communication in voice and spiritual revelations.

I'm so pleased that I live in these last days.

Many of the religious questions asked by ancient intellectuals were answered in 1820 (two hundred years ago) on a clear spring morning after a 14-year old boy (Joseph Smith) was referenced a scripture by a minister, "If any of you lack wisdom, let him ask of God, that giveth to all men liberally, and upbraideth not; and it shall be given him. But let him ask in faith, nothing wavering. For he that wavereth is like a wave of the sea driven with the wind and tossed." (James 1:5-6)

Joseph Smith had been deeply concerned about his relationship with his Father in Heaven and desired to be forgiven of his sins and to know the truth about which religion taught the true Gospel. He knelt down in a grove of trees near his family's farm and approached his God in prayer. He received the answer to his personal concerns (he was forgiven of his sins) plus was given knowledge of truths that man had been debating since the beginning of time.

1. God our Father is a personal being, and men and women were made in His image.

2. Jesus is a personage, separate and distinct from the Father.
3. Jesus Christ was declared by the Father to be His Son.
4. Jesus was the conveyer of revelation, as taught in the Bible.
5. The promise of James to ask of God for wisdom was fulfilled.
6. Joseph learned of the reality of an actual being from an unseen world who tried to destroy him.
7. There was a falling away from the Church that was established by Jesus Christ—Joseph was told not to join any of the sects, for they taught the doctrines of men.
8. Joseph Smith became a witness for God and His Son, Jesus Christ.

"We must bear in mind that all such religious acts as reading the Torah, praying and the performance of other precepts, serve exclusively as the means of causing us to occupy and fill our mind with the precepts of God" Maimonides… *"If any of you lack wisdom, let him ask of God, that giveth to all men liberally, and upbraideth not; and it shall be given him."* Jesus Christ

I believe God has communicated with man throughout history and that the spirit has been felt by those seeking understanding and guidance to live by correct principles of the Gospel. I'm sure some of my thoughts are out of context but I feel there are many similes comparing ancient revelations and the knowledge we receive during these latter days.

60

WHAT GIVES MY
LIFE MEANING

College class assignment request from my grand-daughter Kaili for her 76 year-old grandpa: What Gives My Life Meaning?

Work—Everyone needs to work. I fortunately, as of yet, don't need to spend all day working just to stay alive and reasonably healthy. I have had health set-backs that have shown me the dangers of boredom and depression.

I currently work four half days a week in my chosen profession. There are times when I have things that I would rather do than work, but by the end of my shift I usually find myself uplifted. My family and their children have pretty much moved away and the family I have left are the clients I have gotten to know for the last 46 years working in the same location. I know two and three generations of some families and many relationships have been sealed when bad as well as good things have happened to their pets.

Working has been good for my brain plasticity. Keeping current and relying on practice experiences that spark lights of wisdom memories is much better than inactivity and the feeling of brain fog over taking my soul.

I am stimulated by doing the work of volunteerism for those less fortunate than me or helping others make a social or church activity a success. It may involve working in a park or charity facility, setting up and taking down tables and chairs, assisting in planning an activity or furnishing a food dish.

Two days ago, I went over to a friend's house and visited with him so his wife and mine could attend a "ladies-function" for a couple of hours. He had a stroke and can't recognize letters -so reading or writing is a blocked function in his brain. My friend and I had a delightful visit and he lifted my spirits.

I attend ROMEO'S (RetiredOldMenEatingOutSingle) and have a made "from home lunch" once a week with a bunch of over the hill buddies. We visit a couple of hours and talk about near anything boring to younger generations. One of our older seniors gives us a ten-question quiz he finds in the newspaper.

Friendship—everybody needs a friend that they can call on anytime and trust their loyalty and love. Fortunately, my most trusted and caring friend is my wife. Nothing is more miserable or depressing than not have a team mate that is playing the same game.

Special lasting friendships tend to be established when we are young. Leaving home, marrying, establishing a career and having children involve people that we get close to. At least for me, friendships in my youth are the ones that are the most vividly stuck in my mind. It's like calling my brother or one of my sisters. Time has gone by but it seems like we were never apart from each other.

Attending my 50th high school reunion I ran into a friend I'd known from grade school, through high school and a couple of years in college. We played catchup on our lives and then went looking for our wives. We found them embraced in conversation laughing and with smiles on their faces. We had a hard time pulling them away from each other. Before the reunion finished, we were in a car reserving a spot for them with a cruise we were going on -we had a great cruise together. We even renewed our wedding vows on board the ship and started a tradition celebrating our wedding anniversaries on the same date.

Writing—most people want to leave something of value to their children and folks they've known throughout their lives. I know that if I left a journal few if any of my children would read it and there would probably be a lot of their using some of their own imagination interpreting my inner thoughts and motives.

I started writing letters after being asked by a member of my faith to contact members that were not active &/or do not contacts. Visiting was not productive and I felt texting or emails were not very personal. So, I started sending letters with hopefully an uplifting message to the families and related it to some of my personal experiences. I also send them to family members, clients that are special friends or those that have been struggling with personal issues.

I keep these articles, periodically compile them, and have given them to my family for Christmas. I have also placed some of these articles in a book that I have written.

Here again -it helps my brain plasticity. Visiting with clients often brings up memories that are shared in the articles. I am fortunate in having a long-term employee still working with me that helps make sure stories are correct as far as we can remember.

I feel there is a much better chance that my progeny will read these stories and get to know more about my inner thoughts and actions than if it were read in a journal.

Family—it begins and ends with family. Their mother and my goal during the twenty plus years of raising five children was that we were going to make the effort to raise good citizens, educated with a satisfying career; and knowing who they are, where they came from, why they are on this earth and understanding that loving their God, family and others will bring happiness beyond silver or gold.

If successful, the last twenty or thirty years of our lives would be enjoying the fruits of our labors rather than dreading the mistakes we made when our children were at their informative years. The mother of my children did a wonderful job. Unfortunately, she passed just at the time we were just starting to see our children blossom.

I didn't list family first because mine has learned the principle of work and are taking good care of their families. They show friendship with their brothers and sisters and there are no bridges to be mended in their relationships. They are good citizens and I see service from their family and community activities.

My children's relationship within their families of peace, respect and love for God and each other, those around them, and me; gives my life meaning, less anxiety and concern about their welfare, and time to float my boat at work, with friends and writing life stories to keep my brain plasticity and from two of the evils of old age (boredom and depression). I can truly say the last thirty years of my life have been the best and I'm optimistically looking forward to each present day. After all it is a gift.

61

DARK NIGHT OF THE MIND AND SPIRIT

I recall the Christmas Eve 2000 just after the wedding of my oldest daughter Jana, at Good Samaritan Hospital, sitting at the foot of the bed of my unconscious wife, Sheryl, receiving an IV drip with morphine, picking at the Velcro on my watch band, and waiting to hear the x-ray results from the doctor.

I remember, out of frustration, calling down to the radiology department and asking for the report and being told that the doctors were not in the hospital. I responded by telling her that this was Dr. Hoge, that I needed the radiologist's report for a Sheryl Hoge, and her connecting me with the recorded results; "colon cancer—stage four." I was stunned!

Watching her fade in and out of consciousness, I felt inspired to ask if a surgeon could be available to do surgery, even though it was Christmas Eve.

As I was in the surgery waiting room my thoughts were whether I should pray that Sheryl should die under the anesthetic or survive and go through the shock of knowing she was dying from cancer and then having to go through all the pain and suffering.

She didn't die during surgery, did suffer, but I know she would have never traded death for all the wonderful experiences she had with our family during the next 2 ½ years.

How do you best respond when mental or emotional challenges confront you or those you love? The Apostle Peter wrote that disciples of Jesus Christ are to have "compassion one of another." In that spirit I wish to speak to those who suffer from some form of mental illness or emotional disorder, whether those afflictions be slight or severe, of brief duration or persistent over a lifetime. We sense the complexity of such matters when we hear professionals speak of neuroses and psychoses, of genetic predispositions and chromosome defects, of bipolarity, paranoia, and schizophrenia. However, bewildering this all may be, these afflictions are some of the realities of mortal life, and there should be no more shame in acknowledging them than in acknowledging a battle with high blood pressure or the sudden appearance of a malignant tumor.

In striving for some peace and understanding in these difficult matters, it is crucial to remember that we are living—and chose to live—in a fallen world where for divine purposes our pursuit of godliness will be tested and tried again and again. Of greatest assurance in God's plan is that a Savior was promised, a Redeemer, who through our faith in Him would lift us triumphantly over those tests and trials, even though the cost to do so would be unfathomable for both the Father who sent Him and the Son who came. It is only an appreciation of this divine love that will make our own lesser suffering first bearable, then understandable, and finally redemptive.

Let me leave the extraordinary illnesses I have mentioned to concentrate on MDD - "major depressive disorder"—or, more commonly, "depression." When I speak of this, I am not speaking of bad hair days, tax deadlines, or other discouraging moments we all have. Everyone is going to be anxious or downhearted on occasion. The Book of Mormon says Ammon and his brethren were depressed at a very difficult time, and so can the rest of us be. But today I am speaking of something more serious, of an affliction so severe that it significantly restricts a person's ability to function fully, a crater in the mind so deep that no one can responsibly suggest it would surely go away if those victims would just square their shoulders and think more positively—though I am a vigorous advocate of square shoulders and positive thinking!

No, this "dark night of the mind and spirit" is more than mere discouragement. I have seen it come to an absolutely angelic man when his beloved spouse of 50 years passed away. I have seen it in new mothers with what is euphemistically labeled "after-baby blues." I have seen it strike anxious students, military veterans, and grandmothers worried about the well-being of their grown children.

And I have seen it in young fathers trying to provide for their families. In that regard I once terrifyingly saw it in myself. At one point in our married life when financial fears collided with staggering fatigue, I took a psychic blow that was as unanticipated as it was real. With the grace of God and the love of my family, I kept functioning and kept working, but even after all these years I continue to feel a deep sympathy for others more chronically or more deeply afflicted with such gloom than I was. In any case we have all taken courage from those who, in the words of the Prophet Joseph, "search[ed] . . . and contemplate[d] the darkest abyss" and persevered through it—not the least of whom were Abraham Lincoln, Winston Churchill, and Elder George Albert Smith, the latter being one of the most gentle and Christlike men of our dispensation, who battled recurring depression for some years before later becoming the universally beloved eighth prophet and President of The Church of Jesus Christ of Latter-day Saints.1

Columbus left many statements in his journals and other personal writings in which he boldly declared that he believed the Lord directed him in his great undertaking. Referring to his first voyage to America, he once stated, "With a hand that could be felt, the Lord opened my mind to the fact that it would be possible to sail from here to the Indies . . . This was the fire that burned within me . . . Who can doubt that this fire was not merely mine, but also of the Holy Spirit" (West and Ling 105; Columbus most often referred to the New World as the Indies.)

The "dark night of the mind and spirit" of depression struck Columbus somewhere near the coast of Central America Columbus wrote about an experience he had:

". . . Mercifully, the sailor's prayers for rain were answered, and Columbus quickly took advantage of the higher water to get the ships out of the river to the open sea. Three of the ships were successfully floated over the bar; the Gallega and about twenty men under the command of Bartholomew and the intrepid Diego Mendez stayed behind to guard the compound. With the three ships gone and only a few men left behind, the Indians saw their chance. About four hundred of them rushed into the little village. One of the Spaniards was killed and several were wounded, including the Adelantado, who suffered a wound to the chest. But the Spaniards, though few in number, were better armed, and after three hours of intense fighting, the Indians finally retreated.

In the meantime, Diego Tristan, captain of the Capitana, had been sent by Columbus to obtain fresh water, Tristan witnessed the fight from his boat but could do nothing. When the conflict ended, his men advised him to quickly get back to the safety of the ships, but Tristan responded that he had been ordered by the Admiral to obtain water, and he would do so. They rowed a short distance up the river to a point where the water was clear but were quickly ambushed. Tristan was killed by a spear hat pierced his eye. All his men were killed with the exception of one who was able to swim underwater long enough to escape and take the sad news back to the Admiral.

While all this was taking place, Columbus was alone on board the Capitana anchored some distance offshore. He was suffering with a high fever. The Admiral (Columbus) heard the sound of gunshots and realized that his men, including his brother, were under attack. Knowing the overwhelming number of Indians, he could only assume, when the sound of the muskets died down, that all had been killed. Adding to his weak physical condition was the distress of fearing that his men and his brother were dead. What followed was one of the seminal experiences of the Admiral's life:

"I was completely alone outside on this dangerous coast in a high fever and a state of great exhaustion. All hope of escape was dead. I struggled up to the highest point of the ship, weeping and calling in a trembling voice to your Highnesses' Lord of Hosts in every direction for comfort, but there was no reply.

Exhausted and groaning, I fell as if asleep and heard a very compassionate voice saying: 'O fool, slow to believe and serve thy God, the God of all! What more did he do for Moses or David his servant than he has done for thee? Sine thou wast born, ever has He had thee in His watchful care. When He saw thee at an age that pleased Him, He caused thy name to sound marvelously in the land. The Indies, which were so rich a part of the world, He gave thee for thine own; thou hast divided them as it pleased thee, and He enabled thee to do this. Of the barriers of the Ocean Sea, which were closed with such mighty chains, He gave thee the key; and thou wast obeyed in many lands, and among Christians thou hast gained an honorable fame.

What did He do more for the people of Israel when He brought them out of Egypt? Or for David, who from a shepherd He made to be King of Judea? Turn thyself to Him, and know now thine error; His mercy is infinite, thine old age shall not prevent thee from achieving all great things; He has many inheritances very great. Abraham was over a hundred years old when he begat Isaac, and Sarah was not a young girl.

Thou criest for help, doubting. Answer, who has afflicted thee so greatly and so often, God or the world? The privileges, letters and promises that God gives are all fully kept, and after receiving service his favors increase and

He grants his servants paradise. I have spoken of that which thy Creator has done for thee and does for all men. Now in part He shows thee the reward for the anguish and danger which thou hast endured in the service of others.'

I heard all of this as if I were only partially conscious, and I had no answer to give to words so true, but could only weep for my errors. He, whoever he was who spoke to me, ended by saying: 'Fear not; have trust; all these tribulations are written upon marble and are not without cause." Recorded April 6, 1503. 2

Interesting month and day for members of the Church of Jesus Christ of Latter-Day Saints. They celebrate Christ's birth as April 6 (D&C 20:1) and the church was organized on April 6, 1830.

Joseph Smith also had a "dark night of the mind and spirit", as recorded while a prisoner in the jail at Liberty, Missouri, March 20, 1839: full text found in section 122 of the Doctrine and Covenants:

The ends of the earth shall inquire after thy name, and fools shall have thee in derision, and hell shall rage against thee; While the pure in heart, and the wise, and the noble, and the virtuous, shall seek counsel, and authority, and blessings constantly from under thy hand, God shall stand by thee forever and ever.

If thou art called to pass through tribulation; if thou art in perils among false brethren; if thou art in perils among robbers; if thou art in perils by land or by sea; If thou art accused with all manner of false accusations; if thine enemies fall upon thee; if they tear thee from the society of thy father and mother and brethren and sisters; and if with a drawn sword thine enemies tear thee from the bosom of thy wife, and of thine offspring, and thine elder, son, although but six years of age, shall cling to thy garments, and shall say, My father, my father, why can't you stay with us? O, my father, what are the men going to do with you? and if then he shall be thrust from thee by the sword, and thou be dragged to prison, and thine enemies prowl around thee like wolves for the blood of the lamb.

And if thou shouldst be cast into the pit, or into the hands of murderers, and the sentence of death passed upon thee; if thou be cast into the deep; if the billowing surge conspire against thee; if fierce winds become thine enemy; if the heavens gather blackness, and all the elements combine to hedge up the way; and above all, if the very jaws of hell shall gape open the mouth wide after thee, know thou, my son, that all these things shall give thee experience, and shall be for thy good.3

So how do you best respond when mental or emotional challenges confront you or those you love? Above all, never lose faith in your Father in Heaven, who loves you more than you can comprehend. As President Monson said to the Relief Society sisters so movingly last Saturday evening: "That love never changes. ... It is there for you when you are sad or happy, discouraged or hopeful. God's love is there for you whether or not you feel you deserve [it]. It is simply always there." Never, ever doubt that, and never harden your heart. Faithfully pursue the time-tested devotional practices that bring the Spirit of the Lord into your life. Seek the counsel of those who hold keys for your spiritual well-being. Ask for and cherish priesthood blessings. Take the sacrament every week, and hold fast to the perfecting promises of the Atonement of Jesus Christ. Believe in miracles. I have seen so many of them come when every other indication would say that hope was lost. Hope is never lost. If those miracles do not come soon or fully or seemingly at all, remember the Savior's own anguished example: if the bitter cup does not pass, drink it and be strong, trusting in happier days ahead.

In preventing illness whenever possible, watch for the stress indicators in yourself and in others you may be able to help. As with your automobile, be alert to rising temperatures, excessive speed, or a tank low on fuel. When you face "depletion depression," make the requisite adjustments. Fatigue is the common enemy of us all—so slow down, rest up, replenish, and refill. Physicians promise us that if we do not take time to be well, we most assuredly will take time later on to be ill.

If things continue to be debilitating, seek the advice of reputable people with certified training, professional skills, and good values. Be honest with them about your history and your struggles. Prayerfully and responsibly consider the counsel they give and the solutions they prescribe. If you had appendicitis, God would expect you to seek a priesthood blessing and get the best medical care available. So too with emotional disorders. Our Father in Heaven expects us to use all of the marvelous gifts He has provided in this glorious dispensation.1

My "dark night of the mind and spirit" occurred during the terminal illness and for months after the passing of my kid's mom. We had a picture of Christ hung on our bedroom wall that stated, "I didn't say it would be easy, I said it would be worth it." I would often look at the picture on the wall, as my wife lay on the bed, with her life slowly slipping away and I wanted to throw my shoe at the picture.

Voicing some of my thoughts, a guest author wrote, "for years I had looked at depression clinically, like a scientist examining a foreign virus under a microscope. I had relatives and friends who had experienced depression— some had received treatment in mental hospitals, others who had avoided treatment and even others who had suffered such pain for a prolonged period of time that they took their own lives.

Despite my familiarity with these people, I couldn't understand what they were experiencing. I had a lot of theories about the reasons behind depression, but little real understanding and little desire to understand more.

Then, some years ago, I suffered some substantial setbacks which, at the time, I thought were insurmountable. I couldn't imagine a way forward. I felt as though I had been abandoned by my colleagues, my friends, family and even abandoned by God. I sunk into a depression that lasted several years. Some days it was so hard to get out of bed (I could not sleep), even with my wife and family surrounding me and selflessly supporting me. I believed that no one could understand what I was going through.4

Though we may feel we are "like a broken vessel," as the Psalmist says, we must remember, that vessel is in the hands of the divine potter. Broken minds can be healed just the way broken bones and broken hearts are healed. While God is at work making those repairs, the rest of us can help by being merciful, nonjudgmental, and kind.1

But the Comforter, which is the Holy Ghost,
whom the Father will send in my name, he shall
teach you all things, and bring all things to your
remembrance, whatsoever I have said unto you.

Peace I leave with you, my peace I give unto you: not
as the world giveth, give I unto you. Let not your heart
be troubled, neither let it be afraid. John 14: 26-27

1. *Like a Broken Vessel, Elder Jeffrey R. Holland, October 2013.*
2. *From Christopher Columbus, A man among the Gentiles, Clark B. Hinckley, page 177-179, 2014.*
3. *Doctrine and Covenants: D&C:122.*
4. *How Elder Jeffrey R. Holland's Account of His Struggle with Depression Changed My Life, Guest Author, 03-29-2021.*

62

YOUR MOTHER SHERYL— PREPARATION FOR 10TH ANNIVERSARY FAMILY GET TOGETHER OF KID'S MOM PASSING 2013-07-11

I don't know what I did to attract your mother's attention. I was pretty much a geek. Skinny, dressed with little thought, enrolled in the Future Farmers of America (agriculture) classes instead of seminary, loved animals, rode my horse in the river bottoms, hunted, fished, was easily distracted from studies, into sports and had a father that at the time was inactive in the church.

However, I can tell you what I found attractive about Sheryl:

She spoke correctly and seemed a little more "refined" than most of the other girls I knew in Blackfoot.

1. She knew how to sew.
2. She sang with a group of her friends as well as in the high school choir.

3. Played the piano and organ.

4. I sat next to her in typing class. She was very fast and made few errors. I was slow and made several errors.

5. She knew what she wanted to do. She planned on going to college at UCLA or So Cal, move to California where her cousins lived and be close to Disneyland. She did not like pick-up trucks, gun racks or hats. She wanted her life to be a little better than it was growing up on the farm or being around cowboys.

6. She was very focused on studies and had good grades. And just for your information, Mr. Clark (retired Navy and our high school physiology instructor) commented in his classes that he felt the best mating pair in Blackfoot High School to have advanced offspring (he was very Darwinish) would be my sister Pat and me. Since Pat and I were too close a genetic match his second choice would be Sheryl and me. I think Sheryl may have been #1 if she hadn't fainted during rat dissection lab. So, how do you like being born of superior stock?

7. There will be no play until the studies were done. That's right—she made me sit at the table with her and finish my home work as she did hers. Want to go to the movie? Great, but get the studies done first. Funny thing my grades began to soar my junior and senior year in high school. Your mom made me smart.

8. Also, Ivan hired me to help out with the farm and he befriended me. He would drop me off in the fields, pick me up at noon and take me home and feed me one of Jean's great lunches. I got to know Lance and Mark quite well and they made me feel a part of their family at a time when I needed a father figure. I would

talk Ivan's ear off about when he knew to plant, water, harvest and sell the crops. I would also ask him about finances, insurance, equipment maintenance etcetera. He was always cordial and forthcoming and never made me feel stupid or unappreciated. Even when I cut into a sprinkler line with the windrower, knocked off a water mainline hookup, hit a truck with the header on the grain combine, sprayed the potatoes (along with his hired man—Carlos) with 24-D. I'm sure Ivan was glad to see the sun go down as we checked out the sprinkler lines for leaks. He knew he would soon drop me off at the house and I would be out of his hair.

9. Her parents were active in the church. I didn't really know why this was important but I had a warm something (I'll bet it was the Holy Ghost) feeling that I was making the right choice when we attended church. It may be of interest for you to know that your mom refused to go to church unless her parents would let her ride her horse on Sunday.

10. Sheryl did not like my friends. That would include my cousin Tom Bithell. She would keep me out as late as possible on the weekends to help prevent me from going out "with the boys." Your Uncle Tom had converted an old grain shed into what he called the Blu (sp ?) Room. Some of his dad's home brew + other stuff + girls from time to time would be found there especially on the weekends. Just to give you one example of some of the questionable activities going on there—to be initiated into the Blu room you had to have your crotch packed with snow (male or female). You can probably guess the

rest. I didn't like what your mom was doing at the time; but, the result was a good thing.

First met:

Sheryl was in one of my classes our sophomore year. She was a couple of rows in front of me and to my right. I couldn't help but notice that she kept looking my way. When I looked at her she shyly looked away. I asked some of her friends about her and began noticing her during campus activities. I remember noticing her playing volleyball in the gym and how cute her legs were and how shy she seemed when she hit the ball or made a play. It reminds me of how your sister Janalyn acted when she accidently scored a goal in soccer.

After I got brave enough through the help of others, we met and became good friends. However, I soon found out that another classmate thought that she was his special friend. Lewis Blake called me out after school and was going to fight for the rights of Sheryl Gardner's friendship. He was a tough kid and I knew that my 120# body didn't have a chance. If there would be love—all was lost before it began.

Chicken Little had a friend (Ron Reimer's) who wrestled and played football (varsity in both sports) and as per chance didn't like Lewis Blake very much. He said, "I'll take care of it" and he did. Fortunately, there was no fight and geek Walter looked like a looser to most but not your mom.

Oh, by the way, the person Sheryl was looking at wasn't me. It was Alan Packer the son of another MD in town.

I just happened to be in the line of sight when she was looking his way (maybe at the time she thought I was a looser).

First date:

We were at dinner with a group of friends before going to a dance. We had all been seated around a large table at a nice restaurant with table cloths and fine silverware. About half way through the dinner I needed to be excused to go to the restroom. I felt so self conscious that I was afraid to ask to be excused from the table. The meal seemed to never end, my legs were cramped, sweat was on my brow and my bladder was sure to explode before we got up from the table. I don't remember anything about that date except your mom wore a beautiful dress and everyone seemed to have a good time, except for me.

Times with Sheryl in Blackfoot:

- After school and on weekends Sheryl worked in the bakery department at Albertson's grocery store. Several of the close friends she stayed in touch with over the years worked in the store with her. I loved to go over and visit her at work. She would have flour and grease on her apron, hot oil burns from cooking donuts and the best smell of fresh raised dough.

She glowed with perspiration, her hair was tied back and covered with a cap and she always seemed upbeat and was glad to see me.

- It seemed that we spent most of our time together babysitting your mom's siblings. Jean always seemed to have a calling in the church and the kids needed to be watched. During these times I got a little taste of what to expect when we later got married.

She didn't put up with much. Lance mostly stayed out of trouble but Mark was always at it with Sheryl. I remember one time when Mark got so mad during a confrontation that he climbed up a tree in the back yard and said that he was not coming down and was going to "kill himself".

- Peggy came on the scene when I was about sixteen and what a spoiled brat. One Sunday I was asked to drive her to church. The Rose Chapel is about a mile from the Gardner's old home. From their home to the church Peggy screamed and screamed. I couldn't get her to stop. I tried screaming at her, stopping the car, threatening her, offering her goodies in the future etcetera—you know all the bribes. Non worked! When I see Peggy to this day I think about that trip to the church.
- Also, if you look at our wedding pictures you will see Peggy wearing black shoes. Jean insisted on white ones, white ones were on her when they went to the church, but somehow the shoes became black for the photos.
- During those days Sheryl knew how to cook two things—steak and spaghetti.

- The north/south freeway (interstate highway 15) was being built north of Blackfoot when we were in high school. The road was graveled and waiting for the black top. In the center of the road gravel was pilled a couple of feet high. I had dad's old Cadillac (1955 I think) and was showing off driving back and forth across the gravel in the center of the road. I came in at a bad angle and the car became high centered on the gravel. Sheryl and I had to walk back to her house and ask Ivan to help get the car off the gravel. Chains in hand and tongue in cheek he drove his tractor to the spot and pulled the car off the pile of gravel.

- Another story about dad's old Cadillac. I had purchased a birthday present for your mom. I parked off a secluded road to give her the gift and I'm sure in hopes of lucking out on a kiss or two. No longer had I stopped when a spot light shown through the window. It was a highway patrol police officer wondering what we were doing. He mentioned that there was a storage yard nearby that had been broken into several times and wanted to know if we were about to invade the yard again. I explained to him what we were doing and showed him the unwrapped gift. He said we had best be on our way.

I turned the car key and nothing happened. The car was dead. So, the nice police officer was more than happy to push my dad's car to a "more appropriate location," take us to Ivan and Jean's house and drop us off where we were seen by all the family. Here again Ivan, chain in hand and tongue in cheek, was more than happy helping me get the car going good enough to get me home without my dad finding out.

- I hinted to Sheryl that she was going to get a diamond for Christmas. She was concerned that it may be true and since we were still in high school how would she respond.

The big moment came. The entire family was present, there was a fire in the fireplace stoked on by wrapping paper and all attention was placed on your mom and the gift I had for her. As she opened the box there was the sound of a hiss and a rubber rattle snake appeared from inside of the box. As you know there is not one of the Gardner's that isn't afraid of snakes. What a great gift and the response was every much what I had hoped for. So much so that Peggy grabbed the box and threw it into the fireplace. (another strike against Peggy).

- Good old Uncle Tom had gone with a bunch of classmates to Boise State University for a school function. While there he walked into a jewelry store and stole a wedding ring (later it was given to a friend of mine to marry a girl that was pregnant while in high school). I borrowed it and with my friend (here again Ron Reimers) lying between the front and back seats of my car proposed to Sheryl.

We were seniors in high school and she began giving me all the reasons why marriage would be a very stupid option at that time in our lives. It got pretty thick until Ron could hold back no longer and began to laugh. Your mom should have sent both of us on our way to never be seen again.

- I first discussed marrying Sheryl with my mother. She only gave one negative comment about Sheryl from that time until both of them passed. She said, "Sheryl doesn't seem to smile very much. Do you think she is a very happy girl?" Of course there were times during our relationship that I did wonder if she were happy. Those thoughts came mostly when I wasn't doing things the way your mother wanted them done.

I think Sheryl was mostly happy in her own way. She wasn't a "Good morning to you, good morning to you, we're all in our places with sun shinning faces—for this the way to start a new day". Or "Good morning Merry Sunshine, how did you wake so soon? You scared away the little stars and shined away the moon."

I know some of you also aren't this type of person. Just ask Jana about the summer she worked with me at Camden Pet Hospital. Sheryl did have some depression problems (as did several of the Gardner family) but I felt she worked through them once she understood what it was.

- We were married by Sheryl's bishop (08-24-67) just before our senior year at the University of Idaho. The primary reason was that dad was not able to go to the temple and we didn't want to stir the pot. I'm sure it was just for fun, but dad offered us

$500.00 cash if we would get married and forget about the reception.

During the previous three years of college I drove a turquoise and white 1957 Mercury Monterey to school. The tires were bad and lucky for us as we got off the freeway at Ivan's old home during a trip from the University of Idaho was the time the battery chose to short out.

The engine had been rebuilt by a high school friend of mine, and it always started but the rest was questionable. We would drive all night from Idaho through Montana and over Lolo pass back into Idaho and over to Moscow.

I had a car load of students after Christmas vacation, it was below zero in Montana, the roads were ice covered and slick and sand/gravel had been placed on the road. In the middle of the valley, Big Sky country, we had a flat tire. There was no one for miles, the gas tank was below half full, it was several hours before the sun would come up and we were cold.

Long story short—we got to a service station and found out that the car's tires were so thin that the gravel placed on the roads was penetrating the tires and making them flat. I needed to replace two tires and the only ones they had were oversized. We took them and completed the trip.

The reason I bring this up is that as soon as we got married dad became very concerned about our welfare. In fact he gave us one of his cars so that travel to school would not be "so risky."

- Our wedding reception was held at the LDS church on South Meridian near where Grandma Jean

Gardner is currently living (898 South Meridian). Both families were well known in Blackfoot and there was a line going outside of the cultural hall onto the sidewalk for a couple of hours as people waited to visit with us and our parents. I was exhausted when the evening came to a close and I planned on taking Sheryl to a nice hotel on the hill just off the freeway going into Pocatello. The next day we would be driving to I believe Winnemucca NV where I was to be best man at my friend Ron Reimers' (the guy who protected me from Luis Blake when Sheryl and I first met in high school) wedding.

I pulled into the hotel entrance, walked into the lobby all prettied up with and asked for a room that would be appropriate for a newly married couple. At the front desk a lady ask for my reservation in which I had none. She called around and found us a hotel across the street from Idaho State University.

It was a real dive and I suspect many a single college student tried to talk a girl into staying there. Of course, your mom was not pleased but accepted our fate. Guess what we did just before going to bed. No, we didn't have a family prayer. Sheryl proceeded to turn on the hot water into the sink, wet a wash cloth, place soap on it and show me how to wash my face. No kidding—true story.

- The next year before we left for Purdue University we were sealed in the Idaho Falls Temple. I had been given a draft number of A1 and we did not know whether I would be in graduate school after the summer. Anyway, it all worked out and we began our life really away from home.

Days at the University of Idaho:

- During our senior in high school thoughts became more focused on attending college. I planned on going to the U of I for several reasons. It was the best science education option, there was a degree offered in animal science - science (I could take all the classes pre med and pre dental students took + take my elective classes in horse, cattle, pig etc production instead of humanities and social sciences), I received a Union Pacific scholarship, it was a well known land grant university, dad had been a graduate student in bacteriology there, and finally I knew that Moscow was far away from home and I thought I had some oats that needed to be sown.

This option proved to be a good choice for me. I was accepted at Purdue University for graduate studies upon the reputation of the U of I and members of the staff in the animal science dept. I was given an NEA scholarship for my research after speaking to the professor I was to be assigned only once on the phone.

Also, we could go directly to Purdue after graduation from the U of I. This would reduce my chances of being drafted into the armed forces.

- Sheryl's parents wanted her to attend Rick's college. She would be close to home and the cost would be much more affordable for Ivan. Coming to the aid was Uncle Tom Bithell's mother Nondus and my dad's sister, Bingham county's agent. She helped your mom get a scholarship to the U of I in home economics. Sheryl had not taken any home economic classes in high school (could only cook steak and spaghetti), so I'm not sure how my aunt Nondus got it done. But I do know she was quite well known in the state of Idaho as a county agent and supporter of home economics.

Ivan was overwhelmed that his daughter got a scholarship to a university and it wasn't long before he got behind her wishes. He and Jean were the ones that took us up to Moscow and dropped us of at our dorms.

I think this action by Nondus pretty much sealed our fate as to one day marrying. As a side note it may be of interest to you to know that when my mother and her sister (Aunt Ruth) went up to Moscow for summer school aunt Nondus tipped dad off that they were coming and that he should really get to know Barbara Rich when she was there. Therefore, Nondus was kind of a match maker for dad and me.

- Every time Sheryl got into my car to go back to school Ivan would give me that look as if to say, " If you mess up my daughter in any way you will pay dearly." You know something? I believed him.

- We lived in university housing with two wings built in a Y shape from the dining and lounge building. The girls were on one side and the men on the other. Remember there were no cell phones, but we could see each other's room across the way and "know when you've been sleeping and know when you're awake". Your mom studied hard and at times the lights didn't go out until time to take a test or finishing an assignment. I tried one "all nightery" and the results weren't as rewarding for me as it was for your mother.

- We would have dinner together in the dorm and study at the library almost every night. The library desks were made of cold noisy metal. My routine upon arrival was to place my head down on a book that was lying on the desk. I would fall asleep until the saliva found its way out of my mouth and woke me up.

Sounds gross, but I have always been amazed how much I could learn after I had a power nap with a little juice to get the brain going. We would study until the library closed and walk back to the dorm together.

- A short story on why I mentioned walking. In the state of Idaho the auto license plates were renewed annually. When the fees were paid a new set of license plates were sent to the owner. The owner would take off the old plates and put on the new ones. My dad had the car registered in Blackfoot and the plates each year were sent there instead of Moscow.

Having lived in Moscow and attending the university there dad didn't want us to do a lot of driving the car around and not attending to our studies. Mom and dad were so concerned that we keek our noses to the grindstone that the didn't even let us know when Grandma Hoge passed away. He knew that the U of I was a tough school (on average only ½ the freshman returned as sophomores) and that it would be easy to fall behind. Uncle Tom (again) and his brother Walter Bithell let me know that grandma had passed and we flew together to attend her funeral.

- Once dad got a copy of my grades (mid-term and final) he would send the car's license plates so we could come homefor summer, Christmas or spring break. Also, we didn't have to walk to the restaurant on Sundays to buy the least expensive meal we could find—spaghetti.
- When we returned to the U of I after vacation or summer work Ivan would always place a trunk full of frozen beef to get us by until the next visit.
- When Grandma Hoge passed I was very remorseful. She was the one that often baby sat us kids and read books about far away interesting places. Every time mom sent me a letter she would ask if I had sent Grandma Hoge a letter. She was living alone and interested in what was going on in my life. Finally, I felt guilty enough to send her a letter. I wrote a

fairly long letter (for me) in my best penmanship and sent it to grandma.

A couple of weeks after her death I got a letter that said, "Return to sender, deceased". Over the last twenty years I have not been able to find it. I had kept it in an attaché case with resumes and other high school and college materials, but couldn't find it (the letter has been found and hasn't been opened).

This failure to respond in a reasonable length of time taught me a very important lesson. Never put things off or you may lose the opportunity to get it done. I sure hope that I can find that letter.

- A side note. Making phone calls intrastate was very expensive. Therefore, you kept in touch by writing to your parents. I got a lot of my letters back. Mom would write back and include my letters with correct spelling and punctuation changes. It got very hard to write home. I needed money, my license plates etcetera and if I did write the humiliation of poor use of the English language glared at me. Sheryl usually wrote to help make sure her checking account wasn't off balance.

- One night on our way from the library a giant rat tried to chase us back to the dorm. It was one of my roommates dressed up like a rat and hollering, "Life is nothing but a rat race". Of course, this guy and I were kind of made for each other.

The saying at the U of I was that the farmers sent their daughters to market and their pigs to Moscow. Working on this theme we decided to steal some pigs from the agriculture department and place them in the girls side of the dorm. We soon found out that the pigs were hard to capture, made a lot of noise and would be hard to transport. So, second choice was to pick up a few goats from the dairy science department and lead them to the dorm. This went off very well thank you. If I remember right we placed five goats in the elevator and sent them up to the floor that your mother lived on. It didn't go off as we had hoped. The goats were very friendly and the girls thought it was a great prank and didn't get the message. As years have gone by I wish we had of put numbers on the goats something like this—1,2,4,5 and 6. Do you get it?

- Sheryl decided that she was not interested in home economics during her first year of college. What really brought it a head was chemistry. On a cold wintery day we were walking back from the library. The snow had been blown off the sidewalks and piled up to about chest high along the path. Your mom was talking in a fashion that should have given me a warning for the future—look out when she gets mad. She had just done very poorly on a chemistry test. She was not used of doing poorly in anything and this wasn't going to continue. She lifted the chemistry book into the air and, with words I don't recall and if I did remember they wouldn't be written on this paper, threw it over the snow bank. I retrieved the book and with wet shoes and snow covering my pants above my knees tried to consul her—which as I'm sure you know also isn't a good idea. Therefore, for her it was enrollment in the education department.

- Sheryl had always worn my senior ring after high school. I noticed the guys seemed to be having a good time dating the few girls there were at Moscow and they encouraged me to get my ring back and "have some fun."

We even went over to Washington State University in Pullman drove into the parking lot of a girl's dorm and honked the horn. Wow, there were tons of girls that came to the windows and spoke to us. WSU was overloaded with females—the U of I had mostly men since it was primarily an engineering school (land grant colleges emphasis was engineering, home economics, law and agriculture).

Anyway, I got up the nerve to ask for the ring back and I quickly found that approaching these wonderful young ladies wasn't easy and my approach was having little luck. There were also rumors being fed to me about how much fun Sheryl was having, doing pretty good and thank you very much.

It didn't take too long before I asked your mom to take the senior ring back. No thank you was the reply. If you want to make a commitment with me I expect an engagement ring from you. We drove to Spokane and bought an engagement ring to be placed right away on her finger and a wedding band saved for next summer's wedding.

- During her senior year she drove to Lewiston Idaho to do her student teaching. It was here that she saw real poverty, single or no parent families and kind of a don't really care about my child's education attitude. This seemed to affect her a lot and I'm sure it had something to do with her dedicated interest in your education and success.

- I joined Farm House Fraternity my junior year. The grades were beginning to get better and Sheryl and I prepared for marriage during that next summer.

- Our senior year we lived in married student housing and started to learn to get a long together. I probably shouldn't tell you this story and to be honest I don't remember the incident, but Uncle Tom Bithell (again) insists that it is true.

He was over visiting us and your mom was preparing dinner. It was about ready and she told us that it was done and would soon be over cooked. We kept talking and she got more vocal about food. Finally, she said it was ruined and I'm sure was letting us know how displeased she was. Tom said that I got up picked up the pan and dumped it in the sink saying, "If it's no good then throw it away".

Can you imagine me doing something like that? I'm sure with Tom there that my courage was up and I wanted him to see how stupid of a trick I could pull. For your information, I found out after Uncle Tom left.

Purdue University:

- Why did we decide on going to Purdue University? During the application process for graduate school two schools showed interest, Purdue and Cornell University. I had phone conversations with each institution and Cornell sounded much farther away than West Lafayette Indiana.

It must have been a phone connection because if you look at a map they are both a long way from Blackfoot Idaho. Also, I mentioned above how I was given a scholarship from Purdue after a short visit with the major professor with whom I would be working with.

However, the main reason I chose Purdue was your mom. She told me that she felt I needed to be at Purdue. Inspiration, Holy Ghost, or because of the mascot of Purdue Pete and the train I don't really know. Of course, your mom wasn't about to tell me. As you know, she tended to keep her private thoughts to herself.

- As soon as we graduated from -the U of I we returned to Blackfoot and began packing for our move to Indiana. I was scheduled to start summer school and Sheryl wanted to secure a teaching position. The car dad gave us was questionable for the trip and Ivan offered to sell Lances Pontiac Tempest.

Lance was on his mission to England and the car was in storage. I'll never forget walking with your mom and Ivan into that dusty old shed and watching all the seed peas and rat/mouse poop come rattling out of the engine hood as Ivan lifted it during our inspection. The pests had taken up home in our soon to be home on the road. It was obvious that Ivan felt the car was best used and not kept waiting for Lance.

The Tempest is a small car, had as I recall only two forward gears and I was concerned about it being able to pull a trailer. It wasn't long before we were on the road and everything seemed ok until we went over a mountain pass in Wyoming. The car overheated several times and we weren't sure that we would make it. Fortunately, that was the only pass that challenged Lance's car.

- We settled again into married student housing, Sheryl found an elementary teaching position and began readying the class room. I started graduate summer school and discussions about research with my major professor (Dr. Malvin).
- Some of my classes were taken at the veterinary school and it wasn't long before I wanted to become a doctor of veterinary medicine. I realized that if I decided to continue research and teaching there would be more opportunities if I had a DVM.

I started veterinary school the next year (1969) and was registered as a graduate student finishing my thesis and first year veterinary student. When I received my M.S. I was approached about becoming a PhD. The project they were working on was a new area of anti-inflammatory medications called prostaglandins. This type of medication helped revolutionize the field of pain relief. In fact your mom took one of these products—Celebrex.

- Your mom read a lot of books. I always thought they were trash novels and written for people who wanted to turn off their mind and waste time. However, I recall looking very stupid among my friends over a discussion about snakes. We were talking about poisonous snakes and the venom they produced. Sheryl mentioned that there was a cobra that spit poison into the eyes of its pray.

In front of our friends I told her that was ridiculous. The argument went on until a dictionary was located and I was found to the ignorant one.

I asked her how she knew about these snakes and she calmly told the group the information came during the reading of one of those stupid books.

My first test in horse science was a disaster. I basically flunked it. There were questions about famous race horses, how many inches is in a hand, where the frog was, how many feet was in a furlong, and it went on and on. I brought the test home and asked Sheryl the questions. She would have gotten an A on the test. Here again the knowledge about horses came from her reading some of those stupid timewasting books.

- When it came time to type my Master's thesis I had a great idea. If your mom would do the typing it would save us enough money to buy an electric typewriter. The thesis was titled "FACTORS AFFECTING THE SECRETION OF PROLACTIN BY ECTOPIC PITUITARY TISSUE". There were a lot of words like hypophysectomized, prolactin, ectopic, pituitary, ergocornine, estrodiol etcetera that were repeated numerous times in the transcript.

Sheryl didn't really want to type the thesis and was to say the least a little put out. Let's put it this way—I knew when she was working on the thesis by the words expressed and the sound of ripping paper in the next room.

The document was finally done and I was in the process of receiving oral questioning and presenting my work to the faculty when a comment was made that there were some of the pages missing. Sure enough, my wife and your future mother had gotten tied up in the repetition of words that she didn't know what they meant or really care and in her frustrations left out several pages of the thesis.

It took a bit of time but I had it printed by a "professional typist" and all sixty-four pages were soon where they should be, I received my MS degree, a copy was placed in the Purdue University library and Sheryl had an electric typewriter.

- In veterinary school I was hired to teach my classmates the endocrinology portion of our physiology class. One section was on pregnancy tests. There was the frog, rat and rabbit test. In a nut shell the test involved exposing the animal with urine from a woman that was suspected to be pregnant. After a period of time the frog would assume a mating posture with another frog, and the rat and rabbit would show changes in the reproductive structures (that means they needed to be sacrificed and then opened up for a look).

1969 was the time your mother first got pregnant. So, guess what? You got it—I used her urine for the pregnancy tests. And it worked just great. Only problem was that your mom was a little embarrassed about my class mates knowing she was pregnant and that the test sample was her urine. And, worst of all after a couple of months she lost the fetus and this would not be a private event.

We had several false starts during our five years at Purdue. During a visit to Blackfoot dad gave Sheryl an antibiotic called tetracycline. This seemed to help her carry Bradley Gardner Hoge to term. He also gave some for Janalyn Hoge and Karalee Hoge. Jeremy Rich Hoge was a surprise and Sheryl didn't get any antibiotics before her pregnancy.

Jeremy got all the size and stature in the family and pretty much everything he wanted (this was because he was the last child and the most demanding + we were getting exhausted as parents). Mom's left elbow was never the same after raising Jeremy. When he didn't want to be held, he would just drop to the ground pulling on his mom's arm. She developed tennis elbow even though she had never played tennis.

- Sheryl developed a fever, couldn't keep food down and became very lethargic. I took her to the doctor and he said that she had the flu. It was the time of the year that the church had volleyball tournaments and teams winning basketball and volleyball (there may have been others) would compete in the stake, regions etcetera and if you were good enough you would find yourselves in Salt Lake City playing for the church championship.

We had won several tournaments and drove to St Louis Missouri to play in the next bracket. We didn't do so good, which means we lost, and I returned home to find Sheryl in the hospital awaiting my permission and signature so that she could have surgery. Her flu diagnosis had changed to appendicitis. The appendix had burst and so during surgery she had to have a drain placed in the abdomen for several days. I felt terrible, she had nearly died while I was off playing sports. Her peritonitis further concerned us as to whether she would ever be able to have children.

- Let me share with you an incident that could have been a terrible accident into a fun (for me) memory. I don't know whether you noticed at one time or another how your mom walked when she was mad. She would kind of pound the pavement and slide her feet along.

We lived in an upstairs apartment at married student housing. There were about ten cement steps to the sidewalk below. One morning she was late for work, had an armload of corrected papers and assignments and wasn't in a pretty mood. I had gotten the car ready with the door open awaiting her presence. She angrily came out of the door, stomped towards the first step caught the heel on her shoe and tumbled down the stairs. When she got up, apparently all right, I couldn't help but laugh, which didn't help the situation. Fortunately, she had to work and I needed to be in class or we may have parted ways never to have the opportunity of having you little kiddo's.

California:

- During my senior year of veterinary school Sheryl and I began to look beyond the hallowed halls and into what to do with my education. She was well into her career as a teacher, was comfortable with daily schedules and the demands it placed on our lives and had received an MS at Purdue. I was thinking a lot about Florida. No cold winters, lots of old folks with pets, Disney World (which would take care of her Disney needs) and I thought clients with lots of money to spend. There was a practice there for sale for over a million dollars which was a lot of money at the time. So, I thought there must be lots of money in the sunshine state. Sheryl still wanted California because Florida was so far from home and her family.

During Christmas vacation my senior year a friend of mine (Rich Barrett) and I flew to Salt Lake City where Ivan Gardner met us at the airport and loaned us one of his cars to visit practices and investigate job opportunities in California. We had found a couple of job leads in northern California and headed to Oakland.

Rich had relatives there and we used their home while looking for work. It was there that I first got exposed to marijuana. During the early sixties birth control pills and drugs came on the scene. Fortunately, Blackfoot offered only booze and tobacco at the time so we didn't get exposed to hard drugs.

At the U of I and Purdue it was becoming more prevalent but the schools were "hard liners" and when caught students found themselves looking for another place to pursue their higher education (probably in California).

We had had a nice visit with Rich's extended family and then the pipes and other paraphernalia came out. I excused myself and told them that I wanted to go for a walk. I walked to the top of the hill and found myself in the parking lot of the Oakland Temple. The sun had just gone down, the air was cool and crisp and I could see for miles. The night lights made everything look clean and new. I could see the high radio tower on the hill across the bay, the Oakland Bay and Golden Gate bridges and large ships in the bay between San Francisco and Oakland. I stood there for several minutes just gazing in wonder at such a beautiful site. I then had an epiphany of knowledge realizing that this beautiful area could be enjoyed by me and our future family. I wanted what Sheryl wanted—California.

- This wasn't southern California but it was California. Rich Barrett and I found a clinic on East 14th Street, running right down the middle of Oakland, that was owned and for sale by Doctor Koller (sp?).

He took us to his home on top of a hill looking over the Bay Area one night and wined and dined us. If you recall where East 14th street is you will know that the area was not a good place to practice veterinary medicine. There were more drugs outside the practice than within.

Rich was from New Jersey and more street smart than me and by the time we moved to California we knew it was not a good move for two young vets. We both ended up working for practices in the area after passing our boards. It may be of interest to you that my first job was with Rob Yelland, owner of Lewelling Pet hospital in San Leandro. He was a good friend and classmate of Tom Miner, Chris's eventual father-in-law, while attending veterinary school at the U C Davis.

- Rich Barrett, his wife, dog, my cats and me rented a U-Haul for the move to California. Sheryl stayed behind to finish up her teaching commitments and later flew out to Oakland. Somewhere near Elko Nevada the U-Haul lost its transmission going up a hill. We had to stay a couple of extra days locating another truck, unloading and loading a new one and getting on our way.

I had with me Ming Tau, Maui Ti and a semi wild non-Siamese kitten that we had befriended just before graduation. At a rest stop the kitten got away. I'm sure glad that I didn't lose the Siamese cats or your mom may have stayed in Indiana.

When we arrived in Oakland California I found a small rental home on Sheetz Street which happened to be at the base of the hill which the Oakland Temple had been built. I could get to the temple in ten minutes, attend a morning session and be to work on time. We got Beau as a puppy during the time I worked at Lewelling Pet Hospital and we were living in Oakland.

- I wanted to work in a practice that I could sink roots and be involved in an ownership. Lewelling didn't work out and I went to work at Eden Pet Hospital (Dr. Brown) in Hayward the next year. I had an agreement to stay for one year and then we would make plans for a partnership or purchase of the practice. It was during this time that we purchased home in Fremont.

Still childless we began working with the church social services in hopes of adopting a child. We did not foster children because at that time you couldn't foster and adopt. Your mom began going to a fertility specialist, Dr. Nuddleman, in hopes of "getting it figured out."

One day he informed us that he had a patient who was expecting, would probably be giving up the child for adoption and that he felt it would be a "good match" for us. His question was, "Are you interested". And we replied with a strong yes. As the weeks went by we put the thoughts of an adoption out of our minds. We had a number of disappointments with the church social service and didn't want to be let down again. Your mom's biggest worry was that it may be a boy. She didn't know if she could start with a boy.

A day after May 17, 1975 my receptionist disrupted me in an exam room and said that someone needed to speak with me "right now." I was put out at the interruption and answered the phone in not my best tone of voice. On the other end was Dr. Nuddleman and he said, "Your baby boy has been born. Would you like him circumcised? And, by the way if you can't pick him up tomorrow, I have another family ready to take him home."

I finally got a hold of Sheryl at the school she was teaching (she substituted only while in CA. She didn't want sign a year's contract in case we got lucky having or getting a baby) and gave her the news. The next day we were parked in our new Datsun 260Z sports car in front of the hospital. After what seemed forever our attorney, a nurse and what was to become Walter Christopher Hoge emerged from the hospital. They gave us a change of diaper and a fresh bottle and stated that we needed to make arrangements to have a doctor's visit at a certain time.

We had few things for Chris at home and we didn't think we knew what to do next. So, I called dad. He asked me to tell him what a mother dog would do if Chris were a puppy. I told him and his reply was, "treat him like you would a puppy, but remember that you need to burp him after feeding and you don't need to lick his rear end to make him go to the bathroom." It worked and the rest is history.

We finalized Chris's adoption on Christmas Eve 1975. Sheryl and I were concerned about the judge signing the papers for the adoption because your mom was noticeably pregnant. She wore a long coat and "sucked it in" as much as possible when we went into the office. Trying to be friendly I put out my right hand to the judge. He shook my hand with his left hand. No, he wasn't a boy scout! He was a judge with no right hand. Embarrassed we sat down after the judge motioned us to do so.

The event was a wonderful Christmas Eve experience. The judge began by discussing the first part of his day by mentioning that there was a couple that came into his office to give up their children. Imagine that—on Christmas Eve. He then mentioned how fortunate we were that we had found Chris and were willing to share our lives with him. When we were deciding on a name for Chris my thoughts followed the family creed. Walter first, name of mother's middle name second and the last name last. It had been tradition for several generations. Sheryl did not agree. She thought Walter was bad enough and if you added a Gardner what on earth would he be called?

Negotiations went on until we decided on Christopher. And what do you know? He became legally a part of our family on Christmas Eve. Moms always know best. Gardner for a middle name would definitely not fit in with Christmas.

- After a year with Dr. Brown at Eden Pet Hospital I began negotiations on purchasing his practice. It became evident that he was really not quite ready to make a move at that time and I put out the word with drug salesmen what I was looking for.

Again, a strange call came into Eden Pet Hospital from a client that needed to speak with me right now. When I got on the phone it was Dr. Jack Hylton the owner of Camden Pet Hospital in San Jose informing me that his practice was for sale and asked if I was interested?

I went to San Jose, visited the practice and decided that I was not interested. There were things that needed updating and file cards were all over the place. I didn't know how they could keep track of things with such a mess. Jack called a few days later and invited your mom,

Chris and me to his home. There we visited at his home on "Pill Hill" in Almaden Valley San Jose and discussed our futures. He wanted to back off and enjoy life a little more and I wanted to sink roots where my family could be well fed and I could have clients that I would eventually get to know as family. It worked out and with the tetracycline and a settled in mom we all of a sudden had five children ages five and under.

- The home you grew up in on 6889 Serenity Way was found when mom was pregnant with Brad and hauling around a < one year boy.

We had been with a realtor house hunting in Los Gatos and other communities in the area. For lunch we stopped at a McDonald's type restaurant. Sheryl and I couldn't help but notice young kids pulling out $20.00 bills to buy their food. We talked about it during lunch and told the realtor that we didn't want our children growing up around rich kids. After lunch we eventually worked our way into Almaden Valley and Serenity Way.

It was hot, your mom was not far from delivering brad and she was worn out. When we were shown 6889 Serenity Way she sat down on a chair in the front room and said she could "go no farther". We placed an offer on the house and the Wisdom's accepted. The realtor was surprised since the family had been hard to set up appointments or accept an offer. I'm sure the reason they seemed to like us was because of mom being full of Brad and that cute little boy we were adopting.

The Wisdom's even stayed at the home in an RV to watch over the house until we could move in. FYI, the first owner lost the home to gambling and the Wisdom's were a little weird. They would burn all their garbage in the fireplace and then bury it in the back yard. I found all kinds of items not burnable in the back yard for many years.

The addition on the house was done during 1980 and at the time your mom was pregnant with Jeremy. Construction seemed to take a long time, the weather was damp and cold and Jeremy was the worst child to carry and the last time Sheryl wanted to get pregnant.

- I signed a contract with Dr. Hylton in 1976, purchased Camden Pet Hospital in 1980 and the building in 1982. We finally settled into our permanent home, a practice that I could sink roots in, started a family and began having many wonderful experiences and memories that will carry us through the eternities.

Hopefully you have had experiences living with Sheryl that you would like to share. Time passes, memories fade, people with whom we lived those experiences pass and we don't take the time to write things down. Remember the most important part of us lies between the date we were born and the date in which we passed. The dates are pretty much all you will find on the grave stone. It will be a special gift to our posterity if future generations can read our memories of Sheryl and get a feeling who she was and what she has done for us.

Other comments about Sheryl's personality:

- Your mom did get upset at times and I would say had a temper. I've already mentioned her handling of her brothers as a baby sitter and Mark's climbing up a tree to commit suicide and Sheryl falling off the top step while living at married student housing during our stay at Purdue.

- While we were at a party during our pre child days I told the group I could make Sheryl mad at me in less than one minute. They took me up on it and you guessed it—I won and of course lost in the end for several weeks. My favorite phrase was, "If I were you or my mother would." Each one said would bring back a quick angry toned, "Well you are not me or I'm not your mother."

- During my extensive interest and studying of nutrition I became convinced that I should be a vegetarian (I'm kind of reversed now). I would sit at the table and eat everything but meat. Sheryl finally blew and let me know in so many words that if her cooking wasn't nutritious I might consider not coming to the table. My reply was if she wasn't concerned about my health then I wasn't either and I became a meat eater again.

- Nancy Itri, receptionist and business manager for years, mentioned she would always remember Mrs. Hoge's response when I asked her to call Sheryl and see if she would bring over the minivan to the hospital. Her response was, "I don't drive the minivan. The car I drive is a Camaro."

- Your mom was banking with at least two children in tow. That means that Kara and Jeremy were with her. As she was doing her banking transactions a teller approached her and mentioned that she shouldn't bring in her children if she couldn't control them. Mom took offense of this statement and removed all her deposits from the bank.
- Another good one was when she had seen the doctor and mentioned that she was concerned about her body weight. The stupid doctor looked at her and said, "Mrs. Hoge you are just having a hard time accepting who you are."
- During a soccer game Brad took a hard shot to the head. Sheryl was sure that the player should be red carded and that he had hurt Brad. She made enough of a stink that she was ejected from the game with instructions not to return to any more games until she had classes to learn about the rules in soccer and have anger management discussions.
- One morning just before school started Sheryl and I were in the car and had just crossed Almaden Expressway and were about to the PW parking lot turn in. I noticed a kid riding his bike fast and the wrong way down the side walk. He ran smack into the side of a Cadillac pulling out from the parking lot.

The bike stopped and he flew onto the hood of the car. The driver of the car was a friend of mine, Dr. Rick Watson DVM, and the kid was none other than Mr. Jeremy Rich Hoge. Your mom told me to stop the car, she raced across the street without any regard to oncoming traffic, and with anger and concern safely (I don't know how she didn't get hit) got to the accident.

Dr. Watson was very apologetic for what Jeremy had done. Mom cooled down, Jeremy was okay, Rick insisted that we not worry about the car and I hope Jeremy apologized for causing the accident.

- During a trip to Rocky Point Mexico with the Gardners, Hoges and Retfords I decided to see if I could grow a beard. Mom got so mad at me that I shaved after a couple of days to stop her attention and the rest of the family's snickers.

- Your mom was a bit afraid of dad and I think a little annoyed at the structure of our visits when we were at my home. A few years before Sheryl became ill she would periodically get irritated at what I was doing and said that I was acting more and more like him. Of course, I kind of took this remark as a complement—but I never said that to Sheryl.

- When your mom started a project she could become very focused. She would get started making costumes for recitals, wrapping Christmas gifts, making a quilt etcetera and not stop until the project was done.

What really bothered me was that she liked to read in bed. In fact it was common for her to read an entire book during the night and as the sun came up fall fast asleep. You probably remember the piles of books she had under and around our bed.

She would start a book before I came to bed and I would awaken during the night from time to time because the light was still on. I would let her know that I had to work in the morning, she would kind of hint that there was a couch downstairs and it was waiting for me any time I wanted to use it.

- Probably the most conflict between your mom and me was over you children and when I came home at night. She felt that I took my work too seriously and that I often wouldn't let the staff take care of things that I insisted on doing. I also would be the last one out of the hospital and since we closed at 7pm that meant that I would be home late.

She would often have the children in bed and settling down for the night. Getting home I wanted to play with the kids and read or tell stories. Mom would get very hot under the collar because she had just finished a long day with you brats and she wanted some peace and quiet. Once I got you going it was often very late before you got to sleep.

- Your mom had a definite feeling for what was right or wrong. During the time she was ill my mom and dad loaned money to one of their grandchildren and it looked like it wasn't going to be paid back. Sheryl got very hot under the collar. She mentioned how Pappa and Barbara had loaned us money to buy our houses, Camden Pet Hospital and its building. And, at the time we bought the business property the interest rate we paid was 15% (the market rate was 18% + closing costs) and we paid "every penny back".

Also, that we did not refinance the loan when the rates went down because dad was retired and I wanted mom and dad to have a guaranteed monthly income. I still have several letters she wrote mostly to her and me as to why my brother and sisters should go after the scoundrel and get the money back. This topic kept her busy even when she didn't feel good.

- Sheryl's philosophy on money was that no matter what the accountant said it did not exist unless it was in your hand or in a checking account and you had plenty of checks. She was even known to start adding after the subtracting went past zero while paying bills.

She was always taken care of financially by Ivan in her youth. While we were at the U of I Ivan always sent us meat when we left to go back to school and when Sheryl's checking account got low a call to dad and it was quickly reconciled. I had her start helping write checks for Camden Pet Hospital (she would type them and I would sign them).

Don Dooley and our accountant noticed that profitability and value of the corporation was going down. Checking back through quarterly reports it was found expenses had been taken out for family use. Sheryl was writing checks, passed them my way and without my noticing it I signed them. She owned half the corporation, so what could I say? I'm sure at the time she felt I was starving the family and she needed more money to function.

I couldn't say much but what I did was starting writing and signing the checks all by myself.

- After we had graduated the credit card became a new source of money for Sheryl. In fact periodically I would get phone calls from our credit card company asking if someone was using our card. They would go down the lists of Toy's R Us or Baby whatever in Utah and I would say something like, "looks pretty bad, doesn't it?" Then I told them that the trail of charges belonged to my wife.

One time we were leaving on vacation when I opened up a credit card bill that I couldn't pay. When I found Ivan, I asked him why he hadn't taught his daughter how to handle money. His reply was that it looked like she did know how to handle money and that he taught her how to spend, "so I would be more successful." I was never more angry or disappointed with Ivan than on that day.

I approached my accountant about taking the check books and credit cards away from Sheryl. He told me that if I felt demoralizing her in such a way would help our relationship, go ahead. Then he said why don't you save out a little bit of money at work and set up a slush fund. When things are over drawn and Sheryl approaches you on bended knee, you could then discuss the consequences of being in debt and how the Lord councils us to not become a slave to money, and how our children may suffer if we lost the house. I set up a kind of secret account and the money over time became a fairly good stash. It is because of this fund that I have been able to help you with finances from time to time. So, thank your mom if you have been helped.

- Sheryl's entire life was centered around having a family. As soon as we started living in the same house she began nesting activities. She concentrated on changing the atmosphere in our home by getting ready for children. New drapes, wall hangings, sewing receiving blankets, nice bed spreads, decorating the extra bedroom, putting baby things in extra drawers, cooking meals more often, staying home more, and the constant desire to find a better home or area in town to live. It wasn't long before I understood that these changes were an indication that she was preparing at this point in her life to make her efforts into raising children.

- She wasn't a hugging kissing type of person. She was focused and driven on being sure you had every opportunity to be successful and good citizens in this life and also understood that you have a Heavenly Father that loves you and wants to have you return to Him. She was done with working outside of the home. It was understood that she felt if we did our best raising you that in twenty years we would not have to worry about how you were taking care of our grandchildren.

The results of your mom working with you 24/7 really paid off. You are all college graduates with good careers that take care of your temporal needs or are taking care of you own families.

- After being diagnosed with cancer the only thing she told me that she regretted was not being able to see all of her grandchildren born and watch them grow up. I'm sure that she has had an opportunity to meet all her grandchildren before they came into your homes. And, she probably knows more about them than you or they do at this point in their lives.
- When Sheryl was healthy I didn't see much of her. She wanted to be with you and her grandchildren. The last couple of years of her life she was especially focused on Kara and Jeremy. We had lots of talks about her hopes for their future. She had begun to soften and I felt try to look to the future and what she could do to help them be where they needed to be.
- Kara, Jeremy and I will never forget the wonderful time we had in Hawaii during the Christmas/New Years break 2002/2003. Sheryl had been able to have her colostomy bag removed, was off treatment for several weeks and felt again like a "whole person". I get moist eyes when I see the pictures of kara, Jeremy and your mom in swimming suits laying on the warm sand together without a care in the world.

These few months were the best Sheryl had felt for a long time. She continued to have many good months during the first half of 2003. Even though we knew that the treatments had begun to fail and she was feeling so good because she was off the drugs, we kept these thoughts under wraps. It may seem strange to you but her best of times being sick were in Hawaii and when she made the final decision to not make any more attempts at treatment and signed her care over to Hospice. It was like a rain cloud had finally moved on and the sun began to shine again. After the Hospice decision we went out for dinner and were more relaxed than we had been for a long time.

- The only real regret during my relationship with Sheryl was that she was very private about her personal life and never really talked about her inner feelings. Many years before she became ill I had asked her why she would never really tell me her private inner thoughts. She answered, "When you don't let a person know your inner thoughts - they can't hurt you."

As you well know she would always let me know how she felt outwardly but I was often perplexed as to what brought out the outer emotions. Even when she was terminally ill I rarely knew where she was coming from.

For example, I was making arrangements to sell Camden Pet Hospital (or try to management it from home and not work) and she put her foot down and said that I should continue to work, she would be okay during the day if I came home for lunch, she would like me to go to treatments with her and that she would be fine. One day the social worker approached me and mentioned that she got lonely at home and wished I could be there more often.

- I'm sure you knew that Sheryl was a person that could not say goodbye. She told me that she stayed away from those about to say goodbye because she didn't want to become emotional and she always wanted to have hellos.

When she died I felt very bad that I was in Arizona with Jeremy when he had his shoulder operated on. I had discussed leaving with Hospice. They said that she was in good flesh, not dehydrated and felt that she would be fine for another week or two. After I got home and spent some time thinking about her passing, I realized that Sheryl being as private as she was and that she didn't like to say goodbye probably had chosen this moment in time to leave.

Final thought:

I want to take a moment and let you know what I know. Over the years I have been on this earth the only thing that has not changed in the world around me is the Gospel of Jesus Christ. I know that I have a Father in Heaven that cares about all of us no matter how "good or bad" we think we are. He allowed our brother Jesus Christ to come to this earth and atone for our sins and gave us the Law of Repentance. We are fortunate to be able to come to this earth since one third of our brothers and sisters exercising their agency are not going to have this opportunity.

We have a great heritage from those who have gone before us. If it weren't for our parents and their parents we could easily be floating in a mass of confusion as to where we came from, why we are here and where we will find ourselves when we leave this earth.

We have been privileged to be baptized and received the Gift of the Holy Ghost. This gift is ours and we have every right to receive knowledge, even hidden knowledge if we only ask and are in tune with the Spirit.

We have been taught to be square and honest with those around us, to follow a compass (I prefer to think of it as the Liahona used by the ancients) to guide us to the iron rod (the word of God), to look after our temporal, mental and spiritual needs and to always recognize that Jesus Christ is the only one to worship.

We share the priesthood (government of God) with our wife and family and have living honorable men who use that priesthood as prophets, seers and revelators in our behalf.

I know that it is easy to fall away and we need to constantly renew our covenants by receiving the sacrament on a regular basis and studying, pondering, fasting and praying to stay strong in these days.

I am pleased how you have been sealed together as husbands and wives and the course you are taking in the care and teaching of your children to understand who they are and what they can become if they will only heed the promptings of their conscience and the Holy Ghost.

I am overcome that you are able and willing to take a few hours to honor your mother. She should be an example in your home as to how to raise worthy sons and daughters in Zion. As I mentioned above, she was a very private person. I don't ever recall her ever bearing her testimony. However, I knew she had one by her actions when around me and the results of her efforts in helping you become the wonderful people you are.

One final thought:

"Wherefore, men are free according to the flesh; and all
things are given them which are expedient unto man.
And they are free to choose liberty and eternal life,
through the great Mediator of all men, or to choose
captivity and death, according to the captivity and
power of the devil; for He seeketh that all men might be
miserable like unto himself."
2 NEHPI 2:27

HOME

She didn't need a suitcase
or a toothbrush or a comb
nor money for a ticket
to see her safely home.

She didn't mind that it was time to go
no tear drops dimmed her eyes
she just kinda slipped away
there were no sad good-byes.

I'll not say that I won't miss her
that sometimes my heart won't ache
but I'll never wish that she had stayed
just for my own selfish sake.

I know how long she waited
for the day that she could go
all her life she'd planned the trip
to me it wasn't such a blow.

I know she's not really sleeping
and she certainly isn't dead
we've been building this home in heaven
and she just went on ahead.

She's busy up there getting ready
for the day I shall slip away
what a joyous, glad reunion
and her words, "You're home to stay".

Poems to Ponder, Ruth Sutherland, page 9

63

PAPA AND BARBARA'S LIFE STORIES

2018-08-08 Walter Grimmett Hoge and Barbara Rich Hoge Life Stories

February 22, 1997
Thoughts after visiting my parents on 02-15-97:

I challenged mom and dad to record or write information about their lives. Dad has prepared a life story, but it mostly talks about where he has been and the things he's accomplished. What I asked them was to answer questions about their personal lives in hopes of getting to know who they are inside and the good and tough experiences that have helped mold their character. I will attach these thoughts with the questions I gave them. I also asked them to consider the questions as a guide and to add or remove suggested questions.

Both mom and dad were very open and we had a good discussion as we went over the questions. Dad mentioned: 1- His mother and father didn't have a real close relationship.

Walter S. Hoge spent most of his free time fishing. When Sarah planned Sunday activities Dr. Hoge went fishing. He often fished during the week.

2- Grandpa Hoge was a very honest man with unquestioned integrity. I have felt the same about dad. Dad was often "taken" by the business community but he rarely had unpleasant comments about others. Dad always told me that if I had problems with a teacher, the law etc. it couldn't only be their fault. He felt if I was at the wrong place at the wrong time there was some fault on my part for being in that atmosphere. He always stressed the importance of education. It was something that could never be taken away from me. On the other hand, he stressed that just because I was educated it didn't mean that I had wisdom or that I was better or more important than others. A degree meant responsibility not superiority.

I remember the respect dad gave to the nurses and staff at the hospital and his office. I never got that arrogant feeling when around dad at his work. He would usually explain to the nurses what he was during and answer questions they had. One time I cut my knee diving under a canal bridge at Tom Bithell's house. There were party phone lines at the time and I remember kind of loosing it when I asked the people to hang up so I could call for help. When dad started to work on the knee' I told him I didn't want any anesthetic. He said that was OK the sedative might only encourage infection anyway. So' he sewed it up without any local anesthetic. I was holding onto a nurse's hand and almost broke it. If I remember correctly, she soon placed a towel in my hand to squeeze.

During my visit last week, we were discussing the prophets and the need for us to follow their council. Dad mentioned that the thing that holds most men from doing right is pride (as President Benson had counseled).

3- Dad mentioned that one of his greatest concerns was the misrepresentation there is about who Sarah Hoge was. Most of her writings and the memories from others were when she was ill and not her true self. She had depression for many years and received electric shock treatment several times (which seemed to help for a while). I remember as a very young child her reading us stories. She always had my full interest and the words seemed to flow from her lips.

One summer she let Tom Bithell and me stay with her in Paris Idaho. She stayed there off and on until she needed more care. I remember the hallway to her apartment and the glass high above the door for ventilation. It was during that summer that I took a hammer and exploded caps (a roll at a time). The ringing in my ears took a long time to go away and I think I had some hearing loss from then on.

After that I remember being trouble for her when she lived at our home. She loved oranges slices and I would eat all I could find. At times she would turn on the vacuum at 1-2 AM and what I thought at the time were other strange activities. I feel if I were more mature at the time many of her activities would not have been strange to me.

I can remember the first time I saw grandma showing severe mental difficulties. Tom Bithell and I were at his home in Wapello Idaho and had gone in to check up on grandma in her bedroom. We were commenting about two sparrows copulating on a power line (my first exposure to bird reproduction) when grandma awoke and thought I was my father. Her total recall was when my father was a young man my age.

After that she began to have more problems as the years went by. I remember Nondus Bithell (her daughter) having to forcibly take grandma to her home to clean her up and wash her hair. At one time grandma ran for city council with her main theme "repair the cracks in the sidewalks of down town Blackfoot" (dad was sure glad when she lost the election). She had been a public activist in the years past and was instrumental in the building of Blackfoot's first swimming pool.

I remember one New Year's Eve when Tom Bithell and I ran around saying that everyone on the TV had "shit for hair". This greatly upset grandma and only encouraged us to press on.

Grandma stayed a portion of her last years in an apartment in downtown Blackfoot. She had, I believe a stroke, and for several days lay in her room without food or water. I remember one of our last visits she kept asking me if she were going to die. I reassured her that it wasn't going to happen.

While I was at the University of Idaho, I kept thinking that I needed to write to grandma. I finally got around to sending her a short card. She never received it. The card came back saying "return to

sender deceased". When I think of Grandma Hoge's life I can't imagine what she must have gone through living so many years without a husband to share her life with.

4- Dad mentioned that when he told his father about plans to marry my mother he said, "the Richs are good hard working people with beautiful daughters - it's only too bad that you have to marry a democrat".

Mom mentioned:

1-She pointed to the picture of her when she was eight years of age dressed in Indian clothing. In the was a grainery and old cars. The grainery is still there. It was used to store ice collected in the winter for use in her aunt Rich's refrigerator. Mom stated that straw was placed over the ice and it would last until the river froze again the next year. Mom's family didn't have a refrigerator. The cold background water from the spring and using their closed in porch as a cooler during the cold season was enough.

They would hang meat in the porch and it would freeze much of the year. When you wanted some meat for dinner, you would take it down and cut off what you needed. I can still remember meat hanging in the porch when I visited their home.

2- The home mom grew up in was just built before she was born. She was born in that house. They used the spring for water. They had a cement water retainer (it is still there today) that collected water into a pipe. Hooked to the pipe was a "ram" that would go up and down with the water pressure. Somehow it would create enough pressure to move the water up the hill into a storage tank on top of the house. This supplied pressure for indoor water to the sinks and bath. At the side of their wood stove there was another holding tank. The water was constantly heated by the stove and hot water was provided to the sinks and bath. Her family had the only running water in the area. They had a stove in the family room and the stove in the kitchen for heating. At times the water would freeze over in the spring. During those times mom mentioned that they had to carry water to the house in buckets.

3- For light they used kerosene lamps. During my visit mom got one out and showed me how to trim the wick and control the flame so there wouldn't be soot forming on the glass. Later there were also carbonate? lamps used. There was a water reservoir that could be sealed tight and a long pipe that ended in a V shaped hole. You would add a white hard material to the water, seal it and then light the gas coming from the V at the end of the pipe. Dad remembered there being such a light in the stairway at his home. He described how his dad would prepare and light the lamp at night. Dad thinks the material used was the same as that used in the water canons you used to be able to buy. They had a water chamber and you pushed down a lever to cause a spark which resulted in a loud bang. Mom told me how all her studies were done in front of one of these lamps.

4- There was no electricity in mom's house as she was growing up. The first electric lines were being strung to her home when she and dad were coming home from Germany in 1947. I would have been one year old at the time. It amazes me how much we have lost the ability for self-preservation. If the electricity is out, the computers down, grocery stores on strike, a natural disaster etc. we would be doomed. With that thought, this is one of the two reasons I bought the RV. The other reason was in hopes our family would use it to become closer. So far, I'm not sure the RV has made any difference. No disasters (that's good) - little use (that's bad).

Questions I asked my parents to respond to:

A). Early life through high school

1. Describe the neighborhood you grew up in.
2. What events outside your home had an effect on you as you were growing up (war, depression, fire flood)?
3. What was your home life like (mom/dad always home, close, loud, quiet)?
4. Describe your father.
5. Describe you mother.
6. Do you remember your grandparents? Describe them.
7. What were your likes and dislikes in school?
8. Were their any particular challenges or difficulties you remember having to overcome?
9. What influenced you to go into the career you chose?
10. Any good stories about pranks or trouble you got into?
11. Any special stories about good deeds that helped influence your life?
12. How would you describe the events and feelings that occurred when you left home?

B.) Education past high school.

1. What influenced you to go to college?
2. Were there any events going on around that made it more difficult to go to college?
3. Describe what it was like going to college (admission, classes, campus life, housing).
4. Any good stories about pranks or trouble you got into?
5. What helped you decide what you really wanted to be when you grew up?
6. What were the sins of the day? Did many participate?

7. What colleges did you attend and what degrees did you receive?

8. Military experiences you would like to share.

C.) Courtship and marriage

1. At what age did kids your age start to date?

2. Did they usually pair off or was there a lot of group dating?

3. At what age could you drive a car?

4. Did you ever date in anything other tan a car?

5. How did you meet your future spouse?

6. Any thoughts about what attracted him/her to you?

7. What made you decide that you wanted to spend your life with your future spouse?

8. Were there any special events or experiences during your courtship that you would like to share?

9. How did your parents take it when you told them you were going to marry and to whom?

10. Where were you married?

11. Any honeymoon?

12. Any special experiences or stories about the wedding or honeymoon?

D.) Married life till children left home

1. Are there any funny stories about adjustment to married life (bath tub rings, how toothpaste was squeezed, how dishes were to be washed)?

2. How did you decide where you wanted to live?

3. Any difficult or tough experience you remember while children were living at home?

4. any special events or experiences you remember while children were living at home?
5. What adjustments needed to be made when your last child left home (empty nest syndrome)?

E.) Retirement

1. At what time in your life did you first start to consider retirement?
2. What made you start thinking about retiring?
3. What did you go through preparing yourself emotionally for retirement?
4. When the day of retirement came what thoughts and emotions did you feel?
5. What adjustments did you need to make after retiring?
6. How long did it take before you felt comfortable in retirement?
7. If you were to retire again what would you do different?

F.) Thoughts about your life

1. What would you change in your life it you could?
2. To you, what event stands out the most in your life?
3. What words of advice would you give about what it takes to be happy?
4. Was there any time in your life which you enjoyed the most?

Barbara Rich Hoge (born December 18, 1915)

5. March 1997 1035 Riverton Road Blackfoot, Idaho 83221 Rich, at your request, I shall try to tell you about

some of the experiences of my life since I first arrived at the ranch located on the bank of the Snake River across from the Fort Hall Indian Reservation. Ab Jenkins, a race car fanatico from Salt Lake, came to Blackfoot to build houses and fish and hunt on the river bottoms of the Snake River near the little village of Pingree, Idaho. He became very well acquainted with my father through his activities and sports. My parents were living with grandfather, Heber Charles Chase Rich, Sr. and Edna Shepherd Rich. My brother, Mythen Layne Rich, was born in their home 9 July 1913.

My father made arrangements for Ab Jenkins to come out to the ranch to fish and hunt and build us a new home. It wasn't long before a red brick home was completed with a bath tub, sink and wash basin which had water furnished by a hydraulic ram situated in the spring below the spring house, and with pipes buried under ground to the house and the attic where a large tank was installed to furnish water pressure.

Another large tank was placed in the corner of the kitchen on the wood and coal stove to heat the water and furnish hot water for washing, bathing and kitchen. We also had a reservoir on one end of the kitchen stove to give us extra hot water.

A bathroom with a toilet and bath tub also got their water from the ram. Grandfather's house and ours were the only two families in the whole area who had running water in their homes. The others had to pump water from a well and carry what water they needed to their homes. The ram continued to be used until a well was dug after father's death, 13 September 1957.

I was the first to be born in the new house. one week before Christmas, 18 December 1915. I missed being an Indian by a mile, I slipped into this world without an announcement. Grandma Davis, who was staying at grandpa's home, came over to our home, tied the cord, spanked my bottom, and no birth certificate was prepared. I never had to show a birth certificate until 1945 when Bill and I were getting ready to leave for Germany. He had a two year assignment with the army, following World War II. I was glad my parents were still living and able to prove that I had been born.

A- EARLY LIFE THROUGH HIGH SCHOOL

1. I did not grow up in a neighborhood. We had a largo ranch of about 1,000 acres adjoining the Snake River on the east and the desert west of us. Grandfather had homesteaded it when my father, the first child of the family, who was born in Paris, Idaho, 12 October, 1989, was seven years old. There were nine children in my father's family: five boys, Heber Charles Chase, Lafayette Shepherd, Dean Shepherd, Terrell Shepherd and Don Carlos. Four girls: Edna Clara, Oral Shepherd, Arretta and Editha Emeline, Three of the children were born in Paris, Idaho, one in Logan, Utah, where grandfather practiced law, and five were born at the ranch in Rich, now Pingree.

We had a most wonderful early life on the ranch. Most of father's family were still at home. The river, springs, horses, animals, fishing, hunting, swimming, trips and celebrations kept us busy and interested.

Father was anxious to take us to Fourth of July celebrations so we could win the foot races. We were all fast runners and did our best to please father. Baseball was father's favorite summer sport. The community had an excellent team. Dad was the pitcher. He took us to the games in our Ford touring car to watch the game. With the top folded down we really had a good seat. Mother always enjoyed sports and went with us.

2. Events outside my home did not have much effect on me. World War I of 1914 didn't make much difference to us in our family. We were self-supporting, had everything we needed, and didn't have to depend on anyone for help. The only problem I remember was the "flu" in 1918. The Spani family, friends of my parents who lived in Oregon, came to visit us. Almost everyone became ill with the flu. We had beds crowded in the living room, and mother was a good nurse. It was many days before the whole family was well enough to go home,

3. My dad and mother were always at home. Farming the large farm kept the men busy, and mother had her full job of preparing three meals every day. We had a well-balanced breakfast, lunch and dinner; however, when we rode horses to school, we always carried a lunch. Mother had food ready for us when we returned from school each school day.

She was always at home to greet us. The girls helped with the duties of cleaning the house, doing the dishes and whatever was needed. We were a close family and worked and played together, Dad always liked to take us on trips, visiting Salt Lake, Boise, Montana, Wyoming, and best of all a trip to mother's uncles' ranch in Monida, Montana to fish, hunt grouse and have fun every August before school started in September. All of us children, including mother, aunt Leva, grandma Gutting and others who didn't have fishing poles were given a long willow with a hook on the end of the line. We caught grasshoppers for bait. The fishing was great! We never went home without fish for a fish fry. We also had many wonderful grouse dinners. Mother, grandma and aunt Leva were the best cooks ever.

We attended most of the general conferences at the tabernacle in Salt Lake in April and October. Dad always had to attend because of his church positions. He never went without the whole family, and we always had a fairly new car to drive. Dad traded cars almost every two years.

4. My father was a handsome man in his younger years. He had curly, black hair and hazel, blue eyes. He graduated from the Blackfoot High School and the Rick's Academy. At both schools he was a champion basketball and baseball player, participating in other sports, too.

At age 19 he served a mission in London, England without purse or script. He had a friendly, pleasing personality which helped him to make friends with everyone he met. After his mission term, he traveled to Brussels, Belgium to attend the world's fair.

Dad never became very heavy in his build, always athletic. He was an excellent farmer and rancher, His animals and crops were of the best. He was always faithful to his church and his family. There was nothing more enjoyable to him than a good sports event, hunting and fishing trips and doing things with his family. No one could have had a better dad.

5. My mother was a beautiful woman. She had black, thick hair, brown eyes and a fair complexion, and was blessed with an unusual musical and dramatic talent. Mother had a most wonderful, calm, loving personality.

Her father, Daniel August Gutting, was born in Patterson, New Jersey 25 January 1862. Her mother was born in Hyrum, Utah 14 December 1867. There were four children in the family: Campton Daniel Gutting, who changed his last name to Gooding, born in Hyrum, Utah, 29 October 1888, Leva Barbara Gutting born in Lima, Montana, 15 November 1890, Valine Ellen Gutting Born in Salt Lake City 21 November 1893, and Benjamin Clifford Gutting born in Hyrum, Utah 23 June 1896.

The family moved to Lima, Montana just before mother was born there. Grandfather was an engineer on the Oregon Short Line Railroad. He had his eye injured by a hot cinder, forcing him to retire from the railroad. The family moved to Blackfoot, Idaho where they purchased the Commercial Hotel.

Mother began her education in Blackfoot schools and graduated from the Blackfoot High School. She was the captain of the girls' basketball team and was very active in the music in the school and community. She played for the silent movies when she was 13 years of age. She could look at the picture and play suitable music for each scene without reading music from a copy.

She had a great talent for playing by ear, transposing from key to key without any difficulty. After high school she studied music with John M. Williams who wrote books of study for piano students for many years. While there she studied dramatics. Aunt Leva let her stay with her in Tacoma, Washington while she attended school. Her talents really helped us as a family. She taught us all to sing parts at a very young age. We sang for many occasions with mother accompanying us on the piano. We were known as the Rich Sisters, Barbara, Elna, Ruth and Monna.

While we were young growing up in Pingree, there was always a community dance band. Mother played the piano, Myrthon the drums and we had teachers in our school who played various instruments which added to the band. There were many dances in the communities around, which gave our band the opportunity to play for many weddings, parties, church functions, etc. Later on, I played the banjo, Ruth the guitar and Myrthon the violin. Mother would gather all of the young and old people together in the community and we would put on plays, musicals and programs. There were no radios or televisions for amusement. We made our own fun.

6. Grandfather and grandmother Rich lived on the Rich ranch when I was born. They were well educated. They both graduated from the B.Y.U. Grandfather with a law degree and grandmother with a teaching degree. Grandfather practiced law in Logan for a while, but he wanted to raise his children on the ranch in Pingree which they had homesteaded.

He was a tall, handsome man with black hair and eyes. His personality was one of the best and he made friends with everyone he met, even the Indians across the river from the ranch.

A swarm of bees came buzzing by one day and gathered in one of the large trees. With the help of beating on metal pans, smoke screens and homemade hives, the bees were captured to furnish the family with honey.

Grandfather loved to fish and hunt. He was always ready to tell an interesting story. He was the son of Apostle Charles Coulson Rich and Emeline Grover, their first child. Grandmother was the daughter of Marcus De Lafayette Shepherd a member of the Mormon Battalion and mayor of Beaver, Utah for many years. The family was quite wealthy and the children were members of the elite. They were able to go to school and get an education.

Grandmother was a beautiful, sedate lady with blond hair and blue eyes. She was an excellent school teacher and mother. At the ranch she liked to make real cheese from milk in a cheese press. When it was time to remove the cheese from the press, we all gathered around to sample the trimmings, which were most delicious.

Her banana flavored apple jelly and hot fresh bread were handed to us when we went over to her house to see her. We loved to listen to music played over the Victrola. A handle had to be turned to wind the motor before each disk was played. Grandmother was a great story teller. We had so much fun living on the ranch with our grandparents and some of their family.

There was always the latest car of the times on the drive way when automobiles replaced horses, wagons and buggies.

We did not know grandfather and grandmother Gutting as well as our other grandparents. Grandfather, Daniel August Gutting, and Ella Karene Halversen, moved from the Commercial Hotel which they owned in Blackfoot to Yuma, Idaho, now Sterling, Idaho, before I was born.

Mother was the mail carrier and rode her pony to deliver the mail. Grandfather, Daniel, died of stomach cancer when I was five years old, two months before the twins, Ruth and Roland, were born at the ranch.

When grandmother was left alone, she came to stay with us often and did the sewing for our family. We did not have dresses from the store until we were in high school. Grandmother was a beautiful designer and sewed very well. We all loved what she made for us, Grandmother was of Norwegian descent and grandfather was from Germany. Grandfather had black hair and eyes, and grandmother's hair was blond and her eyes were blue. They were both very talented in music and drama, performing in numerous musical and dramatic events. Grandfather died in Sterling, Idaho, 3 Oct. 1920. Grandmother died of a heart attack at Wapello, Idaho where she was staying with my sister Ruth who was teaching school in Wapello, 4 Apr. 1941.

7. I always liked school very much. It was fun to get back to school in the fall, see everyone, participate in the activities, sports and learn many things. We had such excellent teachers. In grade school we had no running water in the school nor electric lighting or heating. We had to pump our water to drink by holding our one hand under the spout and pump as we drank the cold water. It is a wonder that we didn't die from germs on the spout. We had two toilets on the rock pile and a cover to tie our horses under.

8. Life went on as usual without any problems. Every winter we were snowed in for several weeks because of the heavy snow storms and no mechanical equipment to remove it. Our car was put in the garage until spring.

We didn't mind. Everyone had the same problem. Our basement was full of supplies.

We had horses, cattle, turkeys, chickens, pigs, geese, ducks, fresh milk, butter, and everything we needed to survive until spring came,

9. I always loved teaching children in church. Teaching school seemed to be a worthwhile profession for a woman.

10. We were always too busy at the ranch to think of mischief, and if we did, our father would have really let us have it. He was very strict about what we did. We were never allowed to stay at a friend's house overnight. Father wanted us under his own roof every night.

11. No, there were always ways we helped our neighbors and friends when it was necessary, but this didn't influence my life too much.

12. I didn't really leave home until I was 25. When I taught school for three years near my home, I stayed with my parents, They were glad to have me there because I helped with many of the farm and household duties.

B- EDUCATION PAST HIGH SCHOOL

1. I had always wanted to go to college. The Southern Branch of the University of Idaho was at Pocatello, and I thought it would be wonderful to go learn to be a teacher, My father and mother were very encouraging Father wanted to help me in any way.

2. There were no difficulties in the way which would inhibit me from attending college. Everything was in my favor.

3. Going to college was just like a continuation of high school. There wasn't excess red tape, no struggling to get enough money to be admitted, classes were not over crowded, there was not a large enrollment, and life on the campus was just like one big family, friendly. Students could either live in the dormitory or batch in an apartment with others. I stayed in an apartment with a good friend of mine from Thomas High School. Our rant was only $15.00 a month. We did our own cooking, and most of our food supplies were brought from our homes, Book prices were very reasonable, and other activity fees were small. It was a wonderful opportunity to attend college. I was active in the acapella choir, women's athletic association, service club, physical education and dance groups, member of the L.D.S. Institute, was the queen of the ball one year, played the piano and sang in groups, took private vocal lessons, and I lived a busy, most interesting and wonderful life.

4. I have no stories, prank or troubles to share with you. We just had a good time and enjoyed all events with modesty, kindness and fun in our souls.

5. My early experience with teaching children in a Sunday school class and taking care of my brothers and sister's helped me to decide that teaching was a good profession for a woman.

6. There were not too many sins of the day. It wasn't easy to travel miles to participate in gangs and wrong doings. Cars were not had by everyone. Roads were full of rocks and mud. There was some drinking of moonshine and smoking. We had just a few in our community that thought they were "smart." Mary Merchant, a large, cross eyed, garlic eating, with high laced boots, a straw hat, gingham

cotton dress, woman lived on a farm in the sage brush and made moonshine that she peddled whenever there was a dance or entertainment in Pingree. She drove a team of horses hitched to a hay rack to make her deliveries.

7. I attended the Southern Branch of the University of Idaho in 1935 to 1937 where I received a teaching certificate which was good for five years. During the summer of 1937 I attended a twelve weeks summer school at the BYU. My sister Ruth, who had just finished her junior year at the Thomas High School, went with me and finished her senior year at the experimental high school at the BYU. This put her one year ahead of her twin brother, Roland. She had to return to the Thomas High School the following spring to graduate with Roland and get her diploma, while Ruth and I were attending the summer session at the BYU, we were ask by Dr. Holliday, head of the music department, to accompany Dr. Franklin Harris, president of the BYU, to the Duchesne Indian fair where he was going to speak and furnish a musical number for the program with our accompaniment. We rode with Dr. Harris to the fair.

I graduated from the University of Idaho June of 1941 with a BS Degree in Education. Bill and I were married 6 August 1940. He was an instructor of bacteriology at the university, and I was not charged any tuition or fees of any kind. I was a wife of an instructor. The only expense I had was the cost of the books.

It was fun being a faculty wife. We were asked occasionally to chaperone a social unit's party. When Dr. and Mrs. Glen Holm were gone during the summer, we were asked to live in their apartment in the Idaho Men's House and for Bill to be in charge of all the men. We had to eat every meal with the men in the dining room, I was certainly in a minority.

When I graduated, my parents and three sisters came for graduation. There were a few empty rooms available as some of the students had gone home for the summer. My family were all able to stay at the Idaho Club, we could have been house parents for another men's house, but Bill had decided to attend Northwestern University School of Medicine in the fall.

8. I was not in the military service, but I followed Bill around while he was in medical school and in the array, too. We were together through his training and "permanent" assignments, which didn't last very long before he was sent to Germany. It was wonderful that Barbara Ann, Rich and I were able to join him in Fulda, Germany.

C- COURTSHIP AND MARRIAGE

1. We did not go on dates much until we were in high school, and then it had to be a very special occasion.

2. It was much more fun to go in a group and not be tied down with only one person for the whole evening. Variety was much more pleasing. None of us wanted to get serious.

3. I started to drive a car at age 12. Of course, we were not allowed to get very far away from our home. Mostly I drove the car to run an errand or help on the farm.

4. Sometimes we would go to various church or dance functions in a sleigh when the roads were impassable in a car. We all played basketball and had to go in a sleigh sometimes.

5. I met Bill for the first time when Myrthon, Elna and I moved into Blackfoot where dad had rented a house out by the fairgrounds where grandma Gutting could keep house for us while we attended the Irving Grade School. It was too hard for Elna to ride behind me and the saddle four and one half miles to Pingree Grade School. She was a first grader, Myrthon was in the fifth grade and I in the third. We had a primary program at the tabernacle where I sang a duet with LaVon Monson. It happened that Bill was on the same program and played a piano solo.

Later on in life while I was at Thomas High School, we had a girls' basketball team which played against Blackfoot High School every year. I became very well acquainted with Bill's sister Nondus. Bill's father loved to go fishing out at our ranch and knew my family. He said the Rich girls showed him where to catch minnows. Bill played some of the time in a dance band with my brother, Myrthon. I did dance with him at the Alaskan Dance Hall in Blackfoot before he left for Hawaii where he was going to get his master's degree. Several years later Ruth and I, who had been teaching school, decided to attend summer school at Moscow. It was graduation time at Moscow and all of the Hoge families were there to see Nondus and Olga graduate. We later met Bill several times. His sister was always anxious for us to get together. Well, he invited me to go to church at the Institute one Sunday morning. He kept asking me to go here and there.

6. I believe that Nondus encouraged him. He was getting older and I guess he felt it was time to settle down.

7. Ruth and I had made arrangements to teach at the same school the next year. We had many plans about what

we were going to do together. Bill couldn't see why I still wanted to teach another year. He had other plans and then, too, I could finish school and get my degree. I finally weakened and wrote to my family. My father wrote back and said, "Remember, love is as blind as a bat!" Of course, my parents knew the Hoge family and respected them so they weren't too alarmed.

8. One day Bill asked me to go bicycle riding with him over the hills in Moscow. Well, I had never ridden a bike, only horses. Myrthon had a bicycle but none of us were permitted to use it. I accepted the offer and tried very hard to stay up right. It wasn't too bad, and I did well until going down a steep incline the bike took off to the side of the path and ran over a woman's pink rose bush. I jumped off and tried to rescue the bush and decided I didn't know how to control a bicycle. Another day he invited me to go to Pullman with him for dinner. He loved his steak rare. They brought mine in cooked the same. I felt it would not be courteous to complain and ate it. We did have a good summer at Moscow.

9. My parents were pleased with my choice, and of course my sisters and brother were happy over my decision.

10. We were married in the Logan Temple 6 August 1940. Ruth and I brought Bill back to Blackfoot with us after we finished summer school,

11. Yes, we did have a honeymoon down through the parks in southern Utah and the Grand Canyon. After the trip, we went back to Moscow where we had an apartment and continued with our school work.

12. I believe Bill told you about how he was struck by a horrible allergy attack when we were standing out on

Bright Angel Point looking over the Grand Canyon of the Colorado. He had to ride home with his head in my lap while I drove. It wasn't too comfortable in a coupe.

D- MARRIED LIFE TILL CHILDREN LEFT HOME

1. NO, I can't think about any funny stories or adjustment to married life. We were both so busy with his teaching and my going to school that we didn't have time to be funny. Couse we were too old for such things.

2. We didn't have to decide for a long time where we wanted to live as school came first. After finishing school and our service with the army we had an opportunity to stay in Chicago and work with Dr. Sumner L. Koch, a hand surgeon, etc. We felt that Chicago was not the place to settle and raise a family.

Little by little we got pushed back to Blackfoot. We are most happy to be here on Riverton Road where we have been for over 40 years.

3. No, we did not have any tough or difficult experiences while our children were living at home. Everything seemed to carry on with an even keel.

4. We were always so pleased with our children and what they were doing. They received many different honors throughout their school years. Each one did well in school and was active in various sports, music, ag and 4H clubs, cheer leaders, beauty queens, valedictorian, (Patricia), salutatorian, (Barbara Ann), scholarship, (Rich), dean's list in pharmacy, (John). Both John and Rich were both runners in track. Rich's track team won the state meet.

Both boys attended Boys' State at Boise. John won the Gem Boys State Pentathlon Championship - 1969. We are proud of our children and what they did in the church assignments.

We are most happy that all four of them have married in the temple and continue to be active in the church programs. It was so much fun to take them on trips and go camping with all of them. Every year we attended the Idaho Medical Association convention in June or July at Sun Valley. Every September when the Idaho State Fair was in Blackfoot, the children participated with various projects and entries for the fair. They always received ribbons and money for their efforts. We even had pigs, horses, garden produce, canning and cooked items, and sewing articles to enter.

5. We never had an empty nest syndrome when our last child, John, finally completed his education and got married. Never-the-less, we missed him, but he didn't move very far away. It is wonderful that two of our children and their families live near us. We see them often, and even Rich and Patricia come home every chance they are able to get away from their busy schedules. We are so pleased with our 24 grandchildren, 12 boys and 12 girls, and their spouse of those who are married. Now we have 6 great grandchildren, 2 girls and 4 boys.

E- RETIREMENT

1. We did not even think about retirement until Bill reached 70. At 75, 1 May 1989, he closed his doors at 53 Poplar Street, sold the office building to Dr. Gail Fields, an

orthopedic surgeon, sold a few of his medical equipment treasures, and moved the remainder of the left overs to our basement at 1035 Riverton Road.

Here we are—stacked high with memoirs. Barbara has not been able to retire. "Life goes on just the same as before. She hopes she can survive to carry on all traditions and daily chores."

2. Age seemed to be the main factor to influence retirement. We had accomplished our main desires of life, to prepare for the future, build a practice and a home and prepare to raise and educate a family.

3. We did not go through any emotional problems after the decision was made to retire, I feel that it was harder for Bill than it was for me, He missed his practice and his patients who were so kind to him.

4. I had many thoughts about the many wonderful 39 years we spent at 53 Poplar Street. Our practice was so well managed with Bill's knowledge, kindness and love for his patients, and the marvelous nurses, receptionists and others on the staff who served with respect and honor.

5. We did not make any adjustments after retirement, Everything moved on as usual, every day a new day.

6. We had no problems in any way.

7. Well, we will only retire again when the good Lord calls us to greener pastures, we hope. It should be different from the first retirement.

THOUGHTS ABOUT YOUR LIFE

1. There doesn't seem to be anything in my life that I would change to improve what has gone before these

past 81 years. We have been so involved and so busy with what we have had to do life has really clipped by more quickly than we expected. Our whole life has been so full of enjoyment, happiness, minor problems and fulfillment. It doesn't seem possible we have climbed the ladder to success and are now almost down on the last rung of the ladder.

2. There have been many exciting events in my life. In grade school I was the top speller and participated in the county spelling "B". "I just about made it to the top, down two. When I was a sophomore in high school, I won a newspaper contest as Miss Bingham County and was given a. trip on the train from Blackfoot Depot to San Francisco, a boat trip to Los Angeles, a boat trip to Catalina Island, a complete wardrobe of clothes, hotel Lills, meals, transportation, etc, for two weeks during Christmas vacation. Another girl from Blackfoot, Pauline Falk, was Miss Idaho and he went with me.

We were met by escorts whenever we arrived at our destinations. When we completed our tour, the train brought us back to Blackfoot and let us off at the depot to meet our families.

Another big event was to be Gold and Green Ball Queen when I was attending the Southern Branch of the University of Idaho at the L.D.S. Institute. I earned a student pilot's license 7 May 1964. I represented the Idaho Flying Farmers as their Queen in Miami, Florida, August 1964.

I forget to mention that another high light of my days in high school was when I was salutatorian and plaque honor student of the Thomas High school. My name is still on the plaque at the school. Of course, all of my basketball playing from the fifth grade to the second year in college, as a forward, was a big event as were the musical choirs, programs and singing with my sisters for many, many special events with our mother accompanying us on the piano,

3. To be happy one has to have a positive attitude and not always looking at the bad and discouraging situations. Keep a happy expression on your face. Be pleasant and understanding with others. Keep busy, have time to smell the roses, and enjoy life, your friends, enemies and your family.

4. To me, life has been full of enjoyment. I feel that I have lived my life to the fullest. When we were children and grown-ups at the ranch, it was great! Attending school for many years was exciting and full of pleasure and work, but rewarding. It was thrilling to teach school and watch the children learn and have fun. To me, teaching was enjoyable. I have really been happy as a wife and mother of our four children. Together I feel that our lives have been successful thus far. We have lots to be thankful for: our homes, families, the church which has done so much for helping us raise our family and the good health we have been blessed with. May we continue to carry on until we are called home.

Walter Grimmett Hoge (born March 13, 1914)
Dear Rich,

This is an attempt to answer the questions you ask to get data for the family history. Note above that this is 22 Feb, an important date in the history of our nation.

Tomorrow will be the 23 Feb, an important date in our family history. Remember, Barbara and I talked to you on the phone this morning, and we are so happy we could visit with you last Saturday and Sunday. We really look forward to and cherish those times when we can visit.

I made a sincere attempt to do this on the audio tape, but it turned out I was leaving out important things and not using just the right words.

Question A-1- I, Papa, grew up in the northeast part of Blackfoot with my father, Walter Smith Hoge, my mother, Sarah Louisa Grimmett Hoge and my Sister, Nondus Hoge, four years younger than I, born on '12 May 1918. Originally, we lived on the west side of Shilling Avenue; then soon after Nondus was born we moved to a fairly new house on the east side of the street at 342 N. Shilling, where we lived until I started going away to college, Nondus did the same. Dad died and mother sold the house. We were comfortable and happy there.

In the first house we were members of the Blackfoot Stake, first ward, and I can remember that below-zero January morning when our church burned down, just a block or two from our place. We were in a very nice area with nice neighbors and a few children available for playmates.

In our second location we were members of the second ward, and we walked about four blocks south to our church, which was across the street from the court house. We met a lot of people, parents and children, living in the south part of town, particularly on South Shilling Street. They were mostly good kids, and we could not blame all of our mistakes onto "peer pressure." There was very little crime, and I think not much sin. People in this area mostly had adequate incomes, where pleasant, and mostly easy to get along. with.

A-2-The great world-wide depression, beginning in about 1930, ruined the "adequate income" situation for just about everybody. The people in the west seemed to adjust very well because of family gardens, home sewing, ability to work long, long hours, most being unspoiled, helpful religions, etc. Not many people in our area were going hungry, but we had to abandon luxuries. Looking back, I realize it was good training for us and I am grateful to have been involved. I didn't think so at the time. The depression got blamed for all disasters. I must admit that though I realize that this was a very valuable experience, I would not like to repeat it, I feel the same about my Army experience, which is described a little in the autobiography.

A-3-Mostly our home life was functional and pleasant. The family had breakfast and dinner together, and often we would have lunch together, but we two kids went to school and Dad went to work. In any event we had three "square" meals per day, well-prepared and nourishing. We said blessings on the meals. We were civil to each other and there was definitely "love at home.

The siblings got into arguments, as I consider normal. Dad and Mother did too, and there was some yelling. There was no actual violence. Dad's friends were mostly the fishermen, did a little drinking, etc. Mother's friends were the ward and stake members, so there was not much socializing between them in groups.

A-4-Father was a good-looking man weighing about 160 pounds, a little shy, with good manners, liked by about everyone. He was not an eloquent speaker and did no public speaking. He communicated very well with one or two people at a time, however. Rather dignified, competent in his work as a dentist, honest. Lots of fishing, even sometimes on weekdays, Shotgun hunting. One elk/deer hunt per year, lasting about one week. He was killed 1 Dec 1940 pulling a shot gun thru a fence by a wound in the axilla causing hemorrhage. The friends with him described him as extremely careful with guns, and couldn't understand how it happened.

A-5-Mother was a pretty woman of average size, the oldest of a family of 9 children, 4 boys and 5 girls. One of the boys died as a child and one died of a heart condition at age 18. The girls were all very popular, and one young man made the remark "You can't beat those Grignette girls." Mother never had to do house work or wash the dishes because of her skill as a seamstress. She made and repaired clothes for the whole family, and kept this talent and obligation throughout her married life. She was a school teacher before she was married, after some college training at the University of Utah. She was a very faithful Latter Day Saint, holding a good many leadership positions. She was very competent and bright, and wrote short personal histories of her mother, father, Grandpa Hoge and likely others. She used good grammar and could spell about anything. No one got around to writing about her. She wrote some talks and essays; one that I remember was entitled "The Holy Ghost." It was inspiring. I am trying to locate those papers and distribute copies. I did actually distribute copies of the biographies to each of my children.

Sarah Louisa Grimmett was held in great respect. She was very strict about what her children did. No baseball on Sunday and even no movies. She finally did let me go to a Sunday movie. It was entitled "The Ten Commandments." Her circle of friends was mainly within the church. The words that would describe her are kind, competent, reliable.

During the later part of her life Mother developed a fairly severe depression, unipolar type, and the therapy that was used destroyed much of her memory. Since then, she was not the same person and the grandchildren and other younger persons do not remember her as the bright, helpful, thoughtful, pleasant person she really was. Things she wrote after that time would make you think she was retarded in some way, not at all like the real Sarah.

A-6-Mother wrote short biographies of John Henry Grimmett, Louisa Neat Grimmett, and Walter Hoge. You probably have these, Grandma Hoge was Amelia Ann Smith Hoge. I knew all but Waltor Hoge well, because Mother took us children to Paris, Idaho, where they all lived, for a week or two each summer.

Grandpa Grimmett was successful building contractor. He was very strict with his family, perhaps too strict. This started with mother, but he moderated gradually until by the time of Aunt Jennic, youngest girl, she could do about as girls outside the family. His reputation was that "His word is as good as his bond. He was a prominent citizen and devout church member. He served in the Idaho State Legislature for two terms and took Mother to the inaugural ball.

Grandma Grimmett was a very good mother and wife, an example to her children. Everyone ate breakfast and the evening meal at home. All of the children enjoyed living at home and loved one another. She was very sweet, competent and pretty. Grandma Hoge was known as a great lady, very dignified and with English mannerisms. She knew all about etiquette and manners and put these things into strict practice. She was a rather small lady, always well-dressed and polite. She had a daughter, Aunt Rhoda, who was born a semi-invalid, who lived with grandma all her life. Aunt Rhoda was interested in all her nieces and nephews, and we always thought of "Grandma Hoge and Aunt Rhoda" together. They lived in a beautiful, old, brick home that I would call a mansion.

A block north Grandma's house was "Aunt Sarah's" house. She was Sarah Beck Hoge, Grandpa's other wife in polygamy. Both wives raised fine families. The families respected each other and got along well together.

Grandpa Hoge came from England near the Scotland border when he was a lad of 18 years, looking for gold. Check mother's short biography of him. He served as owner and editor of the "Paris Post", a sawmill owner, sheriff—I think two terms, and served in the state legislature. Held church positions. He was in Boise during the Idaho State Constitutional Convention to try to get a Constitution that did not mention polygamy. This was at the risk of being served a warrant as a polygamist. He performed a valuable service, but finally had to leave Boise in a hurry. See "Idaho's Constitution, the Tie that Binds" by Dennis C. Colson, 1991, University of Idaho Press, Moscow, Idaho, 83843.

A-7-I think that in grade school my likes and dislikes were about the same as any average kid. I liked all of my teachers and respected them.

In high school I did not particularly care for sports, but earned my football letter as a senior, mostly to show myself and my peers I could do it. I liked debate and was on the state championship team in my junior and senior years. I served as class president in my junior year.

I loved the science courses and took all the math courses available. We had excellent English courses because of excellent teachers, and this served me well all my life, both in the universities and afterward. I attended the important Social Eumotions such as the Junior Prom and the Senior ball. We had a group of fellows and girls who tended to run together.

A-8-Negative.

A-9-As a child I noticed that everyone seemed to respond to the doctors. They were trusted, and what they uttered was pretty much gospel. They all had 2 cars and they were rather expensive models. They could deduct one car from the income tax. They seemed to have good incomes. Most of all medicine was based upon science, and I loved science. I greatly respected a doctor who lived across the alley east from us, Dr. Beck, He had 3 boys and actually took an interest in me. His boys and I had the most interesting conversations, almost no subjects barred.

A-10-Probably plenty of stories, but I don't recall any. May insert one later.

A-11-Same as #10. will try to insert one.

A-12-1 left home sort of gradually, so there was no hard reaction. As a freshman, Dee Cox and I had a bachelor's apartment in Pocatello. That meant we were home here in Blackfoot about every weekend. Our mothers would fill a suitcase with prepared foods, as roast beef, cookies and other goodies to take to Pocatello every Sunday afternoon or evening. Also, clean clothes.

Next year I was in Salt Lake City, U. of U. I stayed with Aunt Jennie and Uncle Stan the first half of the term and in a small boarding house the second half. The next 2 years I was in a boarding house with Dee Cox and Bruce Barclay in Provo, at the BYU played with both in a dance orchestra there as I had done in Blackfoot for several years previously, and not much chance for home-sickness.

After graduation I lived at home again for a year, working as a chain-man surveyor, helping to build the diversion dam just upstream from Blackfoot on the Blackfoot river. Leaving home was gradual.

After accumulating some real savings on the surveying job I entered the Graduate School of the University of Idaho, with a little job in the bacteriology department, I guess I can say I had really left home by this time. Letters to and from Blackfoot were about weekly. There was no shock in leaving home.

B-1-From the time I was just a child my mother made it clear to me that I was going to go to college when I grew up. The question was where and how, but not whether. That was in the days when going to college was more the exception than the usual thing for high school graduates. Mother just knew that that was the thing I was to do. By the time I was ready, I was anxious to go.

B-2-The only events around us that made it difficult to go was the great depression, with the general shortage of money. Actually, with the very low tuition, books and fee costs, it was probably easier to finance school than it is today, with the terrible inflation.

B-3-I have already indicated that I did not stay in any fraternity houses or dormitories, that is, until I attended the University of Hawaii ($60 per month for board and room-depression still going on). I didn't have much of any social life, I was a very serious student. The social life could wait. Getting admission was not difficult until I was ready for medical school, but in my case they accepted me first try, I would go to a movie or something with one or two fellows, and that was about it.

B-4-Deferred. will try to think of something.

B-5-See A-9. When I was at the University of Utah I often studied with 2 medical students, from Blackfoot, Norman "Bus" Beck and Ralph Hegsted and Lee Beck, also a sophomore. The Becks older brother was in his third-year medicine at the University of Pennsylvania Medical School.

I was fascinated by the stories I heard about the classes, examinations, etc. I admired the students and decided I would just have to study medicine. I just needed that knowledge to reach my goal in life.

B-6-The sins of the day were pretty much the same as today, except use of street drugs was almost unknown, whereas it is rampant today, and perhaps the greatest threats to the individual and to the nation. There was plenty of drinking amongst all social classes including students, and many lives were ruined by alcohol. Smoking was very common. It made the students grown up and sophisticated, and pretty soon they were hooked. My two medical school friends were addicted. Thank goodness I never took up that burden. Sexual sins were commonplace, but I think not nearly the same as now. In those days the movies encouraged this sort of thing, but not in such a blatant way as nowadays. Television gives the impression that "Everyone is doing it," and therefore it is normal and acceptable. violence was evident and there were some gangs, but only a small fraction of what we face now.

B-7-Answered in some detail in my autobiography. Baccalaureate degree with major in zoology and minor in chemistry in 1936, BYU. University of Hawaii, master's degree with major in bacteriology and minor in chemistry in June 1939. University of Idaho, instructor in bacteriology and Bacteriologist, Agricultural Experiment Station 1939-1941. Northwestern University Medical School, Bachelor of Medicine degree 1944; Cook County Hospital, Internship, 1945. Northwestern University Medical School M. D. 1945. Military service, AUS 1945-47. Charter Fellow, American Academy of Family Physicians 1962. Elected to full membership of the Society of Sigma xl Scientific Society, Idaho Chapter, 1940.

B. 8-SCO "Personal History of Walter G. Hoge" Chapter II. C-1-Kids started to date at long intervals, for parties by the time they entered junior high school (7th grade), but more seriously a couple of years later, when they entered high school, about age 16.

C-2-Group dating was the thing for school parties, birthday parties, etc., but they would repeatedly show up as repeat dates, and you might predict who would be with whom. Then there was the Saturday or Friday night date where one, two or three couples would share a car to go to a function or perhaps a movie. Sometimes they would be considered to be "going steady."

C-3-I began driving a car at about age 15 or 16. A friend of my fathers who sometimes served as a mechanic, Reif Christ, taught me in a thoughtful, careful manner.

C-4-We were occasionally able to borrow or rent horses for rides around the area, as Stephen's Peak or along country roads, or to pull us along country roads over the snow, hanging behind on a rope.

C-5-I knew my future spouse, Barbara, from childhood, but never paid any particular attention to her. She had the reputation as a nice girl. In the late summer of 1938, I attended a dance in Blackfoot at an openair dance hall called "The Alaskan." Barbara happened to be there, and I asked her to dance with me; I don't remember if this was more than one time. I told her that I would soon be sailing from San Francisco, on a steamship, "The Matsonia," for Honolulu, where I was to be a Graduate Assistant at the University of Hawaii. We had quite a nice visit, and sometimes I would think of her after that.

After receiving the Master's degree in bacteriology I returned to the University of Idaho, at Moscow as instructor in Bacteriology and Bacteriologist at the Agricultural Experiment Station at the U of I.

My sister, Nondus, was a friend and former basketball opponent of Barbara, and had developed a deep admiration for her. She had often told me what a nice person Barbara was and had hinted that I ought to date her.

When the summer Session of the University of Idaho started, somehow I heard that Barbara and her sister, Ruth, were there for the session. Barbara was there to study mostly music, I remembered about seeing her a year ago at the dance and thought about Nondus' Comments. I thought here was a girl I might actually date seriously. After all, I was 26 years old now. The date was serious. I asked her to go to church at the LDS Institute at the University. Then we went to other places together, and I knew that this was the girl for me.

C-6-Barbara's brother, Myrthon, and I were good friends, having played in various dance bands together. So, I guess there might have been some curiosity about one of Myrthon's friends. I think may reputation was untarnished and I was fairly well thought of. It may be that my position on a university faculty created a good impression. I don't think I had any particular great charm.

C-7-When I began to date Barbara I knew that I was in love with her, and it wasn't long until I knew I wanted to marry her. Certainly, none of the girls I knew could compare with her. . .

C-8-Our courtship was short and serious. There was not time from June until August for anything "unusual."

C-9-Probably the first person that I told that I was going to be married and to whom was my father. I had just gotten to town, and was visiting him at work in his dental laboratory. We were alone at the time.

I explained that Barbara Rich was Chase Rich's daughter, and he seemed to become very thoughtful. He said, "Well, it is certainly a respected family, old Pioneer stock. I may have even seen her. When I was fishing with a friend near Chase's place, a couple of his girls showed us where to catch minnows for bait. That's the only way you can catch trout that time of year. The girls were nice and really helped us. One of them could have been Barbara.

It sounds as though she is pursuing an education. You are both from Bear Lake. Her family all moved from Bear Lake to homestead land in the Snake River valley, and both your mother and I am from Bear Lake, It is nice that you are of the same religion and have the same background. The Rich family has a very good reputation here. It seems that everything points to a successful marriage. But are you sure you want to get mixed up with all those damned Democrats?"

My mother was thrilled at the prospect. When the neighbors and friends heard about it, the usual comment was, "Well, Walter is going to marry one of the Rich girls. Isn't that just wonderful?"

C-10-We were married in the Logan Temple, Barbara's parents and Uncle Smith Hoge and Aunt Bertha were present. Uncle Smith signed our license as witness.

C-11-We had a wonderful honeymoon. In Barbara's old, reliable Chevrolet coupe, we drove from Logan to Salt Lake City and had dinner at the roof garden dining room at the Hotel Utah. From there we drove to the Temple Square hotel, across the street, to spend the first night together.

Next morning, probably not really early, we headed for the St. George area and visited The Grand Canyon of the Colorado, Bryce Canyon, Zion's Canyon and other attractive places. The scenery was just beautiful, comparing favorably with areas in Switzerland, South America, etc., that we saw later.

C-12-We had walked out to Bright Angel Point, a scenic outlook at the Grand Canyon, and by the time we got back to the car I had a frontal headache which did not entirely stop until it was diagnosed and treated in Pocatello. It was diagnosed as an allergic, sinus headache. It hurt for a week, but did not spoil my honeymoon. We traveled with Barbara driving and I with my head in her lap.

D-1-I don't remember any such instances, though undoubtedly such occurred.

D-2-While living in Chicago, we sometimes discussed where we wanted to settle and practice medicine. We planned to have 4 children, hopefully 2 boys and 2 girls, and a primary consideration would be the best place we could find to raise children.

By the time we had left the army and Germany, we had traveled a little in Europe: Switzerland, England, France, and had lived in the east and south of the United States: Carlisle Barracke, Pennsylvania; Augusta, Georgia; Coral Gables, Florida. I had spent time in Greensboro, North Carolina. Before marriage, each of us had traveled in the western states, including California. We were quite familiar with Idaho, Utah, Wyoming, Montana.

I had a wonderful offer, from the professional standpoint, . in Chicago. A nationally known hand surgeon, a professor of surgery at Northwestern Medical School, Dr. Sumner L. Koch, offered to train me in a residency. This meant that I could get the best training in the world and would have every chance for a successful career in surgery in Chicago, or wherever.

We knew that Idaho wasn't the best place in the world to make money, but the more we thought about it, the more sure we were that the Snake River Valley was a wonderful place to live to accomplish what we wanted to do. After we had lived in our house in Blackfoot for 40 years, as was my custom about Thanksgiving time every year, I bore my testimony in our 14th Ward. I was now 82 years old. I related how I thought we were living in about the best place in the world, amongst about the finest people in the world. After just 40 years in our present location, we had decided to settle here permanently. Some of the members told us how glad they were that we had decided to stay and spend our lives here.

D-3-Fortunately, if there wore tough or difficult circumstances while children were living at home, none was 80 bad that I remember it.

D-4-We had fun with the children every summer, when the Idaho State Medical Convention was regularly held at Sun Valley, Idaho. The kids could enjoy the swimming pools, sometimes fishing, hiking, etc., until the scientific meetings were over.

Then, all six of us would take off for a camping trip. We had a tent or two, sleeping bags, and everything needed for a pleasant camp-out. The girls were not too enthusiastic about this kind of living. We would camp out for two or three nights, then spend a night at a motel. Here we would get bathed, rested in a real bed, then repeat the camping experience. By this time we were ready to return home.

We would have accumulated some slide photographs and other memories. The experiences brought us closer together as a family. Of course, we took a lot of other trips together. Be sure to look up my stories on "Fishing and Flying" in the Autobiography: I was 48 years old when I got my private pilot's license.

D-5-We did not really have the empty nest syndrome because we were in rather close contact with our children when they were away at school, but even more so when they were married and started their own families. Barbara Ann and Family, the Lilyas, and John and family, the Blackfoot : Hoges, have been within a mile or four of us, and we would see all members often. Rich and family, the California Hoges, and Pat and family, the Jay Clarks, live in San Jose, California and Mapleton, Utah, respectively. Between their visits to us and our visits to them, we keep pretty good track of one another. Lots of telephone calls.

E-1-This question on retirement is fully answered in my personal history, beginning with the topic "Slowing Down."

E-2 The birthdays made us start thinking about retirement. Also, the health problem discussed in "Slowing Down." We had begun thinking about investments by this time, and one year we made about $65,000 on the stock market, a lot of money in those days.

E-3-Preparing emotionally for retirement turned out to be a real problem. When I would meet friends they would ask "Hey, Doc, how do you like retirement. It was nearly 2 years before I could truthfully answer, "It's just great. I feel relieved." At first there was a little depression, associated with a feeling of uselessness and a loss of status. This was very real. I had to quit going to most of the medical meetings because I could no longer deduct the cost from income tax; I lost other deductions, as the cost of one of the cars.

E-4-We formally closed the office on 1 May 1989. Of course I would still go down there about every day to take care of odds and ends, and it seems I kept one of the girls, maybe both, working for another month or two. I missed their good help when they were gone. I thought I would miss the practice, but I could also draw a sigh of relief.

E-5-It seemed strange not to have to go to the office. I had numerous requests for transfer of patients to other doctors. I had a good copying machine, thank goodness. It is hard to retire from a medical practice without leaving town. There were many, many calls for help and advice. I felt obligated to help all I could, and I am still doing it a little (March 1997).

E-6-About two years before I felt comfortable in retirement.

E-7-I completely retired at age 75. I should have broken off completely by age 70, even though there might have been some guilt feelings. I would have been at least as well off financially, devoted more time to my extended family, family history, etc.

F-1-The main thing in my life I would change, if I could, is my church involvement, I was beyond 60 years old when I began to realize that life had more meaning than professional responsibility, educating the children, paying the bills and being a good husband and father. I should have become involved in church affairs at the same time I began my professional life, ..or sooner.

F-2-I have tried to think about what event stands out most in my life, but there have been so many wonderful things, and important things, that I cannot pick any single event.

F-3-Of course no one could be happy without adequate food, clothing, shelter, liberty and the pursuit of happiness and all the things guaranteed by our constitution, but we will take all of these things for granted.

I will answer that to be happy we need a good marriage with love and with good children. We need to live a righteous, productive life and to help whomever we can. We need most of all to live the commandments of the Lord, in righteousness, and serve him. Some would say that what we need is fortune, fame and power. I may have thought that in my early life, but certainly my observations have taught me differently. The answer is to love the Lord and serve him constantly, for happiness.

F-4-See Q. F-2. If there is any answer to this, I would have to say I enjoyed the period of my married life with Barbara and my 4 children most of all.

Rich, do not consider this adequately edited. That can be done anytime. I am sending it this way in the interest of getting it to you sooner.